George Dimitrov

Liability of Certification Service Providers

George Dimitrov

Liability of Certification Service Providers

How the Providers of Certification Services Related to Electronic Signatures Could Manage their Liabilities

VDM Verlag Dr. Müller

Imprint

Bibliographic information by the German National Library: The German National Library lists this publication at the German National Bibliography; detailed bibliographic information is available on the Internet at http://dnb.d-nb.de.

Cover image: www.purestockx.com

Publisher:
VDM Verlag Dr. Müller Aktiengesellschaft & Co. KG , Dudweiler Landstr. 125 a, 66123 Saarbrücken, Germany,
Phone +49 681 9100-698, Fax +49 681 9100-988,
Email: info@vdm-verlag.de

Zugl.: Leuven, KULeuven, Diss., 2008

Produced in USA and UK by:
Lightning Source Inc., La Vergne, Tennessee, USA
Lightning Source UK Ltd., Milton Keynes, UK
BookSurge LLC, 5341 Dorchester Road, Suite 16, North Charleston, SC 29418, USA

ISBN: 978-3-639-00824-1

TABLE OF CONTENTS

ABBREVIATIONS

ABA	American Bar Association
ASP	Archival Service Provider
AICPA	American Institute of Certified Public Accountants
ANSI	American National Standards Institute
CA	Certification Authority
CA	Trust AICPA/CICS WebTrust Program for Certification Authorities
CC	Common Criteria for Information Technology Security Evaluation
CICA	Canadian Institute of Chartered Accountants
CISA	Certified Information Systems Auditor (ISACA)
CISSP	Certified Information Systems Security Professionals
CP	Certificate Policy
CPA	Certified Public Accountant
CPS	Certification Practice Statement
CRL	Certificate Revocation List
CSP	Certification Service Provider
CSE	Communications Security Establishment
DAP	Directory Access Protocol
DES	Data Encryption Standard
DIRECTIVE	Directive 1999/93/EC on a Community framework for electronic signatures
DSP	Directory Service Provider
DN	Distinguished Name
DNS	Domain Name Services/Server
DSG	The ABA ISC Digital Signature Guidelines

DSS	Digital Signature Standard
DSP	Directory Service Provider
EC	European Commission
ECAF	European Certification Authority Forum at EEMA
ECDSA	Elliptic Curve Digital Signature Algorithm
EDESA	The Bulgarian Electronic Documents and Electronic Signatures Act
EDI	Electronic Data Interchange
EEMA	European Electronic Messaging Association
EESSI	European Electronic Signatures Standardization Initiative
ETSI	European Telecommunications Standards Institute
EU	European Union
FIPS	Federal Information Processing Standard
FIPS PUB	Federal Information Processing Standard Publication
HTTP	Hypertext Transfer Protocol
IA	Issuing Authority
ICSA	International Computer Security Association
IEC	International Electrotechnical Commission
IIA	Institute of Internal Auditors
ISC	Information Security Committee of the ABA
ISO	International Organization for Standardization
IETF	Internet Engineering Task Force
IP	Internet Protocol
IPSEC	IP Security
ISC	ABA's Information Security Committee
ITSEC	Information Technology Security
ITU	International Telecommunications Union
LDAP	Lightweight Directory Access Protocol

LOC	The Bulgarian Law on Obligations and Contracts
LRA	Local Registration Authority – see also RA
NCSA (U.S.)	National Computer Security Association – see also ICSA
NIST (U.S.)	National Institute of Standards and Technology
OCSP	On-line Certificate Status Protocol
OID	Object Identifier
OJ	Official Journal of the European Communities
OS	Operating System
PGP	Pretty Good Privacy
PIN	Personal Identification Number
PKCS	Public Key Cryptosystem
PKI	Public Key Infrastructure
PKIX	Public Key Infrastructure X.509
PP	Protection Profile
RA	Registration Authority
RFC (IETF)	Request For Comments
RSA	Rivest-Shimar-Adleman Algorithm
RSP	Registration Service Provider
SHA-1	Secure Hash Algorithm
HTTPS	Secure Hypertext Transfer Protocol
S/MIME	Secure Multi-part Internet Mail Extensions
SMTP	Simple Mail Transfer Protocol
SSL	Secure Sockets Layer
TSA	Time-stamping Authority
TSP	Trust Service Provider
TSSP	Time-stamping Service Provider
TST	Time-stamping Token
TTP	Trusted Third Party

UTC	Coordinated Universal Time
UK	United Kingdom
UNCITRAL	United Nations Commission on the International Trade Law
URI	Uniform Resource Identifier
URL	Uniform Resource Locator
US	United States of America

"On the Internet, nobody knows you're a dog". Who doesn't know this famous cartoon of Peter Steiner, published in The New Yorker in the summer of 1993? After the explosion of the Internet during the nineties, the absence of effective means to identify people on the Internet in a trustworthy manner was considered as a major obstacle for electronic business. Therefore many observers estimated that, on a short term, there would be a huge demand for "digital passports" issued by trusted third parties. There was certainly some logic in this reasoning. Traditionally, people conclude business transactions by means of paper documents and handwritten signatures. The expectation was that electronic commerce would never break through without a similar solution for the online environment. From a technical perspective, there was also a general believe that this need would automatically lead to a generalized use of digital signature technology and public key infrastructures. Digital certificates are an essential part of these infrastructures.

Political and industrial decision-makers consequently expected that the need for digital certificates would rapidly become a trigger for new profitable business and that the newly created "certification authorities" would play a key role on the Net. One of the major discussions related to the question whether the issuance of the digital identity certificates, if by all means not a task of the government administration itself, at least shouldn't be monitored or supervised by the government in order to protect the citizens against potential risks. Legislators, first in the US and subsequently in other parts of the world, therefore enacted new laws regulating the activities of the certification authorities. In Europe this has led to the adoption, at the end of 1999, of the Directive on a community network for electronic signatures.

From the beginning, liability has been considered as a major issue in the context of the regulation of certification authorities. What happens when someone has concluded an important contract with an unknown correspondent whose signature apparently was based on a false or revoked certificate? Will people trust the certificate if the certification authority doesn't provide any guarantees that the potential damage will be repaired?

The author of this book, George Dimitrov, critically analyzes the regulatory answer to this question, as it has been adopted in the European directive. His research starts with a sharp and clear overview of the various roles and actors in the relevant landscape. One of the conclusions is that the issuance of a digital certificate is only one part of a larger chain. He also carefully examines the relationships between the certification service provider, the signatory and the relying party. For readers, who are not very familiar with the technology and the policy issues related to electronic signatures, this part of the book offers a clear introduction. The following chapter introduces the reader into the complex field of liability law. This chapter is an excellent overview of the most relevant concepts and issues relating to liability. Although it is based on the legal situation according to Bulgarian law, the overview is illustrative for all European civil law jurisdictions.

The central chapter of the book contains the analysis of the European liability regime for certification service providers issuing qualified certificates to the public. In European legal doctrine on the subject of electronic signatures, this book can from now on, without any doubt, be considered as part of the essential reference material for anyone dealing with the liability aspects in this field.

The last chapters of this publication are devoted to a critical evaluation of the specific liability regime established by the European Directive. What are the practical consequences of this regime, once the rules are being embedded in the framework of national law? The author, who is a leading Bulgarian scholar in the field of ICT-law, illustrates this with examples taken from his own jurisdiction, but his observations are not less relevant for every other European country. One of the main final conclusions of the research is that the specific liability rules created for the issuance of digital certificates, do not actually promote trust in the market but, on the contrary, may lead to additional confusion and legal uncertainty.

Today, in 2008, there is a revived interest in the activities of certification service providers. A large number of European countries have introduced or plan to introduce electronic identity cards with authentication and signature features. The business model with regard to the provision of digital certificates may have changed but the fundamental legal questions, e.g. related to the liability of the certification service providers remain. Therefore the publication of this book arrives at an excellent moment.

The book is based on doctoral research performed by the author at the Interdisciplinary Centre of Law and ICT (ICRI) of K.U.Leuven (Belgium). We express our gratitude to George Dimitrov for his contribution to the research of our Centre and our appreciation to the publisher for bringing this book to the interested readers.

Jos Dumortier
Professor of Law
Director of ICRI, K.U.Leuven

JUSTIFICATION OF THE RESEARCH. SOCIAL AND LEGAL RELEVANCE.

In the era of rapidly developing information technologies, electronic communication between people has become an ordinary and preferred method of communication. One of the first problems faced by the market players was the development of a fast and reasonably secure method for data interchange. The purpose of such a method was to promote confidence in the ability to identify the authors of particular messages and to ascertain the integrity of the data which was communicated.

The electronic signature, used within a public key infrastructure (PKI),[1] has become a widely used tool for ensuring secure communication.[2] Sometimes, it is the only instrument capable of establishing with a high level of certainty the authenticity of messages communicated between persons who may be unknown to each other. The providers of certification services related to electronic signatures play a key role in this infrastructure. Either by supporting the electronic signature by issuing certificates or by providing other ancillary services,[3] they are the persons who are trusted by the market actors communicating electronically by using electronic signatures. In this respect the certification-service-providers play a role analogous to that played by the authorities responsible for issuing personal identification cards in the "paper world". The trust in the certification services is a direct result of the work of the certification-service-providers and the attestations they provide, and it is this that makes the functioning of the public key infrastructure possible in the electronic world.

---

[1] Public Key Infrastructure (PKI) is defined as the sum total of the organizations, systems (hardware and software), personnel, processes, policies, and agreements that allow the technology for "signing" electronic communications based on private and public keys to function for a given set of users. See ABA ISC *PKI Assessment Guidelines* – PAG v0.30, American Bar Association, Information Security Committee, Electronic Commerce Division, Section of Science & Technology Law, 2001 (http://www.abanet.org/scitech/ec/isc/pag/pag.html).

[2] The electronic signature shall mean data in electronic form which are attached to or logically associated with other electronic data and which serve as a method of authentication. Some types of signatures (i.e. the advanced e-signature) shall meet certain requirements such as: to be uniquely linked to the certificate holder; to be capable of identifying the certificate holder; to be created using means that the certificate holder can maintain under his sole control; and to be linked to the data to which it relates in such a manner that any subsequent change of the data is detectable. See Article 2 (1) and (2) of Directive 1999/93/EC.

[3] See Article 2 (11) of Directive 1999/93/EC.

Due to the important role played by the certification-service-providers (CSPs), EU Member States should introduce precise regulation of the providers' status, activity, and supervisory regime, as well as define their rights and obligations towards third parties, where necessary. On the other hand, a careful assessment should be made as to the need for legislation to secure protection and to provide guarantees in respect of the lawful interests of the persons relying on the certification services. The creation of a particular legal liability, for example, is a common method of managing the level of legal protection afforded to given groups of subjects in society.

The European legislator has identified a need for introduction of special liability rules and has introduced such on a supranational level by adopting the Directive 1999/93/EC on a Community framework for electronic signatures. The rules of Article 6 of this Directive are meant to establish common minimum level of protection for the users of certification services related to electronic signatures in the Internal market.

However, is there a necessity to establish specific liability rules when public faith in the services provided is, or could be, undermined by the lax conduct of the CSP; or do the general civil liability regimes currently in place offer adequate legal protection over the interests of the users of certification services? This work aims at answering these questions.

Whether there is a need for a specific liability regime for the certification-service-providers is an important question. On the one hand, the existence of clear and specific liability rules would promote greater trust in the certification services among market players, and would thus make them more willing to use these services. On the other hand, electronic turnover could be seriously affected as a result of this. Unbalanced regulation may have a serious negative impact on the market by hindering the competition in provision of certification services. Introducing a redundant specific liability regime or unnecessary exposure to liability might adversely affect the readiness of the CSPs to provide services. Thus, instead of fulfilling its core role of protecting the interests of certification services users by promoting trust in the electronic services market, the specific liability regime may create obstacles and could lead to market fragmentation. When speaking about a nascent market, serious attention should be given to this problem, since the negative consequences flowing from improper regulation could be severe. In such a situation the *acquis communautaire* has introduced specific liability rules for the CSPs, and has obliged EU Member States to transpose those rules into their national legislations as a minimum regulatory regime. How, and to what extent, is the approach of the European legislator justifiable, and how does it affect the electronic signatures market?

This is, for a number of reasons, a difficult question to answer.

The first reason is that diverse and sometimes contradictory theoretical and practical approaches are taken in respect of liability issues in different legal systems. Countries belonging to the Roman law family interpret the nature of tort and contractual liability in a different manner to those belonging to the common law family. Divergence of approach may also be observed between countries that utilize similar legal systems, and even within a single jurisdiction. Furthermore, there is still no harmonization of the general principles of civil liability at Community level. Introducing liability rules on a supranational level without having a shared understanding of general principles could lead to a situation in which national jurisdictions misinterpret the intention of the European legislator while transposing the *acquis* libility rules.

The second reason is that deducing general conclusions valid for all jurisdictions in respect of the liability issue is a difficult task and remains beyond the scope of this work. Depending on their legal traditions, the national jurisdictions of the EU Member States follow different approaches to the systematization of legal rules in codes, general acts, special acts etc. These acts may contain liability rules applicable to the CSPs, but the level of protection offered may not always be easily identifiable, due to the diverse types of social relations or groups of persons protected. Furthermore, those rules – especially the transposed ones establishing specific liability for the CSPs – may overlap with other specific national liability rules. There is another problem in relation to possible conflict between the transposed specific liability rules and the general national civil liability principles. National laws are based on different principles, concepts and legal traditions, and the transposed specific liability rules may be inconsistent with those principles, especially when it comes to problematic theoretical legal concepts like burden of proof, reasonable reliance, limitation of liability etc.

Since the task of researching the impact of transposition in all EU Member States is too demanding, for the purposes of the present work one jurisdiction that has transposed Directive 1999/93/EC and its specific liability rules – Bulgaria – has been selected as a case study. Bulgaria is a relevant subject for examination not only because it belongs to the family of civil law countries, but also due to the fact that as a new member of the European Community it carefully but swiftly transposes the directions of the European legislation in the area of e-signatures, seeking to balance and adjust the new regulatory framework to the needs of the nascent e-market.

Analysis on how the specific liability rules, as transposed, affect the Bulgarian legal environment with regard to the liability of CSPs will synthesize knowledge and provide evidence relevant to the general question posed by this work: in other words, *whether the supranational specific liability rules of the CSPs, as transposed, contribute towards the building of trust in the certification services market?* If numerous problems are identified, this gives rise to a further question: what issues should be taken into consideration when introducing specific liability rules at a supranational level to given groups of subjects?

Promoting a reasoned analysis of the EU Directive liability rules and the problems associated with transposing them into Bulgarian law is a professional challenge and a longstanding aim of the author. He has pursued his academic studies in Bulgarian law and began his academic career as an assistant professor in civil law and the law on obligations, researching, in particular, the civil liability concept under Bulgarian law. As a practicing lawyer, he has faced the practical implications and problems in substantiating civil liability grounds in civil proceedings, and has therefore acquired knowledge of the court practice in respect of liability issues. Furthermore, the author participated in the drafting process of the contemporary Bulgarian legislation in the area of electronic signatures. During the course of this process, together with the other academics involved, he assessed the difficulties inherent in analyzing the CSPs' liability concept under the EU Directive and in harmonizing the national legislation with its rules. He acted as consultant to the first certification-service-providers established in Bulgaria in managing their liability risk, and later to the Communications Regulation Commission – the Bulgarian state body supervising the activities of the certification-service-providers, which gave further experience of and insight into the legal problems subject to analysis in this work.

Achieving the aims of this work was made possible by analyzing the correlation between different groups of problems.

In Chapter I, as a *first step*, a reliable viewpoint for understanding the basic notions of the public key infrastructure was established in order to facilitate understanding of how the electronic signatures work. The different types of electronic signatures were delineated. The signature-creation and signature-verification processes were examined, as were the role of the certification-service-providers and the services they provide in order to make the use of electronic signatures possible. Emphasis was placed on examination of the specificities of the CSPs' rights and obligations and their market role. This proved necessary in order to make a proper assessment of the necessity of a particular regulation relating to the CSPs' liability. The notion of certification services-provider was analyzed in depth, since different acronyms and various terms are used in the different jurisdictions when referring to the same or different kinds of providers of certification services. For this purpose, the relationships of the CSPs with the other market actors were drawn. Thus, the liability exposure of the CSPs to the respective groups of subjects was clearly outlined. Only thereafter did it prove to be possible to determine whether the general civil liability regime of other service providers or of other subjects would be applicable to CSPs and whether a specific liability regime would be required for them.

Making analysis of the issues in this first part of the work revealed complexity, since a number of sources were found to partially examine or regulate the notion of electronic signature, the certification services and the certification-service-provider – standardization deliverables, normative acts, studies and speeches. However, all these sources impact upon the various notions from different angles, in an incoherent and sometimes contradictory way. This problem gave rise to the necessity of using diverse research methods in correlation and combination. Many studies and normative acts, both on supranational and national levels were collected over a number of months, by means of research on the Internet and in different libraries. They were juxtaposed and thoroughly analyzed to give an introduction to the core issues related to the public key infrastructure processes and mechanisms. Applying the comparative analysis to the notion of CSP led to the identification of two main approaches with respect to the meaning of this notion used in different sources – in a broad and in a strict sense. These findings were used afterwards for making a proper interpretation of the notion of CSP under Directive 1999/93 in Chapter III and under Bulgarian law in Chapter V. The author has drawn upon his own previous work, dedicated to analysis of the key notions, which has appeared in different legal publications.

Many legal norms were found to regulate the relations between the main actors in PKI: CSP – signatory and CSP – third relying party. Successful analyzing the meaning of the legal norms resulted in identification of the relationships between these groups of subjects and in understanding of the nature of their liability. Useful deductions were made in respect of issues that have thus far remained unclear or unanswered in legal theory: enforcement of a valid agreement between the CSP and the relying party (thus substantiating a contractual liability claim towards the CSP); the essence of relationships and liability exposure between the CSP and third persons other than those relying on the certificate; the essence of relationships and liability exposure between the CSP and the impersonated damaged persons, etc. Furthermore, since no

16

clear and effective normative base was found in order to define the relationships, and essence of liability exposure, between the CSPs and the other service providers within the PKI, scientific sources and standardization deliverables were mainly analyzed. This method proved to be appropriate for obtaining reliable information about the market roles of the registration service providers, directory service providers, time-stamping service providers, archive service providers etc.

The *second step* in the analysis of the specific liability of the CSPs was the establishment of a reliable viewpoint for understanding the basic legal notions of liability, fault, wrongfulness, causation etc. These notions were outlined in Chapter II against the background of the Bulgarian civil law doctrine, since the analysis of the effects of the supranational liability rules took place in the context of their transposition into Bulgarian national law. This approach seems appropriate since the Bulgarian legal system belongs to the Continental law family. Therefore, its general liability concept is similar to the concepts upheld in those of the EU Member States that follow Roman law traditions. As a result, the analysis and conclusions in respect of the adequacy of the supranational specific liability rules for CSPs proved to be acceptable and reliable.

Since this work does not aim at making an in-depth theoretical analysis of the essence of the liability concept, nor does it aim at analyzing all the theories regarding liability in different countries, the author's chosen method of obtaining information for the purposes of the research has been to summarize and present the prevailing theories on general civil liability that exist within Bulgarian legal doctrine without straying into the realm of scientific novelty. Those theories were inferred from identified and collected publications, studies and works encapsulating modern Bulgarian legal theory. Various studies regarding civil liability in other countries are presented, but only as reference. Furthermore, due to the lack of any reported court cases on the liability of CSPs to date, it was not possible to refer and support the conclusions by practicle examples. Some cases have been identified and referred to, however, with the sole purpose of clarifying the general liability concept - a rich court practice in this respect exists in Bulgaria as well as in other European countries. It should be further noted that for the purposes of clarifying the general civil liability concept under Bulgarian law, different legislative techniques employed throughout Europe were taken into account and compared, as were the variety of codification styles, divergent legal-interpretation methods, the unequal value of court precedent etc. Illustrative examples have been provided to support the author's conclusions and findings.

Where legal theory leaves it unclear whether and to what extent exposure to liability should be regulated by law, and what restraints for liability management should be introduced to the detriment of the freedom to contract, the aim for national jurisdiction, especially that of Bulgaria, should be to achieve a reasonable balance between competing interests. In the dynamic and technology-driven environment of the online world, leaving the liability regulations to the general rules might give unfair advantage to the interests of certification-service-providers. The European legislator has noted the persistence of this problem and has decided to introduce, on a supranational level, particular rules for the regulation of the CSPs' liability. These aim at the harmonization of the national regimes of the EU Member States by creating unified liability exposure. Analyzing whether these rules, as transposed, are adequate and appropriate to bring about the desired balance is made in Chapter III as the *third step* in this work. The specific liability regime in question is contained in Directive 1999/93/EC on a Community Framework for Electronic Signatures. Consequently, thus a substantial part of the research focuses on analyzing the Directive rules. A proper analysis and identification of legal and practical problems not only contributed to the making of a proper assessment of the necessity of a specific liability regime, but also provided useful guidance for the effective transposition of the provisions of the Directive into national law – a process achieved by the end of the work.

Since the research was focused on the examination of one particular rule of one supranational act – Directive 1999/93/EC – the main method of research at this third stage was elaborated on thorough normative analysis and re-interpretation of this Directive rule on a textual basis. The knowledge of and deductions about the general notions of electronic signatures and the role of the CSPs in providing certification services related to e-signatures contained in the first stage serve as the legal bases for the analysis mentioned above, as does the viewpoint on liability concepts set out in the second stage. However, plain analysis of the Directive rules and proper understanding of the intentions of the European legislator would not have been possible without reviewing the historical development of the liability rule of the Directive from the date of the first proposal to the date of enactment of its final text. The historical analysis of the interim drafts proved to be a successful way to trace the metamorphosis of the initial ideas of the Commission and their subsequent essential distortion. The drafts and the opinions of the different European authorities were gathered from Internet sources and from the hard copy library materials at the Commission and at K.U.Leuven. Furthermore, to find the true meaning of the Directive liability rule, various studies, addressing different aspects of this rule, were collated and reviewed. All of these studies are recent and were obtained from Internet sources. Useful information with respect to this topic has also been obtained via the author's attendance at a number of workshops, seminars and international conferences, where speeches and views on liability of CSPs were presented. The author has challenged some of the prevailing theories on the essence of the liability rule (e.g. the claimed presence of the 'presumption of causality', the presence of the effective 'limitation of liability' etc.) while others support the author's deductions. Serious arguments in support of the assertions were produced by means of inducing theoretical assumptions, particularly in respect of the general model behind the qualified signature concept introduced by the e-signatures Directive.

The introduction of specific liability rules for the CSPs by one directive give rise to further questions on how such a regime interferes with other *acquis* rules establishing a protective statutory shield for certain groups of users (consumers, individuals etc.). There are a number of directives and other Community instruments establishing specific liability rules applicable to the CSPs (as a type of service providers) falling outside the regime introduced by Directive 1999/93/EC. The national rules should comply with all Community acts, but the Bulgarian lawmakers face problems in transposing those rules. Thus, the *further logical step* was the analysis of those problems in Chapter IV. The research aims, firstly, at clarifying the scope of the liability rules, applicable to the CSPs, which are set out in different Community acts, to complete the liability position of the CSPs established on a supranational level. Secondly, the work attempts to identify the order of priority to be followed in applying the specific liability rules where there is contradiction as to their applicability. The research of those issues promoted further knowledge in answering the general question on the necessity for a specific liability regime for the CSPs.

In order to elaborate on the research at this stage, information on the enforced normative texts of different directives which are the subject of analysis, and European Commission reports on implementation levels in the EU Member States (where available) were collected. Internet sources were primarily explored for this purpose. Firstly, the normative rules introducing different specific liability regimes for the relevant groups of subjects were themselves thoroughly analyzed. The analysis was also based on a number of selected studies published by prominent scholars, researching *inter alia* the specific liability rules contained in these directives. Those studies were found in various libraries in Belgium, the UK and Bulgaria. Secondly, the information on whether the liability rules contained in these directives conflict with the relevant rules of the main Community instrument establishing liability rules for the CSPs – Directive 1999/93/EC – was synthesized by means of direct comparison of the overlapping liability rules in force.

The *final step* of the research involved making an analysis of some practical problems and effects faced by the Bulgarian legislators following the transposition of the specific liability rules for the CSPs established by the *acquis*. This analysis made in Chapter V explores to the fullest extent possible the issue of whether the supranational rules, as transposed, establish an effective protective legal shield for the interests of certification services users and promote trust in the provision of such services on a national level. In this regard, it is also worth bearing in mind that findings about the effects of the transposition of the specific liability regime established by the *acquis* into Bulgarian national law are likely also to hold true for other European countries.

To assess the practical problems involved in this transposition, the method employed in the preceding chapter – of comparing the normative texts regarding liability from the Directive and the transposed national liability rules was successfully used. Ascertaining fairness in transposition provides a guarantee that the analysis and conclusions on the effects of the transposition will be correct, while unfair transposition might distort the conclusions of the preceding chapters. The premise of the comparison was provided by thorough analysis and understanding of the meaning and the purpose of the specific liability rules contained in the Bulgarian national legislation. Several studies analyzing the liability of the CSPs, either in Bulgaria or at EU level, were referred to in order to lend support to the findings made during the course of the research. Where possible, the identified problems relating to the transposition of the supranational liability rules into Bulgarian legislation were supported by reference to similar problems and effects of Community rules as experienced in the laws of individual EU Member States. Different studies by other academics were found to support the inferences made by the author in this regard. During the course of the research of different problems at this final stage, some parallels were drawn and deductions made on how matters might have been regulated should no specific liability rules had been established for the CSPs. The applicability of the general national liability rules, and their adequacy, induced findings on the core problems inherent in the supranational rules, and especially in its main concepts – the burden of proof, presumption of fault, reasonable reliance, and limitation of liability.

The *conclusive chapter* of the work summarizes the deductions made during the course of the whole work and synthesizes the conclusions supporting the author's assertion as to the lack of necessity for specific liability rules at a national level from point of view of the Bulgarian law.

Carrying out research on a defined single issue such as the liability of certification-service-providers is complicated due to the lack of any thorough studies relevant to this specific area of law in Europe. Different aspects of CSPs' liability have been non-comprehensively analyzed in a few articles and studies (some of them published during the course of preparation of this work).[4] More profound theoretical analyses of the liability of certification authorities have been carried out in respect of certain countries outside Europe. In the United States, an in-depth survey was conducted under the mandate of the American Bankers' Association by Thomas Smedinghoff, and aimed at giving an overview of the CA's liability on a federal level.[5] From the US perspective, the liability of the CSPs in PKI is also a subject of analysis in the ABA's PKI Assessment Guidelines.[6] A scoping study by Michael Sneddon from Clayton UTZ analyzed legal liability and e-transactions, and was prepared at the behest of the Australian National Electronic Authentication Council.[7] The Authentication and Notary Working Group at the Electronic Commerce Promotion Council of Japan (ECOM)[8] prepared a non-comprehensive analysis, which contained a proposal for the introduction of a liability regime in Japan.[9] The particularities of the liability concept of these countries, however, differ substantially from the liability principles used in Bulgaria and in most other European jurisdictions.

The lack of any relevant court cases reported so far makes the research still more difficult. This fact restricts the scope of the research to theoretical analysis and reflects on the applicable methods of research.

Making an academic research by finding numerous sources in the electronic domain of Internet makes the work far more challenging. On the one hand, the researcher faces the difficulty to track all new deliverables and electronic editions on a day by day

---

[4]   See for example: Balboni, P., *Liability of Certification Service Providers Towards Relying Parties and the Need for a Clear System to Enhance the Level of Trust in Electronic Communication*, Information & Communications Technology Law, Carfax Publishing, Vol. 13, No. 3, 2004; also Rinderle, R., *Legal Aspects of Certification Authorities, A Study – Part of the TIE Project*, 2000, (www.tie.org.uk/tie_project.htm); also Hindelang S., *No Remedy for Disappointed Trust – The Liability Regime for Certification Authorities Towards Third Parties Outwith the EC Directive in England and Germany Compared*, Refereed article, The Journal of Information, Law and Technology (JILT), 2002 (1) (http://elj.warwick.ac.uk/jilt/02-1/hindelang.html); also Dumortier, J., Kelm, S., Nilsson, H., Skouma, G., Van Eecke, P. (2003) *The Legal and Market Aspects of Electronic Signatures in Europe, Study for the European Commission within the eEurope 2005 framework* (http://europa.eu.int/information_society/eeurope/2005/all_about/security/electronic_sig_report.pdf).

[5]   Smedinghoff, T., *Certification Authority Liability Analysis*, A Survey Assigned by the American Bankers Associations, (www.bakernet.com/ecommerce).

[6]   ABA's ISC *PKI Assessment Guidelines* – PAG v0.30, *ibid.*

[7]   Sneddon, M., Partner, Clayton UTZ, NEAC – *Legal Liability and E-transactions*, A scoping study for the National Electronic Authentication Council, August 2000 (http://www.noie.gov.au)

[8]   ECOM, *Proposal For Liability of Certification Authority*, Authentication and Notary Working Group Electronic Commerce Promotion Council of Japan (ECOM), May 2000 (http://www.ecom.or.jp/ecom_e/).

[9]   ECOM, *Proposal For Liability of Certification Authority*, Authentication and Notary Working Group Electronic Commerce Promotion Council of Japan (ECOM), May 2000 (http://www.ecom.or.jp/ecom_e/).

basis, since such studies might influence the deductions of the research. On the other hand, using numerous Internet sources like virtual liabraries, electronic journals, electronic books and articles reflects in changes in the academic style of drafting contemporary academic studies, like the present one. The reader will face issues like bookmarks linking to websites, rather to particular pages of paper editions, to which academic works in the past were usually linking to.

Being mostly of a doctrinal nature, the analysis of the specific liability regime of the CSPs and the conclusions thereof could make a contribution, in several directions, to the concept of liability as it applies to certification services.

Firstly, the research aims at producing useful knowledge necessary for making a clear delineation of the various types of CSPs and the role they play in promoting trust in the use of electronic signatures. It also aims at drawing a fair picture of the core legal relationships of the players in the electronic signatures market. Since no serious study in this respect has been carried out to date, the users and the service providers should gain from the presented study a better understanding of the scope of the functions of the different PKI agents. This will enable them to identify the lines of liability if damage is sustained in connection with different certification and other PKI services. Thus, the derived knowledge will help the signatories and the relying parties to efficiently use different legal instruments in order to impose liability upon certification-service-providers in respect of their misconduct.

On the other hand, the provision of services involving new technologies always makes the service-providers cautious about undertaking business risks, especially in view of potential liability exposure. In this respect, the research will enable the certification-service-providers to explore the available opportunities for management of their liabilities, and thus to minimize their business risk, *inter alia* by obtaining adequate insurance coverage for all events involving risk.

Thirdly, the analysis of the practical transposition of the specific liability rules of the main Community act regulating the activity of certification-service-providers will demonstrate the problems faced by Bulgaria – which is the subject of this research. In this regard, the research will provide national legislators, not only in Bulgaria, but also in the other EU countries, with guidelines for the re-interpretation and clarification of the Directive's liability concept. It will also give practical guidance on how to transpose the supranational liability rules in order to make their national e-signature laws compliant to an acceptable extent with Directive 1999/93/EC.

A side-effect of the analysis of the practical transposition of the Directive's liability rules into the Bulgarian legislation, as a case study, is the provision of useful information and analysis for the Bulgarian legal system, particularly in the area of e-signatures. Since Bulgaria has now successfully joined the EU and become part of the internal market, a pressing need for information about the Bulgarian legal system has emerged. This work also makes a modest contribution in that regard.

The identification of the imperfections of the wording of the liability rule in Directive 1999/93/EC should, furthermore, give ideas for future improvements of the Directive as regards revising the specific liability regime established for CSPs. The problems analyzed in this work lead to more general conclusions with respect to the general problems involved in establishing specific liability regimes on a Community level. The research stresses such problems by addressing them to the European legislator.

Finally, the findings of this study may be of use to all legal practitioners who encounter problems related to the liability of certification-service-providers – barristers, solicitors, judges, arbitrators, prosecutors, in-house lawyers, consultants, academics etc. In this regard, the research will be a useful academic source.

Chapter I

ELECTRONIC SIGNATURES AND CERTIFICATION SERVICE PROVIDERS

To properly understand the CSPs' liability and to make an appropriate assessment as to whether a specific liability regime as introduced by the European Directive on e-signatures is justifiable or whether the general national liability rules are sufficient to guarantee the interest of certification services users, as a first step of the research, several basic issues related to electronic signatures will be introduced. These are the concept of trust, the fundamentals of electronic signatures and public key infrastructure, and the role of certification-service-providers.

The first issue to be examined is the *concept of trust*. Trust is the basic pillar on which the functioning of the electronic world rests, especially when using electronic signatures based on public key cryptography techniques. It is related to the reliance that one of the parties places in various facts[10]. These include the question of whether a certain electronic statement is in fact sent by the alleged author; whether it remains unaltered from the moment of signing until the moment of receipt; whether at a later point in time the will of the author can be proven in such a way that he or she cannot repudiate the statement previously made etc. This trust is built on the bases of a set of technical encryption techniques, certain attestations by trusted third parties, adequate legal norms, establishment of a protection shield for the interests of the relying parties by declaring recognition of the electronic statements and signatures, and by legal rules establishing clear effective instruments for the attraction of liability in the event that damages for usage of electronic signatures are incurred.[11] The different types of electronic signatures import different level of trust. Therefore, the basic aspects of the three main types of electronic signatures – basic, advanced, and qualified – will be outlined. The question of why the law attaches different legal value to these signature types will be addressed in the light of the requirements they fulfil in prompting higher levels of trust.

---

[10] McCullagh, A., *'The establishment of 'TRUST' in the electronic commerce environment'*, The 1998 Information Industry Outlook Conference, 7 November 1998 – Canberra, (http://www.acs.org.au/president/1998/past/io98/etrust.htm).

[11] Similarly, Adrian McCullagh, *ibid.*, promotes interesting theory, that in the electronic commerce environment the concept of trust involves the interaction of four disparate components; technology trust, behavioural trust, product trust, and legal trust.

In the second place, while the answer to the questions of whether and how the liability regime is suited to secure the necessary level of trust is subject of research in the forthcoming chapters, at this stage the *role, types and functions of the 'certification-service-providers'* will be analyzed, since these are the key trusted third parties in the trust-building process. The relationships between CSPs and other parties using or relying on certification services must be identified to understand the CSPs' liability exposure. This chapter clarifies the notions 'trust-service-provider' and 'certification-service-provider'. These terms are used with different meanings not only in the legal literature but also in the national laws and the international acts. It seems impossible to interpret the specific liability rules established by the Directive and by the national laws without having a proper understanding of which subjects these rules are addressed to. However, this chapter does not aim at making a thorough analysis of the roles of the different kinds of CSPs, nor does it attempt to investigate thoroughly their liability regimes. It is limited to the examination of the status of the main players for the purposes of researching and studying the specific liability of the CSPs in the chapters that follow.

The analysis of the basic aspects of the electronic signatures, the concept of trust and the CSPs' role in the trust-building process should clarify the subject of the research and thus put in place the first piece of the foundation of this work.

1. Concept of Trust: Electronic Signatures for Building Trust

As mentioned above, one of the main problems in the world of electronic communications in a broad sense, especially within open networks like the Internet, is confidence – whether a given message has been sent by the alleged author, whether its content has remained unaltered from the time it is sent to the time its content is acknowledged, whether it may be kept for a certain period of time for the purposes of proving the intention of the sender at a later point, and whether unintended recipients or interceptors were prevented from obtaining knowledge of the content of the communicated data. These requirements for secure electronic communications are commonly referred to as authenticity, integrity, non-repudiation and confidentiality.[12]

---

[12] See ECAF Model Part 1 – Introduction/Strategy, Introducting the Elements of Cryptography, section 2, p.1. Legal definition of these notions was found in §1 of the Bulgarian Ordinance on the activities of certification-service-providers, the terms and procedures of termination thereof, and the requirements for

Therefore, a mechanism and infrastructure for exchanging and maintaining data should be established to guarantee security and, as a result, to promote confidence.[13]

The handwritten signature proves to be such a secure authentication tool in traditional written communication. The way in which the hand moves in making the signature, the similarity of the shapes made, the various identification signs – letters or names – the fact that the signature is placed under the text of the written statement, and the fact that both the text and the signature are indelibly applied to the same media instils confidence in the relying party as to the authenticity and integrity of the message, and the possibility of proving the intention of the author at a later point in time. The lack of a signature gives rise to difficulties and insecurity in proving the authorship of the written statement.

For the purposes of electronic communications, information and communication technologies have developed an alternative to the handwritten signature – a cryptographic tool designed to achieve the same, or even greater level of security in proving the authorship of electronic statements – the electronic signature.

The European Community has identified the need to introduce a supranational normative instrument in order to recognize the legal value of electronic signatures and thus promote legal security in the use of electronic means of communication for the exchange of electronic statements. At the beginning of 2000, following lengthy consultations, discussions and coordination procedures, Directive 1999/93/EC on the Community framework for electronic signatures[14] (hereinafter referred to as the "Directive") was brought into force. The Directive aims at facilitating the use of electronic signatures and contributing to their legal recognition. It establishes a legal framework for electronic signatures and certain certification services in order to ensure the proper functioning of the internal market.[15] The Directive regulates the main types of electronic signatures, the principles used in relation to the provision of certification services and the activities and liability of the providers of certification

---

provision of certification services adopted pursuant to CMD No. 17 dated 31 January 2002 (Promulgated, SG No. 15 dated 8 February 2002) (available at http://www.orac.bg/en/resources-links).

[13] See Harrison, R., *Public Key Infrastructure: the risks of being trusted,* "Computers and Law", the magazine of the Society for Computer and Law, August/September 2000, Volume 11 issue 3, page 1, (http://www.laytons.com/ publications/rmh_article.htm)

[14] Promulgated in OJ L13/12 on 19 January 2000.

[15] Article 1 (1) of the Directive.

services, related to electronic signatures – the so-called 'certification-service-providers'.

1.1. Types of electronic signatures

Directive 1999/93/EC deals with three main types of electronic signatures, depending on the statutory requirements for their qualification as such and the legal consequences of their usage.

1.1.1. Basic electronic signature

The basic notion of electronic signature is introduced in Article 2(1) of the Directive. It provides that as an electronic signature shall be considered any "data in electronic form which are attached to or logically associated with other electronic data and which serve as a method of authentication".[16]

This definition of an electronic signature is extremely wide and encompasses within its ambit any type of authentication information, including putting a name under an email or SMS.[17]

Any sign, initials, pseudonym, name, scanned signature, and any identification information such as numbers, or other data if presented in electronic form, may serve as an electronic signature. This information should be attached to or logically associated to the electronic statement. Since the technologies for presenting statements in electronic form are numerous, the Directive has attempted to remain neutral as to the issue of which technologies might be involved. Therefore, if a generally recognized standard for visualization of the attached authentication data is used and is accessible for the addressee of the electronic statement, then these data would serve as an electronic signature.[18] Of course, the addressee should be capable of identifying and associating the signature as being that of the alleged author.

---

[16] Article 2 (1) of Directive 1999/93/EC.

[17] Dumortier, J., *DIRECTIVE 1999/93/EC on a Community framework for electronic signatures*, 2001 K.U.Leuven, ICRI, (http://law.kuleuven.be/icri/all_pubs.php?action=pubs_staff&staffid=1&where=).

[18] Kalaydjiev, A., Belazelkov, B., Dimitrov, G., Yodanova, M., Stancheva, V, Markov, D., *Electronic Document. Electronic Signature, Legal Regime*. Ciela Publishing/CID, 2004, p. 133.

As one can see, the basic electronic signature as an authentication tool does not promote much confidence in the electronic world since it does not secure the elements of trust – integrity, authenticity, confidentiality and non-repudiation – in a dependable manner. Therefore, the Directive does not credit this kind of signature with a high legal value. Where such a 'basic' signature is used, the interested party will bear the burden of proving in legal proceedings the authorship of the signed message.[19]

However, in most cases usage of a basic signature is justifiable since a high level of security is not always necessary. For example, if my colleague and I have agreed to communicate electronically, and he has indicated that it is enough for my first name to appear at the bottom of my emails in order for him to have faith that they originate from me, than there is no reason for the law to restrict the legal value of such authentication. In effect, the parties have agreed to use and trust such an authentication as being secure, while in fact it is not. Many people do the same where non-electronic communication is concerned. They trust, for example, in the security of such methods of communication as fax and voice calls which in reality are far from being secure. Where legal complications arise, the party that wishes to prove the authenticity of the statement will have to do this in legal proceedings, which will not always be an easy task.

1.1.2. Advanced electronic signature

The so-called 'advanced electronic signature' is characterized by much greater security in electronic exchange. It is introduced by Article 2(2) of Directive 1999/93/EC, under the auspices of which as an advanced electronic signature shall be considered any electronic signature meeting the following requirements:

1. uniquely linked to the signatory;

2. capable of identifying the signatory;

3. created using means that the signatory can maintain under his or her sole control; and

---

[19] Article 5 (2) of Directive 1999/93/EC.

4. linked to the data to which it relates in such a manner that any subsequent change of the data is detectable.

But what do these requirements mean? They are formulated in a very general and technology-neutral manner. In practice the market only currently offers one solution that meets all four of these requirements: electronic signatures based on the digital signature technique or, in other words, making use of public key cryptography.[20]

The principle of these electronic signatures is based on the usage of two numbers representing algorithmic key pairs. These keys are called respectively private key (or signature-creation data) and public key (or signature-verification data). They are not equal, but each can be used to achieve one and the same mathematical result in applying special cryptographic algorithms. What is essential is that each key pair is unique. In other words, one public key corresponds only to one given private key. Another important fact is that the private key with the most contemporary information and communication technology means cannot be derived from the public key.[21]

The generation of the key pair represents a complicated mathematical process based on special cryptographic algorithms.

The private key, being signature-creation data, should remain secret and accessible only to the signatory. It is used for 'signing' the electronic statement. The public key, being signature-verification data, may be made available to all third parties because it is used for verification of whether the electronic statement is signed by the corresponding private key and whether the statements remain unaltered from the moment of signature to the moment of receipt and verification.

---

[20] Dumortier, J., *DIRECTIVE 1999/93/EC on a Community framework for electronic signatures, Ibid.*, p.8.
[21] Of course, this would depend on the keys lenght.

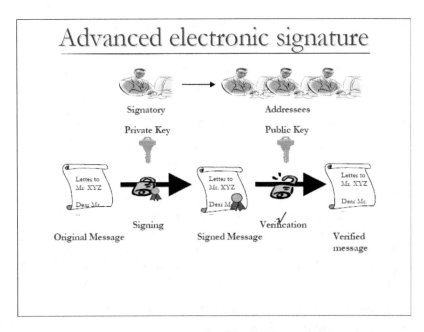

Fig. 1. Advanced electronic signature

The usage of one key for encryption and a different key for decryption is possible due to the different algorithmic methods for asymmetrical cryptography developed in cryptology.

The process of creation of the advanced signature, i.e. the 'signing', is based on the possibility for a signatory to uniquely extract an electronic 'digest' (hash identifier) of a given message (fig. 2, stage 1) by using certain algorithms[22] and one of the keys (the private key) of the key pair to encrypt the electronic digest (fig. 2, stage 2). It is worth mentioning that the electronic digest corresponds to the particular electronic message from which it has been extracted. Any subsequent change to the electronic message will result in another electronic digest. In other words, the message encrypted by the

---

[22] Algorythms for extracting the hash identifier are usually referred to as 'hash-algorythms'. Such algorythms are SHA (Secure Hash Algorythm), MD5 (Message Digest – 5), etc. Algorythms for encryption of the hash identifier are referred to as 'signing algorythms'. Commonly used signing algorythms are RSA (Rivest-Shamir-Adelman), DSA (Digital Signature Algorythm), ECDSA (Elliptic Curve Digital Signature Algorythm), etc.

private key of the signatory electronic digest represents a very advanced electronic signature. Insofar as the electronic digest is unique for every given message, so is the advanced electronic signature.[23] The mechanism for signature creation and verification is illustrated in the following diagram:

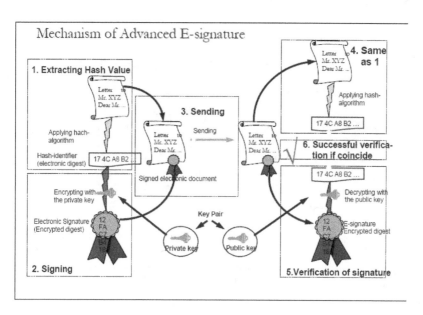

Fig. 2. Mechanism of the advanced electronic signature

The signature is created at the moment of signing only (fig. 2, stage 2). Therefore, it is incorrect to claim that someone 'has an electronic signature'. In fact, no one has an electronic signature – it is uniquely created and differs for every signed electronic message. An individual might have a private key for creating an advanced electronic signature and a corresponding public key for verification of the electronic signature, but this does not amount to having an electronic signature. Confusion over this

---

[23] That is why it is not precise to claim that someone "has an electronic signature". In fact no one has an electronic signature – it is created uniqely and differs for every signed electronic message. Someone might have a private key for creating electronic signature, but not an electronic signature.

matter is frequently reflected in vagueness and inapplicability of various legislative texts.[24]

In fact, after creation of the advanced electronic signature ('signing'), it is attached to the electronic statement using different technology standards.[25] The electronic document and the electronic signature are attached and bundled and may be saved or sent to the addressee (fig. 2, stage 3).

Electronic exchange requires a means of ensuring that the submitted electronic statements cannot be altered by impostors in the period between the moment they are created to the moment they are received. A mechanism should exist to facilitate secure verification of the authenticity of the electronic statements. When using advanced electronic signatures this security is achieved by special cryptographic verification techniques.

In other words, the verification should answer two questions: (i) whether the advanced electronic signature is created by the particular private key; and (ii) whether the electronic message remains unaltered from the moment of its signing to the moment of the verification.

The verification represents a mirror process to that of signature creation. It is achieved by using the public key, which may be made available to all third parties. The addressee firstly decrypts the advanced electronic signature and obtains the electronic digest as it was supposed to be at the moment of creation of the signature (fig. 2, stage 5). If the decrypted electronic digest corresponds to the received electronic statement, then no alternation has taken place from the moment of the creation of the signature to the moment of verification. Any change would result in discrepancy between the electronic digest and the message. Verification is achieved by extracting a new electronic digest from the electronic statement (fig. 2, stage 4) and making a comparison between the digest extracted in this way and the decrypted one (fig. 2, stage 6). Alternation even of a single piece of information in the electronic statement,

---

[24] See for example Article 22, i.(8), Article 28 (1), Article 33 (2) (1) of the Bulgarian EDESA. The law refers to electronic signatute and depending on the context and the systematical place of the norm, the wording would mean either having a private key or a having a public key. Article 212a of the Bulgarian Criminal Code also punishes as a criminal offence "usage of another's electronic signature", which comes to say "usage of another's private key". However, since the criminal norms may not be interpreted broadly, this norm proves to be *de facto* stillborn.

[25] Different standards are available for attaching the electronic signature to the electronic data. They would depend on the very technology for representing the electronic document – electronic mail (S/MIME), MS Word document (.doc), Adobe Acrobat document (.pdf), PKCS#7 format (.p7s), XML format (.xml), etc.

or signing with another private key that does not correspond to the public key made available to the addressee will result in difference between the extracted digest and the decrypted one. Successful verification would promote trust in the integrity of the message and in its authenticity. Currently, 'signing' and verification are achieved quickly and automatically by the software employed,[26] which makes the usage of advanced electronic signatures widely accessible.

The requirements of Article 2(2) of the Directive for advanced electronic signature can easily be understood by considering the matters set out above. These include being uniquely linked to the signatory (created by a private key under sole control of the signatory); being capable of identifying the signatory (verified by using the public key, corresponding to a particular private key in possession of the signatory); having been created using means that the signatory can maintain in his or her sole control (the private key and the signature-creation device); and being linked to the data to which it relates in such a manner that any subsequent change to the data is detectable (the cryptographic verification as described above).

Although the advanced electronic signature gives much greater security as to the authenticity of electronic communications, the Directive still does not grant this type of electronic signature much higher legal status than that attached to the basic electronic signature. A party who wishes to prove the authenticity of an electronic statement signed by an advanced electronic signature in the context of legal proceedings must do so by providing acceptable proof of evidence.[27] The reason for this is that when using advanced electronic signatures there is still no instrument or method which can be used to provide a demonstrable link between the identity of the signatory and the key pair, and no requirements have been established for using infrastructure capable of providing reliable verification of this identity. Such higher requirements are met by the so-called 'qualified electronic signature'.

1.1.3. Qualified electronic signature

The e-signatures Directive attaches the highest legal value to the qualified electronic signature. Its presence in an electronic document is regarded as equivalent to the

---

[26] Signing and verification of of e-mails could be made by most of the pospular electronic mail client applications like Eudora, Microsoft Outlook, Outlook Express, etc. Documents in Windows Word could be signed and verified by the very editor Microsoft Word. Documents in Adobe Acrobat format could be signed and verified by the respective applications develped by Adobe, etc.

[27] Article 5 (2) of Directive 1999/93/EC.

presence of a handwritten signature on a paper document.[28] Signing by means of a qualified signature provides sufficient evidence for the court to accept the authenticity of the electronic message in legal proceedings.[29]

The concept that lies behind the qualified electronic signature reveals the European legislator's desire to protect social relations and to promote greater security and trust in the internal market by introducing a more stringent form of authenticity recognition for certain types of communication. In order to do this, the Directive has established further requirements for the advanced electronic signature.

The qualified electronic signature shall be considered as any advanced electronic signature,[30] which is based on a qualified certificate within the meaning laid down in Annex I, issued by a certification-service-provider meeting the requirements of Annex II, and which is created by a secure signature-creation device within the meaning laid down in the Directive and its Annex III.[31]

How do the above requirements in fact 'qualify' the 'qualified electronic signature'?

In the first place, the signature should be created by a secure signature-creation device (SSCD). This is considered to be configured software or hardware used to implement the signature-creation data (the private key)[32] in a secure manner. The Directive stipulates that such a device must, at the least, ensure that: i) the private key used for signature generation can practically occur only once, and that its secrecy is reasonably assured; ii) the private key used for signature generation cannot, with reasonable assurance, be derived and the signature is protected against forgery using currently available technology; iii) the private key used for signature generation can be reliably protected by the legitimate signatory against the use of others. Secure signature-creation devices must also not alter the data to be signed or prevent such data from being presented to the signatory prior to the signature process.[33] At present smart cards, smart pens, palm PCs, USB tokens, and other

---

[28] Article 5 (1) (a) of Directive 1999/93/EC reads that the qualified signature "(a) satisfy the legal requirements of a signature in relation to data in electronic form in the same manner as a handwritten signature satisfies those requirements in relation to paper-based data; and (b)"

[29] Article 5 (1) (b) of Directive 1999/93/EC.

[30] See section 1.1.2 of Chapter I, *supra*.

[31] See EESSI, *Final Report of the EESSI Expert Team*, 20th July 1999, p.14 (http://www.eema.org/ecaf/ Frep.pdf). This notion is not quite precise. See Chapter III,section 5, *infra*.

[32] Article 1 (5) of the Directive.

[33] Annex III of Directive 1999/93/EC.

tools are used as SSCDs. The internal market should introduce common standards both as to what should be considered a SSCD and on the electronic signature products.[34]

The conformity of the SSCDs with the requirements laid down in the Directive should be determined by public or private bodies designated by Member States, and the results of such determination should be recognized by all Member States. The Commission has established criteria for Member States by which they may determine whether a body should be designated.[35]

In the second place, the Directive introduces requirements for the qualified signature to be supported by a qualified certificate issued by a certification-service-provider.

These requirements in fact establish the key elements for the functioning of a whole infrastructure aiming at promoting trust in electronic signatures (the so-called public key infrastructure - PKI). Analysis of the issue is of utmost importance, since the role played by the certification-service-providers in this infrastructure, particularly in issuing qualified certificates, provides insight into their liability exposure. Therefore, all of the sections that follow are dedicated to analysis of these issues.

1.2. Role of the certification-service-providers

It is apparent from the preceding section that the usage of advanced electronic signatures based on different *encryption techniques* provides a relatively high level of technical security for electronic communications.[36] It has become apparent that these encryption techniques are based on the possibility for the signatory to electronically 'sign' any given message and that the addressee has the possibility to

---

[34] The Commission has published criteria in Commission Decision (2003/511/EC) of 14 July 2003 on the publication of reference numbers of generally recognised standards for electronic signature products in accordance with Directive 1999/93/EC of the European Parliament and of the Council (notified under document number C(2003) 2439).

See also CEN/ISSS CWA 14172-5: "Secure signature creation devices" и CEN/ISSS CWA 14255, WS/E-Sign: "Guidelines for the implementation of Secure Signature-Creation Devices".

[35] See Commission Decision (2000/709/EC) of 6 November 2000 on the minimum criteria to be taken into account by Member States when designating bodies in accordance with Article 3 (4) of Directive 1999/93/EC of the European Parliament and of the Council on a Community framework for electronic signatures (notified under document number C(2000) 3179), OJ L289/42 of 16.11.2000 (http://rechtsinformatik.jura.uni-sb.de/cbl/statutes/dec061100_DigSig_en.pdf)

[36] See *Introduction to Cryptography* in PGP documentation, Network Associates Inc., 1990-1999, Chapter 1, (http://www.pgpi.org/doc/pgpintro/#p1)

carry out cryptographic verification of the signed message. Successful verification by employing different algorithmic techniques creates trust in the integrity of the message and provides evidence that the message has not been altered from the moment of signature to the moment of its verification.[37] In other words, successful technical verification provides assurance for the addressee that the message has been signed by the holder of the private key, which corresponds to the public key, used for the algorithmic verification. Knowledge as to whether the public key is the one of this party's key pair is presupposed by the transfer of the key to the addressee by the signatory in a secure and trustworthy way.[38]

However, the usage of algorithmic techniques and the secure transfer of the public key are not in themselves sufficient to ensure a high level of trust and confidence. It is possible, for example, that the signatory might lose his or her private key or that, as a result of negligence, the key might be compromised by falling into the hands of other parties.[39] Moreover, in an open network environment such as the Internet, trust in the secure transfer of the public key by the signatory is not always easily achieved, especially when millions of users who are unknown to each other communicate daily. A private key could be also generated and used by an impostor purporting to be a genuine signatory.[40]

Therefore, further mechanisms should be developed to promote the proper functioning and usage of the cryptographic keys and security as to the identity of their owners, with a view to minimizing the risk of misuse.[41]

The solution to the problem lies in a third party certifying and guaranteeing the link between the public key and the signatory's identity as a natural person. This link is established by issuing a special electronic document known as a 'qualified

---

[37] Dumortier, J., et al., *The Legal Aspects of Digital Signatures*, Report I, Introductory Report: *The Digital Signature: Technical and Legal Issues*, ICRI, K.U.Leuven, European Commission, October 1998, page 37.

[38] Akdeniz Y. et al, *'Cryptography and Liberty: Can the Trusted Third Parties be Trusted? A Critique of the Recent UK Proposals'*, 1997 (2) The Journal of Information, Law and Technology (JILT). (http://elj.warwick.ac.uk/jilt/cryptog/97_2akdz/)

[39] See Dimitrov, G., *Electronic Signatures: Advanced Electronic Signature*, Market & Law Journal, i.3, 2003.

[40] See Smedinghoff, T., *ibid.*, p.24.

[41] Reagle, Joseph M. Jr., *Trust in Electronic Markets. The Convrgence of Cryptographers and Economists*, First Monday Internet Journal, 1996, (http://www.firstmonday.dk/issues/issue2/markets/).

certificate'.[42] The trusted third party is referred to in the Directive as a 'certification-service-provider'[43].

Although the main function of the qualified certificate is to certify the link between the signatory's identity and his or her public key, it should also attest to other attributes stipulated in the law. Such attributes include *inter alia* an indication that the certificate is issued as a qualified certificate, the identification of the certification-service-provider, an indication of the beginning and end of the period of validity of the certificate; the identity code of the certificate, limitations on the scope of use of the certificate, and limits on the value of transactions for which the certificate can be used etc.[44] The certificate should be signed with the advanced electronic signature of the certification-service-provider.[45] Once the certificate is issued, it is sent to the addressee in a bundle with the electronic statement and the attached electronic signature every time electronic signing occurs. Since everyone is entitled to verify the validity of the publicly available public keys of the certification-service-providers, it is presumed that the certified link between the signatory and its pubic key is valid. Therefore, the relying parties – the addressees of the signed electronic statements – will place trust in the certificate and thus they will have confidence that they verify the electronic signature with the public key of the alleged signatory. In other words, the addressees will trust the authenticity of the electronic statements signed by the signatory. It is obvious that, before issuing a certificate, the certification-service-provider should verify the identity of the signatory and make sure that the latter holds the private key corresponding to the certified public key and that the keys may be used as a key pair (i.e. in a technologically complementary manner). All stages of this process must follow the statutory requirements established for,[46] and the security rules established by, the certification-service-provider. The final stage is the issuance of the certificate. This entails entry of the certificate into a special publicly available directory kept by the certification-service-provider. The directory not only contains a list of issued certificates, but also a list of all certificates which have been revoked, either due to the fact that they have been compromised, or for other reason, prior to expiration of the certificate's period of validity. As the directory is usually open to the

---

[42] Article 2 (10) of Directive 1999/93/EC.

[43] Article 2 (11) of Directive 1999/93/EC.

[44] Annex I of Directive 1999/93/EC.

[45] Annex I (h) of Directive 1999/93/EC.

[46] The duties are described in more details in section 2.2.5, *infra*.

public, any interested party may verify the validity of a certificate at any time, for example by using specialized software which has the functionality to perform verification in an automated regime.[47]

If the advanced electronic signature attached to the electronic statement is followed by a valid qualified certificate issued by a certification-service-provider, the signature shall be considered 'qualified'. Lack of any of the mandatory attributes of the qualified certificate will vitiate the certificate and it accordingly will lose its value of a qualified certificate. Furthermore, an advanced electronic signature followed by an invalid certificate will no longer be regarded as a valid qualified signature. The same consequences will follow if expired or revoked certificates are used. The addressees will no longer trust the signature followed by a revoked certificate, because its revocation would mean that either the private key has become apparent to other people, or its secrecy was compromised by the use of technology, or another reason has emerged. Such a certificate becomes invalid.

Since information technologies in the area of cryptography develop quickly, at a certain period they may be secure enough that the private key will not be compromised (in calculating and extracting the private key from the public key), but at a later stage this may no longer be the case. Therefore, the security policies to be followed by the certification-service-providers for issuing certificates reflect the current state of art of the ICT sector, and certificates are issued with a relatively short term of validity (usually up to one year).[48] Following expiration of this term, certificates may be renewed by the issue of another certificate with the same public key according to the adjusted security policies, should the signatory wish.

Issuing and managing certificates and maintaining the public directory thereof is evidently the main function of the CSP and its role is of the utmost importance for the functioning of the public key infrastructure and the validity of the qualified electronic signatures.

The effectiveness of the CSPs making certain attestations (by providing certification services) with a view to gaining the trust of market actors using or relying on electronic signatures will depend on whether the actors trust such attestations. In other words, why should the CSPs, as third parties, be 'trusted'?

---

[47] For example by using On-line Certificate Status Protocol (OSCP).

[48] All Bulgarian CSPs without any exception issue client certificates with a validity term of 1 year. However, other CSPs (like Globalsign) issue certificates with 3-years validity term.

1.3. Trust in CSPs

Many factors promote trust in CSPs.[49] The mere fact that a person starts providing services related to electronic signatures does not automatically mean that the market players will trust his or her attestations and services. The issue is quite complex,[50] and only the main aspects of it are outlined below.

In the first instance, gaining trust is closely connected to the *statutory rules* establishing requirements for CSPs with regard to the maintenance of certain technology, organizing its management processes in a proper manner, maintaining of financial means and insurance coverage, employing professionals with relevant expertise and experience, meeting certain security levels in view of the vulnerability of the systems etc.[51] Most of the quantitative and qualitative criteria for evaluation of the extent to which these requirements are met is subject to standardization.[52] Should the service providers meet these statutory requirements and standards, it is to be expected that the market players will start to trust the services they offer.

However, when speaking about the statutory requirements, a second question arises – who should supervise the service providers to ensure that these duties are executed, and how should such supervision be done? Governments usually establish *national supervision schemes* under which powers are delegated to governmental or other bodies to control and supervise the activities of the certification-service-providers. The evaluation is typically performed following certain widely recognized standards. The presence of a transparent and effective supervising scheme enhances trust in the services offered by the service provider. National legislation usually

---

[49] McCullagh, A., *ibid*, see *supra* note 11.

[50] A very comprehensive analyss of the trust concept was made by Ed Gerck. The author thoroughly analyses the different of the trust. See Gerck, Ed., *Toward Real-World Models of Trust:Reliance on Received Information*, 1998 by E. Gerck and MCG, (http://mcwg.org/mcg-mirror/trustdef.htm)

[51] On a supranational EU framework see Annex II of Directive 1999/93/EC. In national legislations see for example Article 21 of Bulgarian EDESA.

[52] See *infra* note 106.

establishes different administrative measures and sanctions[53] in order to compel service providers to comply with the statutory requirements.

Another factor that could enhance confidence in the service providers and in electronic signatures is the existence of national *voluntary accreditation schemes*. Accreditation as a principle is based on the attestation that one already trusted party or government body makes as to the reliability and trustworthiness of persons performing certain activities or services. In the area of trust services, 'voluntary accreditation' means an attestation granted upon request by the certification-service-provider concerned, by a public or private trusted body (accreditation body) charged with the development of, and supervision of compliance with, rights and obligations, and certain technology, security management and other standards.[54] Accreditation schemes are voluntary and completely depend on whether service providers will adhere to and benefit from the accreditation or not. Such schemes aim at enhancing the level of services provided and encouraging the development and offering of new services by service providers, in order to meet the levels of confidence, security and quality demanded by the evolving market. By these means, the aim of establishing best practices among service providers is served.[55]

The establishment of different national *licensing regimes* to given groups of providers of goods or services[56] is another means by which trust in service providers is bolstered. A licence is usually considered to be a permission, granted subject to prior verification performed by an authorized state body, which demonstrates that the provider meets given requirements stipulated in the law. The provision of licensed services without a licence is prohibited. The market players trust the licensed

---

[53] See for example the measures and fines provided under Article 45 of the Bulgarian EDESA, Articles 6 and 7 of the Electronic Commerce Act of Ireland, Article 21 and Article 19 of the German E-signatures Act, Article 48 of the Slovenian E-signatures and E-commerce Act etc.

[54] In this respect definitions provided by some supranational instruments like the Directive 1999/93/EC are not quite correct. Under Article 2 (13) of the said act *'voluntary accreditation' means any permission, setting out rights and obligations specific to the provision of certification services, to be granted upon request by the certification-service-provider concerned, by the public or private body charged with the elaboration of, and supervision of compliance with, such rights and obligations, where the certification-service-provider is not entitled to exercise the rights stemming from the permission until it has received the decision by the body.* The main idea of the voluntary accreditation is that the CSP is never deprived of providing services prior the accreditation, because the very accreditation is not a permission *strictu sensu*.

[55] See Recital (11) of Directive 1999/93/EC.

[56] For example for provision of some telecommunication services, for provision of security services, for trading with bonds, etc.

providers in reliance on the facts that the state has verified the activity of the service provider beforehand and the issue of the licence evidences successful verification. In the area of electronic signatures throughout the EU, licensing for provision of certification services is not permitted; while in some countries outside EU licensing regimes for CSPs still exist.[57]

Another effective means of promoting trust in the provision of certification services in the electronic world are the *certification hierarchies* and the *cross-certification*.[58] This is based on the idea of mutual or hierarchical recognition of the certificates being the core instrument for building trust in public key infrastructure based on electronic signatures. Thus, one service provider 'guarantees' that the cross-certified service provider meets certain requirements to the extent that the certifier is ready to bear liability for the activity and the diligence of the other service provider. This issue is analyzed in Chapter III, section 3 (d), *infra* in view of liability allocation.

Trust in the provided services related to electronic signatures could be also promoted by different legislative techniques. One such scenario is the establishment of *mandatory rules* to restrict the autonomy of the parties to negotiate in derogation from the statutory rules.[59] This approach is clearly designed to protect the interests of the weaker party to the contract where unequal bargaining power could lead to economic injustice. This is considered a guiding principle in EU consumer protection law, and is therefore followed by the national legislations. The way in which EU legislation employs this technique to protect the users of certification services will become apparent in the following chapters.[60] However, the discussed approach should be applied with care since it could have an anti-competitive effect. The impossibility for the market players to manage their liability might result in reluctance for provision of certification services which apparently leads to fragmentation of the market.[61]

---

[57] For example China, India, Brasil and others.

[58] Dumortier, J., et al., *The Legal Aspects of Digital Signatures, ibid.*, page 24-31.

[59] On the nature and effects of the mandatory rules see Communication on European Contract Law: Joint Response of the Commission on European Contract Law and the Study Group on a European Civil Code, 2001, (http://www.sgecc.net/media/download/stellungnahme_kommission_5_final1.pdf)

[60] See Chapter IV, Section 6, *infra*.

[61] The problem thoroughly discusses in Capter V, *infra*.

As already mentioned, one of the factors of crucial importance for the trust-building process is the existence of a clear and effective *system of liability*. This means a system that is understandable, user-friendly, coherent, and clear as to the responsibilities its rules impose and the conditions applied for the recovery of compensation.[62] Paolo Balboni accurately outlines the role of liability regimes in the sphere of trusted services provision in his article 'Liability of Certification Service Providers towards Relying Parties and the Need for a Clear System to Enhance the Level of Trust in Electronic Communication':

"If CSPs can be seen now as key elements in the process of building trust in electronic communication, clear and effective liability rules for these 'trust dispensers' would give a strong impetus to the confidence of both consumers and businesses that rely on the certificates and the service providers. In fact, users will feel more confident in using CSPs and the related services when they know that if something goes wrong, someone will be liable and pay the damages. ... Indeed, liability questions play an important role in the relationship between relying parties and CSPs, as well as between two CSPs. A relying party may ask when and to what extent they are entitled to compensation if a CSP has failed to issue a certificate or whether he or she is entitled to a direct action against a CSP that failed to revoke a certificate that they relied on. A CSP established within the European Community may want to know what guarantees exist for a certificate issued by a CSP established in a third country, and when and to what extent it will be liable if the certificate is not accurately provided. In conclusion, the question of who has the burden of proof can be an interesting question for all the subjects involved. If precise answers to these kinds of questions cannot be found, CSPs will not be of any help in building a competitive and trustworthy environment, and there will be no future for a system based on the combination of electronic signatures and CSPs."[63]

The passage quoted above makes it clear that the building of trust is the main pillar for the functioning of the open public key infrastructure.[64] It refers to the confidence that the different parties require in order to rely on the electronic

---

[62] Balboni, P.,*ibid*, p.217.

[63] *Ibid.*

[64] The open PKI model is also referred to as "open system" or "open loop" model. The open system model assumes that signatories will obtain a single "identity" certificate from an independent third-party CA and then use that certificate to facilitate transactions with potentially many different parties. ILPF, A Report Of The ILPF Working Group On Certification Authority Practices, *The Role Of Certification Authorities In Consumer Transactions*, April 1997, (http://www.ilpf.org/groups/ca/draft.htm)

signatures, i.e. as to the authenticity and integrity of electronic statements. The certification-service-providers have an important role in the process of building trust, as they are, in a sense, 'trust service providers'.

The role of the CSPs, and their liability should be examined in the context of relationships with other PKI actors. Thus, the risks that the CSPs undertake and their liability exposure should be properly identified. The elaboration of a comprehensive and comparative overview on how the general liability rules are applied to the CSPs in different jurisdictions lies beyond the scope of this work. The research in this chapter aims to provide a means of understanding the particularities of the CSPs' general duties and relationships.

2. Notion and Types of CSPs.

After introducing the basic aspects of electronic signatures and outlining the important role of the certification-service-providers in promoting trust in the functioning of the public key infrastructure and making the electronic signatures work, the second part of this introductory chapter contains a more detailed analysis of the identity and role of the CSPs. In itself, further knowledge about the notion of CSPs and the role played by different kinds of CSPs in promoting trust within the market would give insight into their liability exposure and thus into the adequacy of the liability rules established by the main supranational act – Directive 1999/93/EC on electronic signatures.

2.1. Trust service provider

CSPs are market players providing a particular spectrum of services to promote the necessary level of trust and confidence in electronic communication. However, there is another notion that is commonly used in the theory and the legislative acts of many countries, which is considered to be the generic term for the provider of any kind of service that promotes trust – the so-called trust service-provider (TSP).[65]

---

[65] See Ganzaroli, A., Mitrakas, A., *Trusted Third Parties in open electronic commerce: The phase of negotiations in the International Trade Transactions model*, EURIDIS, 2002

Various terms are used by different sources to name the provider of trust services related to electronic signatures. There is no generally accepted standard, nor interpreting provision to legally define the TSP. For different purposes, different acronyms are used: 'trusted third parties' (TTPs),[66] 'trust service providers' (TSPs),[67] 'electronic trust service providers',[68] 'certification authorities' (CAs),[69] 'cryptography service providers',[70] 'certification-service-providers'[71] etc.[72]

This fact might lead to confusion as well as incorrect analysis of the role and functions of the different kinds of TSPs. It may also lead to the application of an inappropriate liability regime in different jurisdictions.

The definition of TSP is provided by the European Telecommunications Standards Institute (ETSI) in its document, ETSI TR 102 231 V 1.1.1 (2003-10) 'Electronic Signatures and Infrastructures (ESI) - Provision of harmonized trust service provider status information'.[73] It states that the TSP is a body operating one or more electronic trust services. ETSI finds that this '...*embraces a wide range of services which may relate to electronic signatures and is broader than the provision of certification services alone, and hence is used in preference to and with a broader application than the term certification-service-provider used in the EC Directive 1999/93/EC.*'[74]

This finding of ETSI is not quite precise. By comparing the notion 'trust service-provider' with the notion 'certification-service-provider', it appears that the term 'certification-service-provider' under the Directive only refers to providers of certification services.[75] The Directive provides a clear indication that its rules are not

---

[66] Commonly used in different ISO documents.

[67] See for example ETSI, DTR/SEC 004 010|STF 178 V0.0.14 (D3) (2001-08) (http://www.apectel24.org/down/ESTG/2%20ETSI%20Project%20on%20Status%20of%20TSPs.doc); also the UK's tScheme supporting documents Ref. tSd0042, Ref. 0102 - 107, all ver. 2.0 (www.tscheme.org)

[68] The tScheme Glossary of Terms, Ref.tSd0226, I.1.0, page 4, (www.tScheme.org)

[69] ABA ISC PKI Assessment Guidelines – PAG v0.30, *ibid.*

[70] See the UK Electronic Communications Act, Received Royal Assent on 25 May 2000.

[71] Article 2 (11) of Directive 1999/93/EC.

[72] See Harrison, R., *ibid.*, page 2.

[73] ETSI TR 102 231 V 1.1.1 (2003-10) Electronic Signatures and Infrastructures (ESI); Provision of Harmonized Trust Service Provider Status Information (http://webapp.etsi.org/exchangefolder/ts_102231v010101p.pdf)

[74] ETSI TR 102 231, section 3.1, *supra* note 73.

[75] See section 2.2.2, *infra.*

limited only to the regulation of certification services provided by the CSP, whereas electronic signatures are used in a large variety of circumstances and applications, resulting in a broad range of new services and products relating to or using electronic signatures. The Directive explicitly envisages that '*the definition of such products and services should not be limited to the issuance and management of certificates, but should also encompass any other service and product using, or ancillary to, electronic signatures, such as registration services, times-tamping services, directory services, computing services or consultancy services related to electronic signatures*'.[76] While providing '*any kind of services related to electronic signatures*',[77] the certification-service-provider is not limited to provision of certification services only. Therefore, the notion 'certification-service-provider' under the Directive is used in a broad sense,[78] and to a great extent it tallies with the notion of 'trust service-provider'.

Almost the same meaning is given to the notion of the TSP in the UK Scheme Glossary of Terms.[79] It defines the Electronic TSP as a body operating one or more services which enhance trust and confidence in electronic transactions typically, but not necessarily, using cryptographic techniques or involving confidential material.

The ECAF Model[80] also defines the notion, and recognizes the TSP as an organization that provides one or more of a number of PKI-related trust services, e.g. certification, registration, key generation, key recovery etc.

Taking into consideration the above, for the purposes of this present research, a trust-service-provider will be considered a private or public entity or legal or natural person that provides any kind of certification or other trust services related to electronic signatures enhancing confidence in electronic transactions.[81]

---

[76] Recital (9) of the Directive.

[77] See Article 2 (11) of the Directive

[78] See Dumortier, J., *Directive 1999/93/EC on a Community framework for electronic signatures*, 2001, K.U.Leuven – ICRI, p.10, (http://www.law.kuleuven.ac.be/icri)

[79] See *supra* note 68.

[80] ECAF Model, Part I – Introduction/Strategy, *Section C – PKI Security – A Market Overview*, Version 1 – 12/00, page 1.

[81] See also Groshieide, F., Boele-Woelki, K. , *European Private Law (1999/2000). E-Commerce Issue*, The Netherlands: Molengrafica, 2000, p.36

2.2. Certification-service-provider

Among the large variety of TSPs the main role in the electronic signatures infrastructure and particularly in the PKI, is reserved for certification-service-providers.

Similarly to the notion 'trust-service-provider', there are various interpretations of the notion 'certification-service-provider' used in different surveys, reports, and documents. The laws in the different jurisdictions also vary significantly in the ways they define the term. Misunderstanding the meaning of this notion might create difficulties in analyzing the liability of the CSPs.

2.2.1. CSP in a strict sense

In some jurisdictions, the notion CSP is limited to bodies providing certain (one or several) explicitly envisaged certification services, e.g. issuing certificates, issuing time stamps etc.[82] This player is considered to be a CSP in the strict sense of the term. The Law Governing Framework Conditions for Electronic Signatures of Germany,[83] for example, in Article 2 (8) provides that CSPs are considered to be natural or legal persons who issue qualified certificates or qualified time-stamps. In the same way, Article 19 of the Bulgarian Law on Electronic Documents and Electronic Signatures[84] provides that only natural or legal persons who: i) issue certificates and keep directories in relation thereto, and ii) provide access to the published certificates to any third person, shall be regarded as certification-service-providers. Additionally the CSP may provide services for the creation of private and public keys for qualified electronic signatures.

---

[82] For delineation of the different certification services see section 2.2.4, *supra*.

[83] Promulgated in Bundesgesetzblatt – BGBl. Teil I S. 876 from 21 May 2001

[84] Promulgated in State Gazette №34 from 06 April 2001, in force as of 07 October 2001

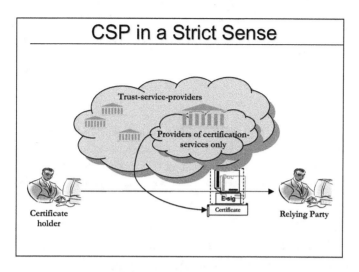

Fig. 3. Certification-service-provider in a strict sense

As one can see, a whole set of ancillary and other certification and trust services, as well as the statute and hence the liability of their providers, remain beyond the scope of these laws.[85] Providers of trust services not falling within the scope of the legally defined notion will not be considered as CSPs in these jurisdictions, and hence will not be subject to any particular liability regime if they appear. Their exposure to liability will be regulated by the general legal regime applicable to any other providers of information or other services.

Whether the provision of such services will in fact be considered as 'services'[86] in legal terms depends on the type of legal system and the statutory provisions in force in the relevant jurisdiction. In any case, it is subject to specific examination. For the EU Member States and for the majority of countries following the continental model, the answer to this question would be positive. Where an EU country is involved, the

---

[85] See also Part 2, Article 3 (9) of the Danish Bill on Electronic Signatures, Bill No. L 229 introduced on 22 March 2000 by the Minister of Research and Information Technology; Article 2 (2) of the Law Concerning Electronic Signatures and Certification Services of Japan; § 2 of the Qualified Electronic Signatures Act (SFS 2000:832) of Sweden, etc.

[86] See Article 50 of the EC Treaty.

activity of the CSPs will fall within the scope of the principles of freedom of establishment and freedom of provision of services enshrined in the EC Treaty.[87]

2.2.2. CSP in a broad sense

In the vast majority of European jurisdictions, and under the meaning of the Directive, the notion of CSP encompasses an entity or person providing a broader set of services – certification services and any other services related to electronic signatures;[88] i.e. the scope of the notion of CSP is much broader. It covers not only provision of certification services, but also other services that could not be considered 'certification' services *strictu sensu*.

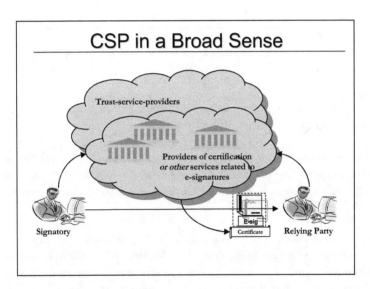

Fig. 4. Certification-service-provider in a broad sense

---

[87] Dumortier, J., et al., *Digital Signatures: A Survey of Law and Practice in the European Union, Report IV*, Woodhaed Publishing, 1998, ICRI – K.U.Leuven, European Commission, Chapter III, Section 2, page 370

[88] E.g. §2, i.10 of the Austrian Federal Law on the Electronic Signatures (Promulgated: Bundesgesetzblatt from 19 August 1999, Teil I); Article 2 of the Electronic Commerce Act, 2000 of Ireland, No.27 of 2000; Article 2 (12) of the Electronic Commerce and Electronic Signatures Act of Slovenia; Article 2 (h) of the Law on Electronic Signatures of Portugal defines, that the CSP shall be natural or legal person that creates and provides means for creating of keys, issues certificates, publishes them and provides other services, related to the electronic signatures. The similar approach is chosen by other states, etc.

Under Article 2 (12) of the Directive, a CSP is defined as any entity or legal or natural person that issues certificates *or provides other services related to electronic signatures*. The UNCITRAL Model Law (2001) also envisages that a CSP is to be considered as any person that issues certificates *and may provide other services related to electronic signatures*.[89] Many countries have transposed literally the definitions of the Directive and of the UNCITRAL Model Law.[90]

The particular restrictions, obligations and specific liability regimes affecting such providers are commonly introduced by the e-signatures laws regulating their activity. Analysis of the liability regime will be made in the relevant chapters below.[91]

By way of conclusion, it could be stated that the definition of the providers of certification and other electronic trust services as 'certification-service-providers' under the Directive, the Model Law, and the laws in certain jurisdictions is to a certain extent incorrect. The reason for this is that it embraces not only certification-service-providers issuing and maintaining certificates, but also registration service providers (RSPs), electronic notaries, directory service providers (DSPs), time-stamping service providers (TSPs), archiving service providers (ASPs), and any other providers of services related to electronic signatures.[92] In this sense, the meaning of certification-service-provider in such jurisdictions is more or less identical to the term trust-service-provider as defined *supra*.

In the literature, similar approaches were found while analyzing the activity of the CSP in a strict and in a broad sense.[93]

The laws in many countries do not clearly delineate the obligations and liabilities of the providers relating to the provision of different certification and other trust

---

[89] See Article 2 (e) of the UNCITRAL Model Law on Electronic Signatures, A/CN.9/WG.IV/WP.88

[90] See *supra* note 88. On the transposition of the rule see Dumortier, J., Kelm, S., Nilsson, H., Skouma, G., Van Eecke, P. (2003) *The Legal and Market Aspects of Electronic Signatures in Europe*, Study for the European Commission within the eEurope 2005 framework (http://europa.eu.int/information_society/eeurope/2005/all_about/security/electronic_sig_report.pdf).

[91] See Chapter III and Chapter V, *infra*.

[92] EESSI, *Final Report of the EESSI Expert Team*, 20th July 1999, p.14 (http://www.eema.org/ecaf/ Frep.pdf)

[93] Winn, J., *The Emerging Law of Electronic Commerce*, page 8 (http://www.smu.edu/~jwinn /mbachapter.htm); Biddle, B., *Digital Signatures Laws and the Electronic Commerce Marketplace*, page 5; European Commission, *Digital Signatures: A survey of law and practice in the EU*, p.49, *supra* note 87.

services. They could be concentrated and provided by one CSP alone but could be also outsourced.

Thus, the CSP can involve, for example, other CSPs to issue certificates, register applications, identify subscribers, maintain directories, or to perform other functions. In such a situation, the relationships between the different parties involved are often complex. Therefore, the role of each of the certification services providers, the relationships they enter into with each other and with other parties, and the obligations arising from these need to be identified and analyzed.[94]

2.2.3. CSP and certification authority

As already mentioned, some sources confusingly name the certification-service-provider 'certification authority' (CA).[95] In other circumstances, CA may be defined as software or software and hardware.[96] Clarity in this respect is of utmost importance since many laws and theoretical research projects mix up these notions, which leads to confusion in understanding their essence.

A 'certification authority' should be considered as the authority (unit) within the structure of the CSP *which issues and manages certificates.*[97] including dealing with their renewal, revocation, suspension, retirement, and archiving. In some circumstances, the CA may be also responsible for generating the key pairs.[98] That is why the CA is sometimes referred to as an 'issuing authority'. The confusion in terminology is a consequence of the fact

---

[94] The necessity identified in The Final Report of the EESSI Expert Team, page 42, *supra* note 92.

[95] See section 1.6. of the ABA's DTI Guidelines, "Certification authority is a person that issues certificates". Also: TTP.NL Framework for Certification of Certification Authorities Against ETSI TS 101 456: 2000, ECP.NL; also *McRoberts' Comments on the UK Consultation Paper of 5th of March*; p.2, also ILPF, *The Role Of Certification Authorities In Consumer Transactions A Report Of The ILPF Working Group On Certification Authority Practices* Draft, April 14, 1997, section 3.4 (http://www.ilpf.org/groups/ca/draft.htm). In some jurisdictions the laws also define the CSP as a CA – Article 3 (9) of the Danish Bill on Electronic Signatures - Bill No. L 229 of 29 May 2000 defines that as "certification authority" shall be understood to mean a natural or legal person who issues certificates.

[96] See *ECAF/EEMA Model Part 1 – Introduction/Strategy*. Section B. Introducing the Elements of Cryptography, p.8.

[97] See Bankservice PLC, CPS, v.1.0, 2003, Article 1.7 (www.b-strust.org); CPS of Globalsign, v.4.0, 2001, Article 3.1 (www.globalsign.net)

[98] *Ibid.*

that in some documents and acts[99] the term used for the issuing unit – CA – is also used to name the service provider itself.

The issuing of certificates is undoubtedly the core certification service. Bearing in mind that pursuant to the Directive and the terminology used below, the certification-service-provider is the entity that issues certificates *or* provides *other services related to electronic signatures*, depending on the scope of certification services offered,[100] the CSP may run a CA but need not necessarily do so. Therefore, not all CSPs act as issuing authorities. This fact should be taken into consideration while examining the liability of the CSP providing CA services.

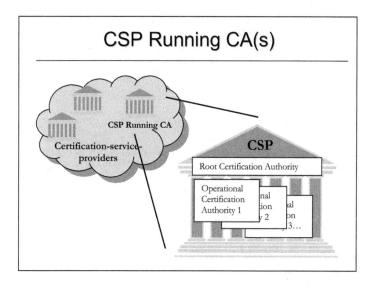

Fig. 5. CSP running certification authority (-ies)

Since public key certificates are the main tool in the PKI that make the use of e-signatures possible, the CA is usually regarded as the 'heart' of the PKI.

---

[99] See *supra* notes 95 and 96.

[100] For identification of different types of certification services see section 2.2.4, *infra*.

The CAs as units[101] have their own certificates attesting their public keys.[102] Furthermore, different CAs may be organizationally separated within one CSP. For example, the CSP may run one CA for the purposes of issuing qualified certificates, another for issuing simplified public key certificates, a third for time-stamping certificates, etc.[103] Hierarchical chains of CAs within one CSP may also be present – a root CA may certify different operational CAs[104]. In all cases, *the CSP as a legal entity will be held liable for the acts or omissions of the CAs*.[105] Therefore, for the purposes of this present report, the CSP running a CA will be referred to as a market player, but not the CA itself. It will be further assumed that the CSP could run one or several CAs.

The laws and technology standards establish certain requirements for the management of the CA, for employing qualified personnel, for the usage of reliable systems, for security management etc, to ensure that the CA operates in a smooth and efficient way. [106]

Despite the fact that in certain jurisdictions CSPs are permitted to outsource their core CA activity, this rarely occurs in practice.[107]

---

[101] See the CA notion in section 2.2.3, par.2, *supra*.

[102] Usually referred to as Operational Certificates, or OperCAs. See for example the OperCA certificates as defined in the CPS of Bankservice PLC (www.b-trust.org) and the CPS of Information Services PLC (www.stap-it.org).

[103] For example the CSP Thawte (www.thawte.com) uses the following certificates for different purposes – Thawte Personal Basic CA, Thawte Personal Freemail CA, Thawte Personal Premium CA, Thawte Premium Server CA, Thawte Premium Server CA, Thawte Server CA, Thawte Timestamping CA, etc. The research shows that many players in the certification services market use one and the same certificate for the purposes of issuing qualified, advanced and other types of certificates, for example Simantec, Swisskey, Servicios de Certificacion – A.N.C., Information Systems, Baltimore, Belgacom, Bankservice, etc. See Kalaydjiev, A., Belazelkov, B., Dimitrov, G., Yodanova, M., Stancheva, V, Markov, D., *Electronic Document. Electronic Signature, Legal Regime*. Ciela Publishing/CID, 2004, p. 177.

[104] The Root CA certificates and the operational (Oper CA) certificates have without any exception different profiles. The Root CA certificates are issued from the CA to itself, while the Oper CA are issued by the Root CA - for example Thawte Personal Freemail CA (root) and Thawte Personal Freemail Issuing CA (operational), StampIP Domestic Root CA and StampIT Domestic CA (operational), etc.

[105] Clear delineation of the liability holder for the activity of the CA is made in the Certification Practice Statement of Bankservice PLC. (www.b-trust.org).

[106] See ISO/IEC TR 13335: Information technology - Guidelines for the management of IT Security (GMITS); BS ISO/IEC 17799 (BS 7799-1): Information technology – Code of practice for information security management; T7&TeleTrusT: Common Industrial Signature Interoperability and MailTrusT Specification (ISIS-MTT Specification): Part 2: PKI Management; CEN/ISSS CWA 14172, Parts 1-5, WS/E-Sign: EESSI Conformity Assessment Guidances, etc.

[107] See ECAF/EEMA Security Best Practice Paper, PKI costs, V.03 final, 2003, p.4. In ECAF Model Part 1 – Introduction/Strategy, Section B Introducing the Elements of Cryptography, Section 6.3. it is envisaged that 6.3 the activity could be outsources to so called "Certificate Manufacturer" that provides certificate management operational services for the Issuing Authority, including creation, renewal, suspension, revocation, etc. ECAF Model identifies these operations to be extremely security sensitive and thus

Different certification services may be identified. The scope of the certification services provided by the CSP running a CA, whether outsourced or not, depends on the certificate policy followed.[108] *Certification services strictu sensu are considered to be those services that are closely related to the issuing and maintenance of certificates.*

Such services *inter alia* may include: the registration service (identity verification of the subscriber), the issue of certificates (the process encompassing all steps from the certificate generation to its publication in the directory[109]), the certificate manufacturing service,[110] the dissemination service (delivery of the certificate to the subscriber[111]), the certificate maintenance (maintaining the certificate during its operational period[112]), the directory maintenance and directory access service (keeping and maintaining the directory and providing access through different technologies[113]),

---

necessitating an extremely trustworthy system operated under carefully controlled policies and procedures, and from a physically secure location. The Model sees the Certificate Manufacturer's role as a service provider to the Issuing Authority, which role in determining certificate content is entirely passive and procedural, whereas it puts in the certificates whatever the Issuing Authority instructs it to denote.

[108] On the essence of the Certificate Policy see Chapter III, section 6.4.1, *infra*.

[109] The certificate issuance is the core certification service (see section 2.2.1, *supra*). The certificate issuance procedure encompasses several stages and services. The procedure is usually initiated upon request of the person seeking issuance of certificate. Depending on the certificate policies followed by the CSP the requests may be placed electronically or in writing. It should reveal certain statements and informaiton on the subscriber and should be supported with resepctive proofs. When certain information is exchanged electronically, like the provision of the private key when the key par is generated by the subscriber, certain standards (i.e the electronic request should be in PKCS#10 standard using formats DER binary X.509/Base-64 encoded .CER file) should be followed. According the certificate policies of the CSP further steps in the certificate issuance process are usually: the proper identification of the subscriber by lawful means (see section 2.2.5.1, *infra*); verification on whether the public and the private key can be used in complimentary manner; generation of the certificate, signing of the certificate by the CA in secured environment; delivery of the draft-certificate to the subscriber for acceptance of the contents (despite of the technological difficulties in performing such a stage, it is applicable in some US states, in Bulgaria, Brasil and other countries); publication of the certificate into the directory; storing of the certificate on smart card, token, or other media; and delivery of the certificate to the subscriber. See Kalaydjiev, A., Belazelkov, B., Dimitrov, G., et al., *ibid.*, p.p.207-219

[110] See *supra* note 107.

[111] The dissemination service is delineated as a separate certification service because it reveals some particularities depending on the mean of disseminating the certificate or the storage media. That especially refers to cases when the storage media is a SSCD that should be handed over to a person residing away from the generation premises of the CA. That is why the dissemination service is frequently outsourced.

[112] See *supra* note 107.

[113] For example through web interface, OCSP (On-line Certificate Status Protocol), LDAP (Lightweight Directory Access Protocol), etc.

the suspension service[114] and the revocation service,[115] the re-key and renewal service,[116] the archiving service,[117] the time-stamping service[118] etc.[119]

The liability exposure of the CSP varies according to the type of certification services provided.

2.2.5. Basic relationships

As already mentioned, the CSP can play one or several roles in the PKI model.

Should the CSP play the role of a CA (running the CA itself or outsourcing this activity) it would enter in different relationships with different players within the PKI – certificate holders, relying parties, other CSPs running CAs, CSPs running RAs,[120] DSPs,[121] TSPs,[122] etc. Thus, different liability lines of exposure could be identified.

The basic lines of relationships of the CSP running CA are shown in Fig. 6.

---

[114] Suspension of a certificate is the process by which a CA temporarily places the operational period of a certificate in abeyance for a specified period. The suspension service proves to be temporary revocation of the certification power of the certificate by placing it in a certificate revocation list (CRL) upon request of the subscriber or other entitled persons (see Article 26 of the Bulgarian EDESA) to shield the interests of the subscriber and the third relying persons when the secrecy of the private key is or could be revealed. Not all CSPs provide suspension service. Upon expiration of the suspension period or upon request of the subscriber the validity of the certificate is restored and the latter is removed from the CRL. For details see ABA's PKI Assessment Guidelines, PAG v0.30, section D.4.9.7, p.176, also Kalaydjiev, A., Belazelkov, B., Dimitrov, G., et al., *ibid.*, p.147.

[115] In divergence to the suspension service the revocation is a irreversible termination of the certification power of the certificate. The revoked certificate is placed irrevocably in the CRL. From this moment forward, the certificate will be considered invalid. Provision of revocation service sometimes remains at discretion of the CSP (See CPS of Globalsign section 12.8, p.71). For more details See *ibid.*

[116] For securing non-disturbed usage of the certificates upon expiration of the operational period certificates could be renewed the by extention of the operational period (renewal) or either with or without re-generation of the key par (re-key). It should be envisaged that depending on the certificate policies of the CSPs not always re-key and renewal will prove to be possible (for example renewal is not allowed by Globaslign for PersonalSign Demo 1 certificates, renewal without re-key will not be further possible before expiration of the operational period of the Certificates Class 1 of Bankservice, re-key after revocation of CA certificates will not be possible, etc.)

[117] See section 2.6, *infra.*

[118] See section 2.5, *infra.*

[119] See ECAF Model Part 1 - Introduction/Strategy, Section B, Introducing the Elements of the Cryptography, p.8; also ABA ISC PAG v0.30 – Public Draft for Comment, section D.1.3.1, p.89.

[120] Registration Authority – See section 2.3, *infra.*

[121] Directory Service Providers – See section 2.4, *infra.*

[122] Time-stamping Service Providers – See section 2.5, *infra.*

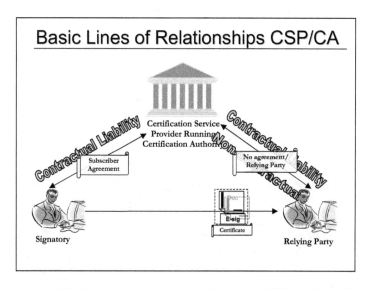

Fig. 6. Basic lines of relationships of the CSP running a CA

Relationships are formed between the CSP running the CA, the subscriber and the relying party. The nature of the relationship between these subjects is the key to understanding the allocation and the scope of the liability within the PKI.

2.2.5.1. Relationships between the CSP running a CA and the subscriber

As it has already been mentioned, the usage of the e-signature is presupposed by the issuing of a certificate attesting the public key to the identity of the subscriber.

The certificate is the key tool for the functioning of the PKI. A reasonable level of trust can only be established between persons who may be unknown to each other based on the use of a public key certificate. The certificate plays an equivalent role in the electronic world as an identity card issued by a state authority. Furthermore, the validity of the certificate is sometimes a prerequisite, from a legal point of view, for the legal validity of the electronic signature.[123]

The process is initiated by the party requesting issue of the certificate. This can be done by submitting a request to the CSP directly or via its registration authority. Provided the identity of the certificate holder and certain other facts are duly ascertained and certain formalities are met,[124] a certificate is issued and a contract between the CSP and the certificate holder is executed.

No disputes have thus far arisen in the realm of legal theory with respect to the fact that the relationship between the certificate holder and the CSP running the CA rests on contractual grounds. The essential elements that reveal the *differentia specifica* of the contract are the obligation of the subscriber to pay a fee to the CSP running the CA, against the obligation of the latter to issue a certificate and maintain it[125] for a certain period of time.[126] Some countries require a written form for the valid execution of the contract,[127] and, even where this is not prescribed as a legal necessity, the CSPs usually choose to follow this practice.[128] Where the written form is not introduced as a precondition for the validity of the contract, other requirements for submission of data in writing are stipulated.[129]

---

[123] Under Article 5 (1) of the Directive an advanced electronic signature will be considered as a qualified electronic signature having the same legal value as a handwritten signature, provided it is based on a qualified certificate meeting the requirements of Annex I of the Directive. For detailed analysis on the legal value of the electronic signatures depending on the validity of the certificate See *infra* Chapter V, sections 3 - 6.

[124] For the particularities of the verification process – see section 2.3, *infra*. See also *supra* note 109.

[125] For thorough analysis of the contract for provision of certification services see Kalaydjiev, A., Belazelkov, B., Dimitrov, G., et al., *ibid.*, p.p. 180 – 189.

[126] The time of the validity of the certificate is usually referred to as 'operational period' of the certificate.

[127] For example Article 22 of the Bulgarian EDESA.

[128] Usually the CSPs choose such form of the contract when undertake issuance of certificates for qualified signatures, certificates with higher value of transactions, CAs' operational certificates, etc. See the policies of Verisign (www.verisign.com), GlobalSign (www.globalsign.be), Thawte (www.thawte.com), Bankservice (www.b-trust.org), Information Services (www.stampit.org), et al. The approach of the CSPs could be easily understood while the liability burden for issuance of certificate to an impostor is quite heavy. Presence of the person before the CSP's staff and sigining in writing before witnesses always plays security role for reducing occurence of frauds.

[129] For example Section 8 of the Danish Bill on Electronic Signatures No. L-229 of 29 May 2000 requires that the certification authorities that issue qualified certificates to submit, as a basis for any customer relationship aimed at the issuance of a qualified certificate, a *written description* of the specific terms of contract for the issuance and any terms and conditions specified for use of the qualified certificate by the certification authority.

The issue of the certificate and its entry in the CA's public register is the final step of the process. From this moment onwards the certificate holder is entitled to use his or her electronic signature.[130]

In fact, the certificate holder enters into a contractual relationship with the CSP because he or she intends to perform legally recognized acts in an electronic form, by addressing signed communications to the intended addressees and thus to have as a legal consequence the binding of his *patrimonium*. The instrument thereof is the electronic certificate. Therefore, the certificate holder expects that the CSP running a CA will provide due care *vis-à-vis* the possibility of the certificate holder to use his or her certificate and the addressees to be able to verify it. Any failure of the CSP running a CA to perform its duties within the scope of the duty of care will constitute a ground for liability.

What is the scope of the CSP's duties?

The scope of the CSP's duties varies between different jurisdictions, so, while regulating the activity of the CSPs, some countries introduce divergent statutory duties and a wide range of imperative norms.[131] It also depends on the provisions as stipulated in the contract between the CSP and the certificate holder. In defining the scope of the CSPs' obligations, the binding value of the certification practice statement (CPS) and the certificate policy (CP) in different jurisdictions will be examined further.[132]

In almost all European jurisdictions, several common duties should be pointed out, which outline the scope of CSPs' duty of care, regardless of whether they are explicitly envisaged in the law.[133] These duties should be carefully identified, since

---

[130] See Kalaydjiev, A., Belazelkov, B., Dimitrov, G., et al., *ibid.*, p. 219.

[131] While most of the EU countries introduce the concept of the qualified signature as established by Article 5 (1) of the Directive 1999/93, the legal value of the qualified signature as handwritten would depend on meeting of certain criteria. One of these criteria is the CSP to meet certain requirements – explicitly listed in Annex II of the Directive. These duties are commonly transposed as imperative and the CSPs cannot deviate from the statutory rules by contractual means. For proper analysis of the duties for CSPs issuing qualified certificates See *infra* Chapter III, section 5. The CSPs that do not issue such certificates have more room for contracual freedom exist in defining the scope of its duties.

[132] See Chapter III, section 6.4, *infra*.

[133] For example in 2000 the British Government has found that the liability of the TSPs both to their customers and to parties relying on their certificates is best left to existing law to providers' and customers' contractual arrangements. Customers will certainly be able to look into their contracts, though these will be subject to exclusion and limitation clauses. The third parties have to rely on the law on delict or perhaps (in Scotland) arguing for a *jus quasitum tertio* (third party right) in their favour – see Groshieide, F., Boele-Woelki, K., *ibid.*, p.38

the omission or negligent performance of any of them might cause damages to the certificate holder, and thus would constitute grounds for holding the CSP liable.

In the first place, the CSP running a CA must provide assurance that successful verification of the certificate holder's identity and other applicable attributes is performed.[134] The scope and the means of verification vary depending on the conditions set forth in the certificate policy, and this will depend on the type of certificate issued (i.e. qualified or advanced certificates, certificates with limits on the value of transactions and key usage etc.).[135] Such verification is of the utmost importance in promoting trust and confidence, since the addressees of the signed messages rely upon it. The verification should be performed only by lawful means.[136] Failure to perform verification with due care may result either in the issue of a certificate to an impostor purporting to be the real signatory or in entering incorrect data as to the signatory's identity or other attributes into the certificate. In both cases, serious harm may occur. A person whose identity is forged may undoubtedly suffer harm – the impostor could make malicious statements on his or her behalf and the relying parties will not be aware that a deception has taken place.[137] The interests of the relying parties in such a scenario could also suffer. Trusting in the CSP's incorrect attestation the relying parties might undertake or omit to undertake certain actions, which could result in harm being caused. Taking the above into account, any failure to perform verification with due care undoubtedly gives grounds for holding the CSP liable regardless of whether or not it issues qualified or other types of certificates.

In the second place, the CSP should usually check whether there is a cryptographic correspondence between the private and the public key when generated by the signatory.[138] The public and the private key constitute a cryptographic key pair. The

---

[134] For the CSPs issuing qualified acertificates this obligation is established on an *acquis* level by Annex II (d) of Directive 1999/93/EC.

[135] Depending on the value of the transaction the certificate could be used for, the insurance coverage, and the type of the certificate (basic, advanced, qualified, enhanced or other), the verification could vary from check-up of the identity requisites provided electronically or sent by mail to personal identification by presence of the Certificate holder before the RA. For example Personal Freemail Certificates of Thawte are issued only based on electronic submission of certain application only, whilst the Personal Certificates are issued after personal attestation by representative of Thawte only (See www.thawte.com).

[136] On the scope of the lawful means see Kalaydjiev, A., Belazelkov, B., Dimitrov, G., et al., *ibid.*, p. 163.

[137] See Smedinghoff, T., *ibid.* See Chapter III, section 4.3, *infra*.

[138] When the CSP provides the key par generation service such verification is senseless. In the later case the CSP will be liable for non-provision of quality key-par generation service. See the CPS and the Certificate Policy for issuing of Class A certificates of Bankservice PLC (www.b-trust.org).

possibility to sign messages with one key (the private key) and verify them with the other (the public key) is the essence of asymmetric cryptography. The issue of a public key certificate instils confidence that the envisaged public key corresponds to the private key kept by the certificate holder and may be used in a complementary manner.[139] The relying party cannot perform successful verification if a certificate is issued where the public key is not part of the key pair. Neither the certificate holder nor the addressee would benefit from use of the electronic signature – they could both suffer harm. The CSP could be held liable for lack of due verification of such correspondence.

The CSP running a CA must further publish and securely keep the certificate available for verification in its register.[140] The PKI principles provide the possibility for the relying party to gain trust by obtaining an attestation on the certificate's validity by a third party – the CSP. This is possible by checking the validity of the certificate in publicly available directories (registers) containing information about the issued certificates and their status.[141] Therefore, the CSP should enter the required information in a timely fashion and maintain an up-to-date register, not only during the operational period of the certificate, but for a long period thereafter. It should also ensure that, even at a later moment, the exact time both of issue and of revocation or suspension of the certificate can be determined in order to assess its validity.[142] The certificate holder expects the CSP to fulfil this obligation and any failure to do so will involve liability.

The CSP should be obliged not only to publish the certificate and keep the register accessible, but should also maintain the certificate and promptly and securely register all changes in its status – revocation, suspension, or restoration of its

---

[139] This is performed by successful verification of a standardized electronically signed request with particular format - PKCS#7 under the Cryptographic Message Syntax Standard. It is a general syntax, developed and maintained by RSA Data Security, Inc., for data to which cryptography may be applied, such as digital signatures and encryption. It also provides a syntax for disseminating certificates or certificate revocation lists. See Windows Knowledge Database, Glossary of Terms, (www.microsoft.com)

[140] For the CSPs issuing qualified certificates this obligation is established on an *acquis* level by Annex II (b) of Directive 1999/93/EC.

[141] The public registers of the CSPs are usually organized in X.500 format with LDAP access. LDAP - Lightweight Directory Access Protocol is a standardized protocol – layer over TCT/IP protocol for access to simplified registers defined in the standard IETF RFC 1777 "The Lightweight Directory Access Protocol". The access could be also performed through OCSP (On-line Certificate Status Protocol)

[142] For CSPs issuing qualified certificates see Annex II (c) and (i) of Directive 1999/93/EC.

validity, upon the certificate holder's request, if its private key is or might be compromised.[143] Failure to register revocation in a timely fashion may result in malicious usage of the compromised certificate holder's private key – thus his or her lawful interests might be threatened. The CSP should bear the liability for such behaviour.

Because the certification services require special knowledge and expertise in the areas of asymmetric cryptography, information security and relevant technologies, the CSP should employ personnel having such expertise and experience.[144] This will ensure the provision of a quality service and reduce the risk of breaches of security. Furthermore, the CSP should establish and follow strict procedures relating to security management and the administration of its activity, which follow national or international standards where available and applicable.[145] Breach of the security caused by CSPs employees' negligence or incompetence, or due to inappropriate management procedures or administrative measures, might lead to the breaching of other obligations (i.e. keeping of a secure register, providing a prompt revocation service, maintaining the secrecy of the private key during the course of the key pair generation, etc.).[146] Any damage caused by such events will involve liability on the part of the CSP.

To promote reasonable trust in the CA's attestation, the CSP should use trustworthy software and hardware systems.[147] There are certain standards, which contain various different criteria, that need to be met in this respect[148]. On the one hand, the systems should be highly secured and protected against intervention and attacks. On the other hand, they should be protected against accidental changes in information stored or communicated within the systems. The systems should be technically operational with respect to the cryptographic processes performed. Furthermore,

---

[143] For CSPs issuing qualified certificates see Annex II (b) of Directive 1999/93/EC.

[144] For CSPs issuing qualified certificates see Annex II (e) of Directive 1999/93/EC.

[145] *Ibid.* See for example ISO/IEC TR 13335: Information technology - Guidelines for the management of IT Security (GMITS); BS ISO/IEC 17799 (BS 7799-1): Information technology – Code of practice for information security management; T7&TeleTrusT: Common Industrial Signature Interoperability and MailTrusT Specification (ISIS-MTT Specification): Part 2: PKI Management; CEN/ISSS CWA 14172, Parts 1-5, WS/E-Sign: EESSI Conformity Assessment Guidances, etc.

[146] Menzel, T., Schweighofer, E., *Liability of Certification Authorities, User Identification & Privacy Protection,* Joint IFIP WG 8.5 and WG 9.6 Working Conference 1999, Kista Schweden, DSV, S. 161-172.

[147] For CSPs issuing qualified certificates see Annex II (f) of Directive 1999/93/EC.

[148] See for example CEN/ISSS CWA 14172-3: "Trustworthy systems managing certificates for electronic signatures"; CEN/ISSS CWA 14167, WS/E-Sign: CWA 14167-1: "Security Requirements for Trustworthy Systems Managing Certificates for Electronic Signatures"; etc.

the CSP should also store the certificates in such manner that they may be duly verified and easily retrieved, and any changes or interventions that could be considered as a compromising event should be made available to the technical staff in charge.[149] In this respect, the CSP should ensure that only authorized persons are entitled to make entries and changes. Any deviation from the standards set forth (if any are relevant) or infringement of the above duties would be considered a breach of duty of care. Therefore, any harm suffered as a direct consequence of this would open the door for exposure of the CSP's liability.

The CSPs will have certain other obligations, depending on the local legislation, the certification practice statement[150] and the contract with the certificate holder., The CSP will be held liable towards the certificate holder on contractual grounds for any negligent breach of such obligations that leads to damage being caused. Among the vast variety of such duties, the following could be mentioned: to maintain sufficient financial funds to meet the operational needs of its activity, to check the authorization of the person submitting a request for the issue of a certificate[151] etc.

In most European jurisdictions, the provision of certain services will be subject to specific consumer protection rules. Such duties will be imposed upon the CSP by the laws on protection of consumers,[152] or by electronic signature laws, for example: to make each party aware, before entering into a contractual relationship, of the exact terms and conditions regarding the use of the certificate, the limitations on its use, the existence of a voluntary accreditation scheme and procedures for complaint and dispute settlement.[153] Sometimes there is even a duty to provide information on such matters in appropriate ways.[154]

Different jurisdictions approach in different ways the CSPs' duties relating to the issue of qualified certificates and the duties of those issuing other types of

---

[149] For CSPs issuing qualified certificates see Annex II (I) of Directive 1999/93/EC.

[150] For the essence of the Certification Practice Statement see Chapter III, section 6.4.1, *infra*.

[151] Under Article 29 (1) (1) of the Bulgarian EDESA the CSP shall be held liable for non-checking the representative power of the person seeking certificate issuance (certificate holder) provided acts on behalf of other person (titular). On an *acquis* level such duties are established by Annex II of Directive 1999/93 EC – see for example paragraphs (h), et al.

[152] Analysed in Chapter IV, *infra*.

[153] See Annex II (k) of Directive 1999/93/EC seeting requirements for CSPs issuing qualified certificates. On a national level see for example Article 21 of Bulgarian EDESA.

[154] Annex II (k) of the Directive provides that such information must be in writing and in redily understandable language)

certificates. Directive 1999/93/EC only specifies the criteria in respect of the CSPs' duties in issuing qualified certificates.[155] These criteria are transposed in a just way into almost all EU jurisdictions and particularly in Bulgaria[156]. The duties are usually transposed into national law as being imperative, so that the parties may not contract out of them.

Most of the duties applicable to CSPs issuing qualified certificates will also prove applicable to CSPs issuing other types of certificates, while it would be against the principles of fair trade and *bona mores* to agree otherwise. It would be inadmissible, for example, for CSPs to manage their liability by agreeing to be contractually exempted, say, from the duty to employ qualified personnel, or to maintain security during the process of generation of the certificate. The scope of the duties and the ability to derogate from contractual duties depends on different factors.

Firstly, the boundaries of contractual freedom set forth by the mandatory rules should be taken into consideration. The parties may not reach agreement in contravention of the mandatory rules set forth in the law.[157] If the CSPs duties are explicitly introduced as being mandatory, no contractual derogations will be possible.[158] They become part of the contractual relationship notwithstanding the will of the CSP. It may decide only whether to enter into a contract or not.

Secondly, even within the scope of contractual freedom, the court in any given jurisdiction will assess what is moral, common, and fair. Should the court find that certain clauses that release the CSP from duties or provide for derogation from certain standards are in conflict with *bona mores,* it will declare them void.[159]

Thirdly, as has already been mentioned, the market status of the certificate holder should be considered. A certificate holder who is a consumer will benefit from greater statutory protection than a certificate holder who is a merchant.[160]

---

[155] See *supra* notes 134, 140, 142, 144, 147, 149, 153, 154.

[156] See Dumortier, J., Kelm, S., *ibid,* p.34.

[157] See Pavlova, M., *ibid.,* p. 142.

[158] On the nature of mandatory contract law rules applicable regardless of the parties' bargain see Communication on European Contract Law: Joint Response of the Commission on European Contract Law and the Study Group on a European Civil Code, 2001, (http://www.sgecc.net/media/download/stellungnahme_kommission_5_final1.pdf)

[159] For detailed analyses of the standard of due care See Chapter II, section 4.1, *infra.*

[160] See Chapter IV, sections 2, 3, and 4, *infra.*

2.2.5.2. Relationships between the CSP running a CA and the relying party

The relying party[161] is a certificate recipient who acts in reliance on that certificate and/or digital signatures which are verified using that certificate.[162]

While the concept of the PKI is based on the building of trust in the identity of the certificate holder or certain attributes thereof, the CSP running a CA plays a key role in this process by providing harmonized status information which attests to the facts about the certificate.[163] Usually it does that by providing access to the directory where it keeps publicly available information on the current status of all certificates issued and those that have been for some reason revoked.[164] The directory is the natural place from which the communicating parties can obtain authentication information about each other.[165]

What is the nature of the relationship between the CSP running a CA and the relying party? By answering this question, we would identify the liability exposure of the CSP towards the relying party.

The relying party does not usually enter into a contractual relationship with the CSP running a CA.[166] It is necessary that a particular fact be ascertained by the relying party, either by checking the records of the issued qualified certificates or by checking the certificate revocation list kept by the CSP. Affirmation of the validity of the certificate is what makes the relying party trust the certificate and thus motivates that party to enter into a relationship with the certificate holder or to perform certain acts (e.g. execution of payment etc.).[167]

---

[161] Often referred to as "*certificate user*" – see ABA ISC PAG v0.30 – Public Draft for Comment, p.285.

[162] See RFC 2527 Internet X.509 Public Key Infrastructure, Certificate Policy and Certification Practices Framework, The Internet Society (1999).

[163] See ETSI TR 102 030 V1.1.1 (2002-03) Provision of harmonized Trust Service Provider status information.

[164] The main protocol used by applications to obtain credentials from the Directory is the Directory Access Protocol (DAP), specified in ITU-T Recomendation X.519 | ISO/IEC 9594-5. There are further protocols developed – LDAP (Lightweight Directory Access Protocol), OCSP (On-line Certificate Status Protocol), etc.

[165] ISO/IEC 9594–8: 1993 (E) Recommendation X.509 Information technology - Open Systems Interconnection - The Directory: Authentication Framework, Introduction, p. iv.

[166] See Communication from the Commission COM (97) 503: Ensuring security and trust in electronic communication: "Towards a European Framework for Digital Signatures and Encryption", *infra* note 503.

[167] See Kalaydjiev, A., Belazelkov, B., Dimitrov, G., et al., *ibid.*, p. 108.

Therefore, any omissions or defects in the certificate or the records for the certificate kept by the CSP that cause damage to the relying party would entitle the relying party to claim damages from the CSP. Examples of this include cases in which, due to the use of a special validity form, the contract was declared void and the party failed to profit, or where by trusting the certificate, the relying party transferred sums to a party other than the alleged certificate holder, whose identity was not properly ascertained by the CSP when issuing the certificate.[168]

The rights of the relying party to hold the CSP liable arise directly from the law rather than from a contract.

Different theories support the view that the relationship between the CSP providing CA services and the relying parties is not based on a contractual relationship. Therefore, liability in this area does not appear to be of a contractual nature.[169] By contrast, it should be borne in mind that the relationship between the CSP and the relying parties may be based on contract.

Some authors[170] assume that the liability exposure to the third relying party arises from a contract between the certificate holder and the CSP for the benefit of a third party.[171] This finding is groundless. First of all, there should be an explicit provision in this respect in the contract between the certificate holder and the CSP.[172] On the other hand, the construction of the beneficiary is inapplicable in the present case. The third party should at least be identifiable at the moment of enforcement of the contract – it is not possible for a contract to be concluded for the benefit of an unlimited number of parties or for unknown parties.[173] This complicated

---

[168] These examples are transposed from the fictitious cases analysed for the purposes of section 2.2.5.2, *supra*.

[169] ECOM, *Proposal for Liability of Certification Authorities, ibid.*, page 13; also Norden, A., *Liability of CSP under the Directive*, Speech before the Legal Workshop of ECAF/EEMA, Brussels, 29-30 November 2001 (https://www.eema.org/legal/norden.pdf).

[170] Hindelang, S., *No Remedy for Disappointed Trust – The Liability Regime for Certification Authorities Towards Third Parties Outwith the EC Directive in England and Germany Compared*, Refereed article, The Journal of Information, Law and Technology (JILT), 2002 (1) http://elj.warwick.ac.uk/jilt/02-1/hindelang.html. Also ABA ISC PAG Public Draft for Comment, Section C.1, p. 42.

[171] Legal regulation of the contract for the benefit of third party can be found in almost all jurisdictions. See for example Article 1121 of French Code Civil, §328–335 of BGB §112–113 of Swiss Civil Code, Article 21 of Bulgarian LOC, etc.

[172] See Kojuharov, A., *ibid.*, p.82

[173] See Kalaydjiev, A., *Contract for the Benefit of a Third Person*, Market and Law Magazine, 2003, Vol.3; also Dikov, L., *Course in Civil Law. Law on Obligations. General Rules*. Vol.III, 1934, p.284-285; also Kojuharov, A, *ibid.*, 1992, p.82

construction would moreover hardly serve the needs of the dynamic PKI e-world. Furthermore, the activity requirements of the CSPs are set forth in the law. It may be considered that the statutory requirements establish an imperative model of behaviour for the CSPs towards all persons.[174] Thus, the CSP is obliged to keep a directory, make this directory accessible, maintain the relevant equipment, ensure the necessary level of security etc. Failure to perform any of these duties may lead to damage being caused to relying third parties, and the behaviour of the CSP will therefore be considered to constitute a tort.[175]

Under the German law, a theoretical possibility exists for the relationship between the CSP and the relying third party to be treated as a contractual relationship between the CSP and the certificate holder under the so-called contract with a protective effect towards a third party ('*Vertrag mit Schutzwirkung zugunsten Dritter*').[176] In such a case, the liability exposure of the CSP towards the third party relying on the certificate would be of a contractual nature, while the latter party would be regarded as falling within the protective ambit of the contract.[177] Because of the isolated nature of such a legal construction, this matter is not explored further in this work.

It is feasible to assume that a direct contractual relationship between the relying party and the CSP could arise.[178] In almost all European jurisdictions, whenever an agreement is reached (coincidence of mutually addressed wills of two parties) and which is intended to establish, settle or terminate the legal relationship between these parties, the contract is regarded as having been concluded.[179] In these jurisdictions, the provision of a service such as delivery of information (online or offline as an obligation of the first party - CSP) against or without payment (as an obligation of the other party – the relying party) will be considered a valid and binding contract.[180]

---

[174] See Kalaydjiev, A., Belazelkov, B, Dimitrov, G., et al., *ibid.*, p. 157.

[175] For the essence of tort liability see Chapter II, section 2.2, *infra*.

[176] Ius Commune Casebook – Tort Law., p. 89.

[177] For thorough analysis of the *Vertrag mit Schutzwirkung zugunsten Dritter* under the German Law and its applicability to the liability exposure of the CSPs see Hindelang S, *ibid.*

[178] In most of the industry standards and guidelines it is also recognized the possibility of the CSP to enter into contractual agreement with the relying party. In this repsect see ABA ISC PAG Public Draft for Comment", *ibid.*, Chapter B.4 and C; also RFC 2527, *ibid.*, section 3.5.

[179] Pavlova, M. *General Civil Law*, Vol.I, Sofi-R, 1995 ed., page 77.

[180] See the Relying Party Agreement of GlobalSign at http://www.globalsign.net/repository/rel_party.pdf

For example, the CSP may establish a web-based procedure whereby the relying party agrees to specific terms in respect of accessing the directory or the CRL.[181] While the web techniques for confirming acceptance of the terms may vary, this access agreement may be executed as a 'click-wrap' agreement[182] or 'shrink-wrap' agreement[183] as known in theory and practice. If the relying party fails to click 'Agree' or 'Accept', scroll the text of the agreement, or perform another similar activity, such as clicking a virtual button that should be considered an electronic statement, and receiving the request by the provider, the relying party will not be granted access to the data kept by the CSP.[184] In this way, the CSP may contractually bind the relying party and hence limit its liability by warnings or disclaimers.[185] Such an agreement is enforceable in almost all jurisdictions.[186]

2.2.5.3. Relationships between the CSP running a CA and third parties

In some cases, a question may arise as to whether the CSP's liability could be invoked by third parties other than the certificate holder and the relying party.

2.2.5.3.1. RELATIONSHIPS BETWEEN THE CSP RUNNING CA AND A PERSON PURPORTING TO BE THE SIGNATORY AND THE IMPERSONATED PERSON

There might be cases when an impostor could obtain a certificate purporting to be the true holder of the signature-creation data, either by obtaining it or by using forged or fake identity documents. Normally, the CSP should verify the identity using the appropriate means prescribed under the national law. However, it is possible for the CSP, due to its own negligence, to be misled and for an erroneous certificate to be issued.

---

[181] Smedinghoff, T, *ibid.*, p.168.

[182] Samson, M., *Internet Law – Click-Wrap Agreement*, 2002, (http://www.phillipsnizer.com/int-click.htm); also Buono, F., Friedman, J., *Maximizing the Enforceability of Click-Wrap Agreements*, 4.3 J. TECH. L. & POL'Y 3, (http://journal.law.ufl.edu/~techlaw/4-3/friedman.html) (2000).

[183] Street, L., Grant, M., *Internet Law*, Lexis Publishing, 2001 ed., page 23

[184] *See* ABA ISC PAG v0.30 – Public Draft for Comment, Section C.5.1.3., p.59.

[185] On the same opinion Biddle, B., *Legislating Market Winners: Digital Signature Laws and the Electronic Commerce Marketplace*, 1997, http://www.acusd.edu/~biddle/LMW.htm

[186] On the click-wrap agreements see also Weigenek, R., *E-Commerce: A Guide to the Law of Electronic Business*, 3rd ed., UK: Butterworths Lexis Nexis, 2002, p.33

The legal consequences with respect to damages will be unpredictable for the relying parties. On the other hand, however, the persons whose names are mentioned in the certificate may also suffer harm. They may find themselves in a situation in which they have to defend themselves against action taken by relying parties that have suffered harm as a consequence of the deception, or as a result of their reputation and trade name being compromised.[187]

It is beyond doubt that the negligent CSP would be liable to the impersonated persons.[188] The liability exposure would be subject to regulation by the national tort liability rules. Some countries might choose to introduce particular rules imposing strict liability for the issue of certificates to an impostor in the name of another person.[189]

The fact that the CSP has acted negligently does not deprive it of the right to claim remedies from the impostor equivalent to the compensation that the CSP is obliged to pay to the impersonated person, on general tort liability grounds.[190]

2.2.5.3.2. RELATIONSHIPS BETWEEN BONA FIDE THIRD PARTIES NOT RELYING ON THE CERTIFICATE

It is possible that third parties may acquire, in good faith, rights from the certificate holder or the relying party following usage of the erroneous certificate. This might occur, for example, where the certificate holder accepts an offer made by the relying party, but the acceptance is supported by an erroneous certificate, and this fact is not detected at the moment of receiving the acceptance. Later on, the contract is declared void, but in the meantime, *bona fide* third parties have acquired property or other rights stemming from the invalid contract. The question arises as to what consequences should flow from such a scenario, insofar as the CSP is concerned.

---

[187] Smedinghoff, T., *ibid.*, page 24.

[188] *Ibid.*

[189] See ETSI TS 101 456 V1.1.1 (2000-12), Annex A, Page 37.

[190] Article 54 of the Bulgarian LOC, for example, provides that the person held responsible for damages caused wrongfully by another person, shall be entitled to a compensation by the latter. Article 4:111 of the Principles of the European Contract Law reads that where a third person for whose acts a party is responsible, or who with a party's assent is involved in the making of a contract: (a) causes a mistake by giving information, or knows of or ought to have known of a mistake, (b) gives incorrect information, (c) commits fraud, (d) makes a threat, or (e) takes excessive benefit or unfair advantage, remedies under this Chapter will be available under the same conditions as if the behaviour or knowledge had been that of the party itself.

Should such third parties lose their rights over property where it has been defectively acquired?[191]

It should be borne in mind that no direct liability can be established between the *bona fide* third parties and the CSP. Those persons enter in to contractual or other relationships with their counterparts. As a result of privity of contract and the relativity of the contractual relationship, the seller (being the certificate holder or the relying party) will be solely responsible towards the buyer (the *bona fide* third party) regardless of the reason for the loss of property rights.[192]

In some jurisdictions, it may be possible to establish grounds for holding the CSP liable.[193] Such liability would be based on a special tort rule according to which all third parties who, as a result of negligence, prevent the execution of a contract would be held liable.[194] Where the PKI is concerned, it seems feasible that cases may exist in which the CSP's tort liability may be triggered on such a ground. The third parties must refrain from intervening in other parties' legal relationships; thus, any negligent intervention in such relationships that causes disturbance and damage would undoubtedly be considered a tort.[195] Liability in such respect would be regulated by the general national tort rules.

2.2.6. Relationships with other PKI actors

In a simple PKI model, there are three market players – the subscriber (i.e. the certificate holder), the relying party and the CSP running the CA or providing the core CA services, which plays the role of the trusted third party.[196] The relationships and liability lines of these actors are identified and analyzed above. Depending on whether the relationships between these three actors involve the usage of qualified certificates, some deviations may exist, and these are discussed in Chapter III, *et seq.*, *infra.*

---

[191] Known as rem habere licere praestare.

[192] Article 188-192 of the Bulgarian LOC. See Rouschev, I., *Liability for eviction*, Regouli, Sofia, 1995.

[193] Article 21 (2) of the Bulgarian LOC.

[194] See also Pound, R., *Jurisprudence*. V. IV, St. Paul, Minnesota, West Publishing Co., 1959, p. 86.

[195] See Pavlova, M., *ibid.*, p. 176.

[196] ABA ISC PAG v0.30 – Public Draft for Comment, Section D.1.3.1, p.89.

In an open PKI, however, these three players will not always have active roles. Sometimes it is possible for another CSP to be involved directly or indirectly in the process of building trust. In cases of direct involvement of these CSPs in relationships with the subscriber and the relying party, their liability exposure will more or less follow the pattern described above.[197] In other cases, indirect involvement will be present, especially when the CSP delegates one or more of its front-end or back-end functions to other entities. In such cases, a question arises about what the liability lines *vis-à-vis* the other actors will be.

A general picture of the lines of the relationship between the actors in the PKI is shown in Figure 7.

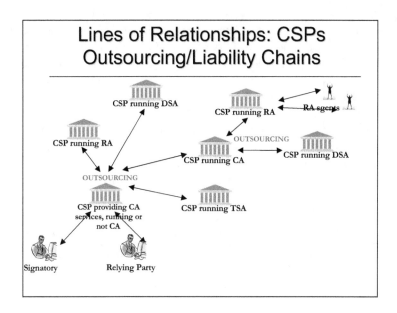

Fig. 7. Outsourcing. Liability chains

---

[197] As an example of CSP entering in privity (direct) relations with the other actors is the Time-stamping Service Provider. See section 2.5, *supra.*

Quite a clear picture of the situation with the spreading of different roles in the PKI is presented in the ABA's PKI Assessment Guidelines. It envisages that:

CA responsibilities can be divided into "front-end" functions involved with having direct contact with certificate applicants and subscribers, and "back-end" functions involved with key operations and management, and certificate management. Front-end functions include facilitating the submission of certificate applications, identification and authentication, certificate application approval or rejection, the initiation of revocations, and the approval or rejection of renewal or re-key requests. Back-end functions can include key management, the signing and issuance of certificates, repository functions, and the revocation of certificates including the generation and publication of revocation information. In some PKIs, the CA may separate front-end from back-end functions by delegating front-end functions to a Registration Authority and retain for itself the back-end functions. An example of this business model would be a CA that retains an RA service to perform front-end functions for it.[198]

Cases might exist in which the CSP outsources all the CA functions. If this occurs, the CSP will not run the CA itself but will instead have a nominal status.[199] Such a situation will not be possible in all jurisdictions.[200] Explicit restrictions on outsourcing certain CA duties exist in some countries.[201] It is also doubtful whether such a scenario will be feasible for providers of certification services for qualified signatures. Annex II of the E-signatures Directive establishes a set of requirements that the CSP must meet in issuing qualified certificates. In EU jurisdictions that have implemented the rule of Annex II,[202] it hardly seems possible for a CSP to outsource all of its CA functions while at the same time meeting the statutory requirements. For example, the CSP cannot delegate to another party the duty to 'maintain sufficient financial

---

[198] ABA ISC PAG v0.30 – Public Draft for Comment, Section D.1.3.1, p.89.

[199] *Ibid.* The outsourced vendor performs the back-end CA functions of minting the certificates. Since the entity outsourcing this function to the vendor is the nominal CA, the vendor cannot be called the CA. In this context, the vendor is sometimes referred to as the "certificate manufacturing authority."

[200] *Ibid.* This seems to be possible in the US.

[201] Under Article 5 of the Bulgarian Ordinance On The Activities Of Certification-Service-Providers, The Terms And Procedures Of Termination Thereof, And The Requirements For Provision Of Certification Services adopted pursuant to CMD No. 17 dated 31 January 2002 (Promulgated, SG No. 15 dated 8 February 2002) it is envisaged that the CSP may ensure, *by own or another person's technical and software means and personnel* (i.e. can be outsourced), the following activities: a) acceptance of the request, the latter containing accurate and complete data on the certificate holder and the owner, and specific attributes thereof, in the cases as provided for in the User's Guide; b) verification of the data as per paragraph (1) (a) above; c) creation of a certificate on the basis of established identity and valid data at the acceptance and during the verification; d) maintanance of the directory. Other activities will not be possible to be outsourced. Under paragraph (2) of the said article such would be a) signing of certificate; b) publication of certificate in the directory; c) management of an issued certificate - entry of changes, suspension, revocation, resumption; d) publication of a list of revoked certificates into the directory.

[202] See Dumortier, J., et al., *The Legal and Market Aspects of Electronic Signatures in Europe, Ibid.,* Appendix 4.

rcsources to operate in conformity with the requirements laid down in the Directive, and in particular, to bear the risk of liability for damages, for example, by obtaining appropriate insurance'[203], nor the duty to '… apply administrative and management procedures which are adequate and correspond to recognized standards'.[204] Other duties such as to 'ensure the operation of a prompt and secure directory and a secure and immediate revocation service'[205] or to 'ensure that the date and time when a certificate is issued or revoked can be determined precisely'[206] or to 'verify, by appropriate means in accordance with national law, the identity and, if applicable, any specific attributes of the person to which a qualified certificate is issued'[207] seems possible to outsource if no particular national restrictions apply.

Where the delegation of responsibilities is possible, it may be further sub-contracted without limitation. For example, the registration authority (RA) functions can be performed by local registration authorities (LRAs), RA agents, etc.[208]

In order to determine liability lines, it is necessary to assess the way in which CA functions are allocated among various entities, and consider the legal form of such a delegation. Some PKI actors may carry out functions of agents for other actors. For example, the RA could be authorized to execute a contract for certification services with a party seeking issuance of a certificate on behalf of the CSP running a CA.[209] In such cases, the basic principles of undisclosed agency law form an essential foundation for the assessment of the PKI's legal duties and the liability of its participants.[210] The legal effects appear directly into the *patrimonium* of the principal – CSP running the CA.[211] Undisclosed agency may not be used in the PKI. In other

---

[203] Annex II (h) of Directive 1999/93/EC.

[204] Annex II (e) *in fine, idib.*

[205] Annex II (b) *idib.*

[206] Annex II (c) *idib.*

[207] Annex II (d) *idib.*

[208] The CPS of Bankservice, for example, allows within the PKI the identity of the persons seeking issuance of certificates to be verified by authorized by the RAs RA-agents (www.b-trust.org). Globalsign allows Local Registration Authorities (LRAs) to perform registration tasks on behalf of a RA. In such a case the RA supervises the LRA. The LRA may have geographical or business connotaion and operates within the framework of Globalsign's accredited procedures. A RA may support several LRAs. See section 3.3. of CPS of Globalsign (www.globalsign.be).

[209] See section 2.3, *infra.*

[210] On the concept of agency see ABA ISC PAG v0.30 – Public Draft for Comment, Section C.2.1, p.44-45. A compative overview on the agency in Europe see Beale, H., Hartkamp, A., et al., *ibid.,* p.914 *et seq.*

[211] Under Article 3:102 of the Principles of the European Contract Law where an agent acts in the name of a principal, the rules on direct representation apply.

cases, the relationship of principal and agent may not exist. The main front-end functions encompassing the making of legal statements may remain at the CSP's discretion and it may fall to the RA to allocate some technical tasks, like the verification of the identity, receipt and archiving of requests etc. In such cases, no agency would exist at all, but only an outsourced technical service.

Should third parties (signatories, relying parties) suffer damage, which is caused by the wrongful acts or omissions of the provider to whom the CA functions are delegated, the entity to be held liable would be the CSP. In other words, the delegation does not relieve the CSP of liability.[212] The CSP will be fully liable, for example, if the delegated RA fails to verify, by durable means, the identity of the person seeking issue of a certificate, and as a result of this a certificate is erroneously issued to an impostor, leading to damage being caused to the relying parties.[213] The CSP will be in a position to be held liable for the conduct of others, which does not mean that it will bear the ultimate business risk. It may seek reimbursement for the damages it is required to pay to the third party that has suffered harm, via the delegated provider's indemnification on contractual grounds. The CSP will not be in a position to agree on relief of liability for the wrongful behaviour of the delegated provider by introducing corresponding clauses in the CPS.[214]

Despite the fact that the general liability of the different CSPs seems to remain outside the scope of this work, a brief overview will be provided of the liability exposure of the main CSPs in the PKI, apart from the CSP running a CA. Focusing on the issue of how and whether the general national liability rules apply will later shed light on the question of whether a specific liability regime is needed.

2.3. Registration service provider

Different terms, initials and acronyms are used for entities performing registration functions. Usage of the term Registration Authority (RA)[215] has become common,

---

[212] *Ibid.* See *infra* note 225. In *Universal Steam Navigation Co. Ltd.* v. *James McKelvie & Co.*, House of Lords, 1923 AC 492, it is envisaged clearly that "a party who signs "as agent" is not personally liable even if elsewhere in the contract he is referred as if he were the principal.". *Op. cip.* Beale H., Hartkamp, A., et al., *ibid.*, p.918.

[213] An example provided in section 2.2.5.3.1, *supra.*

[214] Opposite opinion is supported in ABA ISC PAG v0.30 – Public Draft for Comment, Section C.2.1, p.44-45. On the possibilities for liability management though CPS/CP see Chapter III, section 6.4, *infra.*

[215] Used also as Local Registration Authority (LRA) – see for example the CPS of Gobalsign (www.globalsign.be).

but it could lead to confusion as to what it actually means. 'RA' is sometimes used to refer to the embodied software and hardware employed to perform registration functions.[216] The term is also used to refer to an organizationally detached unit within the CSP that performs registration functions.[217] 'RA' may also denote a separate legal entity that is assigned by the CSP running a CA to perform registration functions on its behalf.[218]

While the present chapter aims to identify the different liability lines brought into existence where different legal entities are involved, the term registration service provider (RSP) will be used to refer to the separate legal entity used to perform RA functions and services upon assignment from the CSP running a CA.

Thus, for the purposes of this work, a registration service provider (RSP) is an entity to which the task of verifying the identity and/or other attributes of the persons seeking issue of a certificate to support their electronic signatures is delegated. The RSP does not usually issue or manage certificates, since such functions are the core activities of CSPs that run CAs.

---

[216] See ECAF Model Part 1 – Introduction/Strategy, Section B Introducting the Elementds of Cryptography, p.8-9. Under the description of RA the ECAF Model reads that "this is a trusted authority, embodied in software (with possible hardware support) … Commonly, the RA software is used by an authorised individual from the community being served (such as someone from the personnel department of a company), whose job it is to ensure that sufficient proof of identity and eligibility is produced before a certificate is issued."

[217] See the CPS of Bankservice (www.b-trust.org), Glossary of terms. In Article 1.8 the RA is defined to be a unit entrusted with the following functions of the CSP: receiving, verification, approval or rejection of request for issuance of certificates, registration of the issuance and revocation requests at the CA, verification of identity of the subscribers in conformity to the CP and CPS, dissemination of the certificates, conclusion of contracts with the subscribers on behalf of the CSP, etc.

[218] ABA ISC PAG v0.30 – Public Draft for Comment, Section D.1.3.2, also RFC 2527 Internet X.509 Public Key Infrastructure Certificate Policy and Certification Practices Framework, Section 2. Definitions.

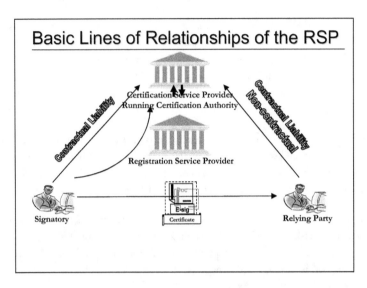

Fig. 8. Basic lines of relationships of the RSP

The RA functions are a subset of the CA functions, which are considered to be 'front-end' functions involving direct contact with certificate applicants and subscribers.[219]

The main RA functions *inter alia* are identified to be: the identification and authentication of individuals or entities who apply for a certificate; the approval or rejection of certificate applications; the initiation of certificate revocations; the identification and authentication of individuals or entities submitting requests for certificates renewal or re-key etc.[220]

Depending on the policy of the CSP running the CA, one or several of the RA functions might be outsourced, while others remain in the hands of the CSP running the CA, or be outsourced to RSPs.

---

[219] ABA ISC PAG v0.30 – Public Draft for Comment, *ibid*.

[220] *Ibid.*, also *supra* note 217. Also ECAF Model Part 1 – Introduction/Strategy, Section B, p.8.

A contractual relationship usually exists between the CSP running the CA and the RSP,[221] which aims at assigning the RA functions to the RSP and allocating the responsibilities between the CSP running the CA and the RSP consistent with the applicable CPS and CP. The ABA PKI Assessment Guidelines state:

The RA agreement will often contain an indemnity provision stating that any breach by the RA in the performance of those duties will entitle the CA to seek indemnification from the RA for any loss or damages suffered by the CA by reason of claim by a third party or otherwise. The RA Agreement may also specify whether or not the RA is considered to be the agent of the CA for certain purposes. If the RA is designated in a limited sense as an agent of the CA then the RA may execute the End Entity Agreement on behalf of the CA.[222]

Some studies show that a separate agreement between the subscriber and the RSP might exist. This will contain the terms and conditions governing the relationship between the RSP and the subscriber.[223] Thus, rights for remedies of the damaged subscriber will stem directly from the contract with the RSP[224] and will have a contractual nature. Such a situation seems to be possible in common law systems, but is unlikely to appear in civil law jurisdictions. This is due to the fact that, in all cases, the RSP acts on behalf of the CSP running the CA, regardless of whether it is authorized to perform legal acts or to provide a technical outsourced service. In this respect, the CSP running the CA will always be liable towards the damaged certificate holder/relying party for its bad choice in assigning the service to a negligent RSP. In other words, it. will be liable for the conduct of others both in contract and tort.[225]

Theoretically, in civil law countries, it is feasible that an artificial application of certain legal techniques and instruments can lead to the RSP being exposed to direct liability towards the subscriber. This will be the case where enforcing a contract between the

---

[221] Commonly referred to as "RA agreement".

[222] ABA ISC PAG v0.30 – Public Draft for Comment, section 2.1.2.1, p.100.

[223] *Ibid.*

[224] In the Australian report to NEAC - Legal Liability and E-transactions it is envisaged that "If there are multiple CAs or a separate CA and RA, each of these parties will have to manage their liability to each other, to S (subscriber) and to Relying Parties". See Sneddon, M., Partner, Clayton UTZ, NEAC - *Legal Liability and E-transactions*, p.9, *ibid., supra* note 7.

[225] In the Notes to the individual provisions of the Danish Bill on Electronic Signatures - Bill No. L 229 of 29 May 2000 it is envisaged that "Section 11 also imposes on the certification authority increased liability for the data in the directory and revocation service being correct and comprising the data required in the provision. The provision does not prevent a certification authority from making an agreement with another certification authority or another company to provide the service. *However, the certification authority continues to be liable under section 11 for any losses incurred in relation to the service*". On the general concept of liability for conduct of others see Chapter II, section 4.4, *infra*.

CSP running a CA and the RSP for the benefit of a third party[226] - subscriber[227] is concerned. In this respect, the subscriber will be entitled to make a direct claim against the RSP, deriving the right to do so directly from the contract between the CSP and the RSP.[228] However, a contract for the benefit of the relying party seems difficult to enforce.

The relationship between the CSP running a CA and the RSP will always be contractual. The term 'contractual relationship', however, should be broadly interpreted. Obligations arise not only when a contract is concluded, but also when the national law provisions stipulates that the rules for contracts apply to unilateral expressions of will (unilateral statements) in those cases where the law permits the creation, alteration or termination of rights and obligations. This rule is applicable in all civil law jurisdictions.[229] For example, when a power of attorney is granted by the CSP running a CA in favour of the RSP (unilateral expression of will) for execution of a contract with the parties seeking the issue of a certificate, then the RSP acquires a right to act on behalf of the CSP running a CA, and the latter must then bear the consequences of the acts performed by the RSP within the scope of the delegated powers.[230] Furthermore, the legal sphere of the CSP running a CA is directly bound by the acts performed by the RSP.[231]

The contract between the CSP running a CA and the RSP should precisely allocate the functions between them, and, by extension, the business risk. Commonly, the RSP will be expected to undertake, in accordance with the applicable law as well as CPS/CP and industry standards *inter alia* to: provide a reliable registration service and ensure provision of accurate information to the CA for inclusion in the certificate;[232]

---

[226] Legal regulation of the contract for the benefit of third party can be found in almost all jurisdictions. See for example Article 1121 of French Code Civil, §328–335 of BGB §112–113 of Swiss Civil Code, Article 21 of Bulgarian LOC, etc.

[227] See Kalaydjiev, A., *Contract for the Benefit of a Third Person*, Market and Law Magazine, 2003, Vol.3.

[228] See Kalaydjiev, A., *Law on obligations, ibid.*, p. 131.

[229] For example Article 44 of the Bulgarian LOC provides that the rules regarding contracts shall respectively apply to the unilateral statements in cases when the law provides for creation, alteration or modification of rights and obligations. In the Principles of the European Contract Law, *ibid.*, Article 1:107 [Application of the Principles by Way of Analogy] reads that "These Principles apply with appropriate modifications to agreements to modify or end a contract, to unilateral promises and other statements and conduct indicating intention."

[230] Thawte is veryfing the identity of applicants for certificate issuance through WOT notaries – special attorneys trusted and authorized by Thawte to act on its behalf (see http://www.thawte.com)

[231] See Pavlova, M., *General Civil Law, ibid.*, p. 169.

[232] See ABA ISC PAG v0.30 – Public Draft for Comment, section 2.1.2.1, p.101, also Annex II (b) to the Directive 1999/93/EC.

verify, by appropriate means, in accordance with national law, the identity and, if applicable, any specific attributes of the person or the entity to which a certificate is issued;[233] employ qualified personnel; apply administrative and management procedures which are adequate and correspond to recognized standards (if applicable);[234] use trustworthy systems and products;[235] record all relevant information concerning the applications for certificate issue, revocation, renewal etc;[236] before executing a contract with the person seeking a certificate to support his or her electronic signature, to act on *bona fide* terms and inform that person by a durable means of communication about all terms and conditions relating to the use of the certificate;[237] to comply with all requirements in respect to the personal data protection regulation, consumer protection, and other applicable rules for provision of certification services.[238]

Usually the RSP must indemnify the CSP running a CA in respect of all that reflects compensation paid to the certificate holders and relying parties who have suffered harm arising from the wrongful behaviour of the RSP. The liability will be contractual and regulated by the general national liability rules, as discussed in Chapter II, *infra*. In civil proceedings, the RSP may be willing to be constituted as a civil accessory to support the defence of the CSP running a CA against the third parties which have suffered harm. Limitations and extensions of the liability of the RSP towards the CSP running a CA are possible within the statutory limits.[239]

Since the subject of this research is the specific liability of the CSPs, and there no such liability is applicable in respect of the RSPs, the question of the applicability of the general liability regime to the RSPs will not be investigated further.

2.4. Directory service provider

The keeping and maintenance of a directory (repository) for certificates, certificate revocation lists, different documents employed by the CSP in the course of provision

---

[233] Per argumentum of Annex II (d) of Directive 1999/93/EC.

[234] *Ibid.*, Annex II (e).

[235] *Ibid.*, Annex II (f).

[236] *Ibid.*, Annex II (i).

[237] *Ibid.*, Annex II (k).

[238] ABA ISC PAG v0.30 – Public Draft for Comment, section 2.1.2.1, p.101.

[239] See Chapter II, section 5, *infra*.

of certification services (certificate policies, certification practice statements, security policies, subscriber agreements, registration provider agreements, etc.) or providing access thereto by employing different techniques (i.e. via different protocols - OCSP, HTTP, LDAP, etc.) can be accomplished by the CSP itself, or can be outsourced in whole or in part to a separate entity known as a directory service provider.[240]

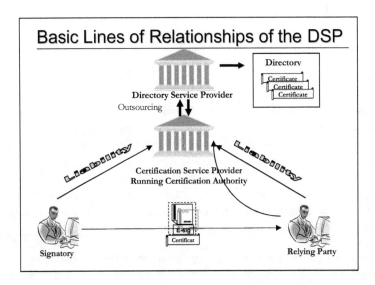

Fig. 9. Basic lines of relationships of the DSP

It is commonly referred to that the repository function is a 'back-end' CA function, while the RA function is a 'front-end' CA function.[241] CAs delegate such functions to

---

[240] In some public documents the DSP is commonly referred to as Repository, or Repository Service Provider – see RFC 2527 Internet X.509 Public Key Infrastructure Certificate Policy and Certification Practices Framework, Section 2. Definitions, also ABA ISC PAG v0.30 – Public Draft for Comment, Section D.2.1.5. In present work "directory" shall be used instead of "repository", thus "Directory Service Provider" instead of "Repository Service Provider" due to the tradition and the usage of the former terms in most of the European industry standards and legislation, especially Directive 1999/93/EC.

[241] ABA ISC PAG v0.30 – Public Draft for Comment, Section D.2.1.5.1, p.113.

DSPs less often than they delegate RA functions. In contrast to the RA functions, the directory can be managed on a centralized basis.[242]

The assignment of the function from the CSP providing CA services to the DSP should normally be addressed in the relevant service contract. The contract may relate to one or several directory services to be delegated, while others will remain a CA function.

The contract usually covers the DSP's obligations[243] to publish the issued certificates in due time, serve the revocation requests,[244] guarantee proper determination of the period for update of revocation information, to ensure that the date and time of a certificate publication or revocation may be determined precisely,[245] to update documents, keep and maintain different access protocols to the directory,[246] guarantee conditions for introducing restricted access to subscribers' certificates in accordance with their instructions,[247] comply with relevant privacy, confidentiality and personal data protection requirements,[248] provide security and usage of trustworthy systems,[249] employ qualified personnel,[250] manage processes in an appropriate fashion etc. In general the DSP should abide by the CA's policy and practices, as set out in the certificate policy and the certification practice statement.

Some studies and industry standards indicate that the DSP can be held directly liable by the parties which have suffered damage. Therefore, it might be possible for it to manage its liability by means of warranties and representations.[251] This seems to be the case in common law doctrine and practice.[252] In jurisdictions following the civil law tradition, such exposure hardly seems applicable.

---

[242] *Ibid.*

[243] See RFC 2527, *ibid.*, P.15.

[244] *Per argumentum* of Article 6 (2) in relation to Annex II (b) of the Directive 1999/93/EC.

[245] *Ibid.*, Annex II (c).

[246] *Ibid.*, Aritcle 6 (2).

[247] *Ibid.*, Annex II (l).

[248] *Ibid.*, Annex II (f) and (g).

[249] *Ibid.*, Annex II (f) and (l).

[250] *Ibid.*, Annex II (e).

[251] See RFC 2527, *ibid.*, p.15, also ABA ISC PAG v0.30 – Public Draft for Comment, Section D.2.1.5.3, p.114 *et seq.*

[252] In Certificate Authority Rating and Trust Guidelines (CARAT), NACHA Internet Council (27 Oct. 1998), (http://internetcouncil.nacha.org/projects/default.html), Sections C.2.1, C.2.5 it is even suggested an

The DSP provides services upon delegation of certification services allocated normally to the CSP running a CA. In this regard, the CSP running a CA 'subcontracts' the provision of certain functions. Should the negligent behaviour of the DSP cause harm to the subscriber and/or the relying party, those parties would be able to recover damages from the CSPs (running CA) on the basis of privity of contract with the latter. The CSP running a CA would be put in a situation of objective liability exposure – it will be held liable for the conduct of others[253] regardless of whether the basis of its liability towards the party which has suffered harm is contractual or tortuous in nature. The contractual relations between the DSP and the CSP running a CA are relative.[254] Therefore, no circumstances could arise in which the DSP becomes directly liable to parties other than the CSP running a CA. Thus, the liability of the DSP should be considered 'secondary' in the sense that the party entitled to invoke it is the contractual party (i.e. the CSP running a CA), once it has suffered harm in terms of the obligation to pay compensation to parties which have suffered harm as a result of the wrongful behaviour of the DSP persons. In this respect the CSP's right to indemnification would stem from the contract with the DSP. The ground for this would be non-fulfilment by the DSP of its contractual obligations, as identified *supra.*

2.5. Time-stamping service providers

In the PKI, it is sometimes necessary to develop mechanisms which allow the creation of a verifiable statement of proof that certain electronic document or data was signed while the signing certificate was valid.[255] The time-stamping service fulfils this role. This service consists in the issue of special types of certificates (time-stamp tokens[256]) by an authority known as the time-stamping service provider (TSSP), which is trusted by the users of the time-stamping services (i.e. subscribers as well as relying parties). In a similar way to the confusion that exists in respect of the notions of

---

implementation model in which the repository function is allocated an equal status to the CA, while its primary focus is on serving the relying party's rather than the subscriber. Op.cit. ABA ISC PAG v0.30 – Public Draft for Comment, n. 263.

[253] See Chapter II, section 4.4 *infra* - Liability for the conduct of others.

[254] On the relative character of the contractual relations see *infra* note 350.

[255] See ABA ISC PAG v0.30 – Public Draft for Comment, section D.4.11.

[256] The time-stamp token is defined to be a data object that binds a representation of a datum to a particular time, thus establishing evidence that the datum existed before that time. See ETSI TS 102 023 V1.1.1 (2002-04) Policy requirements for time-stamping authorities, Section 3.1. It is signed by the TSA'a private key – *ibid.,* section 4.4.

certification-service-provider and certification authority, it should be remembered that two acronyms are in simultaneous use for naming this agent - time-stamping service provider (TSSP) and time-stamping authority (TSA). The time-stamping authority (TSA) is a unit consisting of software and hardware managed under particular procedures to provide time-stamping services, while the time-stamping service provider (TSSP) is the provider of these services.

The TSSP is a certification-service-provider under the meaning of the EU Directive on Electronic Signatures, while it issues time stamp certificates, i.e. provides certification services *strictu sensu*.[257]

The time-stamping service may be provided independently of provision of other certification services, either by the CSP running the CA,[258] or by other entities.[259] It is based on a separate time-stamp policy[260] and a TSA practice statement that should be employed by the TSSP.[261] Under Bulgarian law, provision of a time-stamp service is mandatory for certain types of CSPs.[262]

---

[257] Article 2 (11) of Directive 1999/93/EC. *Ibid.,* sectoin 4.4.

[258] Like Verysign (www.verisign.com), Belgacom (www.belgacom.be), Bankservice (www.b-trust.org), etc.

[259] Such separate TSSP, for example, were found to be Unizeto Certum (www.certum.pl), Surety (www.surety.com), et al.

[260] See the Time-stamping Policy of Unizeto Certum at www.certum.pl.

[261] There is no restriction on the form of a time-stamp policy or practice statement specification. See *ibid.,* section 4.4.

[262] Under Bulgarian law the registered CSPs that issue universal certificates (i.e. a variety of enhanced qualified certificate) are obliged by virtue of Article 40 of EDESA to provide time-stamping service alongside with all other services rendered.

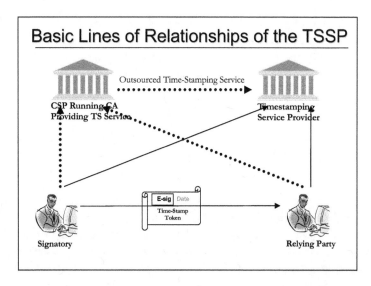

Fig. 10. Basic lines of relationships of the TSSP

Just as with the CSP running a CA, the TSSP should keep and maintain time-stamping certificate lists and other data corresponding to signing certificates, in order to provide the relying parties with assurances that the signed certificate was not revoked at the time of signature.[263]

The TSSP must ensure that all requirements, as detailed in different standards,[264] are implemented as applicable to the selected trusted time-stamp policy. It should provide all its time-stamping services in a manner consistent with the relevant practice statement and ensure adherence to any additional obligations indicated in the time stamp, either directly or incorporated by reference.[265] The TSSP would normally be expected to provide reliable service to a standard of care not less than that applicable to a CSP running a CA. In other words, it must use reliable systems, employ qualified personnel, demonstrate reliability, ensure the operation of a prompt and secure

---

[263] ABA ISC PAG v0.30 – Public Draft for Comment, *ibid.*

[264] For example ETSI TS 102 023 V1.1.1 (2002-04) Policy requirements for time-stamping authorities, Section 7.

[265] *Ibid.*, section 6.

directory and a secure and immediate time-stamp revocation service, ensure that the date and time when the time-stamp token is issued or revoked can be determined precisely, take measures against forgery of time-stamp tokens, maintain the secrecy of its private keys, record all relevant information concerning time-stamp tokens for an appropriate period of time, as specified in the time-stamp policy – in particular in order to provide evidence of data certification for the purposes of legal proceedings – to communicate precise terms and conditions regarding the use of the token with a party seeking issue of a time-stamp token etc. The level of care that must be exercised by the TSSP will be assessed by the national courts in any given case.

The liability exposure of the TSSPs towards the subscribers and the relying parties derives either from contract or from national law.[266] In most countries the liability regime of the TSSP is more or less similar to the liability regime for CSPs running CAs that do not issue qualified certificates, since there is usually no specific liability regime in force for these subjects.[267] Since the liability regime of the TSSPs remains beyond the scope of the present research, the liability exposure thereof will not be analyzed in detail.[268]

However, it should be noted that the TSSPs could manage their liability by introducing related clauses in the services contract or in the time-stamping policy and practice statement. A national law can also establish additional restrictions on liability limitation.[269] Where consumers are involved, statutory protections may also apply.[270]

Should a TSSP choose to outsource certain elements of the time-stamping services to other parties, it will retain overall responsibility for the reliable provision of the services.[271] In such a case, the TSSPs will remain generally liable for the conduct of

---

[266] *Ibid.*, Annex A (Informative) - Potential liability in the provision of time-stamping services.

[267] See sections 2.2.5.1 and 2.2.5.2, *supra.*

[268] For more information on the legal aspects of the time-stamping authotities, see Mitrakas, A., *Legal Aspects of Time Stamping,* Globalsign NV/SA, January 2002.

[269] For example, under Bulgarian law on e-signatures the CSPs that are obliged to provide time-stamping service may not place any liability limitations or exemption for damages arising of non-provision of time-stamping service (arg. of Article 40 EDESA).

[270] See ETSI TS 102 023 V1.1.1 (2002-04) Policy requirements for time-stamping authorities, Annex A.

[271] *Ibid.*, Section 4.2.

others.[272] The TSSP should ensure conformity with the procedures prescribed in its policy, even when the functions of the TSA are undertaken by sub-contractors.[273]

2.6. Other certification-service-providers

Depending on the outsourced CA functions, numerous providers of different certification and other trust services might exist. These include key management service providers,[274] key escrow service providers,[275] archive service providers,[276] etc.[277] The common role of all certification-service-providers is to contribute to the trust-building process in the PKI. This issue is discussed in sections 2.1 and 2.2, *supra*.

Depending on the types of relationships with the main actors – the CSP running CA, the subscriber and the relying party (whether privity of contract exists between them or not) – the duties, and thus the liability, of these certification-service-providers will reveal certain specific features, but will also follow, more or less, the pattern explained in the preceding sections. Since no specific regime regulating the activities, and, by extension, the liability of these providers was found in Bulgarian and in any of the other EU jurisdictions, it falls to the general national laws to regulate these issues.[278] In this regard, analysis of the liability of these actors remains beyond the scope of the present work.

---

[272] See Chapter II, section 4.4, *infra*.

[273] ABA ISC PAG v0.30 – Public Draft for Comment, Section D.4.11. An appropriate example in such respect is provided in ETSI TS 102 023 V1.1.1 (2002-04). It reads that the TSA may sub-contract all the component services, including the services which generate time-stamps using the TSA's key. However, the private key or keys used to generate the time-stamp tokens are identified as belonging to the TSA which maintains overall responsibility for meeting the requirements defined in the current document.

[274] *Per argumentum* of Annex II (j) of Directive 1999/93/EC. Also Article 19 (2) of the Bulgarian LOC.

[275] See Groshieide, F., Boele-Woelki, K. , *European Private Law (1999/2000). E-Commerce Issue*, The Netherlands: Molengrafica, 2000, p.36 Also ABA ISC PAG v0.30 – Public Draft for Comment, Section D 6.2.3.

[276] See Dumortier, J., Van Den Eynde, S., *Electronic signatures and trusted archival services*, in Proceedings of the DLMForum 2002, Barcelona 6-8 May 2002, Luxembourg, Office for Official Publications of the European Communities, 2002; also ABA ISC PAG v0.30 – Public Draft for Comment, Sections D 6.2.5 and D.6.2.6.

[277] EESSI, *Final Report of the EESSI Expert Team*, 20th July 1999, p.14 (http://www.eema.org/ecaf/ Frep.pdf)

[278] There exist, however, industry standards that provide particular range of the due care of these providers – see ETSI TR 102 231 V 1.1.1 (2003-10) Electronic Signatures and Infrastructures (ESI); Provision of Harmonized Trust Service Provider Status Information (http://webapp.etsi.org/exchangefolder/ts_102231v010101p.pdf)

3. Conclusions

The research prepared in this chapter sheds light on the basic aspects of electronic signatures and the infrastructure for using electronic signatures based on public key technologies. Two very important issues for gathering proofs of evidence to substantiate the assertions of the author are analyzed: the concept of trust in electronic communications, and the role of the CSPs in the trust-building process.

The *concept of trust is examined* at the beginning of the chapter (section 1). The overview reveals that trust is one of the engines driving the public key infrastructure and the usage of electronic signatures in open networks like the Internet. The research shows the differences between the main types of electronic signatures – basic, advanced and qualified. The way in which electronic signatures work is demonstrated, and the role of the public key certificate, and how these certificates are used to promote trust, is explained. Emphasis is put on the qualified electronic signatures.

Research on the trust concept leads to three main conclusions:

➢   a key role in the trust-building process is played by the certification-service-providers being trusted third parties;

➢   there are certain factors that promote trust in the PKI, *inter alia*: the existence of an effective supervising scheme, legal rules establishing statutory duties for the activities of the CSPs, mandatory rules, national accreditation schemes etc;

➢   a relevant though not the most important factor, for promoting trust is the existence of a clear and effective liability regime to guarantee the protection of parties in circumstances where trust is undermined due to the negligent behaviour of the CSPs.

Thus, in section 2, the focus of the analysis was on the examination of the *notion and the role of the CSPs*. This led to the establishment of further necessary viewpoints for investigation of the liability of the CSPs, and to the following deductions:

In the first instance, the analysis provided a clear view on the trusted third party, whose liability is the subject of research – the certification-service-provider.

Secondly, the role of the CSPs was examined from the perspective of the relationships with the other PKI actors. The relationships between the CSPs and the other parties using or relying on certification services were identified and discussed. These relationships include those between the CSP and the certificate holder, and between the CSP and the relying party. The scope of the research was narrowed by excluding the relationship between the certificate holder, resp. the relying party with the CSPs providing outsourced services, since no direct liability could arise.

Thirdly, the nature of the relationships between the CSPs and other main actors were precisely identified: the contractual ones with the certificate holder, contractual or non-contractual ones with the relying party, and the contractual with the other CSPs to whom certain functions are outsourced. This analysis provided a viewpoint for proper interpretation of the liability provisions of Directive 1999/93/EC in Chapter III and the Bulgarian national rules transposing the *acquis*.

Although basic knowledge has now been acquired on the concept of electronic signatures, the role of the certification-service-providers in the trust-building process and the relationships between the CSPs and the main actors using or relying on electronic signatures, it is still not possible to commence an analysis of the liability regime of the CSPs. Another basic issue also requires analysis: the concept of of general civil liability.

Chapter II

GENERAL CONCEPT OF CIVIL LIABILITY

The civil liability regime impacts not only on the usage of electronic signatures, but also on the functioning of the whole market. When entering into different legal relationships, people place faith in the rule of law, trusting in the idea that if anything goes wrong 'someone will be liable'[279] for the damage caused to their property as a result of the other party's misconduct. In other words, if the regulations are not followed, the statutory law enforcement instruments and mechanisms will be executed to ensure justice and balance in society.

Therefore, the presence of a clear regime for attaching liability promotes trust for the market players. When relationships between parties come into being, are altered and subsequently terminated in an electronic environment by usage of electronic signatures, uncertainty as to whether and how the general liability regime could be effectively enforced might undermine trust and hamper the usage of electronic means of communications.

Can the general liability regime promote the necessary level of trust in the electronic world? Is it adapted to effectively guarantee the interests of the market players? Is there a need to enforce specific liability rules? Would such rules promote trust, and how would they achieve this?

Answering these questions seems to be impossible without making an overview of the concept of the general civil liability at this stage. Since the chosen method for research is to acquire knowledge and deductions for substantiating the assertions by analyzing the transposition problems of the supranational liability rules in Bulgarian law, the present chapter serves as a short introduction to Bulgarian civil liability law and explains the main theoretical concepts in the Bulgarian doctrine on civil liability.

There are several reasons for drafting this chapter.

---

[279] Balboni, P., *Liability of Certification Service Providers Towards Relying Parties and the Need for a Clear System to Enhance the Level of Trust in Electronic Communication*, Information & Communications Technology Law, Carfax Publishing, Vol. 13, No. 3, 2004, p.217.

In the first instance, the notion of 'civil liability' reveals different meanings in different jurisdictions, particularly in terms of the legal substance of liability. In the *acquis communautaire* certain terminology is used, but no clear directions exist as to what should be considered liability, negligence, reasonableness, fault and so on when these notions are considered on a supranational level. Therefore, the key to the correct understanding of CSPs' liability should be sought by the examination of the *basic aspects of the civil liability concept*. Only after carrying out such an examination can a proper analysis of the specific liability of the certification-service-providers, introduced by the *acquis communautaire*, and its transposition into national legal systems, as well as an assessment of the necessity of such a specific regime, be made.

This task seems to be of utmost difficulty because doctrinal approaches to the issue of liability vary not only between different countries, but even within one and the same country. Therefore, the present analysis will concentrate *only on reviewing the concept of liability from the point of view of the prevalent modern civil law doctrine in Bulgaria* – as the latter has been selected as a case study country for the purposes of the present research. Since the Bulgarian legislation falls within the continental law family and follows the traditions of the French legal system, the conclusions and the findings herein provide a good point of reference for interpreting the provisions of the *acquis communautaire* that establish liability rules for the CSPs.

The author makes reference to the respective approaches to the liability concept of the English, French and German legal systems, representing the three major European law families. However, in order not to lose the focus of the work – the assessment of the specific liability regime for CSPs from the point of view of Bulgarian law – all such references to legal texts in the different national laws and the comparative overviews regarding the general liability concept are restricted to the footnotes. This non-standard academic technique is intentionally followed in Chapter II in order to preserve its reviewing purpose and to refer to other jurisdictions by way of comparison only.

Making an analysis of the basic aspects of the liability concepts seems obligatory, secondly, because the *acquis communautaire*, particularly Directive 1999/93/EC on a Community framework for electronic signatures *does not provide for harmonization of the general rules for liability of the CSPs*. Recital (22) of the Directive explicitly envisages that CSPs subject to national rules regarding liability for non-performance of their statutory or contractual duties beyond the specific liability regime established by the Directive. This relates to the liability of all CSPs regardless of the type of certificates they issue or whether they issue certificates to the public or to closed user groups. In this respect, the chapter aims at outlining the scope of the general civil liability regime so that in the following chapters the scope of the specific regime of the CSPs issuing qualified certificates to the public can be drawn.

Thirdly, the analysis of the general liability regime will justify the *reasons* for introduction of a specific liability regime for the CSPs by the European legislator. Such an analysis will answer the question of whether or not the general liability regimes are suited to guarantee the interests of the users of certification services and, as a result, to promote trust in the world of electronic communications described in chapters IV and V below.

The research made in this chapter is based on several sources[280]. Since the making of a detailed analysis of the general civil liability concept is beyond the scope of the present work, the theories upheld in these sources are strictly followed without presenting novel approaches to civil liability theory.

Finally, not all the aspects and complications of civil liability are examined. The research is focused mainly on the basic liability concepts that are useful in order to understand the specific liability of the CSPs so that a proper evaluation of its necessity can be made.

1. The Notion of Liability. Liability - Obligation Correlation

The notion of liability has different aspects and meanings in Bulgarian legal theory.

Sometimes it is used to name the relationship between two subjects, consisting of the obligation of one of the subjects to repair the damages caused to the other and the correlated subjective right of the damaged subject to claim compensation.[281]

---

[280] The main sources that are used for the elaboration of the analysis in Chapter I are *inter alia*: Kalaydjiev, A., *Law on Obligations. General Part*, SIBI, 2001; Pavlova, M., General Civil Law, Part I, Ciela, 1996; Van Gerven, W., Lever, J., Larouche, P., *Cases, Materials and Text on National, Supranational and International Tort Law*, Hart Publishing, Oxford and Portland, Oregon, 2000; Beale, H., HartKamp, A., Kötz, H., Tallon, D., *Cases, Materials and Text on Contract Law*, Hart Publishing, Oxford and Portland, Oregon, 2002; Short Survey of the Principles of European Contract Law: Introduction to the Principles of European Contract Law prepared by the Commission on European contract law (http://www.cbs.dk/departments/law/staff/ol/_commission on ecl/survey_pecl.htm); European Group on Tort Law, *Principles of European Tort Law*, Text and Commentary, Springer-Verlag/Wien, 2005.

[281] The concept of "subjective rights" ("субективно право", "subjektive Rechte", "droit subjectif") is known to the Continental legal systems like Bulgaria, Germany, France, Italy, etc. The subjective right shall mean the guaranteed by the law possibility of a person to demand certain behaviour or result from the obliged

Other authors use the 'liability' notion to address the very issue of an obligation to compensate.[282]

Moreover, under certain normative acts, 'liability' may also mean bearing the consequences of *force majeure*.[283] It is also used with the meaning of a guarantee.[284]

From the civil procedure point of view, liability is seen as the subjection of the property of the certification-service-provider towards the claim of a damaged person. From a practical point of view, the liability of a CSP is also considered an unfavourable consequence, resulting from the non-fulfilment of certain duties to bear the consequences of execution of compulsory statutory measures and proceedings against its property.[285]

For the purposes of this work, liability will be regarded as the relationship between the creditor, respectively the party who has suffered harm in tort, and the debtor, respectively the tortfeasor, consisting of the obligation of the debtor to make restitution for the harm caused to the creditor as a result of unlawful behaviour.[286]

2. Functions. Types of Liability

2.1. General notes

The debtor's obligation to provide compensation to the creditor for harm suffered by the creditor arises as a legal consequence of the non-performance of

---

person for satisfying his legally recognized interest. The "subjective right" is opposed to the term "objective right" (*"обективно право"*, *"objektives Rechte"*, *"droit objectif"*), which means the law as a set of written rules (general law). Misunderstanding may arise due to the usage of the same word in many languages to name "right" and "law". See Pavlova, M., General Civil Law, Part I, Ciela, 1996, p.p. 152-162. The same concept is followed by most of the civil law families - see Van Gerven, W., Lever, J., Larouche, P., *Cases, Materials and Text on National, Supranational and International Tort Law*, Hart Publishing, Oxford and Portland, Oregon, 2000, p.63.).

[282] See Mazeaud, H., Mazeaud., L., *Traité théorique et pratique de la responsabilité civile délictuelle et contractuelle.*, V. 1. Paris, 1947, p. 2. Also Martine, E., L'option entre la responsabilité contractuelle et la responsabilité délictuell, Paris, 1967, p. 7.

[283] See Article 373 of the Bulgarian Commercial Act.

[284] See Article 6 of the Directive 1999/93/EC: "... Member states shall ensure that ... *by guaranteeing* such a certificate the certification-service-provider *shall be liable* for damage ..."

[285] See Kalaydjiev, A., *Law on Obligations. General Part*, SIBI, 2001, p.40

[286] See Pavlova, M., *ibid*, p. 162, also Van Gerven, et al., *ibid*, p.63.

contractual[287] or statutory duties.[288]

Bulgarian legal doctrine identifies two main functions of civil liability.

The *first* and the main one is the restitutory function – the duty to indemnify in respect of damage caused, which is assigned to the debtor.[289]

In some legal systems, civil liability also has a punitive function.[290] From a theoretical point of view, this function of civil liability rests on the idea of punishing the tortfeasor, or debtor, for the negligent non-performance of its duties, with a view to discouraging future negligent behaviour. In Bulgaria, as in other civil law countries, however, the punitive function of liability is not recognized.[291] The only exception to this is found in cases in which a contractual obligation for liquidated damages[292] is

---

[287] The term contract ("договор", "contrat", "Vertrag") has no one and the same meaning in the different legal systems. Article 8 of the Bulgarian Law on Obligaitions and Contract (LOC) defines that "The contract is an agreement between two or more persons to establish, arrange or terminate a legal relation between them". Under Article 1.101 of the French Code Civil the contract is a species of agreement - convention by which one or more person obligate themselves to one or more other persons to give, or to do or not to do something. (Cornu, G., *Vocabulaire Juridique Henri Capitant*, 8th ed., Paris, PUF, 2000.). Similarly under German law (§305 BGB) it is the name of the legal act to which referense should be made – "For the creation of an obligation by a juristic act, and for for any anlternation of the substance of an obligationm, a contract between the parties is necessary, unless otherwise provided by law". No legal definition of contract was found in English law, but in the US law as representative of the Common law systems the contract shall be considered "a promise or a set of promises for the breach of which the law gives a remedy or the performance of which the law in some way recognizes a duty" (§1 of Restatement of the Law Second, Contracts 2d, 1981, vol.1) – it stresses on the need for the availability for remedy in cases of breach of promise. The present common view in the European countries to the contract since the Roman law is that it is a source of obligations, effected by the will of the parties. See Beale, H., HartKamp, A., Kötz, H., Tallon, D., *Cases, Materials and Text on Contract Law*, Hart Publishing, Oxford and Portland, Oregon, 2002, p.p. 2-3 and 36.

[288] The author will not investigate hereinunder the cases where valid obligations arise from *gestio*, administrative acts, unjust enrichment or other reasons, while they remain out of interest for the purposes of the present research.

[289] See Kalaydjiev, A., *Ibid.*, p.338, also Kojuharov, A., *Law on Obligations. General Doctrine on the Obligation Relations. First Book*, Sofia, 1992, p.256, also Van Gerven, W., et al., *ibid.*, p.69

[290] See Ryan, P., *Revisiting the United States' Application of Punitive Damages: Separating Myth from Reality*, ILSA Journal of International and Comparative Law, Volume 10:1 (2003), Treitel, G., *Remedies for Breach of Contract (Courses of Action Open to a Party Aggrieved). Contracts in General.* Chapter 16. International Encyclopaedia of Comparative Law. Volume VII. J. C. B. Mohr (Paul Siebeck). Tübingen /Mouton/the Hague/Paris, 1976, p. 4.

[291] See Kalaydjiev, A., *Ibid.*

[292] In Bulgaria, like in most of the civil law countries, in contract the parties may agree beforehand that should fault is present, the non-guilty party shall be entitled to liquidated damages at a fixed amount. If such an agreement is reached and respective clause exist in the contract, the court will award the amound agreed if the ground of the claim is proved (i.e. the obligation and the fault) without necessitiy of proving the existence of damage or the value of ths damage. Of course, should the actual damage, as evaluated in money, is higher then the amount of the liquidated damages agreed, the aggrieved party shall be entitled to prove the actual value of the damages and the court will award the excess apart of the amount of the agreed liquidated damage. See Kojuharov, A., *Ibid*, p.321, also Kalaydjiev, A., *Ibid*, p.406-407.

undertaken and no damage *de facto* has arisen from the non-performance of the obligation, or the value of the damage is lower than that falling due under the contract.[293] In certain of the countries following the common law model, the awarding of punitive damages is a more widespread practice.[294]

Some authors identify another function of civil liability that is mostly relevant to tort liability, rather than to contractual liability. This is the function of discouraging the future repetition of the negligent behaviour at issue.[295]

Bulgarian scholars, as well as those in the majority of legal systems following continental legal traditions, view the *corpus* of civil liability as consisting of five elements: the behaviour, the unlawfulness of the behaviour, the damage caused, causality between the behaviour and the damage caused, and fault[296]. In some cases, the *corpus* might miss one of these elements but despite this, liability might arise. As already discussed, this might happen, for example, when liquidated damages are agreed beforehand – in such a case, it is possible that no damage has actually been caused, but the debtor may still be held contractually liable.[297] There are also cases when liability might arise without the debtor having acted with *dolus* or negligence – for example, when he or she has agreed to bear the risk of *force majeure*, or when damages are caused by a subcontractor.[298]

Dating from the Roman times, two types of liability, presently applicable to the CSPs, are recognized – contractual and tortious (delictual).[299]

2.2. Contractual and tortious liability

The distinction between contractual and tortious liability is fundamental in order to make possible the assessment in Chapter III of the specific liability regime of the

---

[293] See Apostolov, A., *Law on Obligations*, p. 178.

[294] Ryan, P., *Ibid*. Punitive damages are awarded as an exception in some civil law jurisdictions like the Netherlands.

[295] See Van Gerven, W., et al., *ibid.*, p.69

[296] See Kalaydjiev, A., *ibid.*, p.338.

[297] In tort such a possibility cannot exist, because penalty damages cannot be agreed beforehand.

[298] See sections 4.3 and 4.4, *infra*.

[299] The other types of non-contractual liabilities remain out of scope of this research since they does not substantially affect the liability regime of the CSPs.

CSPs introduced by the EU Directive on e-signatures.[300]

Distinctions between the two main types of liability exist in the following respects.

In the first instance, a dividing line may be seen in the rules that establish duties and thus give rise to corresponding subjective rights (so-called 'primary rules').[301] From this point of view, the duty not to cause damage established in tort law is always directed to everyone, while the contractual duties are usually directed towards the other contractual party.[302] Furthermore, entering into a contractual relationship always depends on the free will of the parties, while everyone is subject to tortious duties regardless of whether they are willing to be bound or not.[303]

In the second instance, a difference may be identified with respect to the rules giving rise to liability in the case when the established duties in tort or in contract are breached (these are referred to as 'secondary rules').[304] Firstly, the contractual liability usually arises when there has been non-performance of valid obligations, either undertaken in contract or which have arisen under a unilateral transaction. The tort liability arises only when the infringement of established statutory duties not to cause damage is present as a general primary rule,[305] or when such an exposure is explicitly envisaged in particular primary rules.[306] Secondly, the sanctions, remedies and possibilities for specific performance are much broader if the contractual obligations are not fulfilled. Another divergence reveals the nature of the interest to be protected by engaging liability in contract and in tort. In tort, the interest of the damaged person is to have his *patrimonium* restored to the degree it would have been if no tort had been committed, i.e. to be restored in *status quo*

---

[300] As it will become evident from the analysis made in Chapter III, most of the investigated studies incorrectly assume that the particular liability regime established refers to tortious liability of the CSPs only, but not to the contractual one. This most probably results from the incorrect understanding of the general concept of the contractual and tortious liability and the grounds for their appearance.

[301] See Van Gerven, W., et al., *ibid.*, p.32

[302] This concept gives rise to classification of the subjective rights to absolute and relative. See Pavlova, M., *ibid.*, p. 175; also Van Gerven, W., et al., *ibid.*, p.63-67; also the famous case of the Italian Corte di Cassazione *Luigi Meroni*, 26 January 1971, No.174, Foro it. 1971-I-245. See *infra* note 350.

[303] See Clerk & Lindsell on Torts, 15th ed., London: Sweet and Maxwell, 1982, at para.1-05.

[304] See *supra* note 301.

[305] See for example Article 45 of the Bulgarian LOC, §823 of BGB, Article 1383 of the French Code Civil, etc.

[306] The criminal codes list comprehensively cases of tortious behaviour that might raise grounds for civil liability. In civil codes or laws there are also sometimes explicitly listed cases of non-contractual liability. See for example Article 12, Article 21 (2), Article 88 (1) of the Bulgarian LOC, Article 384, 385 and 386 of the French Code Civil, §833-838 of BGB, etc. See section 4.4, *infra*.

ante.[307] In this respect, tortious liability aims at satisfying the negative interest.[308] Contractual liability, on the other hand, shields the creditor's positive interest – the creditor should be placed in the position he or she would have expected to have been in if the contract had been performed fully, accurately and without delay.[309]

In the third instance, the behaviour of the debtor, resp. the tortfeasor under both types of liability could be either action or omission. However, usually the tort liability results from the active behaviour of a party, while omission results in non-fulfilment of contractual obligations, and accordingly leads to contractual liability being incurred.[310]

Fourthly, in some cases of contractual liability (e.g. when the damages are agreed beforehand) the value of the actual damage caused may be less than the sum due under the contract.[311] In contrast to tort liability, the damages in some cases of contractual liability are not necessarily an element of the liability *corpus.*[312]

Fifthly, in contractual law, instruments exist to contractually extend or limit the liability.[313] There is no such possibility in tort.

Further differences may also be identified in the liability for the conduct of others,[314] in respect of such issues as discharge from liability in circumstances of contributive fault, the regime of liability due to default, and the prescription rules,

---

[307] See Howing, P., *Positive and Negative Interest in Law*, Deventer: Kluwer, 192, p.p. 104-113.

[308] See Konov, T., *ibid.,* p.30-34, also Weir, T., *Complex Liabilities.* International Encyclopaedia of Comparative Law, Vol.XI/12: Torts (Tübingen: Mohr, 1976), at 5-6, also *supra* note 307.

[309] See Kalaydjiev, A., *ibid.,* p.339, also Van Gerven, W., et al., *ibid.,* p.33, also Borrows, A., *Remedies for Torts and Breach of Contract,* 2nd ed., Butterworth, London, p.17. As guiding Principle of the European Contract Law Article 9:502 establishes that the general measure of damages is such sum *as will put the aggrieved party as nearly as possible into the position in which it would have been if the contract had been duly performed.* Such damages cover the loss which the aggrieved party has suffered and the gain of which it has been deprived.

[310] See Kalaydjiev, A., *ibid.,* p.341.

[311] Article 9:509 of the Principles of European Contract Law states that where the contract provides that a party who fails to perform is to pay a specified sum to the aggrieved party for such non-performance, the aggrieved party shall be awarded that sum irrespective of its actual loss.

[312] See Kalaydjiev, A., *ibid.,* p.339. See *supra* note 292.

[313] See section 5, *infra.*

[314] See section 4.4, *infra.*

which are not the subject of analysis in the present work.[315]

After noting the above-mentioned theoretical criteria for drawing distinctions between contractual and tortious liability, it is possible to proceed to an analysis of the specific liability regime of the certification-service-providers introduced by the Directive 1999/93/EC on e-signatures. It will become evident that difficulties were encountered by many scholars in analysing the Directive's rules introducing specific liability for the CSPs because of improperly interpreting their nature. This analysis will be made in the following chapter.

2.3. Concurrence

Concurrence is another liability issue that should be outlined prior to entering into thorough analysis of the specific liability of the CSPs and making an estimation of its adequacy. It may happen that the negligent behaviour of a given party (in our case, of the CSP), giving rise to damage, may be regarded as the non-fulfillment of contractual obligations and in the same time as the commission of a tort. In such cases, the question arises of whether the party that has suffered damage has a free choice as to the basis on which the claim is made, or whether pursuing a remedy in tort should be excluded due to the existence of a contractual claim against the debtor/tortfeasor (i.e. – the CSP). This situation is commonly referred to as a 'concurrence'[316] due to the existence of concurrent causes of action in contract and tort.[317]

This issue is of great importance because, as it will become evident, the service providers may be subject to different liability exposure in different jurisdictions. Therefore, the aggrieved parties may have different possibilities when it comes to choosing the grounds on which to base their claim for compensation against the service providers.

---

[315] For thorough analysis of the differences between the tortious and contractual liability See Kalaydjiev, A., *ibid.*, p.p.338-346.

[316] In most of the studies and legal textbooks the concept is referred to as *"concurrence of claims"*. See Koziol, H., Steininger, B. (*editors*), *European Tort Law 2002*, 2004, Springer, p.p. 118, 231. Also Cane P., Stapelton, J., *The Law of Obligations: Essays in Celebration of John Fleming*, 1999, Oxford University Press, p.120, also Zimmermann, R., *Comparative Foundations of a European Law of Set-Off and Prescription*, 2002, Cambridge University Press, p. 84. The concept is also known as *"competing claims"*. See Beale, H., Hartkamp, A., et al., *ibid.*, p.69.

[317] See Cane, P., *The Anatomy of Tort Law*, Hart Publishing, Oxford, 1997, p.22, also Van Gerven, W., et al., *ibid.*, p.34.

The choice of the place of establishment within the EU becomes of great importance in the light of this issue,[318] which has, as a result, become problematic with respect to the CSPs.[319]

Different legal systems choose different approaches to the issue.[320]

The jurisdictions following the English[321] and the German model[322] allow the party that has suffered damage to choose between contractual and tortious claims. French law and the countries following it, including Bulgaria, usually apply the *non-cumul*

---

[318] Richard Harrison in his article PKI: The risks of being trusted (*infra* note 321), provides interesting example in respect to the position of CSPs in view of concurrence of tortiuos and contractual liability. The author states that "Whether or not there is a contract, there may well be a duty to take reasonable care to avoid loss to certain parties. The present position, in so far as it can be summarised, is that the court looks at new duties incrementally and pragmatically. The fundamental premise is that assumption of responsibility to a person who relies on your advice generates liability for foreseeable loss if you do not take reasonable care in giving the advice. This liability in tort arises independently of contract and can exist concurrently with it. If B relies on a digital certificate provided by a certification authority vouching for and paid by A, then it is likely that B can recover against the certification authority if it is negligent. The concept of "assumption of responsibility" will in all probability be applied.". Further the author finds that "There is always a level of risk but if the certification authority feels that the price charged for the services will enable it to make a profit out of its activities, then it will be happy to bear that risk. Equally, it may charge a lower price and qualify the result to be sought. It will incorporate exclusion clauses and liability limitation clauses into its contracts and assuming the business to business negotiation process is not on written standard terms, or more likely assuming that it passes the test of reasonableness, those contractual terms will allocate the risk between the parties. The law of contract in this context is all about risk allocation".

[319] In the Communication to the EU Commission on the European Civil Code COM(2001) 398 final), *infra* note 346 it is identified that "If a German sub-contractor realized that a French producer, whom it supplied and who has become liable under product liability rules, would have a right of recourse against the sub-contractor which the sub-contract cannot defend with the aid of § 447 BGB (limitation of action after six months) – and even more so if the sub-contractor never even suspected it would be liable under the French law of delict (or by way of subrogation) – it would hardly have accepted the order from the French producer on those terms. Further examples are easily found. Can a German doctor who is liable for malpractice under both contract and tort law rules defend himself (like his French colleague) on the basis of the principle of *non cumul des responsabilités*, known in French law, but not in German law, under which the injured party cannot sue in both tort and contract? If not, is it justifiable for a doctor to be dependent on the same financial recompense for the treatment of patients from different Member States on the footing of diverse risks of liability? Agreements on limitation or exclusion of liability are invalid under quite different circumstances. Many contractual parties do not reckon with that and therefore unconsciously run a risk with cross-border contracts which is not factored into the calculation of costs."

[320] See Tunc, A., *Introduction, International Encyclopedia of Comparative Law*, Vol. XI/I, Torts, Mohr, Tübingen, 1974, p.24; also Loubser, M., *Concurrence of Contract and Tort, Law in Motion*, Kluwer Law International, Dordrecht, 1996, p.p.343-353.

[321] For the approach of the English system it is quite famous the case *Hendesron* v. *Merrett Syndycates*, House of Lords [1995] 2 AC 145, and BGH, 24 May 1976 (BGHZ 66, 315, NJW 1976, 1505). Lord Browne-Wilkinson in his speech states: "*I can see no good reason for holding that the existence of a contractual right is in all circumstances inconsistent with the co-existence of another tortious right, provided it is understood that the agreement of the parties evidenced by the contract can modify and shape the tortious duties which, in the absence of contract, would be applicable*". See also Harrison, R., *Public Key Infrastructure: the risks of being trusted*, "Computers and Law", the magazine of the Society for Computer and Law, August/September 2000, Vol. 11 issue 3.

[322] See Weir, T., *Complex Liability, International Encyclopedia of Comparative Law, Torts*, XI/12, Mohr, Tübingen, 1974, p.7–20; also Van Gerven, W., et al., *ibid.*, p.34.

approach.[323]

In the countries granting to the party that has suffered damage the possibility to choose the most advantageous claim for defending his or her legal interest, the option to be preferred depends on weighing up the differences between the contractual and tort liability.[324]

Some authors see those differences in the attitude of the legal system towards the compensation of pure economic loss (*damnum emergens*).[325]

In modern Bulgarian legal theory, proper explanations and guidance exist as to how the issue should be approached.[326] The question of *cumul* or *non-cumul* of tortious and contractual liability should be resolved in the light of the interest which the different liability regimes protect. While contractual liability shields the positive interest (i.e. the interest of the accurate performance of the contract or the interest of entering into a valid contractual relationship etc), tortious liability protects the negative interest (i.e. the interest of not causing harm). An illustrative example of a hypothetical case involving a CSP will be provided, in the light of the basic information about the role and duties of the CSP set out in Chapter I. Let us assume that due to failing to provide access to the directory the CSP has caused damage to the certificate holder, because the relying party failed to verify the certificate and, thus, has not trusted the certificate holder's signature. The extent of the damage for the certificate holder would be related to his or her failure to enter into a beneficial contractual relationship, i.e. his or her positive interest would be harmed. In case damage has also occurred as result of unlawful infringement of property (e.g, a fraudulent act of a deceiver led to money being transferred from his or her bank account), a negative interest would suffer as well. As an exception, it is possible for the same interest of the creditor to be viewed both as negative and positive. Whereas, in the first example, the certificate holder has suffered damage in terms of payment of compensation resulting from failure to enter into a valid contract, in the latter example, there is no space for concurrence of liability – the liability of the CSP would be invoked only on contractual grounds, because the negative interest is

---

[323] Also referred to as 'exclusive liability'. See Beale, H., et al., *ibid.*, p.p.36 and 67.

[324] See section 2.2, *supra in fine*.

[325] See section 3.1, *infra*.

[326] See Kalaydjiev, A., *ibid.*, p.p.344-345.

harmed as a consequence of non-performance of contractual obligations.[327]

2.4. Pre-contractual liability

During the course of negotiations and before the conclusion of a contract for provision of services, and particularly – being the subject of this analysis – of certification services, the parties should act in good faith. Otherwise, they will be liable for any damage caused.[328] The obligation to make restitution in respect of damage is usually referred to as 'pre-contractual liability', or *culpa in contrahendo*. This section outlines some basic features of the issue under Bulgarian legal theory, while analysis of the pre-contractual liability of the CSPs in the PKI world will be made in Chapter III, *infra*.

As it will become clear, certain pre-contractual obligations of the CSPs issuing qualified certificates to the public are introduced by the Directive 1999/93/EC on e-signatures.[329] Some authors deny the necessity of pre-contractual liability.[330] They find, on the basis of the principle of freedom to contract, that parties cannot be held liable for damage which arises prior to the conclusion of the contract. Such theories are untenable.[331] Pre-contractual liability is recognized and regulated not only under the laws of Bulgaria, but also under the general liability laws in all EU jurisdictions.[332] However, pre-contractual liability is treated differently, while it is considered in some jurisdictions to be a specific type of liability.[333]

---

[327] *Ibid.*

[328] See Article 12 of the Bulgarian Law on Obligations and Contracts.

[329] See Anex II of the Directive.

[330] See Pound, R., *Jurisprudence*. V. IV. West Publishing Co. St. Paul, Minn. 1959, p. 429. See also Mehren, A. *International Encyclopedia of Comparative Law. Volume VII. Contracts in General. The Formation of Contracts. Chapter 9.* J. C. B. Mohr (Paul Siebeck) Tübingen. Martinus Nijhoff Publishers. Dordich-Boston-Lancaster, 1991, p. 66.

[331] For critical disproval of such theories see Kalaydjiev, A., *ibid.*, p.p.94-95.

[332] On a *supranational* level it should mentioned the Principles the European Contract Law – *Negotiations contrary to good faith*. Article 2:301 provides in Section 3: [Liability for negotiations] that a party is free to negotiate and is not liable for failure to reach an agreement. However, a party who has negotiated or broken off negotiations contrary to good faith and fair dealing is liable for the losses caused to the other party. It is contrary to good faith and fair dealing, in particular, for a party to enter into or continue negotiations with no real intention of reaching an agreement with the other party.

[333] The English and French laws have same approach by seeing in the pre-contractual liability act of tort. The German law theory stands on the opinion that the pre-contractual liability does not come under tortious liability but constitutes a specific category of liability developed by the courts under §242 BGB – See Beale, H., HartKamp, A., et al. (ed.), *ibid.*, p.36.

In order for the CSP to be held liable on pre-contractual grounds, the *corpus* of the liability should reveal the following elements: behaviour (actions or omissions), the unlawfulness of the behaviour, damage caused, causality between the behaviour and the damage, and fault.[334]

The illicit behaviour of the parties should be viewed through the prism of infringing the requirements prescribed by law for negotiating in good faith in such a way that damage will not be caused.[335] In general, the required *bona fide* behaviour is more or less a moral category for upright, honest and correct behaviour during the course of the negotiations, rather than meeting explicit statutory duties.[336] However, such statutory duties establishing pre-contractual duties might exist.[337]

Likewise the other types of liability, attaching the pre-contractual liability of the CSPs should be presupposed by occurrence of damage. For example, if due to the pre-contractual illicit behaviour of one of the parties a contract cannot be enforced (is has become null or void), the party that is not in fault may suffer damage by entering into a new contract in order to satisfy its interest. This may lead to expenses to enforce the new contract, on one hand, and to incurrence of further damage relating to the period until the new contract is enforced and fulfilled, on the other. The remedy should encompass both the actual damages caused and the lost profits.[338]

Pre-contractual liability may be successfully invoked if causality exists between the

---

[334] See Kojuharov, A., *Law on Obligations. General Doctrine on the Obligation Relations. First Book*, Sofia, 1992, p. 54–56.

[335] See Konov, T., *The Notion Unlawfulness in the Area of Delicts under the Bulgarian Civil Law.* Almanac of Sofia University, Vol. 79, 1986, Book 1, p. 203.

[336] Most academics recognize several main types of conduct that is considered pre-contractual behaviour contrary to good faith, *inter alia*: negotiating without intending to conclude a contract, unjust breaking of negotiations, knowingly concluding an invalid contract, not giving adequate information, disclosing confidential information, causing physical or legal harm to the other party in the course of the negotiations, etc. See Beale, H., Hartcamp, A., et al., *ibid.*, p. 243.

[337] Annex II (k) of the Directive 1999/93.EC establishes explicitly statutory pre-cotnractual duties for the CSPs issuing qualified certificates. They must "before entering into a contractual relationship with a person seeking a certificate to support his electronic signature inform that person by a durable means of communication of the precise terms and conditions regarding the use of the certificate, including any limitations on its use, the existence of a voluntary accreditation scheme and procedures for complaints and dispute settlement. Such information, which may be transmitted electronically, must be in writing and in redily understandable language."

[338] Under the laws of France, Germany and the United Kingdom the pre-contractual liability covers both the damages suffered and the lost profits – See Mazeaud, H., L. Mazeaud, *Traité théorique et pratique de la responsabilité civil délictuelle et contractuelle.* Paris, 1947, p. 127–134 ; Also Anson, B., *Contract Law*, 1984, p. 346.

illicit pre-contractual behaviour and the ensuing damage. Where the provision of certification services are concerned, this may even be common. Another fictitious example will illustrate the issue. Let us suppose that the CSP, before entering into a contractual relationship with a person seeking a certificate to support his or her electronic signature, fails to inform that person by durable means of communication about the precise terms and conditions regarding the use of the certificate (e.g. it is not a qualified certificate), or the limitations on its use (e.g. it can be used only for e-mail), or the information transmitted electronically is not in writing and in readily understandable language.[339] In such a case, if a certificate is issued and used by the certificate holder, it will not have the effectiveness of a valid certificate, and thus the signature that is supported by such a certificate will not have the legal value of a handwritten signature.[340] The negligent pre-contractual behaviour of the CSP is causally linked to the damage that ensues.

The above example focuses attention on another issue - the so-called 'transformation' of the pre-contractual liability into a contractual one. This would be the case when the damage which arises can be causally linked to the illicit behaviour of the CSP during the course of the negotiations, but this damage occurs after the enforcement of the valid contract for certification services. In such cases, the pre-contractual liability will be 'absorbed' by the contractual liability.

Another example would shed more light on this issue. Assume the CSP has failed to perform its obligation to ensure the operation of a prompt and secure directory and a secure and immediate revocation service under given standards.[341] The CSP has assured the person seeking issue of a certificate that it (the CSP) meets the statutory requirements. Neither before nor after entering into the contract for issue of the certificate, however, has the CSP in fact met these requirements. The person seeking issue of the certificate would never have entered into a contract if this fact was known to him or her. In this situation, the applicant assumes that the CSP will fulfil its duties during the term of the contract (i.e. the term of validity of the certificate).

---

[339] See Annex II (k) of the Directive: "before entering into a contractual relationship with a person seeking a certificate to support his electronic signature inform that person by a durable means of communication of the precise terms and conditions regarding the use of the certificate, including any limitations on its use, the existence of a voluntary accreditation scheme and procedures for complaints and dispute settlement. Such information, which may be transmitted electronically, must be in writing and in readily understandable language. Relevant parts of this information must also be made available on request to third-parties relying on the certificate"

[340] Article 5 (1) of the Directive

[341] See Annex II (b) of the Directive.

Due to the illicit pre-contractual behaviour absorbed into non-fulfilment of a contractual obligation, the CSP may cause damage to the signature holder, should the relying party be unable to build the necessary level of trust in the authenticity of the messages due to the impossibility of verifying the validity of the certificate in the CSP's directory.

Pre-contractual liability can only be invoked where culpable behaviour occurs,[342] whether of a wilful or negligent nature.[343] In the pre-contractual liability, culpable behaviour is usually presumed.[344]

Different theoretical views on the nature of the pre-contractual liability exist not only in Bulgarian legal theory, but in all other countries throughout Europe. However, being of more theoretical than practical interest, the matter is not discussed in the present study.[345]

The problem of *culpa in contrahendo* is widely discussed also on a European supranational level.[346]

---

[342] See Kalaydjiev, A., *ibid.*, p.98. Contrary opinion supported by some Bulgarian authors – see Dikov, L., *Civil Law Course, Law on Obligation, General Part*, Vol. III, 1934, p. 236; also the French author Salei – See Mehren, A., *International Encyclopedia of Comparative Law. Volume VII. Contracts in General. The Formation of Contracts. Chapter 9. J. C. B. Mohr (Paul Siebeck) Tübingen. Martinus Nijhoff Publishers. Dordich-Boston-Lancaster, 1991, p. 65.

[343] See Kojuharov, A., *ibid.*, p. 58–59. The said conclusion is derived in the Bulgarian doctrine by interpretation of Article 12 and Article 28 (2) of the LOC, also Article 42 (1) LOC in connection with Article 83 and Article 51 (2) LOC.

[344] See Kalaydjiev, A., *ibid.*, p.98. Contrary opinion supported by Konov, T., *ibid.*, p.204.

[345] The nature of the pre-contractual liability is widely discussed for many years. One century ago Rudolf von Jhering published an article „Culpa in Contrahendo oder Schadenersatz bei nichtigen oder nicht zur Perfektion gelangten Vertragen", Jahrbücher für die Dogmatik des heutigen römischen und deutschen Privatrechts, 1861.IV.1, where he widely supports the idea, that the offeror simultaneously with the offer submission places another offer for negotiating in good faith, which the offeree accepts. That is why, Jhering finds, that the liability has a contractual nature. Prof. Kalaydjiev in his book Law on Obligations, *ibid.*, p.101 criticizes the theory of Jhering substantiating that presence of agreement in this respect should be considered a fiction and there should be a special rule in this respect, which cannot be found in any legal system. The author finds that the theory would be hardly applicable because sometimes it could be applicable to persons that will not be parties to the future contract – i.e. person that seeks a shelter from the rain in a shop. The theory of Jhering would hardly differentiate the potential parties of the future contract. The assumption of the author is that the theory of Jhering is born due to lack of relevant general tort clause in the German law.

[346] In the Communication to the EU Commission on the European Civil Code COM(2001) 398 final, it is identified that "Similar points also emerge sharply when the national laws of the negotiating parties employ differing conceptions of what constitutes a binding offer. The offeror may make an offer on the assumption that it can be freely revoked, only to find that according to the offeree's national law it is irrevocable in the circumstances and the offeree's acceptance suffices to constitute a valid contract, notwithstanding previous revocation of the offer which was effective only under the offeror's national law. A false sense of security may similarly be created by the assumed applicability of one's own national rules on the time or required mode of acceptance of an offer, be it, for example, the time of dispatch of the

3. Damage

When speaking about the liability of CSPs, one of the issues that arise is that, as a general rule, liability only comes into being when damage has occurred. Therefore, damage is commonly considered to be one of the elements of the liability *corpus*.

What should be considered as 'damage'[347]? What is the extent and the chain of the damages that the CSP might be held liable for? At the present stage, it is necessary that the basic views of the Bulgarian civil liability theory be presented. During the course of analysis of the specific liability regime in Chapter III the issue is reconsidered so that proper interpretation of the rules of the E-signatures Directive is achieved.

In the Bulgarian legal literature, different theories on the essence of damage are presented. Some authors find that damage is the unfavourable consequence of the non-fulfilment of contractual obligations, or, correspondingly, of the duty not to cause damage, which affects the rights and interests of the creditor.[348]

For the purposes of the present study, damage caused by the CSP should be considered as any given infringement of subjective rights, any disturbance to the detriment of a third party's goods, or any disturbance of factual relations.

During the course of usage of electronic signatures and provision of certification services within the PKI, it is not only subjective rights that might be harmed as a consequence of infringement of contractual or statutory duties, but also protected goods that are not subject to rights and protected factual status (e.g. possession). In all

---

acceptance by the offeree or the time of receipt by the offeror. In all such cases the freedom to choose the law governing a contract provides no security against the unwitting or premature conclusion of a contract. What matters in such cases is the legal framework for the negotiations themselves, before and leading to the conclusion of the contract. The uncertainties of that environment itself may deter a party from entering into cross-border commerce. Those uncertainties are compounded when one remembers that it is not merely possibly inadvertent contractual liability (in its most limited sense) which is at stake when parties are negotiating: liability may arise in tort due to economic loss in reliance on misrepresentations and according to principles of culpa in contrahendo, all of which may vary markedly from jurisdiction to jurisdiction". See Communication on European Contract Law: *Joint Response of the Commission on European Contract Law and the Study Group on a European Civil Code*, 2001, (http://www.sgecc.net/media/download/stellungnahme_kommission_5_final1.pdf)

[347] European Group on Tort Law, *Principles of European Tort Law*, Text and Commentary, Springer-Verlag/Wien, 2005, Chapter 2, p.2.

[348] See Kojuharov, A., *Law on obligations, Ibid.*, 1992, Sofi-R, p. 264. In the systems following the case law model the theory and the practice recognize the so-called "nominal damages" – See Kalaydjiev, A., *ibid.*, p.347.

these cases, damage may occur.[349] Most scholars of Bulgarian legal theory consider that the damage appears as a consequence of causing harm to goods that are subject either to relative rights (in the case of a contractual liability), or to absolute rights (in the case of a tort liability).[350]

Depending on the possibility for monetary evaluation of the damage, it may be classified into two main types: material and non-material.

3.1. Material and non-material damage[351]

Non-material damage cannot be assessed as it is intangible and cannot be directly perceived by the senses. However, the demand for justice and equity in the society has resulted in most of the jurisdictions to evaluate non-material damage.[352]

Non-material damage encompasses the consequences of the infringement of intangible goods or rights such as dignity, freedom of speech, right to a name, privacy, moral rights, etc.[353]

The right to claim for compensation for non-material damage originates from Roman law.[354] Comparative research shows that there are two models for restitution in respect of such damage.[355] Under the first model (used in France,[356] Bulgaria[357] and

---

[349] See Antonov, D., *Unjust Injury*, 1965, Sofia, p. 49–50; also Gotsev, V., *Contractual and tort liability*, 1979, Sofia, p. 31; also Goleva, P., *Reparation of Victims in car Accidents*, 1991, Sofia, p. 10.

[350] The concept of relative and absolute rights is widely professed in legal doctrines in Germany, Austria, Bulgaria, and others. The doctrine in these countries recognises the dividing of the subjective rights into two main types: absolute and relative. Any subjective right shall be considered absolute provided the obligation towards the right holder falls upon unlimited number of liable persons. For example the property right holder shall be entitled to demand from any third person not to hinder and intrude him to exercise its property rights and to derive benefits from the usage of its property. Such an absolute right is for example the copyright. On the contrary – towards any relative right holder corresponds an obligation of an exact person. Such rights arise from contractual relationships, torts, etc. The buyer as a right holder under a purchase contract shall be entitled to demand the transfer of the title and handing-over of the belonging – subject to the contract, only from the seller but from nobody else. See Dimitrov, G., *Legal Protection of Domains*, WIPO, 2001 (www.wipo.org).

[351] Article 2:101 of the Priciples of Euroepan Tort Law, refers to the two types of damages as "pecuniary damage", resp."non-pecuniary damage".

[352] See Demogue, R., *Modern French Legal Philosophy*, Boston, The Boston Book Company. 1916, p. 556–562.

[353] See Article 10:301 (1) of the Priciples of Euroepan Tort Law. European Group on Tort Law, *Principles of European Tort Law*, Text and Commentary, Springer-Verlag/Wien, 2005, p.9.

[354] The Roman law recognizes the delict that might cause non-material damages – *injura*.

[355] *See* Kalaydjiev, A., *ibid.*, p.p.351-353.

[356] See Art 1382 of the Code Civil.

other countries) there is a general rule introducing the possibility for any non-material damage to be compensated, regardless of the type of infringement or goods harmed. The second model (applied in Germany,[358] Italy[359] and other countries) provides for restitution in respect of non-material damage only when this is explicitly permitted by law. The Principles of European Tort Law provide that restitution shall be monetary (compensation), or in kind as far as it is possible and not too burdensome to the other party.[360]

Under Bulgarian law, as in other countries, a remedy for non-material damage can be claimed in tort. However, the question of whether or not compensation can be claimed in respect of non-material damage caused by breach of contract is widely disputed. In this work, discussion of the issue is limited to breach of contracts for certification services. Different theories can be found in the legal literature. In some jurisdictions such remedies can be claimed,[361] while in others this does not seem to be possible.[362]

It is beyond doubt that non-material damage could arise as a result of using electronic signatures, while such damage may be caused by non-fulfilment of contractual obligations by the CSP. Examples in this respect are provided in section 4.5.1 of Chapter III, *infra*.

As already discussed, material damage can be measured in terms of monetary value. Material damage should be viewed as the difference between the creditors' property (*patrimonium*) after the infringement and the value that the property would have had, provided no infringement was committed.[363]

---

[357] See Article 52 of the Law on Obligations and Contracts.

[358] See § 847 of BGB

[359] See Article 2059 of Codice Civile.

[360] Article 10:101, Article 10:104 and 10.301 of the Principles of European Tort Law.

[361] The French law and the common law jurisdictions allow remedies for non-material damages as a consequence of breach of contract. See Treitel, G., *Remedies for Breach of Contract (Courses of Action Open to a Party Aggrieved). Contracts in General*, Chapter 16, International Encyclopedia of Comparative Law, Volume VII, J. C. B. Mohr (Paul Siebeck), Tübingen/Mouton/the Hague/Paris, 1976, p. 84–87.

[362] For example in Bulgaria the constant court practice denies awarding of such a remedy – See court cases of the Supreme Court №1786–1970–I CD, №197–1997–V CD, etc.

[363] See Kojuharov, A., *ibid.*, p.270. Also Article 10:301 of the Principles of European Tort Law define the material damages by using the term "pecuniary damage".

Most jurisdictions classify material damage as actual damage (an actual realized loss,[364] *damnum emergens*) and loss of profit (an expected future loss,[365] *lucrum cessans*).[366].

Claims may be made in respect of material damage both in contract and tort.[367]

Damnum emergens are the consequences of damage to present goods – decreasing the value or destruction of belongings, bearing of expenses etc,.[368] while *lucrum cessans* should be considered as representing the failure of the property to increase in value.[369] In any case, determination of *lucrum cessans* seems to be more difficult[370] - if there is a lack of certainty in the probable increase in value of the property, compensation would not be awarded.[371] Non-material *lucrum cessans* cannot be awarded.[372]

---

[364] Under the Article 10:201 of the Principles of European Tort Law - "diminuition of the victim's patrimony". European Group on Tort Law, *Principles of European Tort Law*, Text and Commentary, Springer-Verlag/Wien, 2005, p.9.

[365] *Ibid.* - "loss of income or profit".

[366] See court cases of the Bulgarian Supreme Court №2529–1974–I CD, and №1456–1983–I CD. There should be paid attention on 9:501 of the Principles of the European Contract Law. It reads that The aggrieved party is entitled to damages for loss caused by the other party's non-performance which is not excused. The loss for which damages are recoverable includes: (a) non-pecuniary loss ; and (b) future loss which is reasonably likely to occur.

[367] See Kalaydjiev, A., *ibid.*, p.354. In Bulgarian law, relevant provisions that give grounds for such conclusions are Article 51 (3) LOC, and Article 51 (1) (for the tort liability) and Article 82 LOC (for the contractual liability).

[368] Appearance of obligations (for example monetary obligation) caused by the infringement is considered to be *damnum emergens* only should these obligations are actually fulfilled (i.e. the debt is paid). See Kalaydjiev, A., *ibid.*, p.354.

[369] See Lee, R.W., *The Elements of Roman Law* 394 (4th ed. 1956): "There kinds of damages are distinguished by the commentators as *damnum emergens* and *lucrum cessans*, which may be rendered 'positive damages' and 'loss of profit'. The first may be immediate (e.g., my slave is killed or has lost an eye), or consequential (I have lost his services – I have incurred medical expenses – he was one of a troupe of singers and the whole troupe is less valuable in consequence of his death or injury). Where there is no pecuniary loss there is no action. An action does not lie … for striking a slave if his value to me has not been depreciated by the blow nor for trespass to land unattended by damage". *Op. cit* by Black's Law Dictionary, 7th ed., West Group, St.Paul, 1999, p.398.

[370] The future damages are remedied only upon their appearance – Bulgarian Supreme Court cases №23–1960–IV CD, and №2772–1971–I CD – See Iossifov, B., Balabanov, B., *ibid.*, p.67. Furthermore there should exist security that the property increase should emerge - Bulgarian Supreme Court cases №2065–1959–II CD, №1696–1974–I CD, №348–1981–I CD, №13–1997–IV CD – See Tsachev, L, Law of Obligations and Contracts. Text, court cases, literature and notes, 1990, Sofia, p.330. All *op cit.* Kalaydjiev, A., *ibid.*, p.354.

[371] See Bulgarian Supreme Cassation Court case №29–1998-V, Court practice of the Supreme Court of Cassation. Civil law section 1997, 1999, Sofia, p.21.

[372] See Kalaydjiev, A., *ibid.*, p.355.

3.2. Causation

Outlining the causation concept is of the utmost importance for the purposes of the present research, since, as it will become clear in Chapters III and V, the causation concept is sometimes misunderstood and improperly considered to be regulated by the specific liability regime contained in the EU Directive on e-signatures in divergence to the approaches taken by the vast majority of the European jurisdictions.

Causation is a common term used not only in Bulgaria, but in all EU jurisdictions. In the theory of civil liability it is regarded as the casual nexus between the behaviour of the tortfeasor or debtor (the cause) and the damage caused as a consequence of the behaviour (the effect).[373] Different theories try to explain the causation.[374]

The basic theory here is that of *conditio sine qua non* or equivalence.[375] All other theories applied in different jurisdictions seem to use the latter theory as a starting-point.[376] It provides that causation is present only in cases when, if the non-fulfilment of the obligation or the illicit behaviour, as a fact, is hypothetically removed from the sequence of events, preceding the appearance of the result, the latter would not occur.[377] In other words, if the result would have happened anyway,

---

[373] In Bulgarian law it is referred to as "причинно-следствена връзка". In German law the causation is referred under the term "*Kausalzusammenhang*". In France, the term "*lien de causalité*" is commonly used.

[374] Most of the theories are thoroughly analyzed by Kalaydjiev, A., *ibid.*, p.p. 359 – 361. The author distinguishes the equivalence theory (*conditio sine qua non*), the theory of the relevant event, the adequacy theory, the theory of the necessary causation and the material theory. They will not be discussed in the present research.

[375] In Bulgarian – "*теория на равноценността*", in French – "*théorie de l'équivalence des conditions*", in German – "*Äquivalenztheorie*".

[376] In English law it is accepted a two-stage process in establishing the remoteness of the damage. In the "cause-in-fact" stage it is presented as the assessment of whether the conduct of the alleged tortfeasor is a *conditio sine qua non* of the damages appearance. This approach is usually called a "but for" test. At the second stage, called "legal cause", the assessment is focused on establishment of whether the tortfeasor is ought to be liable for the harm. The German law approaches the causality establishment in two aspects: the establishment of causal link between the conduct of the defendant and the result which leads to liability (*Haftungsbegründende Kausalität*) and the determination of the scope of liability (*Haftungsausfüllende Kausalität*). Similarly to the English law the German law uses the *conditio sine qua non* as a starting point for causation assessment. In Germany, however, the adequacy theory is considered to come "on top" of the *conditio sine qua non*. French authors and case-law find that the equivalence and the adequate theory should be applied alternatively. However, the French law also uses as a starting point the equivalence theory – *cit op.* Van Gerven, W, et al., *ibid.*, p.452.

[377] In German law, for example, it is accepted the so called *Kausalität im natürlichen Sinne* being decisive in establishing causation in natural or logical sense, while the German law makes distinction between the *Kausalität im natürlichen Sinne*, which is assessed according to the *conditio sine qua non* and next step –

notwithstanding the behaviour of the debtor/tortfeasor, causation cannot be demonstrated. Therefore, behaviour is a *conditio sine qua non* of the result.

Another theory commonly used as an approach for determining causality is the *theory of the adequate cause* or adequacy theory.[378] Under this theory, the conduct of the defendant is an adequate cause of the damage if he or she could produce the result in question, regularly, typically, adequately and not as an exception.[379] In other words, the conduct of the defendant is in general apt to cause the result or considerably increases the probability of it being caused.[380] All other casual circumstances are of no importance.[381]

The different legal approaches for assessment of the relevant causation that might trigger the civil liability of the defendant based on the above theories are widely applicable – within different jurisdictions or even within one and the same jurisdiction.[382] The common approach followed in Bulgaria and in most of the European jurisdictions is that the tortfeasor/debtor who has not acted in good faith is liable for all direct and immediate damage caused.[383]

Bulgarian law and the laws in some other countries provide that if the debtor has not acted *contra bonos mores*, he or she will be responsible for the foreseeable damage only.[384]

Direct damage results as a consequence of the wrongful behaviour, either in tort or contract. As already mentioned, the causal nexus may be successfully assessed by the application of the equivalence theory. Further the direct damage will be limited by

---

the so called causation in legal sense - *Kausalität im rechtlichen Sinne* – See Van Gerven, W., et al., *ibid.*, p.452-453.

[378] In Bulgarian – "*теория на адекватната причинна връзка*",in German – "*Adäquanztheorie*", in French – "*théorie de la casualité adéquate*".

[379] See Kalaydjiev, A., *ibid.*, p. 360.

[380] See Van Gerven, W., et al., *ibid.*, p. 397

[381] Under Article 3:101 of the Principles of Euroepan Tort Law an activity or conduct is a cause of the victim's damage if, in absence of the activity, the damage would not have occured.

[382] *Ibid.*, p. 466.

[383] The notion "immediate damages" used in the Bulgarian and French law does not have meaning different than the one of direct damages – See Kalaydjiev, A, *ibid.*, p.362.

[384] This is the case with the Bulgarian law (Article 51 LOC). The French law also has promoted such a rule (Article 1150 Code Civil). The remoteness based on foreseeable damages depending on the type of fault is unknown to other jurisdictions – e.g. the German law. Under Article 9:503 of the Principles of European Law should the non-performance was intentional or grossly negligent, the non-performance party shall be liable for all damages, including the unforeseeable.

application of the adequacy theory – it should be estimated as a typical, normal consequence of the wrongful behaviour.[385]

The accidental, casual damage that cannot be identified as a typical and normal result of the behaviour should be considered indirect damage. The latter should not be confused with damage that is a direct consequence of other facts that break the chain of causation (such as where the creditor's contributory negligence is the sole reason for the damage arising), or damage that is a consequence of *force majeure*, or the behaviour of a third party (in cases of liability not based on fault).[386]

Therefore, generally, the tortfeasor and the careless debtor will be liable for all direct damage being *conditio sine qua non* of the illicit behaviour (using the equivalence theory) which also prove to be a reasonable (adequate) consequence of the behaviour.

Many jurisdictions introduce the concept of liability for damage by limiting the scope to foreseeable damage,[387] which is limited to damage that could reasonably have been foreseen.[388]

The concept of foreseeability of damage has been the subject of numerous theoretical discussions. The most relevant is the *theory of the foreseeability assessment* on the basis of due care.[389] In other words,. foreseeable damage is damage that could have been foreseen if due care has been taken.[390] Foreseeability is examined by the court from the point of view of the debtor/tortfeasor, not from the point of view of the creditor.[391] It also refers to the fact that damage has occurred, and does not refer

---

[385] See Kalaydjiev, A., *ibid.*, p. 362.

[386] *Ibid.*

[387] See *supra* note 384.

[388] See Treitel, G., *op. cit.*, p. 65.

[389] An emanation of this theory is the common approach accepted by the academics in all EU jurisdictions while drafting the Principles of European Contract Law. Article 9:503 thereof [Foreseeability] reads that the non-performing party is liable only for loss *which it foresaw or could reasonably have foreseen at the time of conclusion of the contract as a likely result of its non-performance*, unless the non-performance was intentional or grossly negligent.

[390] The English law, likewise the French law, follows the concept of limitation of damages based on their foreseeability. Once it has been established that the defendant was under a duty of due care to the plaintiff, the remoteness of the damages shall be considered only through the reasonable foreseeability, without any further normative considerations – See Van Gerven, W., *ibid.*, p.457.

[391] See Kalaydjiev, A., *ibid.*, p. 363.

to the value of the damage.[392] To assess whether any given damage was foreseeable, the court should investigate the circumstances that could have been known to the debtor at the moment when the obligation arose.[393]

De facto the difference between direct and foreseeable damage is not substantial, because the criteria for the assessment of both types are objective and abstract. Thus the damage that the debtor might foresee when acting with due care is not so different from the damage that might conceivably occur from the point of view of an abstract person.[394]

After the overview of the general concept of damages made from the point of view of the Bulgarian scholars, with a comparative synopsis of the theories upheld in the countries representing the main civil law families in Europe, a follow-up analysis of the rules establishing the specific liability regime in Article 6 of Directive 1999/93/EC could be made.

4. Unlawfulness and Fault

4.1. The concepts of unlawfulness and fault in civil law

The legal norms of the *acquis communautaire* establishing the specific liability regime for the CSPs cannot be understood without achieving clarity on such basic issues of civil liability as diligence, fault and lawfulness. The rules giving rise to specific liability establish the level of behaviour expected from all the actors in the trust building process – CSPs, signatories, relying parties. They outline the scope of the required diligence and behaviour of these actors. However, the legal traditions in different countries see in various ways the essence of the unlawfulness and fault. The Bulgarian legal system, being taken as a case study, also approaches these issues with its own *differentia specifica*. This present section focuses on the main aspects of the legal categories of unlawfulness and fault under Bulgarian law by making a comparative overview where differences with the other EU jurisdictions exist.

---

[392] See Apostolov, I., *ibid.*, p.104

[393] See Kalaydjiev, A., *ibid*, p. 363.

[394] *Ibid.*

For many centuries, liability in the continental civil law was based on the wrongfulness concept.[395] Wrongfulness as a notion is considered to comprise two elements: 'objective' (unlawfulness)[396] and 'subjective' (fault).[397]

Under most of the European civil law jurisdictions, the two notions are considered to be separate elements of liability. However, as it will become evident, fault in a strict sense plays a minor role in most jurisdictions, insofar as it is generally assessed under objective criteria and the types of fault can only increase the burden of liability.[398]

In Bulgarian legal theory, unlawfulness is a basic element of civil liability. It refers to the assessment of whether the behaviour of the alleged tortfeasor or debtor-in-fault has deviated from the standard of behaviour required by law.[399] This standard is commonly referred to as 'duty of due care',[400] and is discussed below in this section.

For centuries, the doctrine has seen culpability (being personal responsibility for reprehensible behaviour) as the essence of fault in civil law. In the course of the twentieth century, this concept has changed, and the 'objective' theory has spread throughout almost all legal systems.[401] It provides an objective criterion - the fault should be understood as acting wrongfully, i.e. in a course of conduct, whether by

---

[395] See Van Gerven, W., et al., *ibid.,* p. 352.

[396] In Bulgarian – *"противоправност"*, in German – *"Rechtswidrigkeit"*, in French – *"illiceité"*.

[397] In many countries the culpability (*"виновност"*, *"culpabilité"*, *"Vershulden")* is considered to be the element, rather than the fault (*"вина"*, *"faute"*, *"Fehler")* itself. In practice there is no difference in the substance of the concept. In most of the systems the fault is referred to as negligence – despite of whether the person has acted intentionally or not.

[398] *Cit op.* Van Gerven, W., et al., *ibid.,* p.353. After thorough comparative research the authors find that under English law, the tort of negligence does not seem to distinguish between these two elements, since wrongfulness (breach of duty) is assessed under an essentially objective standard; nevertheless, subjective factors such as bad or evil motive may play a role under certain torts. However, even in a legal system such as German law, where culpability is still expressly mentioned as an autonomous element in addition to the condition of unlawfulness (at §823 (1) and (2) BGB), culpability retain only limited significance, at least according to the prevailing conduct theory.

[399] *Ibid.*

[400] Article 1:201 sets out as one of the Principles of the European Contract Law "The good faith and fair dealing" – "Each party must act in accordance with good faith and fair dealing". See The Principles of the European Contract Law at http://www.cbs.dk/departments/law/staff/ol/commission_on_ecl/ PECL%20engelsk/engelsk_partl_og_II.htm. The Principles are not binding but are base and considered "First Draft" of the future European Civil Code – See Short Survey of the Principles of European Contract Law: Introduction to the Principles of European Contract Law Prepared by The Commission on European Contract Law (http://www.cbs.dk/departments/law/staff/ol/ commission_on_ecl/survey_pecl.htm).

[401] See Zweigert, K., Kotz, H., *An Introduction to Comparative Law,* Clarendon Press, Oxford, 1987, p. 688–690.

act or omission, in a way that it is in breach of the duties expected by society from an average citizen carrying out the same activity under the same circumstances as the person whose conduct is assessed.[402] In this respect, fault in civil liability recedes from fault in criminal law, where the rule *nulla poena sine culpa* proves to be the main principle.

For this reason, it is sometimes considered that fault in civil law is actually that very unlawful behaviour.[403] Thus, unlawful conduct is enough and fault is not a pre-condition for civil liability to arise.[404]

However, in Bulgaria, as in most of the jurisdictions within the EU, fault is envisaged explicitly as an element of the civil liability *corpus* both for contracts and torts.[405] The same approach is taken by the drafters of the Principles of European Tort Law.[406]

What is fault under the contemporary civil law doctrine?

Clarification of the notion of fault in civil law is related to the clarification of another notion – 'due care', i.e. it is closely connected to unlawfulness as an element of liability.

As discussed, Bulgarian law and most of the national laws establish as a general model for the conduct of the debtor, both in contractual relations and tort, the duty

---

[402] See Van Gerven, W., et al., *ibid.*, p.330

[403] See Kalaydjiev, A., *ibid.*, p. 371.

[404] See Van Gerven, W., et al., Introductory note to the Culpability in the French system, *ibid.*, p.332.

[405] For example, Article 45 (2) of the Bulgarian LOC provides that "In cases of tort *the fault is presumed*, unless otherwise proved". Article 82 of LOC provides that "If the debtor has acted *willfully*, he will be liable for all direct and immediate damages". § 823 BGB provides that "a person who, *wilfully or negligently*, unlawfully injures the life, body, health, freedom, property or other right of another is bound to compensate him for any damage arising therefrom" and "the same obligation is placed upon a person who infringes a statute intended for the protection of others. If, according to the provisions of the statute, an infringement of this is possible even *without fault*, the duty to make compensation arises only *in the event of fault*". In English law the basic rule is often said to be that contractual liability is strict. In *Raineri v. Miles*, 1981, AC 1050, it is famous the speech of Lord Edmund-Davies whereby he states that "*In relation to a claim for damages for breach of contract, it is, in general, immaterial why the defendant failed to fulfil his obligations and certainly to defence to plead that he had done his best*". Op. cit. Beale, H., Hartkamp, A., et al., *ibid.*, p.665.

[406] Article 1:101 (2) of the Principles of European Tort Law reads that "Damage may be attributed in particular to the person ... a) whose conduct constituting fault has caused it." Article 4:101 reads that "A person is liable on the basis of fault for intentional or negligent violation of the required standard of conduct".

of care of a 'reasonable person' in the same circumstances.[407] Since the circumstances will differ, the duty of care also differs.[408] In any case, it will be assessed *in abstracto*, as an objective criterion, not connected to the behaviour of a particular person, but rather to the normal, expected, usual behaviour of people in similar circumstances.[409]

The objective approach to fault also provides an appropriate means to attach liability to legal persons both in contract and tort. A legal person cannot be regarded, in formal terms, as having mental activity, whether one is talking about tort or contract. That is why legal persons cannot act wilfully when they fail to fulfil contractual obligations or commit a tort. As negligence does not amount to fault in the strict sense of the word, but rather unlawful behaviour which falls beneath an acceptable level of care, legal persons would be liable for their negligent misconduct both in contract and tort.[410]

In any single case, the duty of care will have different substance. The duty of care of a merchant, for example, is different from that of an ordinary citizen.[411] Thus the duty of a CSP differs from the duty of the average merchant or information technology service provider.[412] Furthermore, the duty of a CSP issuing qualified certificates differs from the duty of a CSP issuing certificates for advanced e-signatures.[413]

The tortfeasor cannot evade liability by proving lack of knowledge or personal skills; nor financial or intellectual potential. The CSP, for example, cannot defend itself by saying that it failed to keep the directory of the certificates up to date due to lack of knowledge or financial means.[414] Because the model is abstract, it requires a certain

---

[407] This notion varies from jurisdiction to jurisdiction. The Bulgarian law, for example, uses the term duty of care of "the good master" ("*добрия стопанин*").

[408] Under the Principles of the European Contract Law (Article 1:302) reasonableness is to be judged by what persons acting in good faith and in the same situation as the parties would consider to be reasonable. In particular, in assessing what is reasonable the nature and purpose of the contract, the circumstances of the case, and the usages and practices of the trades or professions involved should be taken into account.

[409] See Kalaydjiev, A., *ibid.*, p. 366.

[410] *Ibid.*, p. 371.

[411] Article 302 of the Bulgarian Commercial Act.

[412] See analysis of Directive 2000/31/EC in Chapter IV, section 6, *infra*.

[413] See Annex II of the Directive 1999/93/EC.

[414] Annex II (e) of the Directive 1999/93 EC provides that the CSP issuing qualified certificates to the public must employ personnel who possess the expert knowledge, experience, and qualifications necessary for

level of knowledge, ability and skills on the part of the members of the business sector into which the debtor falls.[415] Otherwise, the model would not be applicable. Even though the standard may be particularized by law,[416] the average standard will always be assessed by the court.

The law can deviate from this general model by imposing higher or lower standards of care on the different market groups.[417]

The law may allow further contractual deviation from the standard of care – the so-called *favor debitoris*.[418] The framework for such deviations should lie, of course, within certain statutory limits, and will not always prove to be possible.[419] This especially refers to the CSPs. As will become later evident from the analysis of the transposition of the specific liability regime of Directive 1999/93/EC into the Bulgarian law in Chapter V, the Bulgarian lawmaker faced problems in the interpretation of the Directive. The drafters of the Bulgarian law saw deviation in the *favor debitoris* principle, which deviation they made applicable to the CSPs by introducing a special rule. The Bulgarian law restrains those CSPs that issue qualified or universal certificates from seeking to rely on contractual clauses giving exemption from liability. The restraint of such clauses applies in respect not only of intentional (*dolus*) or grossly negligent (*cupla lata*) misconduct, but also for any kind of

---

the services provided, in particular competence at managerial level, expertise in electronic signature technology and familiarity with proper security procedures; they must also apply administrative and management procedures which are adequate and correspond to recognized standards. Annex II (h) envisages that it should maintain sufficient financial resources to operate in conformity with the requirements laid down in the Directive, in particular to bear the risk of liability for damages, for example, by obtaining appropriate insurance.

[415] See Kalaydjiev, A., *ibid.*, p. 371.

[416] For example Annex II of the Directive 1999/93/EC establishes statutory standard of care by enlisting the duties of the certification-service-provider issuing qualified certificates.

[417] For example under Article 65 of the Bulgarian Inheritance Act, the inheritor that have accepted the heritage under inventory list, shall take due care for the property as the one he would taken for his own property – i.e. he shall be liable for *culpa levis in concreto*.

[418] Article 94 of the Bulgarian LOC allows the parties to contractually agree on reducing the liability of the debtor, but not for malice (*dolus*) or gross negligence (*culpa lata*). §442 of German BGB reads that in contract the debtor *may not be released beforehand from responsibility for wilful conduct*. § 443 provides that an agreement whereby the obligation of warranty of title imposed upon the seller by §§ 433 to 437, 439 to 442, is released or limited is void, if the seller *fraudulently* conceals the defect. Similarly § 637 BGB establishes a rule that an agreement, whereby the obligation of the contractor as to responsibility for a defect in the work is released or limited, is void if the contractor *fraudulently* conceals the defect.

[419] Article 6 (3) and (4) of the Directive provide that the CSPs may limit their liability for damages that might be caused from the usage of the certificate by placing limitations on the use and value of transactions in the certificate. All other limitations placed in the certificate shall not be binding. See Chapter III, section 6 *infra*.

negligence (*culpa levissima in abstracto*). It is worth noting that the general Bulgarian civil law otherwise allows this.[420]

The debtor/tortfeasor would be considered at fault if he or she has failed to act with due care, regardless of his or her personal subjective attitude towards the reprehensible behaviour or the consequences thereof. In other words, negligence in civil law should not be considered in terms of fault in the subjective sense.[421]

Despite the fact that the fault is assessed *in abstracto* as non-performance of the statutory or contractual duties as against the expected due care of the 'average person', the types of fault are sometimes relevant for gauging the extent of the debtor's/tortfeasor's liability.

When speaking of types of fault, the criteria for classification are based mostly on the subjective attitude of the person, i.e. the psychological position a person has towards his or her own reprehensible conduct. In such a sense, fault has two elements – intellectual and volitional. The intellectual element reveals the consciousness of the person in respect of the reprehensible conduct, and the volitional element reveals the attitude towards the detrimental consequences.[422]

In this respect the intentional fault is the intention of the person not only to pursue the course of conduct which breaches the standard of due care, but also to bring about the detrimental consequences.[423]

Negligence means that the person does not foresee the consequences of his or behaviour, as a result of failing to act with the due care with which he was supposed to act. Some legal systems provide differentiation in view of the consequences of negligence and gross negligence (the negligent behaviour that the most negligent debtor would exhibit).[424]

The other classifications of fault that exist do not seem to be of interest for this research.

---

[420] Article 29 (4) of the Bulgarian Electronic Document and Electronic Signatures Act and Article 94 of LOC. See *supra* note 418.

[421] See Kalaydjiev, A., *ibid.*, p. 371.

[422] *Ibid.*

[423] See Konov, T., *ibid.*, p. 155.

[424] See *supra* note 418.

The type of fault may play a role, often to increase the burden of liability for the harmful consequences of the wrongful conduct or to deprive the exemption clauses of their effect.[425] In view of the type of fault of the CSPs, the legal regime in some countries and particularly in Bulgaria might also bring about such an effect[426] - an issue that is discussed further in Chapter V.

4.2. Presumption of fault

Providing a general overview in relation to the presumption of fault is of key importance for the proper analysis of the specific liability regime of the CSPs. Review of the doctrine in the area of electronic signatures reveals that the presumption of fault is sometimes confused with the presumption of causality. Shedding light on the issue will later provide proof of evidence on a certain inefficiency of the approach chosen by the European legislator in establishing presumption of fault. Most of the EU Member States' general laws literally transpose this presumption, although it will become clear that no such necessity exists. This finding is demonstrated in Chapter V.

The burden of proving the fault derives from the general civil liability rules. Under those rules in Bulgarian law, the alleged tortfeasor will always bear the burden of proving that he or she has acted with due care[427]. That rule is applicable in some systems only in contract, but in others, like Bulgaria, it applies both in contract and tort. Usually, legal systems establish, either explicitly or implicitly, a rebuttable presumption of negligence by allocating the burden of proving the non-culpable behaviour or performance with due care.[428]

---

[425] See Van Gerven, W., et al., *ibid.*, p.332.

[426] From Article 29 of Bulgarian EDESA in connection to Article 82 of LOC it could be deducted, for example, that should the CSPs has proved to have acted with malice (intentionally), he will be liable for all foreseeable and unforeseeable direct and immediate damages, while for negligence it could be held liable only to the foreseeable damages.

[427] It is notable Article 1:305 of the Principles of European Contract Law [Imputed Knowledge]. It reads that if any person who with a party's assent was involved in making a contract, or who was entrusted with performance by a party or performed with its assent: (a) knew or foresaw a fact, or ought to have known or foreseen it; or (b) acted intentionally or with gross negligence, or not in accordance with good faith and fair dealing, this knowledge, foresight or behaviour is imputed to the party itself.

[428] For example Article 45 (2) of the Bulgarian Law on Obligations and Contracts provides that "*In tort the fault is presumed unless contrary is proved*". In contractual relations Article 79 provides that the damages claim of the creditor is presupposed *only* from the non-fulfilment of the obligation and the causality of the damage occurrence. Under the French Civil Code the debtor is condemned, if there be ground, to the payment of damages and interest, either by reason of the non-performance of the obligation or by reason

As already discussed, negligence is not considered to be a psychological attitude, but rather non-compliance with the objective criterion for due care.[429] The unlawfulness of the behaviour should be proved, but this is not necessary for the culpability.

The presumption of negligence means that the illegal result was foreseeable and avoidable by exercising due care.[430] In tort, the party suffering damage would be bound to prove the behaviour *contra lege*, the damages and the chain of causation between the unlawful behaviour and the occurrence of the damage. In a contract, the burden of proving the performance lies with the debtor.[431]

4.3. Liability without fault

Another concept of general civil law that should be outlined for the purposes of proving the assertions of the work is liability without fault. Behind this concept lies the need for society to promote greater trust and security by allocating strict liability to certain groups of subjects. The European legislator sometimes chooses this approach to shield the interests of given groups of person. Whether such supranational rules applicable to the CSPs exist and how these rules interfere with the specific liability regime of the CSPs established by Directive 1999/93/EC is the subject of analysis in Chapter IV. This chapter will provide insights into why and where it is reasonable to introduce specific legal regimes governing over given sets of relationships, where these deviate from the general regimes, and why for the CSPs such an approach is not justifiable.

---

of delay in its execution, *as often as he cannot prove that such non-performance proceeds from a foreign cause which cannot be imputed to him, although there be no bad faith on his pArticle* (Article 1147). In German law there are several provisions establishing presumption in this respect - § 276 BGB [Responsibility for one's own conduct] reads that in contract the debtor is responsible, *unless it is otherwise provided,* for wilful conduct and negligence. Further § 827 BGB [Exclusion and lessening of responsibility] reads that in tort "a person who causes damage to another person .... is responsible for any damage which he in this condition unlawfully causes in the same manner as if negligence were imputable to him; *the responsibility does not arise if he has been brought into this condition without fault.*" – i.e. the alleged tortfeasor must prove such condition.

[429] It is seen that the negligence only is presumed, but not the intentional behaviour – see Kalaydjiev, A., *ibid.*, p. 373.

[430] See Konov, T., *ibid.*, p. 169

[431] See Kalaydjiev, A., *ibid.*, p. 374.

In legal theory this concept is referred to by different phrases – 'no-fault liability',[432] 'risk-based liability',[433] 'strict liability',[434] but is known in the Bulgarian legal system and in all other jurisdictions throughout Europe. It may arise both in contract and tort.

Strict liability in contract applies to, for example, the liability of the carrier,[435] or the liability of the debtor for lack of money.[436]

Strict liability in tort applies to liability for animals, liability for injury resulting from air transport accidents,[437] liability arising from accidents at nuclear installations,[438] environmental liability, liability for damage caused by the conduct of others (i.e. liability for damage caused by children or supervised persons,[439] liability for damage caused by employees and representatives[440]), liability for damage caused by the unsafe state of an immovable,[441] liability for damage caused by defective products[442] etc.

While the principle of *nulla penae sine culpa* is still the main principle of civil law, fault is considered to be an element triggering the liability. Strict liability is therefore an exception to the rule - it arises only in cases explicitly envisaged by law.

The common concept for all situations in which strict liability arises, according to Bulgarian legal theory, is that the detrimental consequences accrue to the

---

[432] In Bulgaria – "*безвиновна отговорност*", in France – "*responsabilite sans fauté*".

[433] In Germany – "*Gefährdungshaftung*". However, in Germany the concept is based not only on removal of the fault, but on the concept of risk.

[434] Used in English law mostly.

[435] Article 373 of the Bulgarian Commercial Act.

[436] Article 81 (2) of the Bulgarian LOC. Same approach followed by Article 9:101 of the Principles of European Contract Law – "The creditor is entitled to recover money which is due". The concept is also accepted in German law (§279 BGB)– see Beale, H., Hartkamp, A., et al., *ibid.*, p.661.

[437] See Warsaw Convention for the Unification of Certain Rules relating to International Carriage by Air of 12 October 1929, 137 LNTS 11, also Regulation 2027/97 of 9 October 1997, OJ L 185/1.

[438] See Paris Convention on Third Party Liability in the Field of Nuclear Energy as of 29 July 1960, The Brussels Convention supplementing the Paris Convention of 31 January 1963, the Brussels Convention Relating to Civil Liability in the Field of Maritime Carriage of Nuclear Material of 17 December 1971.

[439] *Ibid.*, Article 3:104.

[440] *Ibid.*, Article 3:201.

[441] *Ibid.*, Article 3:202.

[442] *Ibid.*, Article 3:204.

debtor/tortfeasor not due to his fault, but because of the occurrence of the damage that is caused by the given unlawful behaviour.[443]

Reasonable justification for imposing liability not based on fault arises where the law is dealing with a situation in which an exceptional risk or danger to society is created. Such situations include the keeping of animals, manufacturing industrial products, operating a nuclear power station etc.[444]

The basic elements for strict liability are the occurrence of the damage, behaviour, the unlawfulness of the behaviour, and the chain of causation between the unlawful behaviour and the damage caused.[445]

The debtor/tortfeasor will be able to avoid liability if he or she has not accepted the risk pursuant to a contract (in cases of contractual strict liability), or where his or her behaviour was not subject to free choice,[446] or because an extraneous cause is shown to exist,[447] or because of the behaviour of the party who has suffered damage or of a third party. However, building a defence by showing an extraneous cause would not be possible in all jurisdictions.[448]

Liability for the conduct of others will be analyzed among the different causes in respect of liability without fault.

4.4. Liability for the conduct of others

Introduction to liability for conduct of others at this stage seems of the utmost importance for understanding the CSPs' liability, and especially for making an assessment of specific liability for 'guaranteeing' qualified certificates, introduced by the EC Directive on e-signatures. Furthermore, in the PKI, as has become

---

[443] See Konov, T., *ibid.,* p. 220.

[444] See Van Gerven, W., et al., *ibid.,* p. 579.

[445] See Konov, T., *ibid.,* p. 219–230.

[446] See Kalaydjiev, A., *ibid.,* p. 375.

[447] The extraneous case is referred to as *"force majeure", "cas fortiut"* (in France), *"Acts of God"* (in England), *"höhere Gewalt"* (in Germany), *"непреодолима сила"* (Bulgaria), etc. See Van Gerven, W., et. al., *ibid.,* p. 582.

[448] *Ibid.* This is the case in France. Under Article 7:102 of the Principles of European Tort Law a person has a defence if the damage is caused by an unforeseeable and irresistible force of nature (force majeure). See European Group on Tort Law, *Principles of European Tort Law,* Text and Commentary, Springer-Verlag/Wien, 2005, p.6.

evident,[449] outsourcing is a common and preferred means of provision of certification services. The CSPs often act through other parties (RAs) in identifying the party seeking issue of a certificate, and even the latter could re-outsource some of the processes to agents;[450] the CSPs may outsource the keeping and maintenance of the public directory,[451] or the online access thereto. Issue of time-stamp certificates is also a preferred way for provision of trust services.[452] Where the CSP bears the obligation to provide certain certification services, either by contract, or by virtue of law, the CSP will also bear the consequences and thus will be liable for the misconduct of the other providers of certification services to which it has outsourced activities.

Under Bulgarian law, liability for the conduct of others is subject to different regimes for contract and for tort. The same approach is taken in most of the European jurisdictions. It is a deviation from the general concept of the liability of a person for his or her own wrongful behaviour in cases of breach of contract or commission of a tortious act.[453]

Liability for the conduct of others arises in cases envisaged by law regardless of whether the personal conduct of the debtor/tortfeasor is involved. The idea of establishing such a liability regime may derive from the particular characteristics of the relationship between the person whose conduct caused the non-fulfilment of the obligation (or tort) and the person whose liability is at issue.[454]

Historically, liability for the conduct of others emerged in Roman law when the debtor made a bad choice or failed to properly supervise the person to whom the given activity was subcontracted.[455] The tort liability for the conduct of others also has its roots in the so-called *actio noxalis* where the master or the father was held liable for a tort, committed by a son, a slave or an animal.[456]

---

[449] See Chapter I, sections 2.2.4 and 2.2.6 *supra*.

[450] See Chapter I, section 2.3 *supra*.

[451] See Chapter I, section 2.4 *supra*.

[452] See Chapter I, section 2.5 *supra*.

[453] See Van Gerven, W., et al., *ibid.*, p.467

[454] *Ibid.*

[455] See Kalaydjiev, A., *ibid.*, p. 377.

[456] Black's Law Dictionary, *ibid.*, p.1092

Liability for the conduct of others should not be confused with similar issues, such as joint liability[457] and the liability of agents.[458]

All contemporary legal systems have developed this institution, but there is a fairly diverse range of regimes. The research focuses on the Bulgarian approach, but some references to other legal systems are made by way of comparison.

The regime for contractual liability for the conduct of others is constructed on the basis of the general rules of contractual liability.[459]

In the first instance, attention should be paid to the fact that in a contract the obligation may sometimes be performed by another person where in other cases it may not.

When contractual obligation should be performed specifically by the debtor, due to the nature of the obligation, by virtue of law, or by agreement of the parties (so-called *intuitu personae* obligations), no activity may be subcontracted whatsoever, and the infringement of this obligation leads to complete non-fulfilment of the obligation (i.e. non-provision of due care).[460]

Usually, however, in contractual obligations the debtor undertakes to provide a result to the creditor. Once the result is delivered, the interest of the debtor should be considered satisfied. In this respect, it is of no importance to the creditor who exactly will deliver the result – the debtor personally, or another party. Failure to deliver the result in the case of subcontracting would lead to civil liability on the part of the debtor, regardless of where the fault lies – with the debtor, or with the

---

[457] *Op. cit.* Kalaydjiev, A., *ibid.,* p. 377. The common carrier will be liable for the further behaviour of other carriers if he had performed the transportation with their participation. However, the liability of the carrier shall not be for the other carriers' conduct, because all carriers shall be jointly liable under the transportation contract.

[458] *Ibid.,* p. 377, Under Article 23 of the Bulgarian LOC the promissor who promises that another person will act or will undertake an obligation shall be liable for his own conduct, but not for the conduct of the other person, should the latter fails to act or to undertake the obligation as promised.

[459] There is no general rule dealing with liability for conduct of others in contractual relations in Bulgarian law. In German law, however, such a provision exists - § 278 BGB [Responsibility for persons employed in performing obligation] reads that a debtor is responsible for the fault of his legal representative and of persons whom he employs in performing his obligation, to the same extent as for his own fault. Under the German law it is irrelevant whether the debtor has exercised due care in making his choice. Same approach is chosen by the Commission drafting the Principles of European Contract Law: Article 8:107 [Performance Entrusted to Another] provides that a party who entrusts performance of the contract to another person *remains responsible for performance.*

[460] See Kalaydjiev, A., *ibid.,* p. 379.

subcontractor.[461] Thus, contractual liability for the conduct of others proves to be objective in nature – it does not depend on the debtor's fault.[462]

Tort liability for the conduct of others arises only in those cases explicitly envisaged in the law.[463] The rationale in this concept lays in the negative interest the tort liability aims at satisfying – the tort leads to unfavourable changes in the *patrimonium* (the property) of the damaged person and the duty to provide a remedy should lie with the person that has caused the damage.[464]

The survey performed shows that in different systems similar hypotheses of tort liability for conduct of others can be identified. *Inter alia,* such hypotheses are: liability for harm caused by employees or assignees, liability of parents for harm caused by their children,[465] liability of guardians for harm caused by persons in their custody etc.

For the purposes of the present analysis – i.e. the specific liability of the CSPs – only liability for harm caused by employees or assignees proves to be of interest among all these hypotheses.[466] The analysis reveals that, in this respect, almost all countries throughout Europe have a common approach.[467]

---

[461] There are exceptions of this rule. For example when a mandate is trusted the mandatary shall be liable for the bad choice of re-assignment of the mandate. However, the bad choice could be contested and the due care in this respect shall be investigated in view of the choice.

[462] This concept is recognized by the Bulgarian law – See Kalaydjiev, A., *ibid.,* p. 379, also Konov, T., *ibid.,* p.114-118. In French law the objective nature of the general civil liability is recognized as well - Cour de cassation. Cass. Crim., 26 March 1997, Foyer Notre-Dam des Flots, Bull.crim.1997.124, No.2, JCP 1997.II.22868, with report of F.Desportes, D 1997.Jur.496, with note by P.Jourdain. Translation by Y.P.Salmon. *Op.cit.* Van Gerven, W., et al., *ibid.,* p.520.

[463] This conclusion shall be valid for jurisdictions like Bulgaria, Germany and England. The French law comprises of general regime of tort liability for others in addition to the general regime governing contractual obligations for others, as well as particular regimes concerning the liability. The general rule is the one of Article 1384 (1) which reads that everyone is liable for the damage caused not only by the one's conduct, but also by the conduct of persons for whom one is responsible or by things in one's care. The drafters of the Principles of the European Tort Law enumerate two groups of cases whereby the alleged person shall be held liabile for conduct of others – see articles 6:101 and 6:102.

[464] See Kalaydjiev, A., *ibid.,* p. 379.

[465] Article 6:101 of the Principles of European Tort Law, *ibid.,* p. 6.

[466] Employee is usually referred to in Germany as "*Verrichtungsgehilfe*", in France as "*préposé*".

[467] Under the English law, liability for harm caused by employees is the only vicarious liability regime, where one can be held liable for injury caused by another, irrespective of whether one was at fault. In all other cases where can be incurred liability for other's conduct the liability shall be based on fault. House of Lords, case *Carmarthenshire Country Council* v. *Lewis* [1955] AC 549 at 566, HL, per Lord Reid. *Op. cit.* Van Gerven, W., et al., *ibid.,* p.514. Under Article 1385 (5) of the French Code Civil principles and employers are liable for the damage caused by their servants and employees in the course of the functions for which they are employed. Under Article 49 of the Bulgarian LOC the person that have

Incurring liability for tort in the case discussed requires certain conditions to be met: a particular type of behaviour by a person is required; the behaviour should be wrongful; damage must have occurred; the damage must have been caused by the wrongful behaviour; the person who has suffered the damage must be a third party, other than the tortfeasor and the liable person; the behaviour should take place during the course of the accomplishment of a task assigned by the liable person; an assignment from the liable person to the tortfeasor should be present.[468]

The assignment of a certain task means that there exists a relationship whereby a person (employee, assignee) performs work for the benefit of the assignor. The assignment does not necessarily mean that an employment contract *strictu sensu* should exist. In this respect, the CSPs will always be liable for the conduct of the other CSPs to which they have outsourced certain services or activities, which are part of the service provision. The subject of the assignment could be both factual and legal actions.[469]

The damage caused during the course of the accomplishment of the task may be caused either by action or omission. It need not necessarily arise in the course of performing the task, but may also occur in relation to the performance of the task – i.e. preparation to initiate the performance of the work.[470] Liability also arises when the employee has deviated from the instructions given by the employer.[471]

The liability for harm caused by employees or assignees is objective - no culpability of the assignor is required.[472] The employer (assignor) may avoid liability if it is possible to prove either that the damage was not caused negligently by the employee (the assignee) or that it was not caused during the course or in relation to the accomplishment of the task assigned.[473] Liability relates both to material and to

---

assigned to another some work shall be liable for the damages, caused by the latter, during the course of performance of the work. In Germany the liability of employees is regulated by §831 (1) BGB [Liability for employees] – Anyone who employees another person for a task is liable for the injury unlawfully caused to a third party by that other person in the accomplishment of the task.

[468] See Kalaydjiev, A., *ibid.*, p. 382, also Van Gerven, W., et al., *ibid.*, p.481

[469] See Kalaydjiev, A., *ibid*, p.382.

[470] *Ibid.*

[471] Bulgarian Supreme Court PP-9-1966, *Op. cit.* Yossifov, B., Balabanov, B., *Tort*, 1989, Sofia, p. 31.

[472] See *supra* note 467.

[473] Under §831 (1), sect.2 BGB no liability shall arise if (i) the employer exercised reasonable care in the selection of the employee and – when the employer himself procures tools or directs the accomplishment of the task – in the procurement of tools and the direction of the employee or (ii) the injury would also

intangible damage.[474] The objective character of the liability is a ground for a claim for redress against the tortfeasor.[475]

Having identified the lines of liability in Chapter I, and having given an overview of the liability for conduct of others, it is apparent that there are practical cases where the CSPs will be held liable for the conduct of others, especially when outsourcing activities to other CSPs.

5. Extension and Limitation of Liability

Managing liability by certain legal means in the PKI directly refers to the management of business risks. The employment of such means is made possible by the introduction of the specific liability regime of the CSPs in the e-signatures Directive. Assessment of whether such means are appropriate is made in Chapter III, *infra*. The following section provides only a brief overview of the general principles of extension and limitation of liability from the point of view of Bulgarian legal theory.

The general concept of freedom of contract in civil law provides means for the parties to divert from the statutory liability burden placed upon them. This refers only to contractual liability. Under Bulgarian legal doctrine, no agreements can be enforced by way of tort liability beforehand.[476]

In the first instance, such divergence may be regarded in terms of extension of the liability causes – i.e. the parties may agree that the debtor will be liable for *force majeure*.

---

have been caused if the employer had taken such reasonable care. Under the French Code Civil once the conditions of Article 1385 (5) are met it is very difficult of the employer to defeat the liability. It is considered an irrefutable presumption of liability. However, the employer can prove that the harm was caused by *force majeur* or there existed say contributory fault, or other defence to exonerate the employee. Same is the case under English law – See Van Gerven, W., et al., *ibid.*, p.469.

[474] Supreme Court Case №340-1988 V, Court practice of the Supreme Cassation Court of Republic of Bulgaria, Civil Department, 1998, 2000, Sofia, p. 30. *Op. cit.* Kalaydjiev, A., *ibid.*, p. 382.

[475] The problems, related to the liability for harm caused by employees or assignees are very complicated and are subject to different approaches and academic debates in different jurisdictions. For thorough analysis of the liability in English, German and French laws see Van Gerven, et al., *ibid.*, chapter 5.1, p.467-513

[476] See Kalaydjiev, A., *ibid.*, p. 382..

In the second instance, the creditor may agree to release the debtor from liability in the case of certain types of negligent behaviour.[477] Such agreements are also enforceable,[478] which is of particular relevance to CSPs.

The introduction of limitations, however, is subject to certain restrictions. The laws sometimes explicitly restrict the parties to agree on exemption for intentional malice or gross negligence,[479] which especially refers to CSPs.[480] Even if a similar rule is not explicitly introduced in certain laws, it is scarcely likely that such an agreement can be successfully enforced in any jurisdiction where it breaches *bonos mores*.[481]

The liability of CSPs can be successfully managed to a certain extent, by making representations before entering into a contract with the subscriber, or by using other legal methods (CPS/CP, placing limitations on use of the certificate or the value of transactions etc), which are the subject of thorough analysis in Chapter III, *infra*.[482]

Furthermore, there are cases in which, both in contract and tort, it is unjust to hold the debtor liable when the creditor has contributed to the occurrence of the damage.[483] It is possible, for example, for the damage to have been caused directly

---

[477] Under the Principles of the European Contract Law established by Article 1:201 (2) the parties may not exclude or limit the duty of acting in good faith and fair dealing. See *supra* note 400.

[478] See Kalaydjiev, A., *ibid.*, p. 383.

[479] Under Bulgarian Law and German law in some cases the parties could contractually agree on reducing of the liability of the debtor, but not for malice (*dolus*) or gross negligence (*culpa lata*). (Article 92 of Bulgarian LOC and § 443 BGB). See *supra* note 418.

[480] Article 29 (4) of the Bulgarian EDESA provides restriction for the CSPs issuing qualified or universal certificates to introduce clauses by CPS or by agreement with the person seeking issuance of certificate for release of liability for any kind of negligence, while the general rule of Article 94 of LOC would allow for such a release (except for willful misconduct or gross negligence) when party is CSP that do not issue qualified or universal certificates. Article 6 (3) and (4) of the Directive 1999/93/EC provides that the CSPs issuing qualified certificates to the public may limit their liability for damages that could be caused from the usage of the certificate by placing limitations on the use and value of transactions in the certificate. All other limitations placed in the certificate will not be binding. See *infra* section 6 of Chapter III.

[481] See Capitant, Terre and Lequette, *Les Grands arrêts de la jurisprudence civile*, 10th ed., Paris, Dalloz, 1996, No.96, reported Civ.com. of 15 June 1959 – "A clause seeking to exclude liability for breach of contract will be disregarded where the relevant breach of contract occurred intentionally (dol) or resulted from gross negligence (faute lourde).". Op. cit. Beale, H., Hartkamp, A., et al., *ibid.*, p.502.

[482] See Chapter III, section 6 *infra*.

[483] This concept is set forth as main principle of the European contract law. Article 9:504 of the Principles of the European Contract Law reads that the non-performing party is not liable for loss suffered by the aggrieved party to the extent that the aggrieved party contributed to the non-performance or its effects. Furthermore, Article 9:505 rules that the non-performing party is not liable for loss suffered by the aggrieved party to the extent that the aggrieved party could have reduced the loss by taking reasonable

by the creditor's behaviour. In such a case, no liability will emerge.[484]

In practice, there are also cases where the creditor may have only contributed to the occurrence of the damage; i.e. they result as a consequence of the behaviour of both the debtor and the creditor. In such cases, the compensation will depend on the contributory 'quota' for the occurrence of the damage. According to this rule, the compensation has to be reduced only to the extent of the actual contribution.[485]

Finally, those cases in which damage is caused by the behaviour of the debtor and by another event – e.g. a natural phenomenon ('acts of god') – are also relevant to the issue discussed. In such situations, the amount of compensation to be paid should be assessed and reduced *pro rata* to the extent to which human behaviour contributed to the damage.[486]

6. Conclusions

This present chapter sets out a brief theoretical overview of the general notion of civil liability under Bulgarian law. The analysis focused on certain aspects of the civil liability theory, relevant to this survey – notion and types of liability (contractual and tortious), concurrence of claims, pre-contractual liability, types of damage and causation, meanings of unlawfulness and fault, particularly presumptions of causality and fault, as well as liability without fault (strict liability) and liability for the conduct of others. Some basic aspects of different legal methods for extending and limiting liability were also summarized. Reference to similarities between the Bulgarian concept and the theoretical approaches in the jurisdictions representing the main law families in Europe was made by way of comparison. Reference to the current version of the draft Principles of the European Contract and the Principles of the European Tort Law was made on the basis that these principles will become in the near future

---

steps. The aggrieved party is entitled to recover any expenses reasonably incurred in attempting to reduce the loss

[484] See Kalaydjiev, A., *ibid.*, p. 80.

[485] §254 BGB, also Article 83 (1) and Article 51 (2) of the Bulgarian LOC, etc. Article 8:101 [Contributory Counduct or Activity of the Victim] of the Principles of European Tort Law reads that liability can be excluded or reduced to such extent as is considered just having regard to the victim's contributory fault and to any other matters which would be relevant to establish or reduce liability of the victim if he were the tortfeasor.

[486] *Op. cit.* Kalaydjiev, A., *ibid.*, p. 384. In the famous French case Lamoriciere the court assessed that the contributive damages are present as a result of behaviour of the debtor (1/5) and the cyclone (4/5) that should be considered a *force majeur* – see Treitel, G., *ibid.*, p. 72.

supranational rules aimed at harmonizing the contract and tort law civil liability principles throughout the EU.

Since the figure of the certification-service-provider was analysed in Chapter I, it has become possible providing at this stage some illustrative examples related to the CSPs to outline the types of problematic issues that will be discussed in the following chapters. At the same time, reference to such examples was made to demonstrate the applicability of the general liability regime to the particular activity of the CSPs in the absence of a specific liability regime.

Making such an analysis was a logical step for the purposes of this research. Firstly, while the main object of the work is to deduct conclusions on the relevance of the approach of the European legislator to introduce a specific liability regime for the certification-service-providers, proper analysis of the Directive 1999/93/EC rules seems impossible without a pre-defined theoretical viewpoint for understanding and interpreting the Directive liability rules. In this connection, no Community instrument was found whatsoever to provide interpreting provisions or proper directions with respect to liability in order to build such knowledge.

Secondly, the liability of the CSPs will be regulated by the general national rules regarding liability.[487] Therefore, it was impossible to analyze the specific liability rules of the Directive and their transposition effects on the national liability regime without having a fair theoretical standpoint. Only then would it be possible to gain an understanding of whether and where differences between the supranational and national rules exist and why problems are faced in the national implementation of the Directive.

Thirdly, the analysis shed light on the general liability regime from the point of view of the Bulgarian legal doctrine, since the transposition of the specific liability rules into the Bulgarian legal system is taken as a case study. The comparative overview demonstrates that the approach chosen seems to be acceptable, since Bulgarian law falls within the continental law families and follows the traditions of the French legal system. Moreover, the references to the draft Principles of the European Contract and the Principles of the European Tort Law, demonstrates that as a matter of principle, the Bulgarian law stays close to the Principles. Therefore, the conclusions and deductions made in this work on the appropriateness of the specific liability rules

---

[487]   Recital (22) of the Directive 1999/93/EC.

and the problems involved in their transposition into Bulgarian law will be adequate and fair to an acceptable extent.

After putting a theoretical fulcrum in place as a means of understanding the general concept of liability, it is possible to proceed further with the analysis of the specific liability regime of the CSPs established by Directive 1999/93/EC (Chapter III) and by other Directives (Chapter IV) and to answer the question of whether the transposed specific liability rules are meant to promote further trust in the electronic communications from the point of view of Bulgarian law, or the general liability regime secures the necessary level of trust (Chapter V).

Chapter III

SPECIFIC LIABILITY REGIME UNDER THE EU E-SIGNATURES DIRECTIVE

The analysis of the special liability rules introduced in the national legislation of Bulgaria and the assessment of the necessity of such rules may be successfully accomplished only by identifying and investigating their source – the *acquis communautaire*. Therefore, the present and the following chapters focus on the examination of supranational liability rules.

As previously noted, the main relevant legislative instrument in the European Union that introduces a specific liability regime for certification-service-providers is the Directive 1999/93/EC on the Community framework for electronic signatures (the 'Directive')[488]. Since the Directive prescribes the introduction of a *minimum* particular liability regime and proves to be the *main* source for the national legislation of Bulgaria, the whole of this chapter is dedicated to the analysis of the liability rules it contains.

A proper understanding of the specific aspects of the supranational liability regulation structure in force can only be achieved by giving a historical overview of the legislative process in drafting the relevant normative text, and by making a thorough analysis of its final version. The deductions derived from such an examination provide an appropriate starting-point for successful analysis of the practical transposition of the Directive's liability rules and an understanding of the implementation problems faced by the national jurisdiction of the country that is the subject of this analysis - Bulgaria.

A thorough study of the specific liability rules would further assist in making an estimation of whether or not those rules promote greater trust in the world of electronic signatures or whether they are doomed to remain merely rules.

The knowledge derived from this research serves as a good basis for the assessment made in Chapter V of the problems of transposition of the specific liability regime

---

[488] OJ L13/12 of 19 January 2000.

introduced by Directive 1999/93/EC and whether this regime, as transposed, results in better protection for the interests of the users of certification services.

The text of Article 6 of the Directive states:

Article 6

Liability

1. As a minimum, Member States shall ensure that by issuing a certificate as a qualified certificate to the public or by guaranteeing such a certificate to the public a certification-service-provider is liable for damage caused to any entity or legal or natural person who reasonably relies on that certificate:

(a) as regards the accuracy at the time of issuance of all information contained in the qualified certificate and as regards the fact that the certificate contains all the details prescribed for a qualified certificate;

(b) for assurance that at the time of the issuance of the certificate, the signatory identified in the qualified certificate held the signature-creation data corresponding to the signature verification data given or identified in the certificate;

(c) for assurance that the signature-creation data and the signature-verification data can be used in a complementary manner in cases where the certification-service-provider generates them both;

unless the certification-service-provider proves that he has not acted negligently.

2. As a minimum Member States shall ensure that a certification-service-provider who has issued a certificate as a qualified certificate to the public is liable for damage caused to any entity or legal or natural person who reasonably relies on the certificate for failure to register revocation of the certificate unless the certification-service-provider proves that he has not acted negligently.

3. Member States shall ensure that a certification-service-provider may indicate in a qualified certificate limitation on the use of that certificate, provided the limitations are recognizable to third parties. The certification-service-provider shall not be liable for damage arising from use of a qualified certificate which exceeds the limitations placed on it.

4. Member States shall ensure that a certification-service-provider may indicate in the qualified certificate a limit on the value of transactions for which the certificate can be used, provided that the limit is recognizable to third parties.

The certification-service-provider shall not be liable for damage resulting from this maximum limit being exceeded.

5. The provisions of paragraphs 1 to 4 shall be without prejudice to Council Directive 93/13/EEC of 5 April 1993 on unfair terms in consumer contracts (1)."

1. General Notes

1.1. Approach of the Directive for building of trust. Qualified signatures.

The Directive role is to ensure security and trust in the electronic communications by establishing a common European framework for digital signatures and encryption so that the national legislations of the Member States could not hinder the free movement of goods and services in the internal market[489]. In order to strengthen confidence in the new technologies, clear rules should be established.

In general, these rules should promote within the Community:

➢ common legal recognition of electronic signatures by outlining objective criteria thereof;

➢ laying down of definite rules for provision of services and performing activity by the CSPs;

➢ encouraging implementation of voluntary accreditation schemes aiming at enhancing the level of trust in certification services offered by the CSPs;

➢ establishment of appropriate national supervision schemes for compliance with the provisions laid down in the Directive;

➢ pushing the Member States to swiftly enable bodies charged with the conformity assessment to be designated;

➢ striking of an appropriate balance between consumer and business needs.

---

[489] *Ibid*, Preamble (3) and (4).

The approach of the Directive to reach the said enhanced level of trust is quite interesting.

The Directive establishes divergent legal recognition of the different types of electronic signatures – basic[490], advanced[491] and qualified. Article 5 promotes legal effectiveness and admissibility of all types of e-signatures as evidence in legal proceedings[492]. The European legislator equalizes the legal value of the qualified signature to a handwritten signature. As a qualified signature will be considered the advanced electronic signature supported by a qualified certificate, meeting the requirements of Annex I of the Directive, issued by a certification-service-provider, meeting the requirements of Annex II of the Directive[493]. The aim of most of the rules of the Directive is to provide necessary framework to achieve security and trust in usage of qualified signatures in public environment.

In this respect, it is noteworthy that the Directive establishes statutory mandatory requirements *only* with respect to the CSPs issuing qualified certificates (in Annex II)[494] and statutory mandatory requirements for the requisites *only* for the qualified certificates in order to be considered qualified (Annex I)[495].

Furthermore, the Directive also prescribes that the Member States must ensure the establishment of an appropriate system that allows supervision of CSPs, established on its territory that issue qualified certificates to the public *only*[496]. Supervising the activity of the CSPs would deliver to the market the confidence that the State

---

[490] Under the meaning of Article 2 (1) of the Directive - data in electronic form which are attached to or logically associated with other electronic data and which serve as a method of authentication.

[491] Defined as such in Article 2 (1) of the Directive to be an electronic signature which meets the following requirements: (a) it is uniquely linked to the signatory; (b) it is capable of identifying the signatory; (c) it is created using means that the signatory can maintain under his sole control; and (d) it is linked to the data to which it relates in such a manner that any subsequent change of the data is detectable.

[492] Article 5 (1) (2) and paragraph 2.

[493] See *infra* note 546.

[494] The criteria will be analysed in section 3, *infra*.

[495] Under Annex I of the Directive qualified certificates must contain: (a) an indication that the certificate is issued as a qualified certificate; (b) the identification of the certification-service-provider and the State in which it is established; (c) the name of the signatory or a pseudonym, which shall be identified as such; (d) provision for a specific attribute of the signatory to be included if relevant, depending on the purpose for which the certificate is intended; (e) signature-verification data which correspond to signature-creation data under the control of the signatory; (f) an indication of the beginning and end of the period of validity of the certificate; (g) the identity code of the certificate; (h) the advanced electronic signature of the certification-service-provider issuing it; (i) limitations on the scope of use of the certificate, if applicable; and (j) limits on the value of transactions for which the certificate can be used, if applicable. Further analysis on the rule is made in section 3 *infra*.

[496] Article 3 (3) of the Directive.

controls this activity and has an active role in making the CSPs conform to predefined statutory norms and standards, thus the CSPs would provide trustworthy services and the security of the usage of electronic signatures would be achieved. The supervision could be performed through state or private bodies[497].

In order for the legal value of the qualified signatures to be equalized to a handwritten signature, the signature should be further created by a secure signature-creation-device (SSCD). The internal market should have common standards on what should be considered a SSCD and on the electronic signature products[498]. Thus, the standardized qualified e-signatures should merely give users a presumption that a signature complying with this standard will be presumed equivalent to handwritten throughout Europe[499].

The conformity of the SSCDs with the requirements laid down in the Directive (in Annex III) should be determined by public or private bodies designated by Member States. The determination of conformity should be recognised by all Member States. The Commission established criteria for Member States to determine whether a body should be designated[500].

To promote further trust in usage of e-signatures the Directive encourages the Member State to introduce and maintain voluntary accreditation schemes. All conditions related to such schemes must be objective, transparent, proportionate and non-discriminatory. Member States may not limit the number of accredited certification-service-providers for reasons which fall within the scope of the Directive[501]. The accreditation was already discussed *supra*.[502]

---

[497] *Ibid.*

[498] The Commission has published criteria in Commission Decision (2003/511/EC) of 14 July 2003 on the publication of reference numbers of generally recognised standards for electronic signature products in accordance with Directive 1999/93/EC of the European Parliament and of the Council (notified under document number C(2003) 2439).

See also CEN/ISSS CWA 14172-5: "Secure signature creation devices" и CEN/ISSS CWA 14255, WS/E-Sign: "Guidelines for the implementation of Secure Signature-Creation Devices".

[499] Dumortier, J., et al., *The Legal and Market Aspects of Electronic Signatures, ibid*, p.12

[500] See Commission Decision (2000/709/EC) of 6 November 2000 on the minimum criteria to be taken into account by Member States when designating bodies in accordance with Article 3 (4) of Directive 1999/93/EC of the European Parliament and of the Council on a Community framework for electronic signatures (notified under document number C(2000) 3179), OJ L289/42 of 16.11.2000 (http://rechtsinformatik.jura.uni-sb.de/cbl/statutes/dec061100_DigSig_en.pdf)

[501] Article 3 (2) of the Directive.

[502] See Chapter I, Section 1, *supra*.

Finally, the Directive introduces specific liability rules addressed to the CSPs issuing qualified certificates to the public. By this the Directive aims at establishing further trust in using qualified electronic signatures in the Community market. The way the liability regime of given relations may impact the trust-building process was already discussed in chapter I, section 1, *supra*.

From the above analysis it becomes evident that except for the accreditation, all other measures provided for by the Directive to enhance trust in the electronic world aim at securing the usage of *qualified* signatures. Therefore here comes the reasonable question: is the introduction of specific liability regime for the CSPs issuing qualified certificates to support qualified signatures necessary to enhance further the trust or the other measures provided are enough to secure the trust in usage of electronic signatures? The analysis of the liability rules introduced by the Directive in this and the forthcoming chapters will give an answer to this question.

1.2. History of the Directive's liability rules

On October 8th, 1997, the European Commission adopted a key document for the future electronic signature legislation – Communication COM (97) 503 "Ensuring security and trust in electronic communication: "Towards a European Framework for Digital Signatures and Encryption"[503].

In Section 3.2 of the Communication the Commission envisages that clear liability rules would contribute to the acceptance of the certification services[504]. However, divergent levels of protection at a national level could potentially act as a cross-border barrier to the provision of goods or services or to the use by public administrations of on-line services in a cross-border context. Liability questions may play a particular role in the relationship between users and CSPs or between two CSPs as well as licensing authorities (licensing CSPs).

The document states further that in all Member States, there are contractual rules connected to appropriate liability rules between the user and the CSP. Liability very

---

[503] Communication from the Commission COM (97) 503: Ensuring security and trust in electronic communication: "Towards a European Framework for Digital Signatures and Encryption", available at http://www.swiss.ai.mit.edu/6805/articles/crypto/eu-october-8-97.html.

[504] The exposition of the findings of the Commission herein below are deliberately kept very close to the original text of the Communication due its key importance to the analysis and the interpretation of the final text of the Directive's liability clauses. Some of the italic highlights are mine.

much depends on concrete single cases. For instance, liability problems can be better managed if digital signatures are used within specific closed user groups.

An extremely important finding of the Commission is that the liability largely depends upon the concrete service offered by the CA as stipulated in the contract. A *legal catalogue of requirements could form the basis for the contractual duties. It would also provide for both minimum and maximum liability of the CSPs or guarantees*, for example, the accuracy of the certificate or the correctness of the key directory. Certification practice statements, being detailed descriptions of how policies are implemented by a particular CSP, could also play an important role as orientation for liability issues.

Further, the document recognizes that *normally* there is no contractual relationship between a CSP and third parties, like the recipients of a digitally signed message or other CSPs, who have confidence in the validity of certificates. Therefore, Member States should examine whether there is a need for special liability rules.

In view of the liability exposure of the State, the Commission recognizes that errors made by a licensing authority in the licensing process can be damaging to the user, the CSP and third parties. Since the licensing authority has no contractual obligations and since the extra-contractual liability of public authorities is usually strictly limited, Member States should examine whether special rules for liability are necessary.

The first impression is that these initial notes of the Commission are widely influenced by the developments and the discussions of the liability issues in the United States[505].

---

[505] See Biddle, B., *Legislating Market Winners: Digital Signature Laws and the Electronic Commerce Marketplace*, 34 San Diego Law Review 1225 (1997) (modified version in 2:3 World Wide Web Journal 231 (1997)). (http://bradbiddle.com/LMW.htm).

Also David G. Masse and Andrew D. Fernandes, Economic Modelling and Risk Management in Public Key Infrastructures P 178 (Version 3.0, Apr. 15, 1997) (visited Jan. 17, 1998) (http://www.chait-amyot.ca/docs/pki.html).

Also Biddle, B., *Misplaced Priorities: The Utah Digital Signature Act and Liability Allocation in a Public Key Infrastructure*, 33 SAN DIEGO LAW REVIEW 1143 (1996). (http://bradbiddle.com/MP.htm).

Also Goldman, E., Maher, T., Biddle, B., *The Role of Certification Authorities in Consumer Transactions: A Report of the ILPF* [Internet Law and Policy Forum] Working Group on Certification Authority Practices, published by the ILPF and online at http://www.ilpf.org (1996). <http://www.ilpf.org/groups/ca/draft.htm>

Thus, after analyzing these initial findings of the Commission, the essence of the principles of the future normative act should be summarized as follows:

1.   Clarification of the liability CSPs may play an important role in the relationship between users and CSPs by enhancing the trust in certification services;

2.   Liability is better managed in contractual relationships;

3.   Liability is better managed in closed PKI rather than in open PKI;

4.   A legal catalogue of requirements for the activity of the CSPs could form the basis for the contractual duties, and thus would provide for clarification on both the minimum and maximum liability of the CSPs;

5.   Certification Practice Statements play an important role in the liability exposure of the CSPs;

6.   *Normally* there is no contractual relationship between the CSPs and the relying parties, thus the liability exposure should be examined from this point of view;

7.   The licensing regime of CSPs would create large problems in respect to the liability.

It should be pointed out that these initial notes and directions of the Commission are quite practical and rational. They reveal the key problems in the liability of the CSPs. It should be noted that the Commission on this first stage *does not* have intention of introducing specific liability rules, but rather raises the problems that should be taken into consideration during the drafting process. As will become obvious, some of the issues pointed out by the Commission undergo an interesting metamorphosis.

Following the meeting of the Council on December 1st, 1997, where the plan of the Commission was accepted, two documents were issued by the Commission: i) a Proposal for a Directive on a Community Framework for Electronic Signatures and ii) a mandate to the European standardization bodies to analyze the needs for standardization activities in relation to electronic signatures[506].

---

[506] See Dumortier, J., *The European Regulatory Framework for Electronic Signatures: A critical Evaluation at* Nielsen, R., Jacobsen, S., Trzaskowski, J. (editors), *EU Electronic Commerce Law*, Djof Publishing (2004), p.69

In the Proposal for a European Parliament and Council Directive on a common framework for electronic signatures several important amendments are proposed by the Parliament that should be noted[507].

The first amendment was to the rule of Article 6 (1) (b) advising that instead of the CSPs being liable for compliance with all the requirements of this Directive in issuing the qualified certificate, a *"compliance with all the requirements of Annex I to this Directive in issuing the qualified certificate"* should be clarified[508]. Despite the fact that the Parliament's proposal has not been accepted, it can be inferred that the essence of the liability rule is in fact establishing statutory obligations for the CSPs – those listed in Annex I. The liability comes only after those duties are infringed[509].

The text of the next two amendments of Article 6 (3) is self-explanatory[510]. Member states shall ensure that a certification-service-provider may indicate, in the qualified certificate, limits on the uses of a certain certificate. The certification-service-provider shall not be liable for damages arising *from the contrary use of a qualified certificate, which includes limits on its uses*. The next amendment provides that Member States shall ensure that a certification-service-provider may indicate in the qualified certificate a limit on the value of transactions *for which the certificate is valid*. The historical development of the text demonstrates that the main idea and rule of Article 6 (3) and (4) is actually to provide a possibility for the CSPs to issue certificates under certain conditions (key usage and value of transactions) and usage of these certificates beyond the denoted purpose leads to disqualifying the qualified e-signature and thus to exemption of the CSP of liability rather than to its limitation[511].

The above considerations seem to be reasonable and grounded by the analysis of the Opinion of the Economic and Social Committee (ESC) on the 'Proposal for a European Parliament and Council Directive on a common framework for electronic signatures'. In the said document, it is stated that in respect to the liability provision of Article 6, it prescribes *a set of obligations for the certification-service-provider*, who must ensure

---

[507] Proposal to the European Parliament and Council Directive on a common framework for electronic signatures (COM(98)0297 - C4-0376/98 - 98/0191(COD)) - http://europa.eu.int/information_society/topics/ebusiness/ecommerce/8epolicy_elaw/law_ecommerce/legal/1signatures/index_en.htm

[508] See Amendment 20 of the Proposal.

[509] See Chapter V, sections 2.4 and 2.7, *infra*.

[510] See Amendment 21 and 22 of the Proposal.

[511] See Chapter III, sections 6.3.1 and 6.3.3 and Chapter V, sections 2.6 and 2.7, *infra*.

the information is accurate, comply with the provisions of the directive, and check that the certificate holder fulfils the necessary technical and technological requirements. Another important understanding of the ESC is, however, that the rule of Article 6 provides for *exemptions from liability* in the case of mistakes in the original information, and *provides for the possibility of limiting both the uses of the certificate and the sum certified*[512].

In the Opinion of the Committee of the Regions on the 'Proposal for a European Parliament and Council Directive on a common framework for electronic signatures',[513] the view that the common liability rules as proposed by the Commission should exist is substantiated. By this the trust-building process for both consumers and businesses that rely on certificates and for service providers would be supported, and thus, the wide acceptance of electronic signatures would be promoted.

It becomes obvious from the submitted Opinion that the Committee of the Regions stresses mainly on the protection of consumers and business, rather than on the market development and the readiness of the CSPs to undertake the specific liabilities as would be imposed should the Directive is enacted[514].

Following the remarks and opinions of different authorities in charge, an Amended Proposal to the European Parliament and Council Directive on a Common Framework for Electronic Signatures the Commission was issued, which addressed the Parliament in a perfunctory manner and stated that the Proposal introduces liability rules for the CSP in order to support the trust-building process for both

---

[512] The original text of the opinion on the liability could be found in section 3.6.: "*Article 6.* With regard to liability, this article prescribes a set of obligations for the certification service provider, who must ensure the information is accurate, comply with the provisions of the directive, and check that the certificate holder and certifier fulfil the necessary technical and technological requirements. The article also lays down exemptions from liability in the case of mistakes in the original information, and provides for the possibility of limiting both the uses of the certificate and the sum certified."

[513] Opinion of the Committee of the Regions on the 'Proposal for a European Parliament and Council Directive on a common framework for electronic signatures' (1999/C 93/06) - http://europa.eu.int/information_society/topics/ebusiness/ecommerce/8epolicy_elaw/law_ecommerce/lega l/1signatures/index_en.htm

[514] To a contrast – one of the main problem stressed by the American experts and academics was the risk of closing the market of services in open PKI due to levying of too heavy liabilities to the CAs. Most of the American authors also stressed on the balance between the allocation of the liability between the users and the CAs. See Goldman, E., Maher, T., Biddle, B., *ibid.*

consumers and businesses that rely on the certificates[515]. On the basis of the proposal, the CSP will, in particular, be liable for the validity of a certificate's content[516].

In the Report on the Communication from the Commission to the Council, the European Parliament, the Economic and Social Committee and the Committee of the Regions on Ensuring Security and Trust in Electronic Telecommunication - Towards a European framework for Digital Signatures and Encryption of the Committee on Legal Affairs and Citizens' Rights,[517] it is noted that a solid regulation of liability is essential for achieving confidence in the use of cryptographic products, but believes that *for the time being there is no need for supplementary rules on liability at the European level, given that the present rules in this field are still adequate, although this does not mean that Member States may not draw up supplementary rules on liability.* The Committee advises that introduction of supplementary rules in the national legislations of the Member States may be allowed, as long as this does not create any obstacles to the import of goods and services from other Member States. Thus, the Committee advises the Commission to keep an eye on the developments in this field, and, if necessary, to propose appropriate supranational measures on a European level[518].

The Report expresses a view on the clear assessment of the Committee on Legal Affairs and Citizens' Rights about the lack of necessity for supplementary liability

---

[515] Amended Proposal for a European Parliament and Council Directive on a common framework for electronic signatures, COM (1999) 195 final, 98/0191(COD) - http://europa.eu.int/information_society/topics/ebusiness/ecommerce/8epolicy_elaw/law_ecommerce/lega l/1signatures/index_en.htm.

[516] The amendment refer to Article 6 (3) as follows: "3. Member States shall ensure that a certification service provider may indicate in the qualified certificate limits on the uses of a certain certificate. The certification service provider shall not be liable for damages arising from a contrary use of a qualified certificate which includes limits on its uses."

[517] Report on the communication from the Commission to the Council, the European Parliament, the Economic and Social Committee and the Committee of the Regions on ensuring security and trust in electronic telecommunication - towards a European framework for digital signatures and encryption (COM(97)0503 - C4-0648/97) Committee on Legal Affairs and Citizens' Rights - http://europa.eu.int/information_society/topics/ebusiness/ecommerce/8epolicy_elaw/law_ecommerce/lega l/1signatures/index_en.htm

[518] The original text of the opinion of the Committee on Legal Affairs and Citizens' Rights to the liability rules and the opinions provided by the s: "Noted that a water-tight regulation of liability is essential for confidence in the use of cryptographic products, but believes that for the time being *there is no need for supplementary rules on liability at European level, given that the present rules in this field are still adequate, although this does not mean that Member States may not draw up supplementary rules on liability,* related amongst other things to the volume of the contracts, as long as this does not create any obstacles to the importation of goods and services from other Member States, and calls on the Commission to keep a close eye on developments in this field and, if necessary, to propose appropriate European measures."

regulation at the moment of drafting the Directive – an opinion that should be firmly supported[519]. `

On December 13th, 1999, the Directive 1999/93/EC on a Community framework for electronic signatures was adopted and entered into force upon its publication in the Official Journal in January 2000[520].

The historical review of the development of the liability issue reveals quite a deviation of the initial bases of the Commission as noted in the Communication of the Commission entitled "Towards a European Framework for Digital Signatures and Encryption". Identification of the deviations and conclusions thereof would be possible only after a thorough analysis of the enacted provisions of Article 6 of the Directive.

1.3. Scope of the necessary analysis

The Directive aims at harmonizing the legislations of the different Member States by introducing rules regulating the status of the electronic signatures and their legal recognition and the status of the providers of certification and other services related to electronic signatures.

The Directive does not provide any rules regulating the liability of the certificate holders and the third relying parties. Their liability will be regulated by national general or specific liability rules where applicable.

The scope of the Directive covers only the liability of the CSPs before the certificate holders and third relying parties. It does not provide for a comprehensive regulation of the CSP's liability, neither regulates the activity of the different kinds of CSPs apart of those issuing qualified certificates to the public.

As mentioned above, before examining the substance of the issue, attention should be paid to the different terminology used by the Directive in defining the 'Trust Service Providers'. The Directive regulates a subset of TSPs legally defined as 'certification-service-providers'[521]. To the extent that the definition encompasses providers not

---

[519] See Chapter V, section 2.7 and Chapter VI, *supra*.

[520] Directive 1999/93/EC of the European Parliament and the Council of 13 December 1999 on a Community framework for electronic signatures, JOCE L13/12, 19 January 2000.

[521] Article 2, i.(11) of the Directive.

only of certification services, but also of all services related to electronic signatures, the use of this term is not quite precise[522]. Its meaning, to some extent, coincides and is embraced by the term 'trust-service-provider'. Herein below, the terminology used by the Directive will be observed.

Article 6 of the Directive establishes the minimum regime that the Member States should introduce and ensure as statutory regulations in governing only the *liability of the CSPs issuing or guaranteeing qualified certificates to the public.* [523] That is to say the Member States must secure that under the national laws the CSPs shall be held liable at least for the causes envisaged in the Directive. The provision does not restrict Member States in introducing a heavier liability regime and hence to provide priority to the third persons to the detriment of the CSP's interests.[524] Such restrictions could be effective both in the contractual and/or delictual liability regimes. However, the heavier national liability regime, if introduced, should not hamper or place barriers for provision of certification services within the internal market.

Beyond the scope of Article 6, and hence of the Directive, remains the relationship between the CSP and the persons relying on the certificate in respect to the limitation of liability based on effective notice, the possibilities on aggregate limitations, or based on liability caps, etc.

The said rule will be examined in different directions.

a)   First, the subjects targeted by the provision should be determined. In other words, it is necessary to deduct which persons will be liable under those rules.

b)   In order to understand correctly the rule of Article 6, the persons entitled to engage the liability of the CSPs should be analyzed - it should be clearly answered before whom the CSPs will be liable.

c)   Further, the scope of the liability and its nature in view of the relationships between the different actors in the electronic trust service infrastructure should be

---

[522] See Chapter I, sections 2.2.1 and 2.2.2, *supra*.

[523] Norden, A., *ibid.*

[524] See Dumortier, J., et al., *The Legal and Market Aspects of Electronic Signatures in Europe, ibid.*, p.51, also Rinderle, R., *Legal Aspects of Certification Authorities*, A Study – Part of the TIE Project, 2000, (www.tie.org.uk/tie_project.htm), p.48.

determined. Analyzing the duties of the CSPs is of utmost importance for the proper understanding of their liability.

d) Finally, the possibilities for limitation of the liability by different legal instruments should be examined.

2. Liability under the Directive

The Directive provides that CSPs should be liable to the other actors relying on certificates in both contract and tort (delict). The legal doctrine firmly supports this conclusion[525]. Being simultaneously legal grounds for contractual and delictual liability, the liability rules of the Directive reveal a dualistic nature[526].

Not all relationships and respective liability arising thereof are covered by the specific liability regime, established by the Directive. It regulates only the relations between the CSP and the certificate holders and between the CSP and the third relying parties. It does not address the member states rules regulating the relationships and hence liability between the different CSPs and other TSPs (unless being third relying parties), neither on the liability arising from the relationship between the CSP and the third damaged parties who are not relying on the certificate, but suffering damages thereof – the "victims"[527]. These will be subject to national regulation[528].

Under national general contract rules, the liability of the certificate holder before the CSP will be regulated, as far as the legal relationship between them arises under a contract. The reasons for such liability exposure could be numerous (e.g. the intentional provision of inaccurate or false information or data, etc.)[529].

The Directive further does not cover the liability exposure of the certificate holder to the relying party and *vice versa*. The certificate holder could, for example, intentionally or negligently provide inaccurate information to the CSP that results in the issuance of a qualified certificate intending to mislead the relying party to perform certain acts,

---

[525] See Harrison, R., *PKI: The Risks of Being Trusted, ibid.*; also European Commission, Digital Signatures: A Survey of Law and Practice in the European Union, Report I, Part 4, *ibid.*, p.p. 111-114.

[526] See *infra* section 4.2. While the Directive liability rules are transposed into the Bulgarian legislation, the said opinion is supported by Kalaydjiev, A., Belazelkov, B., Dimitrov, G., et al., *ibid.*, p. 248.

[527] Smedinghoff, T., *ibid.*, p. 22.

[528] Thoroughly analysed in Chapter I, section 2.2.5.3 , *supra*.

[529] See *supra* Chapter I, section 2.2..5.1, *supra*.

etc[530]. The relationship between the certificate holder and the third relying party could be based both on contract, or not[531]. They will be governed respectively by the national contract or tort rules.

Beyond the scope of the Directive also remains the regulation of the liability of the certificate holder and the relying party towards the CSP[532], the liability of the CSP towards third *bona fidei* parties[533], the liability of the CSP towards the impersonated persons[534], the liability of the impostor towards the CSP[535], etc. All these relationships and the liability arising thereof will be governed by the national liability rules on contract or tort.

2.1. Relationship between the CSP and the certificate holder

As already mentioned the relationships between the CSP and the certificate holder are contractual[536]. This concept has been undisputable so far in theory and the respective national laws[537]. However, certain wrongful behaviour might constitute, at one and the same time, the non-fulfilment of contractual obligations and conduct of tort. Under different jurisdictions the concurrence of claims would be resolved according to the national rules allowing or not choosing the way of defence[538].

The very Directive provides a clear direction on contractual grounds for the relationship. Annex II (k) rules that the CSP is obliged to disclose certain information *"before entering into a contractual relationship with a person seeking a certificate to support his electronic signature …"*

---

[530] For more details about the relations and the liability between the subscriber and the relying party and between the subscriber to unrelated third party see ETSI 101456 V1.1.1 (2000-12) Policy Requirements of CA, Annex I, p. 37.

[531] On the opposite opinion Norden, A. Liability of CSP under the Directive, *ibid.*

[532] See respectively Chapter I, sections 2.2.5.1 and 2.2.5.2 *supra.*

[533] See Chapter I, section 2.2.5.3.2 *supra.*

[534] See Chapter I, section 2.2.5.3.1 *supra.*

[535] *Ibid.*

[536] See Chapter I, section 2.2.5.1 *supra.*

[537] Article 36 of the Slovenian Electronic Commerce and Electronic Signatures Act; §12 of the Qualified Electronic Signatures Act of Sweden; Annex II (k) of the Electronic Commerce Act 2000 of Ireland; Article 23 of the Bulgarian Law on Electronic Document and Electronic Signature, etc.

[538] On concurrence of claims see Chapter II, section 2.3 *supra.*

The Directive does not rule a specific regime for the contracts to be established by the Member States. On the contrary – Recital 13 clearly envisages that the Directive *"does not seek to harmonize national rules concerning contract law, particularly the formation and performance of contracts ..."* Further, Article 1 (2) provides that it does not cover aspects related to the conclusion and validity of contracts or other legal obligations where there are requirements as regards the form, prescribed by national or Community law, nor does it affect the rules and limits contained in national or Community law governing the use of documents.

However, by providing a special minimum liability regime in Article 6 and particular obligations in the Annexes for the CSPs, the Directive establishes directions on implementing national imperative rules concerning:

a)   the obligations of the CSPs towards the certificate holders and hence specific liability grounds;

b)   delimiting the possibilities of the CSPs to manage their liability by imposing an obligatory minimum regime.

Therefore, the particularities of the liability of the CSP towards the certificate holder under the Directive could be viewed in its *differentia specifica* contractual nature.

The question of whether the certificate holder falls within the scope of Article 6 of the directive is clarified *infra*.[539]

2.2. Relationship between the CSPs and the relying parties under the Directive.

The relationship between the CSP and the relying parties will be subject to regulation by the Directive, despite their nature[540]. The Directive provides indirect clues in this respect.

With respect to the contractual liability, however, complications could arise in view of the fact that the minimum Directive's liability rules cannot be applied *per se* to the cases when a contract between the CSP and the relying party has been executed.

---

[539] See section 4.1, *infra*.

[540] On the possibility to be established contractual relationship between the relying party and the CSP see Chapter I, section 2.2.5.2 *supra*.

None of the CSP's duties pursuant to Article 6 could be regarded as contractual obligations of the CSP towards the relying party. It is doubtful whether the "failure to register revocation" under Article 6 (2) of the Directive could be undertaken as a contractual obligation towards the relying party. The main duty of the CSP under such a contract would be to provide information[541], i.e. the CSP would be contractually liable for "not providing information" or "providing untrue information" but not for "failure to register revocation". The same conclusion could be made for the liability grounds prescribed in Article 6 (1).

The CSP may not take advantage of the possibility to contractually limit its liability towards the relying party beyond the transposed liability clauses of the Directive. The rules of the Directive as transposed into the national legislations should be considered mandatory[542].

3. Liable Persons

Who will be liable under Article 6 (1) and (2)?

The above mentioned rules do not regulate the liability regime of all CSPs. They only cover the regime of the certification-service-providers issuing or guaranteeing qualified certificates to the public.

Who are these CSPs?

a)   The scope of Article 6 (1) and (2) covers only the certification-service-providers *strictu sensu*, in other words, only CSPs providing CA services[543] notwithstanding whether this service is outsourced or not.

b)   These would only be certification-service-providers under the meaning of Annex II of the Directive[544]. They should meet the requirements of the said Annex, e.g.:

---

[541] By providing information service the CSP would be considered an information society service provider – its activity is subject to regulation of the national rules transposing Directive 2000/31/EC on E-commerce. See *infra* Chapter IV, section 6. See also Lodder, A., Kaspersen, H., eDirectives: Guide to European Law on E-commerce, Kluwer International, The Netherlands, 2002, p.82.

[542] See section 6, *infra*.

[543] See Rinderle, R., *ibid.*, p.48

[544] See Dumortier, J., Kelm, S., Nilsson, H., Skouma, G., Van Eecke, P., *ibid.*, p.52

1. to demonstrate the reliability necessary for providing certification services;

2. to ensure the operation of a prompt and secure directory and a secure and immediate revocation service;

3. to ensure that the date and time when a certificate is issued or revoked can be determined precisely;

4. to verify, by appropriate means in accordance with national law, the identity and, if applicable, any specific attributes of the person to whom a qualified certificate is issued;

5. to employ personnel who possess the expert knowledge, experience, and qualifications necessary for the services provided, in particular, competence at the managerial level, expertise in electronic signature technology and familiarity with proper security procedures; they must also apply administrative and management procedures which are adequate and correspond to recognized standards;

6. to use trustworthy systems and products which are protected against modification and ensure the technical and cryptographic security of the processes supported by them;

7. to take measures against forgery of certificates, and, in cases where the certification-service-provider generates signature-creation data, to guarantee the confidentiality during the process of generating such data;

8. to maintain sufficient financial resources to operate in conformity with the requirements laid down in the Directive, in particular, to bear the risk of liability for damages, for example, by obtaining appropriate insurance;

9. to record (even electronically) all the relevant information, concerning the qualified certificate for an appropriate period of time, in particular for the purpose of providing evidence of certification for the purposes of legal proceedings;

10. not to store or copy signature-creation data of the person to whom the certification-service-provider provided key management services;

11. before entering into a contractual relationship with a person seeking a certificate to support his electronic signature, to inform that person by a durable means of communication of the precise terms and conditions regarding the use of the

certificate, including any limitations on its use, the existence of a voluntary accreditation scheme and procedures for complaints and dispute settlement. Such information, which may be transmitted electronically, must be in writing and in readily understandable language. Relevant parts of this information must also be made available upon request to third parties relying on the certificate;

12. to use trustworthy systems to store certificates in a verifiable form so that:

➢   only authorized persons can make entries and changes,

➢   information can be checked for authenticity,

➢   certificates are publicly available for retrieval in only those cases for which the certificate-holder's consent has been obtained, and

➢   any technical changes compromising these security requirements are apparent to the operator.

An interesting question arises in relation to the cases when the certification provider has issued a qualified certificate meeting the requirements of Annex I, but the very provider does not meet the requirements of Annex II. Would the provider be held liable under Article 6? The answer to this question should be positive and the provision of Article 6 should be broadly interpreted.

This conclusion has been reached, considering the fact that if we assume the contrary, than any CSP issuing or guaranteeing qualified certificates could avoid liability by pretending it does not meet a given requirement of Annex II. The interests of the relying parties and of the certificate holders should be given priority to the ones of the CSP that has formally issued or guaranteed a qualified certificate. The relying parties and the certificate holders are not in a position to verify whether the CSP meets the requirements of Annex II, for example – "to maintain sufficient financial resources" or "to employ personnel who possess the necessary expert knowledge". They may possess no qualified knowledge to do that. Furthermore they have no rights to request proofs of evidence from the CSP for meeting the statutory requirements nor have they rights to supervise the activity of the CSP (which is normaly a state competence). The relying parties and the certificate holders could only check the fact of whether the certificate meets the requirements of Annex I. They could easily verify, for example, whether the certificate holds "an indication whether it is issued as qualified" (Annex I (a)) or whether "limits for the value of transactions for which the certificate can be used" are set (Annex I (j)). These indications are easiliy verifiable.

The certificate holder could check them at the moment of acceptance of the certificate issued. The relying party should make a verification each time when it receivs a signed message supported by a qualified certificate. The conformity assessment of the CSP's activity with the requirements of Annex II could be performed only *a posteriori* by supervising bodies within the meaning of Article 3, i.(3) of the Directive[545]. Under this rule each member state shall ensure the establishment of an appropriate system that allows for supervision of certification-service-providers which are established on its territory and issue qualified certificates to the public. Nonetheless how the supervision is performed, it is considered to be a state competence for controlling the activities of the CSPs. Should a given CSP fail to meet the requirements set forth by the law, it would be subject to fines or other sanctions as established in the different countries. The users of certification services feel safe and trust the CSPs knowing that the state supervises the activity of the CSPs on an ongoing base. Therefore, since the verification whether the CSP meets *de facto* the requirements of Annex II lays out of the due care of the users, the CSP would not release itself of civil liability under Article 6 if he does not met the requirements of Annex II.

Opposite doctrinarian views to the presented above conclusion exist. A team of EESSI experts in their Final Report dated 20th July 1999[546] found that the liability regime of Article 6 is applicable "only for the CSP *in the sense of Annex II*, issuing certificates to the public in the sense of Annex I". That is to say these scholars assume that Article 6 is applicable only to CSPs that meet the requirements of Annex II (*"CSP in the sense of Annex II"*). Having in mind the above stated arguments, it should be deducted that this conclusion could not be supported. A CSP that has issued qualified certificate to the public will be held liable under Article 6 of the Directive despite of whether it meets or not the requirements of Annex II.

c)   Article 6 (1) covers those CSPs that issue qualified certificates. The requirements for a certificate to be considered 'qualified', are provided in Annex I. If the CSP has not issued a certificate as qualified or has issued a certificate that does not meet the requirements of Annex I, then a question arises whether the certification-service-provider can be held liable under the regime of Article 6?

[545] Dumortier, J., Kelm, S., Nilsson, H., Skouma, G., Van Eecke, P., *ibid.*, p.39

[546] EESSI, Final Report of the EESSI Expert Team, *ibid.*, p.25

Issuing a certificate 'as qualified' has a technical aspect. The fields in the certificate are defined by a special formal language known as ASN.1 (Abstract Syntax Notation One)[547]. The applications usually read the formal descriptions and visualize the values set. The industry standards define that marking of the certificate 'as qualified' could be done by setting of one of its fields[548]. Once this field is set the software application of the users identifies the certificate 'as qualified' and performs given actions depending on its functionality. The indication could be also identified by mere opening the certificate with a respective viewer[549].

It is reasonable to assume that those CSPs that have issued certificates *as* a non-qualified cannot be held liable under this regime[550]. This conclusion is deducted *per argumentum a contrario* of the rule. The meaning of the provision of Article 6 (1) is clear – the liability regime prescribed will be applicable only to CSPs issuing qualified certificates or guaranteeing such.

But what about the CSPs that have issued a certificate indicating that it is qualified, but the certificate actually lacks, for example, its identity code, or the identification of the State where the CSP is established?

It could be concluded that the liability regime of Article 6 (1) would be fully applicable to those CSPs. A careful examination of the wording of the rule undoubtedly supports that conclusion. The European legislator has envisaged that the CSP shall be liable for causing damage to any entity "by issuing a certificate *as qualified*", i.e. the certificate does not necessarily need to be qualified by meeting the requirements of Annex I[551]. Furthermore the provision of Article 6 (1) (b) clearly states that the CSP

---

[547] Abstract Syntax Notation One (ASN.1) is a formal language for abstractly describing messages to be exchanged among an extensive range of applications involving the Internet, intelligent network, cellular phones, ground-to-air communications, electronic commerce, secure electronic services, interactive television, intelligent transportation systems, Voice Over IP and others. It has streamlined encoding rules. The ITU-T X.509 Recommendation specifies a certificate using ASN.1 and encodes it using DER. For more information on ASN see the ASN.1 Information Site at http://asn1.elibel.tm.fr/.

[548] See ETSI TS 101 862 V1.2.1 (2001-06) Qualified Certificate Profile; IETF Qualified Certificate Profile, RFC 3039 [4] и RFC 2459 [3] also ITU-T Recommendation X.509 [2]. The industry standards define that marking of the certificate 'as qualified' could be done by check of the boolean critical field "esi4-qcStatement-1".

[549] While most of the software tools does not provide for possibility to read and identify properly this field (ETSI TS 101 862 was adopted only in June, 2001) the notification is sometimes done by making relevant note in any of the non-mandatory fields (like OU) – see the CP of Bankservice (www.b-trust.org).

[550] Ridnerle, R., *ibid.*, p.48

[551] See Lodder, A., Kaspersen, H., *eDirectives: Guide to European Union Law on E-Commerce*, Kluwer Law International, The Netherlands, 2002, p.57, also Rinderle, R., *ibid.*, p.48; also Dumortier, J., Kelm, S., Nilsson, H., Skouma, G., Van Eecke, P., *ibid.*, p.52

shall be liable for damage "... *as regards the fact that the certificate contains all the details prescribed for a qualified certificate*". The certificate holder and the relying party usually do not have the means and enough technical knowledge to control whether the certificate is 'qualified' or not under the meaning of the Directive. They usually trust the attestation of the CSP just because the certificate is issued as qualified[552].

d)   The scope of Article 6 (1) covers not only CSPs that have issued certificates as qualified, but also those that have *guaranteed* certificates as qualified to the public.

The conclusions stated above should be considered fully valid for these CSPs. However, there are certain particularities with respect to the interpretation of the exact meaning of the rule.

Firstly, the certificates should be guaranteed to the public and not for closed group purposes, and secondly, they should be guaranteed '*as qualified*' but the certificates do not necessarily need to meet *de facto* the requirements of Annex I[553].

The figure of '*guaranteeing of certificate*' is used further in Article 7 (1) (b) whereby the Directive rules that Member States shall ensure that certificates which are issued as qualified to the public by a CSP established in a third country are recognized as legally equivalent to certificates issued by a CSP established within the Community, if a CSP which is established within the Community and fulfils the requirements laid down in the Directive, *guarantees* the certificate.

The notion 'guaranteeing' should be clearly analyzed while the Directive does not specify exactly how such a 'guarantee' could be provided. It is of no doubt that the conventional meaning of the word known in the legal theory as a 'security' cannot be used, but rather proper interpretation should be searched in the semantics of the word and in the peculiarities of the PKI.

In the first place, a guaranteeing in the terms of the Directive would mean the recognition of other CSPs operational or root public keys. This concept is known in

---

[552] Lodder, A., Kaspersen, H., *ibid.*, p.58.

[553] See *supra* note 551.

PKI, depending on the model chosen, as 'cross-certification'[554] or 'bridge-certification'[555]. In the terms of building a hierarchical, cross (mesh), or bridge certification, a chain of trust is developed within one or different PKIs. Thus, 'guarantee' in this respect, will be considered the certification of the public key certificates by or between CAs. Should a CSP undertake to 'guarantee' the qualified certificates to the public, issued by another CSP, they would be jointly liable within the limits of liability of the issuing CSP[556].

However, the scope of Article 6 goes beyond the simple cross-certification[557]. The reason for such a conclusion is given in the provision of Article 7 (1) (b). In such a sense, the 'guaranteeing' could encompass any other legal means or instrument of providing 'security' given that the CSP acts according to certain national rules, particularly by issuing qualified certificates to the public. The research shows that such a regime of 'guaranteeing' is established in some jurisdictions. For example Article 44 of the Bulgarian EDESA provides that a foreign certificate shall be recognized on the territory of Bulgaria, provided a Bulgarian certification-service-provider, that has been accredited or that has been registered, *has taken an obligation to be liable for actions or failure to take actions by the certification-service-provider, established in another country, in cases falling under Article 29*[558]. This fact shall be ascertained by the Bulgarian national supervisory body – The Communications Regulation Commission (CRC). Only upon ascertaining this fact, both the certificate of the foreign certification-service-provider, for which the liability has been undertaken, and the certificate of the Bulgarian certification-service-provider that has undertaken the liability and conditions upon which the liability has been undertaken, shall be entered into a special register kept by the CRC. No cross-certification is needed. The Bulgarian CSP shall be jointly liable with the foreign CSP for the performance of the obligations as set forth by Article 29 of

---

[554] See Kalaydjiev, A., Belazelkov, B., Dimitrov, G., et al., *ibid.*, p.201. See also Turnbull, J., Cross-Certification and PKI Policy Network, Entrust, 2000, p. 3 (http://www.entrust.com/resources/download.cfm/21143/_cross_certification.pdf); Network Certification Authority WG, *Cross Certification Guidelines*, Japan, (http://www.ecom.jp/ecom_e/report/summary/wg08-2.pdf); Government of Canada PKI Cross-Certification Policy (www.cio-dpi.gc.ca/pki-icp/crosscert/crosscert_e.asp).

[555] See Polk, W., Hasting, N., *Bridge Certification Authorities: Connecting B2B Pubic Key Infrastructures*, National Institute of Standards and Technology (http://csrc.nist.gov/pki/documents/B2B-article.pdf).

[556] On the joint liability in contracts see Kalaydjiev., A., *ibid.*, p.p.482-498, in tort – Van Gerven, et al., *ibid.*, p.430.

[557] Lodder, A., Kaspersen, H., *ibid.*, p.58.

[558] Article 29 of Bulgarian EDESA is transposing the minimum liability regime of Article 6 of the Directive, but even goes beyond by establishing more grounds for engaging of CSPs' liability. See Dumortier, J., et al., *The Legal and Market Aspects of Electronic Signatures in Europe, ibid.*

EDESA only upon a unilateral statement towards the regulatory body and the public[559].

e) The rule of Article 6 further addresses only the CSPs issuing or guaranteeing certificates *to the public.'* certificates in 'a publicly accessible directory'[560]. Other authors consider that the expression 'issuing to the public' should be interpreted as referring to certification services that are open to verifiers that *do not have a prior relationship with the CA.*[561]

The interpretations in such respect are not correct. Recital (16) of the Directive defines the scope of t private law between a specified number of participants. Further, Recital (16) envisages, that "the freedom of parties *to agree among themselves* on the terms and conditions under which they accept electronically signed data, should be respected to the extent allowed by national law". In this way, the Directive clearly delineates the meaning of expressions 'to the public' and 'not to the public'. In a case when one of the parties issues certificates to itself or to its contractual party, to be used within the relationship among them, no issuance 'to the public' will be present. In this case, even if the issuing party maintains a publicly available register and provides public access to any interested person, this will not mean the certificates are issued 'to the public', despite the fact that no prior relationship between the party accessing the publicly available certificates exist. A CSP may be considered to be issuing qualified certificates to the public if the certificates are not restricted to uses governed by voluntary agreements under private law *among* the participants.[562]

In such a sense, the explanatory memorandum to the draft Directive states that *"there are obvious applications of electronic signature technology in closed environments, e.g. a company's local area network, or a bank system. Certificates and electronic signatures are also used for authorization purposes, e.g. to access a private account. Within the constraints of national law, the principle of contractual freedom enables contracting parties to agree among themselves the terms and conditions under which they do business, e.g. accept electronic signatures. In these areas there is no need for regulation".*[563]

---

[559] See Kalaydjiev, A., Belazelkov, B., Dimitrov, G., et al., *Ibid.*, p.p. 334-340.

[560] Lodder, A., Kaspersen, H., *ibid.*, p.58

[561] Rinderle, R., *ibid.*, p. 50, also Lodder, A., Kaspersen, H., *ibid.*, p.58

[562] See ETSI TS 101 456 V1.1.1 (2000-12), Annex A, p.35.

[563] See Proposal for a European Parliament and Council Directive on a common framework for electronic signatures: Communication from the Commission to the European Parliament, the Council, the Economic and Social Committee and the Committee of the Regions; COM (98) 297 final, Official Journal C 325 of 23/10/98. Cit. on Dumortier, J., Kelm, S., Nilsson, H., Skouma, G., Van Eecke, P., *ibid.*, p.28.

The liability of a vast group of CSPs remains beyond the scope of the regulation of the Directive.

a)   In the first place, outside the scope of Article 6 (1) remain the certification-service-providers that do not issue or guarantee certificates to the public.[564] As such will be considered banking or financial institutions, companies and organizations, etc., that issue certificates within closed systems - to their customers, employees or counteragents for the purposes of their internal or business correspondence and relationships.

b)   Article 6 (1) does not establish a liability regime of those certification-service-providers that do not issue or guarantee certificates. As it became obvious from Chapter I, the notion "certification-service-provider" under the Directive has a broad sense. It encompasses not only the persons that issue certificates, but also all other entities or legal or natural persons that provide other services related to electronic signatures[565]. Article 6 is meant to regulate the liability of those providers that *issue* or *guarantee* certificates. Therefore registration service providers, directory service providers, key escrow service providers, key generation providers, archival service providers, etc., when these *do not issue* or *guarantee* certificates, will not be covered by this regime. However, the Member States are not deprived of introducing a specific liability regime for such providers.

c)   Further all certification-service-providers who issue or guarantee certificates, but not as qualified, remain out of the scope of the rule. Such providers would be those issuing and maintaining certificates for advanced or other electronic signatures[566].

All the above rules will be valid for Article 6 (2).

---

[564] See ETSI TS 101 456 V1.1.1 (2000-12) *Policy requirements for certification authorities issuing qualified certificates*, Annex A (informative) - Potential liability in the use of electronic signatures, 2000, p.36 (http://portal.etsi.org/sec/ts%5F101456v010101p.pdf)

[565] Article 2 (11) of the Directive.

[566] Rinderle, R., *ibid.*, p.49

Apart from the minimum regime prescribed by the Directive, the liability of the certification-service-providers providing certification-services to the public shall be regulated by national rules regarding liability[567].

4. Exposure to Whom?

Article 6 (1) of the Directive provides that by issuing or guaranteeing a certificate as qualified to the public, the CSP shall be liable for causing damages to *"any entity or natural or legal person that reasonably relies on that certificate"*.

In order to understand correctly this rule, the relationship between the CSP and the other actors who might rely on the certificate should be analyzed.

The liability of the CSP will not be exposed to all legal subjects, but only to those that reasonably rely on the certificate, i.e., that participate and have a role in the electronic signature infrastructure by having trust in the attestations made in the certificate and its validity.

4.1. Liability before the certificate holder

Will the CSP be liable before the certificate holder under Article 6 (1)?

Some authors find that the scope of Article 6 (1) excludes certificate holders[568]. They state that as far as the relationship between the CSP and the certificate holder are contractual, the liability of the CSP would be governed by the general civil liability rules. Furthermore, they find that the rule of Annex II (k) provides that the CSP needs to communicate limitations on liability, which seems to indicate that this is different from art 6. Following that position, they deduct that the rule of Article 6 (1) is intended to provide protection only to third relying parties because the certificate holder would, in any case, be protected by the general liability rules.

---

[567] See Recital 22 of the Directive.

[568] Norden, A., *ibid.*

Other authors also try to analyze the issue, but do not provide a clear answer on whether the certificate holder should be protected by Article 6 (1)[569]. They identify that it is not quite clear from the wording of Article 6 (1) if the certificate holder is included or not, and provide some arguments pointing in both directions. They see that on one hand, if the certificate holder enters into a contract with the CA regarding the issuance of the certificate, it could be argued that the liability of the CA to the certificate holder is governed by the terms of that contract or the national contract law. Thus, the specific liability rules do not apply to the certificate holder as far as they do not apply to closed systems and therefore to contractual situations[570]. On the other hand, these authors find that another possibility exists – to treat the liability provisions of the Directive as a default rule and as far as there are no prevalent contractual regulations in the CSP – certificate holder relationship, then Article 6 (as nationally transposed) would apply. However, they see this approach inconsistent with the specification of the liability provisions as 'a minimum' in Article 6[571]. Thirdly, these authors consider that the rule of Article 6 should be regarded as a minimum liability rule, thus the certificate holder cannot be deprived by contractual terms, but later provide a contest that one of the aims of the Directive is to ensure the security of the certificate market through a concept of 'liability instead of supervision'[572].

It cannot be supported that the will of the European legislator was to exclude the certificate holder from the scope of minimum liability protection as established by Article 6 (1). We should look at the very purpose of the Directive and the difference in the approaches of the different jurisdictions in providing contractual freedom. Some national laws leave broader rights for the parties to negotiate exemption of liability, while others provide limitations[573]. The Directive aims at providing *minimum liability statutory requirements* to be introduced by the Member States in order to have equal minimum protection for *all entities and persons that rely on qualified certificates* in the EU States[574]. The parties would not be able to negotiate an exemption of liability

---

[569] Lodder, A., Kaspersen, H., *eDirectives: Guide to European Law on E-commerce*, Kluwer Law International, The Netherlands, 2002, p.57. The chapter on liability is based on a report drafted by Regina Rinderle, researcher at K.U.Leuven ICRI in the context of the TIE project (www.tie.org.uk/tie_project.htm).

[570] *Ibid.*, p.59.

[571] *Ibid.*

[572] *Ibid.*

[573] See Chapter II, section 5, *supra*.

[574] Communication from the Commission COM (97) 503: Ensuring security and trust in electronic communication: "Towards a European Framework for Digital Signatures and Encryption", available at http://www.swiss.ai.mit.edu/6805/articles/crypto/eu-october-8-97.html, Section 3.2.

beyond the established limits, unless negotiated under the hypotheses of paragraphs (3) and (4). If the legislation provides such minimum liability rules, they should be of 'imperative' nature so the parties cannot deviate from them. If they, irrespective to this, agree otherwise, then the imperative rules would apply[575].

Apart from the said above, the norm of paragraph (5) of Article 6, which unequivocally supports the conclusion, should be analyzed. As we have already clarified, the CSP and the certificate holder enter into a contractual relationship for the certificate issuance. If the certificate holder, as a contractual party, falls beyond the scope of Article 6 (1) then the norm of paragraph (5) becomes senseless providing that the provisions of *paragraphs 1 to 4* shall be without prejudice to Council Directive 93/13/EEC of 5 April 1993 on unfair terms in *consumer contracts*. It is clear that the Directive envisages that there might be a contractual relationship between the CSP and the certificate holder, being a consumer, and the terms of this contract cannot contain unfair terms.

In this respect, it is reasonable to assume that the scope of Article 6 covers the CSP's liability with regard to the certificate holder.

The contrary would lead to the erroneous conclusion that the CSP would be able to widely limit its liability by the very contract and there would not be statutory guarantees for protecting the interests of the certificate holder.

Furthermore, by excluding the certificate holder from the scope of Article 6 (1) it appears that as far as the Directive provides protection for the third relying parties by introducing a minimum liability regime, their interests will be better protected than the interests of the certificate holders. This does not seem to be the case. Giving an example would be appropriate to support the assertions of this work:

Let us assume that a certain jurisdiction provides a special validity form for certain acts – an electronic document signed with a qualified electronic signature[576]. The certificate holder has requested issuance of a qualified certificate for using it to sign a formal contract. The CSP has issued the certificate, but due to its negligence, say the name of the state where the CSP is established is omitted on the certificate (Annex I (b)). Due to the fact that the certificate omits one of its details, it cannot be

---

[575] See *supra* note 158, also Chapter II, section 2.2.5.1, *supra*.

[576] See Article 7 (3) of the Bulgarian Law on Electronic Document and Electronic Signatures.

considered as 'qualified'. Therefore if the certificate is used to support the certificate holder's signature, the contract between the latter and the relying party would be null due to the lack of the prescribed validity form. The certificate holder would suffer damages and loose profits because of the CSP's negligence. He is deprived of concluding a binding contract.

Is the certificate holder suffering damages due to the fact that the certificate does not contain all the details prescribed? Yes. Has the CSP issued the certificate 'as qualified'? Yes. Is there a missing mandatory field as ruled by Annex II? Yes. Has the CSP acted negligently? Yes. Is the certificate holder a "person who reasonably relies on that certificate" to enter into a contractual relationship? Yes. Since all these questions deserve a positive answer, it could be implied that there is no any reason to exclude the certificate holder from the scope of Article 6. The notion "*any* person who reasonably relies on that certificate" should not be interpreted strictly in view of the term "relying party" which is broadly used in the theory and different studies and reports. In the cases when the Directive addresses an issue to the "relying party" as a person with which the certificate holder enters into a contractual or other relationship, it uses the term "*third parties relying on the certificate*"[577].

The above conclusion is equally valid for the rule of Article 6 (2).

4.2. Liability before the third relying parties

The other group of persons, the CSP will be liable to pursuant to Article 6 (1) and (2) are the third relying parties other than the certificate holder. These are the parties with which the certificate holder enters in a relationship and uses its certificate to support its qualified electronic signature.

Several studies can be found to treat the liability between the CSP and the relying party[578]. In general, all the authors reach the same conclusion – the CSP will be undoubtedly liable towards the relying party under the Directive. The general view is that the nature of this liability is non-contractual (delictual)[579].

---

[577] See Directive, Annex II (k) *in fine*.

[578] See ECOM, Proposal for Liability of Certification Authorities, *ibid*; also Norden, A., Liability of CSP under the Directive, Speech, *ibid*; also European Commission, Digital Signatures: A Survey of Law and Practice in the European Union, *ibid*; also EESSI, Final Report of the EESSI Expert Team, *ibid*.

[579] See Chapter I, section 2.2.5.2, *supra*.

On the other hand, as already mentioned above, in almost all jurisdictions the relationship between the relying party and the CSP could be "dressed" in the form of a contract. Therefore, the liability would be contractual.[580]

Does Article 6 (1) and (2) of the Directive cover both regimes? The answer to this question should be positive. In this respect the rules of Article 6 reveal a dualistic nature.

If no contract is enforced, Article 6, as transposed, would apply to any wrongful behaviour of the CSP falling within the scope of the outlined duties that has caused damages to the relying party. The norm establishes criteria that should be considered requirements for due care in provision of certification services under the Directive. Any adverse wrongful behaviour to the prescribed criteria that causes damages would trigger the liability of the CSP because the latter would be considered non-abiding to a particular obligation "not-to-damage". Therefore Article 6 will have the character of a tort rule.

Should a binding contract[581] between the CSP and the relying party be enforced, the liability will be attached on contractual grounds, i.e. on Article 6 as nationally transposed. In this respect, they will have the nature of mandatory rules regulating specific contractual relationships. Any contrary opinion makes the presence of Article 6 senseless. If we assume that it does not apply to contractual relationships with the relying party, then the CSP can easily contractually release itself of any specific liability within the limits of the general national liability regime to the detriment of the relying party[582]. That was definitely not the idea of the European legislator in introducing a specific liability regime. Member States are obliged to make sure that a CSP issuing qualified certificates to the public is liable for damage caused to *any person who reasonably relies on the certificate*[583] both in contract and not. Therefore should the contract is enforced, the parties may not deviate from the prescriptions of Article 6. The imperative nature of the rules will prevent such a scenario. They will be considered as mandatory part of the contract despite the will of the parties'[584] and

---

[580] On the same opinion, see Biddle, B., *Legislating Market Winners, ibid.*

[581] See section 2.2, *supra.*

[582] See Chapter II, section 5, *supra.*

[583] EESSI, The Final Report of the EESSI Expert Team, *ibid.*, p.22.

[584] On the nature of the rule of Article 6 see section 4.1, *supra.*

regardless of whether the duties of the CSP as outlined in Article 6 (1) and (2) are contractually introduced accordingly or adversely.

That issue cannot bring difficulties for the transposition of Article 6 (1) and (2). Although the liability exposure of CSP to the third relying party is based on contractual or delictual grounds under the respective national law, the Directive establishes the minimum regime for this liability. Member States are directed to establish such a minimum liability regime. Provided the respective jurisdiction recognizes the possibility of the relying party to enter into a contractual relationship with the CSP (e.g. for requesting information regarding the certificate or for duties coinciding formally with the liability grounds of Article 6 (1) and (2)), then it is a duty of the national legislative body to transpose the provision of Article 6 in a way that would keep its protective shield for the relying parties in both a contractual and delictual relationship with the CSP.

Besides, from the point of view of national jurisdictions, an issue can arise when one and the same rule would constitute grounds for both contractual and non-contractual liability for one and the same behaviour[585]. This concept is known in legal theory as "concurrence of claims"[586].

For example: the CSP and the relying parties, within the scope of their contractual freedom, could agree that the CSP while providing information would be liable: as regards the accuracy at the time of issuance of all information contained in the qualified certificate[587] and as regards the fact that the certificate contains all the details prescribed for a qualified certificate; or for assurance that at the time of the issuance of the certificate, the certificate holder identified in the qualified certificate held the signature-creation data corresponding to the signature-verification data given or identified in the certificate; or for assurance that the signature-creation data and the signature-verification data can be used in a complementary manner in cases where the CSP has generated them both; or that the CSP would be held liable if it had failed to register certificate revocation. In such cases the relying party will be entitled to base its liability claim towards the CSP on grounds of the contract. At the same time,

---

[585] In cases when an agreement between the CSP and the relying party is enforced.

[586] Pavlova, M. *General Civil Law*, Vol.I, Sofi-R, 1995 ed., p. 193.

[587] See for example Article 4 of the Relying Party Agreement of GlobalSign at (www.globalsign.be). "GlobalSign recognizing its trusted position shall use best efforts to ensure the Relying Party that information contained in its certificates is accurate and correct. GlobalSign shall take all reasonable steps to ensure the Relying Party that information contained in its records and directories is adequate, i.e. by updating them timely."

however, the relying party may see grounds for engaging the CSP's liability on the particular tort rule (transposing Article 6) while all elements thereof are present – wrongful behaviour, unlawfulness, fault, damages and causality[588].

Would the contractual claim be given priority to the tortious one, or should the damaged relying party be given the freedom of choice to decide on which grounds to base its claim[589]?

Clarity on how to deal with the issue could be derived from the general national liability rules. While the Directive does not provide direct regulation, guidance in this respect is given by Recital (22) – "*certification-service-providers providing certification services to the public are subject to national rules regarding liability*" beyond the specific liability of Article 6. The issue of concurrence in the general civil liability theory and the approaches of the different jurisdictions was already discussed *supra[590]*.

4.3. Liability before the third damaged parties not relying on the certificate

As mentioned above, there might be cases when an impostor could obtain a certificate purporting to be the true holder of the private key either by obtaining it or by using forged or fake identity documents[591]. In such cases, the impersonated persons could suffer damages from the fraudulent usage of their identity.

Does the Directive provide a minimum liability regime for the protection of those persons? The answer to this question is negative. Article 6 (1) and (2) provides the CSP liability exposure only to persons that reasonably *rely* on the certificate. The impersonated damaged persons do not rely on the certificate. They might not even know that their name has been inappropriately used. The persons that rely on the certificate and thus are covered by the Directive in that case would only be *bona fidei* relying persons – i.e. the certificate holder and the third relying party[592].

---

[588] See *supra* Chapter II.

[589] In some jurisdictions, the court states that in situation of "concurrence of claims" the contractual claim precludes the realization of the delictual claim.

[590] See Chapter II, section 2.3, *supra*.

[591] See Chapter I, section 2.2.5.3.1, *supra*.

[592] See sections 4.1 and 4.2, *supra*.

4.4. Reasonable reliance

The certificate holder and the third relying parties might not in all cases hold the CSP liable under Article 6 (1) and (2). They should have *reasonably* relied on the certificate.

The rule of Article 6 implies a construction based on the theory of reliance, i.e. what is normally expected by the relying person based on his awareness of all circumstances related to the certificate and its usage[593].

Some authors exclude the certificate holder from among the persons that the reasonable reliance should refer to, while the relationship between them and the CSP are contractual, and the liability of the CSP in general is governed by the terms of the contract or by the national contract law only. They consider that the liability of the CSP under Article 6 does not apply to the certificate holder. As already justified above, the signature holders and the third relying parties should be considered 'any person relying on the certificate' under the meaning of Article 6 of the Directive[594]. This conclusion refers to all provisions of Article 6.

Where are the limits of the "reasonable reliance"?

4.4.1. Limits of the "reasonable reliance"

4.4.1.1. Reasonable reliance – general criteria

The "reasonable reliance" would differ depending on the person and his relationship with the CSP. One would be the reasonable reliance of the certificate holder, other than the third relying party. One would also be the reasonable reliance of the certificate holder being himself a CSP, and another - if he was a natural person willing to communicate safely by using electronic signature.

If the relying person is mentally diseased and could not understand the meaning and the legal consequences of his behaviour, it would be difficult to assume that he has

---

[593] The theory of reliance is a concept that may be traced back to Ihering's theory of interests. The modern theory of reliance is built by Fuller and Purdue in "*The reliance interest in contract damages*" (46 Yale LJ 52, 1936), later developed by Aliyah, P., *The Basis of Contract*, 46 Harvard LR 553, 1986. *Cit op.* Beale, H., Hartkamp, A., et al., *ibid.*, p.p. 120-122.

[594] See section 4.1 of present chapter, *supra*.

reasonably relied on an obviously erroneous certificate and has performed certain acts.

The reasonableness would depend further on the knowledge of certain facts by the relying persons and their expectations about the usage of the certificate. For example, if the certificate holder has informed the third relying party that his private key was stolen or compromised, that would debar the CSP from its delictual liability of failure to register revocation of the certificate (Article 6 (2)); if the certificate holder has provided the CSP with untrue information about its attribute at the moment of issuing the certificate (for example by using fake identity documents) and the CSP has negligently verified "by appropriate means in accordance with national law" its attributes without having noticed the falsification, it is obvious that the negligent certificate holder cannot engage the CSP's contractual liability by pretending that he has suffered damages due to defects in the certificate (Article 6 (1)).

Furthermore, non-reasonable should be considered any relying party that obtrudes the CSP to provide the certification service. If, for example, the third relying party has requested access to the directory and upon the attempt of the CSP to submit information it becomes obvious that the relying party's systems have installed filters which do not allow the delivery of information from the CSP's server, the latter would not be able to provide the service. Such a relying party would not be able to invoke the CSP's liability, for example, due to damages caused by not timely providing information on the revocation of the certificate.

The above examples show that beyond the reasonable reliance remains the negligence or knowledge of certain facts by the relying persons or acting in a way to obtrude the CSP to perform its obligations. In such cases the possibility of engaging the liability of the CSP would be blocked, even though an act of negligence is present.

4.4.1.2. Reasonable reliance under Article 6 (1)

Should there be no negligence of the certificate holder or the relying party present that could exclude the reasonable reliance, the scope of the 'normal' reasonable care of using e-signatures should be identified. It does not seem to be within the due care of the certificate holder or of the third relying party to require a special care on checking the completeness of the information as included in the certificate or its validity[595].

However, some implications on the scope of a behaviour that should be considered reasonable care could be found in the very rule of Article 6 (1). It provides clearly that the certificate holder and the relying party should check at least whether the certificate is issued *as qualified*. Otherwise, the whole rule of Article 6 would have no sense. Denoting the certificate as such, would make the certificate holder *rely* on that certificate by using it intentionally (i.e. reasonably) to invoke certain legal consequences, namely because the certificate is issued *as qualified* (he would presume that it conforms to Annex I) and thus the e-signature would be considered *as handwritten* (Article 5(2)). The third relying party would *rely* on the certificate to be *qualified* and thus the e-signature to be *as handwritten* by performing a simple control, whether the certificate is issued *as qualified* or not.

The construction of the provision of Article 6 (1) and its logical and systemathical interpretation would also support that conclusion. The CSP shall be held liable for issuing the certificate *as qualified,* envisages paragraph (1), if certain duties had not been fulfilled at a given moment in the past (listed below in three letters). The application of the rule would be possible only after the damage has occurred (the liability can be invoked only after contractual or statutory obligations are not fulfilled and damages have occurred[596]). This means that the parties have had the knowledge that the certificate was issued *as qualified* but have not been aware, for example, that the information contained in the certificate at the time of its issuance was inaccurate, or that the certificate did not contain all the details prescribed for a qualified certificate. If they were aware of those facts (while knowing that the certificate is issued as qualified), they would never have used or trusted the certificate - they would have relied on the certificate unreasonably.

---

[595] See Rinderle, R., *ibid.,* p.51. The author finds that it is questionable if the recipient of the qualified electronic signature can be said to have reasonably relied on the respective certificate if the information specified in Annex I of the Directive is missing. The author gives a priority to the technical knowledge of the person. See also Skouma, G., *ibid.,* p.54

[596] These rules are known in the theory as "secondary rules". See Van Gerven, W., et al., *ibid.,* p.32

4.4.1.3. Reasonable reliance under Article 6 (2)

The above arguments apply to Article 6 (2).

However, the scope of the reasonable reliance of the relying parties under the latter provision is different, because it refers to other types of behaviour due. The examined rule of the Directive refers to damages caused to the relying parties due to the CSP's failure to timely register revocation of the certificate[597].

With respect to the certificate holder, a hypothesis could hardly be seen whereby he would unreasonably rely on the certificate due to the CSP's failure to register revocation. The CSP would always be held liable for such negligent behaviour towards the certificate holder.

In respect to the third relying party, however, the Directive identifies certain duties that could be considered as due in view of assessing whether the relying party has reasonably relied on the certificate. Within such duties falls the requirement that the relying party at least verifies the validity of the certificate by checking the CRL and directory of the CSP. Without such a control, the CSP's liability could hardly be invoked despite the fact of whether he had registered revocation in due time or not. The rule of Article 6 presupposes that the relying party has consulted the directory of the CSP, and having trusted the information entered, has performed certain acts that have caused damages.

4.4.1.4. Reasonable reliance under Article 6 (3) and (4)

The rule of Article 6 (3) and (4) do not refer to reasonable reliance, but they affect indirectly the statutory criteria for reasonableness of the relying parties for the cases in paragraphs (1) and (2).

Thus, the certificate holder should also ascertain the limits of the qualified certificate use and the limits of the value of transactions for which the certificate can be used before using the certificate, regardless of whether this information included in the certificate is accurate or not (Article 6 (1) (a)). The third relying party should also control these facts and not trust the certificate without prior verification. Failure to perform these duties would debar the certificate holder and the relying party from

---

[597] See section 5.2. of present chapter, *infra*.

the right to invoke the CSP's liability on the grounds of Article 6, paragraphs (1) and (2) provided damages have occurred. They should not be considered as persons reasonably relying on the certificate.

Some authors find that it will be up to the courts to decide on whether the relying party has reasonably relied on a certificate if that certificate excludes the liability of the issuer in a respect that is not covered by Article 6 (3) and (4)[598]. Such a finding cannot be supported.

If we assume that the above motivated conclusions are not correct and there is no due care for controlling the limits of the certificate use, then any person might pierce the liability limitation shield of the CSPs as established by paragraphs (3) and (4) by pretending that he had no knowledge of the marked limitations and had no due care of controlling these facts. Obviously this was not the will of the European legislator.

The above does not mean that beyond the analyzed cases it should always be considered that the relying party has reasonably relied on the certificate and thus, the CSP would always be held liable. Besides the explicitly envisaged statutory criteria for reasonable reliance, the dividing line between the reasonable reliance and the non-reasonable should also be searched in determining a more general objective criterion.

4.4.2. Objective criterion

The Directive introduces an objective standard of *reasonable reliance* as a prerequisite for the CSP's liability exposure. The reasonable reliance should be analyzed from the viewpoint of the reasonable trust that a person of ordinary prudence would have in the same or similar circumstances while communicating electronically.[599] In order to establish whether this person has acted reasonably, it should be estimated whether he has assessed the risk and behaved with a degree of care like any other person engaged in the same line of activity would have done. This is known in

---

[598] Rinderle, R., *ibid.*, p.51

[599] Black's Law Dictionary 1265, 6th edition, 1990.

theory and practice in almost all jurisdictions as a "reasonable person" objective standard.[600]

The degree of care determines the *differentia specifica* of this standard in its applicability in the area of the electronic communications. It is proportional to the degree of risk of harm in performing an activity through electronic means and especially within open networks.[601]

In applying the said objective standard, the court should analyze whether a person has reasonably relied on a certificate in respect to all the circumstances and particularities of the case.[602]

Any failure of the relying person with respect to the verification process (e.g. to check the revocation list, to check the limits of use placed on the certificate, to use an insecure viewer, knowledge of certain facts, etc.) may render its reliance on the certificate unreasonable under the circumstances, exempting the CSP of liability under the Directive provisions[603].

4.5. Scope of damage compensation

Under the Directive the relying party should have suffered damages in order to engage the CSP's liability.

What is the scope of these damages?

4.5.1. Material and non-material damages

The rule of Article 6 does not specify the type of damages to be compensated. It refers only to the fact that the CSP shall be liable for "*damages caused*". In my opinion

---

[600] Smedinghoff, T., *ibid* , p. 37.

[601] *Ibid.*, reported *Welsh Mfg. V. Pinkerton's, Inc.*, 474 A.2d 436, 440 (R.I. 1984), *later app.*, 494 A.2d 897 (R.I. 1985); See also *McMillan v. Michigan State Highway Commission*, 344 N.W.2d 26 (Mich. Ct. App. 1983), *aff'd in part, rev'd in part on other grounds*, 393 N.W.2d 332 (Mich. 1986) (duty required of actor is to conform to legal standard of reasonable conduct in light of apparent risk).

[602] *Ibid.*, reported *Glatt v. Feist*, 156 N.W.2d 819, 829 (N.D. 1968) (the amount or degree of diligence necessary to constitute ordinary care varies with facts and circumstances of each case).

[603] ETSI TS 101 456 V1.1.1 (2000-12), Annex A, Page 36.

the rule of Article 6 covers both material and non-material damages of the persons relying on the certificate[604].

The reason for this conclusion flows from the very purpose of the Directive[605]. The liability exposure of the CSP for causing *material damages* to the certificate holder is undeniable[606]. The said finding could easily be proven by examination of some fictitious cases: Provided that pursuant to law the certificate holder has electronically submitted to the court its duly signed statement of claim against its debtor with a qualified signature. During the process of admission of the claim the court has found that the qualified certificate supporting the electronic signature appears not to be valid due to the lack of details. While the communication is not in the prescribed statutory form[607], the court has considered the claim not to be validly submitted. If due to that fact the certificate holder has missed a preclusive statutory term to submit its claim, and his subjective right has been precluded, he would be entitled to claim material damages against the negligent CSP in the amount equal to the value of the claim towards his debtor. In the same way, the certificate holder would hold the negligent CSP liable when the latter has missed to revoke the certificate in the due time and an impostor has used the compromised public key to successfully withdraw money from the certificate holder's bank account. In the latter case, if the relying party has suffered damages for incorrect payment to the fraudulent impostor, he would be entitled to hold the CSP liable too.

In all of the above cases, the claims towards the CSP should be conferred for reparation of material damages. They prove to be a result of lessening the *patrimonium* of the person relying on the certificate or the impossibility for its increasing (*lucrum cessans*) due to the negligent behaviour of the CSP. Without doubt these damages are material, having real tangible value, and falling within the scope of Article 6.

In other hypotheses, the person relying on the certificate could suffer not only material damages but also *non-material* ones. Due to the negligent behaviour of the CSP, its good name and reputation could be harmed. To illustrate this, the following

---

[604] Awarding of non-material damages would depend on the general liability rules of the respective jurisdiction. In some countries remedies for non-material damages caused by non-fulfillment of contractual obligation may not be considered. See Chapter II, section 3.1, *supra*.

[605] See Communication from the Commission COM (97) 503: Ensuring security and trust in electronic communication: "Towards a European Framework for Digital Signatures and Encryption", available at http://www.swiss.ai.mit.edu/6805/articles/crypto/eu-october-8-97.html. Also section 1.1, *supra*.

[606] See Chapter I, section 2.2.5.1, *supra*.

[607] Such form is envisaged under the draft amendments to the Bulgarian Civil Procedure Code.

example could be examined: Due to the CSP's failure to register revocation in the due time, the publisher has trusted a signed mail with attached novel of the author he was expecting to be submitted. Believing this is the work of the author, he has trusted the certificate by verifying its operational status at the registry and the CRL kept by the CSP, and has published the work. Afterwards, after publishing the book, it has become evident that the work was not the one written by the author, but of an impostor purporting to be the real author. The good name and the reputation of the real author were harmed. Being such legally protected non-material personal rights and interests, the good name and reputation of the certificate holder should be defended against the CSP, which has caused the harm due to the negligent non-processing of a certificate revocation request. Non-material damages should be repaired and there is no any reason for it to be excluded from the scope of Article 6.[608]

The purpose of the Directive is to establish a protective shield for the interests of the persons relying on the certificate. Whether for tort or contractual liability, the rules of Article 6 as transposed entitle the persons relying on the certificate to claim both material and non-material damages from the negligent CSP. This would be the case in most of the countries following the French model[609]. However, in some jurisdictions, the literal transposition of Article 6 cannot constitute grounds for claiming non-material damages unless specific rules in this respect are introduced[610].

4.5.2. Direct damages

Where should be drawn the line for the limits of the liability, provided there are no limitations introduced by the CSP in the certificate pursuant to Article 6 (3) and (4)? Would the CSP be liable for all damages or just for the direct damages? Should the scope of the damages be limited to the foreseeable ones or not?

---

[608] In some jurisdictions the courts are still reluctant in awarding non-material damages arising of non-fulfilment of contractual obligations. See court cases of the Supreme Court of Bulgaria №1786–1970–I CD, №197–1997–V CD.

[609] French law (Art 1382 of the Code Civil) and Bulgarian law (Article 52 of the LOC) for example provide general tort rules for compensation of damages despite of whether of material or non-material nature.

[610] The legal traditions in countries like Germany, Austria, Italy, et al., provide for compensation of non-material damages should special provision is present. See Chapter II, section 3.1, *supra*.

The answer to these questions could be found in the general regime and theories of the delictual and the contractual liability[611].

In the normal course of business, the contractual liability and hence the scope of the damage compensation, would be limited only to the foreseeable and highly casual damages.[612] This encompasses only those damages that come about as a normal, adequate consequence of the default[613]. Therefore, in the majority of the cases, the contractual liability for damages under the Directive as transposed would be limited to the damages that the CSP could or must have foreseen by exercising due care[614].

The case would be different, however, when under a contract the CSP has acted by wilful default and has intentionally cased damages. In such cases, in my opinion, the CSP could be held liable, not only for the foreseeable but for all direct and immediate damages[615]. Therefore, the scope of the damages under the Directive as transposed and depending on the jurisdiction should be interpreted depending on the form of the fault – negligence or wilfulness[616].

As discussed *supra*, with reference to tort, the liability of the CSP under the Directive in most of the jurisdictions would not depend on the type of fault. The CSP would be fully liable before the third relying party when there are no prior contractual relationships and damages are caused due to fault. The damage would usually encompass all direct and immediate damages - foreseeable and not foreseeable[617].

4.5.3. Indirect damages

Under the meaning of the Directive, the CSP cannot be held liable for indirect damages caused as a consequence of its negligent behaviour, notwithstanding whether in contract or in delict.

---

[611] See Kojuharov, A, *General Study of the Obligation,* Volume I, New Edition by Gerdjikov, O., Sofi-R, 1992, p. 264; also Kalaydjiev, A., *ibid.*; also Konov, Tr., *Grounds for Civil Liability,* University Publishing House 'St.Kliment Ohridski', 1995; also Chapter II, section 3, *supra.*

[612] ECOM, Proposal for Liability of Certification Authorities, *ibid., Page 10.*

[613] On establishment of the causation link and the types of damages see Chapter II, section 3.3, *supra.*

[614] *Ibid.*

[615] Not in all jurisdictions. See *supra* notes 383 and 384.

[616] On the types of fault see Chapter II, section 4, *supra.*

[617] See *supra* notes 383 and 390.

If we assume the contrary, this would lead to an unforeseeable chain of results causing a huge risk to the CSP's business. Undoubtedly, there would be no CSP ready to undertake such a business risk; hence the development of the whole electronic trust business would be hindered.[618]

The concept of indirect damages liability is inapplicable so far in the EU jurisdictions[619].

5. Liability Grounds

What facts can constitute grounds for holding the CSP liable? The Directive provides those facts in Article 6, paragraphs 1 and 2, which will be the subject of the following analysis.

5.1. Grounds under Article 6 (1)

Under Article 6 (1) the CSP shall be liable for several reasons:

5.1.1. Inaccuracy of information

The CSP shall be held liable for the inaccurate information contained in the qualified certificate at the time of its issuance.

One of the main obligations of the CSP is to attest the accuracy of the information contained in the certificate. In its position as a party trusted by all actors, it should exercise due professional care in verifying and checking the information by all appropriate means under the respective national law[620]. If the information is not correct then CSP's main role of a trusted party will be compromised. It should be held liable for being negligent in performing its duties.

This accuracy of information does not concern all the details prescribed for in Annex I, but:

---

[618] ECOM, Proposal for Liability of Certification Authorities, *ibid.*, p. 11.

[619] See Weigenek, R., *E-Commerce: A Guide to the Law of Electronic Business*, 3rd ed., UK: Butterworths Lexis Nexis, 2002, pp.60-63.

[620] See Chapter I, section 2.2.5.1, *supra*.

1.　　　regarding the fact that the certificate is issued as qualified[621], as already mentioned above, issuing the certificate as qualified by denoting the certificate as such, would make the relying party trust to a greater extent[622]. The issuance of a qualified certificate presupposes that the CSP meets the requirements of Annex II, i.e. it uses trustworthy systems, it employs qualified personnel, etc. On the other hand, marking the certificate as qualified would motivate the certificate holder to use it and the relying party to trust it whenever the law requires a special form of validity of the transaction signed with a qualified electronic signature. In both cases the parties would be misled, provided the certificate contains untrue information that it is qualified, but formally does not meet the requirements of a qualified certificate. As a consequence, damages could occur;

2.　　　regarding the identification of the CSP[623] – its full name and other requisites as required by the national law which would be necessary for the CSP to be identified properly. Mistakes and omissions in the requisites or the identifiable peculiarities of the CSP would lead to the loss of trust;

3.　　　regarding the state of establishment of the CSP[624]. Depending on the State of establishment, the regime for legal recognition of certificates issued in EU states and in other countries and also the different liability regime, the scope of their duties, supervisory regime, etc. will vary. A possible inaccuracy of this information would affect the legal value of the certificate[625];

4.　　　regarding the name of the certificate holder or its pseudonym[626], this information concerns the most important requisite. The CSP should establish a strict and comprehensive procedure for the reliable verification of the identity of the certificate holder. Improper verification or untrue records could bring the most serious negative consequences for the relying parties. Given that the certificate holds the pseudonym of the certificate holder, the CSP should keep information about its

---

[621] The Directive, Annex I (a)

[622] Marking the certificate as qualified is performed by setting the non-critical field "Qualified Statements". The procedure and the requirements are set forth in ETSI 101 862 - Qualified Certificate Profile. Due to functional imperfection in older versions of software to recognize and read properly this field, the CSPs usually note that fact in other appropriate fields (i.e. one of the OU fields) – see the CPS of Bankservice (www.b-trust.org).

[623] Annex I (b) of the EU Directive

[624] Annex I (b) of the EU Directive

[625] See Kalaydjiev, A., Belazelkov, B., Dimitrov, G., et al., *ibid.*, p. 194.

[626] Annex I (c) of the EU Directive

true identity. Some countries do not recognize the possibility for the certificate to hold a pseudonym only[627];

5.   provision of specific attributes of the certificate holder to be included if relevant[628], depending on the purpose for which the certificate is issued. Such attributes depend on the legal status of the certificate holder. These attributes may vary depending on the requirements as established by the national laws – address, national personal identity number for the natural or legal persons, fiscal numbers in certain jurisdictions, etc. A collection of such information should be without prejudice to the restrictions and rules for collection, storing and processing of personal data as provided by the national laws;

6.   regarding the fact that the listed signature-verification data corresponds to the signature-creation data under the control of the certificate holder[629], it should be noted that the inaccuracy in respect to the signature-verification data (for example an erroneous public key) constitutes a separate and different ground for the CSP's liability exposure than the inaccuracy of the fact of whether the signature-creation data was under the control of the noted certificate holder.[630] The later fact is provided as a different, separate ground in subparagraph (b) in Article 6 (1). Erroneous signature-verification data might lead to an impossibility for the relying party to verify the qualified electronic signature and hence to trust the certificate holder. Therefore, damages could occur for both the relying party and the certificate holder;

7.   regarding the indices of the beginning and end of the period of validity of the certificate[631], only exact information would motivate the relying party to trust the certificate and to enter into a relationship with the certificate holder or to perform certain acts. If the qualified signature is used before or after the validity term of the certificate supporting the signature, the so signed document will not be considered signed with a qualified signature at all which might lead to invalidity of the contract or to difficulties for the certificate holder to prove in legal proceedings

---

[627] See Dumortier, J., Nilsson, H., et al., *ibid.*, p. 142.

[628] Annex I (d) of the EU Directive

[629] See Annex I (e) of the EU Directive

[630] See section 5.1.3, *infra.*

[631] See Annex I (f) of the EU Directive

its authorship[632]. Therefore this requirement is of utmost importance for the interest of the relying parties and the certificate holder;

8.   regarding the identity code of the certificate[633], the uniqueness of the certificate should be ascertained in order to avoid issuance at a later stage of one and the same certificate with different data. Inaccuracy of such information would lead to invalidity of the certificate as qualified and to unfavorable consequences as described pursuant to the preceding paragraph;

9.   regarding the advanced electronic signature of the issuing CSP[634], such would be the cases when the CSP has used a wrong or an electronic signature that does not meet in any respect the requirements of an advanced electronic signature under Article 2 (2), or there are defects in the supporting CA certificate. These facts would invalidate the certificate because it would not be considered signed. The provision, however, should be broadly interpreted. By mentioning "advanced electronic signature", the Directive does not mean such a signature only. *Per argumentum a fortiori* any kind of signature meeting the requirement for advanced signature and revealing enhanced levels of security and trust (qualified – under the meaning of Article 5 (1) and enhanced - under the meaning of Article 3 (2), or variations thereof) will be considered validly used;

10.   regarding the limitations on the scope of use of the certificate, it is difficult to find cases whereby the inaccuracy of that information might expose the liability of the CSP. This is due to the fact that the CSP could *only* be held liable if the certificate has been used within the scope as explicitly mentioned *in the very certificate*. Even if we assume that the certificate has been issued with an erroneous scope of use, the rule foreseen in Article 6 (3) would prevail – the CSP shall not be liable for damages arising from the use of a qualified certificate, which exceeds the limitations placed on it. If an erroneous purpose of the certificate is noted then the relying party would never trust that certificate if used in any other way by the certificate holder. In such a case, should the relying party trust the certificate, it would not be able to engage the CSP's liability beyond the scope of limitations formally placed into the certificate. Hence, the CSP's liability exposure for inaccurate information regarding the limitations on the scope of use of the certificate would be

---

[632] See Article 5 of the Directive

[633] See Annex I (g) of the EU Directive

[634] See Annex I (h) of the EU Directive

applicable only towards the certificate holder. It could be mentioned as an example the case when the certificate holder has requested and paid for issuing a certificate for the signing of e-mail messages, but in the certificate, it has been noted that it is intended for signing of objects (i.e. software or files)[635]. Any attempt of the certificate holder to use it for the purpose he intended would be hampered, hence he might suffer losses. Therefore, grounds for the certificate holder would arise to hold the CSP liable;

11.   regarding the limits on the value of the transactions for which the certificate can be used, the case is almost the same under the preceding paragraph. Provided the transaction value limits were wrongfully indicated on the certificate due to the negligence of the CSP, it would be impossible for the relying party to engage the CSPs liability. Article 6 (4) provides that the CSP shall not be liable for the damage resulting from the maximum limit placed on the certificate being exceeded. Therefore the CSP shall be liable solely towards the certificate holder and only in cases where the CSP has placed a lower transaction value than the one expected and contractually agreed upon with the CSP. Given that the certificate holder has failed to enter into a transaction due to this reason, he would be entitled to engage the liability of the CSP on that ground.

It is important to pay attention to the fact that the information should be accurate at the moment the certificate is issued. The CSP cannot be held responsible for the accuracy of the information after that moment, as it might change[636]. There are numerous examples in this respect - if the personal name of the certificate holder has changed after the certificate issuance (due to marriage or other reason) the information of certificate holder's name at this later stage would differ from the one at the moment the certificate was issued. The CSP has duly verified and attested the identity of the certificate holder before issuing the certificate, but it cannot be held liable for keeping this information up to date because this duty falls beyond its reasonable professional care.

---

[635] See for example the Certificate Personal Class 2 (for signing of e-mails) and Object Sign (for signing of objects) of Bankservice (www.b-strust.org).

[636] See Kalaydjiev, A., Belazelkov, B., Dimitrov, G., et al., *ibid.*, p.204-205

5.1.2. Lack of details

Other grounds for exposing the liability of the CSP under Article 6 (1) (a) would be the fact that the certificate does not contain all the details prescribed for being a qualified certificate. The mandatory requirements for a certificate to be considered a qualified are explicitly enumerated in Annex I, namely: an indication that the certificate is issued as a qualified certificate; the identification of the certification-service-provider and the State in which it is established; the name of the certificate holder or a pseudonym, which shall be identified as such; provision of a specific attribute of the certificate holder to be included if relevant, depending on the purpose for which the certificate is intended; signature-verification data which corresponds to signature-creation data under the control of the certificate holder; an indication of the beginning and end of the period of validity of the certificate; the identity code of the certificate; the advanced electronic signature of the certification-service-provider issuing it; limitations on the scope of use of the certificate, if applicable; and limits on the value of transactions for which the certificate can be used, if applicable.

The lack of any of the above listed details would lead to the certificate losing its qualification as a "qualified" certificate. Unfavorable consequences might be numerous. Some of them have already been analyzed and supporting examples have been provided[637].

5.1.3. Non-holding the signature-creation data

Another fact that would expose the CSP to a liability is the assurance that at the time of the qualified certificate issuance, its holder held the signature-creation data corresponding to the signature-verification data given or identified in the certificate.

Undoubtedly one of the main principles and keys to the trust service infrastructure and particularly to the PKI, is the usage of certificate whereby the CSP has bound the identity of the certificate holder with the signature-verification data (e.g. the public key) by *a priori* verification of the identity of the certificate holder and the fact that he holds the corresponding signature-creation data (e.g. the private key). Based on that certification, the relying parties build their trust and perform transactions, or enter into other relationships with the certificate holder.

---

[637] See section 4.1 and section 5.1.1. (1), i.1.

Therefore, one of the main and most important duties of the CSP is, before issuing the certificate, to check: i) whether the data or public cryptographic keys, which will be used by the relying party for the purpose of verifying an electronic signature of the certificate holder, corresponds to the data or private cryptographic keys, which will be used by the certificate holder to create an electronic signature, and ii) whether the signature-creation data (the private key) is held by the certificate holder. If the certificate holder does not hold them, then another person purporting to be the certificate holder would be able to use the certificate and hence might threaten the interests of the third relying parties reasonably relying on the certificate. Therefore the CSP should perform due verification.

Provided, due to negligence, the certificate has not been issued to the real signatory, the CSP would be held liable under Article 6 (1) (b) towards the damaged persons that have relied on the certificate – i.e. the third relying parties. As already mentioned above, the rule of Article 6 does not provide grounds for engaging the liability of the CSP towards the impersonated damaged persons[638].

The verification could only be done at the moment the certificate is issued. This is the time-line limit for the CSP's due care and hence for its liability. After that moment, the signature-creation data might be compromised – it might be made available to other persons due to negligence of the certificate holder or might be stolen. In no way can the CSP be aware of that fact unless advised.

5.1.4. Inconsistence

The CSP can provide the service of algorithmic generation of the signature-creation and the signature-verification data. This function must be performed in a way that the signature-creation data and the signature-verification data could be used in an algorithmically complementary manner. Otherwise the third relying parties would not be able to verify the digital signature of the certificate holder and hence would not trust the signed data. Obviously, the lack of trust may do harm both to the certificate holder and the relying party.

Lack of correspondence between the signature-creation data and the signature-verification data can result of different negligent actions of the CSP. It be caused,

---

[638] See section 4.3, *supra*.

for example, of usage of systems that do not meet the security management standard criteria[639] leading to the compromising of its trustworthiness due to software bugs, hardware incompliance, or low security mechanisms (for example, allowing intentional intervention of unauthorized persons), etc[640]. Incompliance could occur due to incorrect application of cryptographic algorithms and technologies leading to mismatches between the public and the private keys, etc.

5.2. Grounds under Article 6 (2)

Another ground invoking the CSP's liability under the Directive is the negligent failure to register revocation of the certificate that has caused damages to the persons who have reasonably relied on the certificate. The said ground is introduced by a separate rule in Article 6 (2) of the Directive. It corresponds to one of the main duties of the CSP provided in Annex II (b) – to ensure the operation of a secure and immediate revocation service.

The revocation mechanism is a protection shield for the interests of the certificate holder and the third parties in case the signature-creation data has been compromised. It could be used against fraudulent actions of impostors or persons that have come to know or have stolen the signature-creation data of the certificate holder[641]. Upon expiration of the operational term of the certificate, it further protects the certificate holder from the risk of the cryptographic algorithms being cracked and the signature-creation data (the private key) being derived from the signature-verification data. The development of the information and communication technology presupposes the risks of vulnerability of signature-creation data to cryptanalytic attacks.[642]

Therefore, the CSP should provide a reliable mechanism for prompt certificate revocation. Failure to immediately process a revocation request and to register the revoked certificate with the respective CRL might generate the possibility for the potential impostor to misuse the signature-creation data and to cause unpredictable damages to the certificate holder and/or the third relying parties. For causing damages

---

[639] For example under ISO 15408 (http://www.iso.ch), or Common Criteria (http://www.commoncriteria.org/cc/cc.html)

[640] ECOM, Proposal for Liability of Certification Authorities, *ibid.,* p. 16.

[641] Smedinghoff, T., *ibid.,* p. 26.

[642] ABA ISC PKI Assessment Guidelines – PAG v0.30, *ibid.,* p. 106.

due to such a negligent behaviour, the CSP would be exposed to liability towards all the persons relying on the certificate.

"Failure to register revocation" should be broadly interpreted. It could encompass different negligent actions of the CSP: the delayed processing or non-processing of the certificate holder's revocation or suspension request; the improper reporting of the certificate to be operational while the operational period has expired; the CRL is not accessible by the third relying parties due to malfunction of the CSP's equipment; the CSP has found the information in the certificate to be untrue but has failed to immediately revoke the certificate; the CSP has registered erroneous revocation information; etc.[643]

6. Limitation and Exemption of Liability

The CSP will not be liable in all cases before the persons relying on the certificates under the liability regime established by the Directive. There are hypotheses under which the Directive provides exemption or limitation of the CSP's of liability.

6.1. Exemption of liability

A precondition for the liability of the CSP to be engaged under the Directive is its negligent behaviour. Both paragraphs (1) and (2) of Article 6 state that the CSP shall be liable unless he "*proves that he has not acted negligently*".

6.1.1. Due care

Article 6 (1) and (2) of the Directive only envisages liability grounds for the CSP's exposure due to its negligence as a type of fault[644]. It does not cover strict liability as it exists in product liability law[645]. It is questionable what kind of negligence the

---

[643] ECOM, Proposal for Liability of Certification Authorities, *ibid.*, p.26. On the fault in the general legal theory see Chapter II, section 4, *supra*.

[644] The notion of negligence shall have different meaning in the theory and in the different legal systems. Many systems distinguish three types of negligence gross negligence, ordinary negligence and slight (less) negligence, while others refer just to two types – gross and ordinary.

[645] See Rinderle, R., *ibid.*, p.52; also Lodder A., Kaspersen, H., *ibid.*, p.61; also Dumortier, J., Kelm, S., Nilsson, H., Skouma, G., Van Eecke, P., *ibid.*, p.55. See also Wegenek, R., *ibid.*, p.67.

provision refers to – gross negligence (*culpa lata*)[646] or ordinary negligence (*culpa levis in abstracto*)[647]? While not addressing the type of negligence and in view of the purposes of Article 6 - to protect the signatories and the relying party in building trust by using certification services, it should be assumed that the will of the European legislator was to cover both types of negligence.

While discussing the provision, another question arises. Does the provision refer to negligence only? As already discussed, the provision should not be strictly interpreted. *Per argumentum a fortiori* it should be assumed that the liability of the CSP could be exposed when the latter has also acted by wilful default (*dolus*)[648].

If we manage to apply the generally accepted legal theories[649] to the certification service provision, the negligence under the Directive would mean a fault of the CSP to exercise due care while performing its duties, i.e. to meet certain professional standards in providing certification services in issuing qualified certificates to the public[650].

The minimum duties of the CSP issuing qualified certificates are thoroughly enlisted in Annex II of the Directive. Hence, whether it has exercised due care in performing its duties, i.e. has acted diligently could be determined by analyzing the performance of each of the duties. The duties of the CSP are provided cumulatively with respect to the expected conduct. If fulfillment of any of them was not performed with due care, the result would be either accurateness or completeness of the information contained in the certificate (Article 6 (1) (a)), or improper control in making sure the certificate

---

[646] Gross negligence is considered to be failure to use even the slightest amount of care in a way that shows recklessness or wilful disregard for the safety of others interests. Usually that would be the level of care of the debtor under contracts made for the sole benefit of the debtor. See The 'Lectric Law Library's Lexicon (http://www.lectlaw.com/def/g020.htm).

[647] Ordinary negligence shall be considered the failure to use ordinary reasonable care of something which a reasonably prudent person would not do, or the failure to do something which a reasonably prudent person would do under like circumstances. The ordinary negligence is the want of ordinary diligence. Usually that would be the level of care of the debtor under contracts which are for the benefit of both parties. Some legal systems distinguish also a variety of the ordinary negligence - slight negligence. That would be negligence less than the ordinary negligence. It is the want of great diligence in performing certain duties. In those contracts made for the sole interest of the party who has received and is to return the thing which is the object of the contract, the slightest negligence will invoke liability. See The 'Lectric Law Library's Lexicon (http://www.lectlaw.com/def2/n010.htm).

[648] In this respect shall be considered that the CSP has acted *in dolus* if by non-fulfilling its obligations he is aware that he will cause damages but doesn't do anything to prevent that or is intentionally willing to do harm. See Kalaydjiev, A., *ibid.*, p. 370.

[649] For example, ECOM, Proposal for Liability of Certification Authorities, *ibid.*, p. 17; also PKI Assessment Guidelines – PAG v0.30, p. 43, *supra* note 9; also Smedinghoff, T., *ibid.*, p. 95.

[650] See Chapter II, section 4.1, *supra*.

holder identified in the certificate held the signature-creation data corresponding to the signature-verification data at the moment of issuance of the certificate (Article 6 (1) (b)), or if he has provided the key-generation service – creating the impossibility for the key pair to be used in a complementary manner (Article 6 (1) (c)). If because of this fact, damages were caused, the overall result would be negligent behaviour of the CSP resulting in liability exposure to damages.

The notion of "due care" is an abstract standard of behaviour. While determining whether the CSP has acted negligently or not, the court should apply the standard as a pattern in any single case in view of the applicable law[651]. The standard would differ depending on:

a)   the duties of the CSP with respect to the type of the certification service provided. One would be the professional standard of the CA, another would be that of the TSA, RA, etc.;

b)   the particularities of the service, the environment and the infrastructure. The standard of the CSPs processing on-line inquiries for certificate verification through OCSP would differ from the one of the CSPs not providing such a service - the level of trust in the different types of verification is variable;

c)   the professional level of the services provision[652]. The standard of the accredited CSP issuing qualified or enhanced certificates would be higher than the one of the non-accredited one. Obviously, the accredited CSPs would be required to meet higher standards.

d)   whether there are stipulations contractually agreed upon limitation of the due care (where applicable and recognizable)[653];

e)   whether the relying on the certificate persons have also exercised due care in consuming the service and have not obtruded the CSP to provide the service. This is the border of their reasonable reliance.[654]

---

[651] The applicable standards may vary from state to state depending on the different statutory approaches in regulating the activity of the CSPs.

[652] See Article 3 (2) and Recital (11) of the Directive.

[653] See sections 6.2 and 6.3, *infra*. In some countries the exemption is not possible for malice and gross negligence (see *supra* note 418), while in others the exemption is not possible for any kind of negligence (see Article 29 (4) of the Bulgarian EDESA – " *"The agreements by which the certification-service-provider's liability for negligence is excluded or limited shall be invalid"*; *supra* note 480).

In any case, the standard of care of the CSP would be higher than the standard of care of the other service providers. It must possess respective level of special knowledge and skills necessary to act as a CSP, and must have the obligation to act as a reasonable member of the profession would in a given circumstance.[655]

Being an objective criterion, the due care of the CSP will be examined by the courts in determining whether there are industry standards or customs applicable thereto (i.e. policy requirements, constant trade custom, etc.)[656]. In some documents it is stated that in most Member States failure to comply with an industry standard, may be a *prima facie* evidence of negligence of the CSP.[657] In my opinion, the courts should not make an *a priori* conclusion in such cases, but should examine all particular circumstances, the conduct of the CSP, and the conduct of the damaged persons relying on the certificate.

6.1.2. Burden of proof

The provision of Article 6 establishes a refutable presumption of fault by explicitly allocating to the CSP the burden of proving that he has acted diligently. The CSP would be the one to prove that the reason for his conduct is not its negligence but factors beyond his reasonable control and due care. The negligence shall be presumed both in tort and in contractual relationship[658].

The approach of the Directive seems to be in line with the approaches of most of the national legal systems. The recipient of signed document would hardly be in a position to investigate the matter and to backup his claim, should the signature prove to be invalid. The CSP has the necessary management and organization to investigate the issue[659]. On the other hand, sometimes the security policies of the CSP deprive possibilities of any compulsory investigation by court experts.

---

[654] See section 4.4, *supra* and Article 6 (1) and (2) of the Directive.

[655] Smedinghoff, T., *ibid.,* p.30, reported W. Page Keeton, et al., *Prosser and Keeton on the Law of Torts* § 32, at 187 (5th ed. 1984).

[656] See Ius Commune Casebook – Tort Law, (http://www.rechten.unimaas.nl/casebook/), p.68/3

[657] See ETSI TS 101 456 V1.1.1 (2000-12), *ibid.,* Annex A, p.36.

[658] See Kalaydjiev, A., *ibid.*

[659] Rinderle, R., *ibid.,* p.52

However, taking into account the general principles of law of the major part of the EU legal systems, it seems that the rule in this respect does not seem to be indispensable, while it establishes burden of proof of fault rather than burden of proof of causation[660].

As it will become evident from the forthcoming Chapters IV and V, introducing rebutable presumption of fault would prove to be unnecessary.

6.1.3. Exemption grounds

To avoid liability, the CSP could prove that the relying person has not reasonably relied on the certificate due to respective conduct – failures, omissions, knowledge of certain facts, etc. In such a case, the courts should examine the limits of the causality in the occurrence of the damages and whether there are co-causing reasons.

Further, should the CSP prove that he has not acted negligently, i.e. has exercised the due care in performing his duties, he will be exempted of liability, although damages have occurred and formally were caused by the reasons as listed in Article 6 (1) and (2). For example such would be the cases when:

a)   *Force majeur* circumstances were present. The CSP shall not be held liable under Article 6 provided wars, earthquakes, floods or other acts of God have occurred, provided the CSP has made all his efforts to reduce the damages.

b)   The CSP has exercised the due care to fulfil his duties, but despite that, damages have occurred. For example, it has used all appropriate under the national law means to verify the identity of the person requesting issuing of a qualified certificate, but the forged identity documents were done in a way that the verification was proved to had been successful and a certificate was issued to an impostor purporting to be the real certificate holder;

c)   The reasons for non-fulfilment of the duties were beyond CSP's control. For example, if the CSP was providing on-line verification of the status of the qualified certificates issued and the communication lines connecting the party willing to

---

[660] Thorough analysis of the "burden of proof" concept under the Directive is provided in Chapter V, section 5, *infra*.

access on-line the status and the CSP were malfunctioning due to fault of the telecommunication operator – proprietor of the lines;

d)   The relying persons were not reasonably relying on the certificate and this was the main reason for the occurrence of the damage. For example the relying person was aware of the compromising of the certificate holder's private key, but nevertheless has trusted the non-revoked certificate.

e)   Other cases falling beyond the due care of the CSP.

6.2. Liability limits under Article 6 (3)

The Directive prescribes that Member States shall ensure that the CSP may indicate in the qualified certificate limitations on the use of that certificate, provided that the limitations are recognizable to third parties. By this the CSP shall not be held liable for damage arising from use of the qualified certificate, which exceeds the limitations placed on it.

There are several legal issues that should be addressed.

6.2.1. Hypotheses covered

There are two completely different hypothesis covered by Article 6 (3). The first refers to the possibility of the CSP to limit the usage of the certificate by placing such a note on it. In this way, the certificate shall be considered qualified only when used for the denoted purpose. Usage for other purposes would disqualify its legal effectiveness of a "qualified certificate" [661]. The CSPs follow strict Security Policy while issuing different types of certificates. The validity of the certificate as a 'qualified' one and the consequences arising thereof require the certificate to contain certain requisites – the ones listed in Annex II. In order for the CSP to issue the certificate by placing the note "qualified", he performs certain controls and verifications following the security procedure. By placing the limitation on the usage of the certificate, the CSP practically announces to the third parties that the security

---

[661] See Kalaydjiev, A., Belazelkov, B., Dimitrov, G., et al., *ibid.*, p. 200. The authors find that the usage of a signature beyond the limitations on its usage or on the value of transactions disqualifies the electronic signature as meeting the requirements of Article 5 (1). On the opposite opinion – Hindelang S, *ibid* - the author suggests interpreting the clause of the Directive as limiting the liability only. The finding of Hindelang cannot be supported.

controls are performed within certain limits and the relying parties should trust the certificate only if the signature is used for transactions within the limits (denoted purpose) indicated in the certificate. Usage of signature beyond these limits means that no valid attestation (certification) on behalf of the CSP exist. Such certificate shall not be trusted, thus the signature is no longer supported by a valid qualified certificate.

The second hypothesis covered by the rule of Article 6 (3) addresses the liability exposure of the CSP in case of usage beyond the noted limitations. In fact, such a usage would exempt the CSP from its liability. Some studies incorrectly interpret the rule of Article 6, para 3 to provide "limitation of liability". The same is valid for paragraph 4. In fact, the rule refers to placing of limits on the use of the certificate beyond which the liability of the CSPs cannot be engaged. In other words, the CSP shall be liable under Article 6 (1) and (2) only in the cases when the certificate is used for the purposes and within the limits explicitly noted in the certificate.

Therefore, by introducing an option for the CSP to place limits on the certificate usage, the rule provides a legal instrument for the CSP to control its liability exposure and hence to control its business risk.

6.2.2. Scope of CSPs

In respect of the liable persons, similarly to the provision of Article 6 (1) and (2), the Directive addresses the rule only to CSP issuing *qualified certificates* to the public[662]. Nevertheless, the rule does not explicitly envisage this fact in a way it does in the preceding paragraphs (2) and (3), it should be systematically and logically interpreted.

With respect to the notion 'to the public', no doubt could exist on what the EU legislator has meant. As already mentioned above, the Directive regulates the activity and the regime of CSPs providing certification cervices to the public only[663]. When issuing certificates to closed groups, the relationship between the CSP and the relying parties hence the liability exposure, are governed by a contract. The introduction of minimum liability requirements in a closed model is not likely to be the appropriate approach. Such a liability regime shall be governed by the contractual will of the

---

[662] See Section 3 of present chapter, *supra*.

[663] See Recital (16) of the Directive.

parties, the general contract national rules, and the ones concerning the consumer contracts.[664]

Beyond the scope of paragraph 3 remain the CSPs guaranteeing qualified certificates. To my opinion, the rule cannot be broadly interpreted. Precise analysis of the wording of the rule supports such a conclusion. The norm envisages that the CSP *"may indicate in a qualified certificate limitations ..."* It is obvious that by using a verb meaning introducing details into the certificate and while such introducing could be done only at the moment of the certificate issuance implies that *only* the CSP *issuing* certificates can *indicate* limitations.

The European legislator does not explicitly give the CSP guaranteeing the certificate a possibility to limit its usage and hence liability apart of the limitations placed on the guaranteed certificate. While guaranteeing the qualified certificate, the CSP will be jointly liable with the issuer of the certificate for damages within the usage limitations placed on the very certificate. However, in some jurisdictions such limitations prove to be possible[665].

6.2.3. Enforceability against whom?

Unlike paragraphs (1) and (2), the rule of paragraph (3) does not addresses explicitly towards whom the limitations of the use and hence of the liability shall be enforceable. Some unclear directions on the potential scope of persons could be derived from the ruling that the CSP may indicate limitations provided they are *"... recognizable to third parties"*.

Does the said provision limit its protective shield only to third relying on the certificate parties or encompasses the certificate holders too?

It should be assumed that the idea of providing the CSP with an instrument to control its liability by introducing limitations on the certificate usage and hence of its liability should be effective towards both the certificate holder and the third relying

---

[664] The same view supported in ETSI TS 101 456 V1.1.1 (2000-12), Annex A, p. 36 *in fine*; and ECOM, *Proposal for Liability of Certification Authorities, ibid.*, page 4-5.

[665] Under Article 44 (4) (2), *in fine* it is envisaged that in cases of recognition of the legal value of certificates issued by foreign CSPs the Bulgarian CSP that guarantees the certificate can place "... *conditions upon which the liability is assumed*". This limitation is entered into the special register kept by the Bulgarian supervisory body in charge – the Communications Regulation Commission. See Kalaydjiev, A., Belazelkov, B., Dimitrov, G., et al., *ibid.*, p.339.

parties. Therefore, the notion *"third parties"* is used by the Directive to address the persons other then the very CSP.

It is true that the meaning of the rule at first glance appears to cover the relying parties only. The CSP and the relying party are usually not in contractual relationship. Therefore, it is difficult for the CSP to legally address the valid recognizable limitations on its delictual liability towards the relying party. By introducing limitations on the usage of the certificate, the Directive provides the possibility for the CSP to clearly and securely address the relying parties not to trust the certificate provided if used beyond the noted limitations. If they have trusted the certificate anyway, then they shall no longer be considered persons reasonably relying on this certificate and would not be entitled to engage the CSP's liability[666].

What about the certificate holder? The situation could be clearly and easily solved when the contract or the CP/CPS holds the limitations on the use of the certificate and the contract refers to it. The limitations placed by the CSP shall be enforceable against the certificate holder as any other clause unless the respective national law does not recognize certain limitations. If, however, there are no limitations placed in the CPS or agreed by contract, the only way for the CSP to limit its liability for usage of the certificate remains their placement in the very certificate. That way, the certificate holder shall be positioned as non-reasonably relying on the certificate, if used beyond the limitations for its usage[667]. As already analyzed *supra*, within the reasonable reliance of both the certificate holder and the third relying party would be to verify the limits of the usage of the certificate.

An interesting hypothesis would be faced when the certificate holder has requested a certificate expecting it to have a certain scope of usage but the CSP has issued it with wrong usage note. Shall the CSP's liability be limited pursuant to paragraph (3) to the so introduced limitations placed on the certificate? The answer would be negative. In such a case, the CSP shall be contractually and without limit liable for negligent non-fulfilment of its obligations to issue a qualified certificate with accurate information on the grounds of Article 6 (1) (a).

---

[666] Same idea is supported by the UNICTRAL Model Law on Electronic Signatures. In Section 79 of the Draft for the Enactment it is envisaged that the relying party "should take reasonable steps … to observe any limitations with respect to the certificate".

[667] See section 4.4.1.4 of present chapter, *supra*.

Further, it should be pointed out that the limits on the certificate's use should be recognizable under the national legislation to third parties.[668] The national laws may introduce a stricter liability than the one prescribed by the Directive. Thus, they could exclude the possibility of the CSPs to reduce their liability by placing limitations on the certificate.

6.2.4. *Key usage*

Clear distinction should be made between limitations on the use of the certificate and the limitation on the value of transactions for which the certificate can be used.

Limitations on the usage would refer to the purposes for which the certificate may be used and trusted and hence to be considered a qualified certificate. From a substantive legal point of view, the certificate shall not be considered qualified at all if used beyond the scope of the key usage[669]. Therefore, any liabilities arising therefrom cannot be assigned to the CSP's account.

The purpose of the certificate can be referred to as: secure e-mail[670], server authentication[671], website authentication, code signing, hardware driver verification[672], etc.[673]

Some studies assume that there are further possibilities for indicating limitations on the use of the certificate by having the certificate only used for a certain type of transaction or only being used within one company, one country or within the EC[674]. There is no provision disabling the application of such an approach whatsoever, and thus it should be supported. However, some difficulties would be faced in view of interoperability and thus possibilities that such an indication could be identified with

---

[668] EESSI, Final Report of the EESSI Expert Team, 20th July 1999, p. 64.

[669] See Kalaydjiev, A., Belazelkov, B., Dimitrov, G., et al., *ibid.*, p. 199.

[670] See Personal Freemail RSA 2000.8.30 Certificate

[671] See MS SGC Authority Certificate

[672] See Microsoft Hardware Driver Compatibility Certificate

[673] The usage of the certificate is indicated in the "Key Usage" Field. The later field is critical. Details on the purposes of the usage of the certificate are indicated in another critical field - "Extended Key Usage". Some of the common key usages are: Digital Signature; Non-repudiation; Key encipherment; Data encipherment; Key Certificate Signing; CRL Signing; and others.

[674] Rinderle, R., *ibid.*, p.52, also Lodder, A., Kaspersen, H., *ibid.*, p.62.

respective software by the relying parties. Development of industry standards in this respect is recommended.

6.3. Limits of liability under Article 6 (4)

Another limitation of the CSP's liability could be achieved by indicating in the qualified certificate a limit on the value of the transactions for which the certificate can be used, provided the limit is recognizable to third parties. Needless to say, the norm envisages transactions between the signature holder and the third relying parties.

As regards the scope of the CSPs and the third parties against whom the limitations shall be applicable, the conclusions of the section 6.2 *supra* shall be fully valid.

6.3.1. Types of transactions

An interesting assumption in some studies was found that the rule of Article 6 (4) encompasses commercial transactions only[675]. There is no such indication in paragraph (4). The provision refers to the '*value of transactions*'. In my opinion, there is no reason to exclude from the scope of paragraph (4) the transactions between natural persons, NGOs, or any transaction having monetary value that does not have a '*commercial*' nature *strictu sensu* under the national laws. If the provisions of paragraph (3) and (4) should be considered as "CSP friendly"[676], then why limitations should be introduced for the CSP to manage its liability in such transactions by placing limits of their value in the certificates?

It is obvious that the scope of the Directive is not meant to cover commercial relationships only. Recital (9) provides that "*electronic signatures will be used in a large variety of circumstances and applications ...*", and even "*will be used in the public sector ...*" (Recital (19)). Thus the provision of paragraph (4) should be interpreted broader.

---

[675] Rinderle, R., *ibid.*, p.53, also Lodder, A., Kaspersen, H., *ibid.*, p.62.
[676] *Ibid.*, p.49.

6.3.2. Indication

How the limitation on the value of the transactions should be indicated in the certificate? The deliverables setting out the techonology standars provide a clear direction in this respect. It should be done by a statement of the issuer indicating the specified monetary amount. [677]

6.3.3. Legal consequences

Similarly to the limitations on the usage of the certificate, provided the certificate is used in a transaction exceeding the limits placed on it, from a legal viewpoint it shall be considered that the certificate does not meet the requirements of a qualified certificate as prescribed in Annex I. Such certificate shall not have the legal value of a qualified certificate[678].

By placing limitations in the certificate, the CSP provides trust by "certifying" certain facts only within these limits. Therefore, it would be entirely at the risk of the relying party to trust such a certificate and to enter into a transaction or to perform certain acts. The CSP cannot be held liable for the incorrect usage of the certificate in such cases. It is exempted of liability. In this respect the conclusions made in section 6.2.1, *supra* are fully valid.

In the Report to the European Commission entitled "The Legal and Market Aspects of Electronic Signatures"[679] it is envisaged that *"to avoid liability for potential conflicts regarding the legal validity of a digital signature in certain context, the CSP may wish to make clear that he does not guarantee the legal effect of an electronic signature that bears this certificate"*. Such notifications would undoubtedly enhance the clarity of the liability exposure of the CSP. However, the rule of paragraph 4 provides enough clarity in this respect – the CSP may indicate in a qualified certificate a *limit of the value* of transactions for which the certificate *can be used* …". That is to say, the certificate cannot certify any fact placed on it if used beyond the noted value. It *cannot be used* beyond such limits at all.

---

[677] ETSI TS 101 862 V1.1.1 (2000-12) "Qualified certificate profile", section 4.2.2, p. 7 (http://portal.etsi.org/sec/ts_101862v010201p.pdf)

[678] Kalaydjiev, A., Belazelkov, B., Dimitrov, G., et al., *ibid.*, p. 194.

[679] Dumortier, J., Kelm, S., et al., *ibid.*

Should the certificate lose its certification value, the supported signature also loses its validity as being a qualified signature[680].

In such a sense, the wording of the Directive should be noted. It says that the CSP may place *limits on the value of transactions*, not *liability limits*. The Directive should be interpreted very carefully. Article 6 (3) and (4) does not refer to "reducing" or "limiting" the liability of the CSP to a certain extent, but rather placing limits, i.e. conditions upon which the CSP may be held liable. Thus the CSP may be held liable for the usage of the certificate *within these limits*, not *up to these limits*. Paragraph (4) explicitly envisages that the CSP *shall not be liable* for damage resulting from these maximum limits being exceeded, i.e. the CSP shall not be held liable at all if the maximum limits placed are exceeded by the use of the signature.

The grounds for such a conclusion could be derived not only by proper interpretation of Article 6 (4), but also by analysing of the rule of Article 5 (1)[681]. The said article provides that a qualified electronic signature (having the effect of a handwritten signature) shall be considered any advanced signature which is based on a qualified certificate[682]. The requisites of the qualified certificates are listed in Annex I. As one of the requisites, the said Annex envisages "(j) limits on the value of transactions for which the certificate *can be used*" (again not limits of the liability of the CSP!). Should such limits on the value of transactions be placed by the CSP, the qualified certificate can be used under these conditions, and thus, it has a legal value as such *only* within these limits. Beyond the noted limits it shall not be considered a qualified certificate. That is to say, the advanced signature supported by such a certificate shall not be considered "qualified" and thus shall not have the effect of a handwritten signature.

It is easy to reveal the real will of the European legislator by reviewing the historical process of the drafting the Directive. In the second Proposal from the Commission to the European Parliament, the text of the provision as accepted by the Parliament was: "4. Member States shall ensure that a certification-service-provider may indicate in the qualified certificate a limit on the value of transactions *for which the certificate is valid*. The certification-service-provider shall not be liable for damages in excess of that value

---

[680] The opposite opinion supported by Hindelang S, *ibid.*

[681] See section 1.1, *supra.*

[682] Dumortier, J., *The European Regulatory Framework for Electronic Signatures: A critical Evaluation* at Nielsen, R., Jacobsen, S., Trzaskowski, J. (editors), *EU Electronic Commerce Law*, Djøf Publishing, 2004, p.71.

limit"[683]. The final version of Article 6 shows that it was elaborated under this idea, whereas only revisions in the wording, not in the meaning of the text were made.

Now, if we turn back to the liability clause of Article 6 (4), it is easy to understand the idea of exemption of liability of the CSP should the latter have placed limits on the purposes of the certificate, rather than placing limitation to a certain extent.

Therefore, a conclusion could be made that the CSP's liability could be engaged only in the cases when the certificate *is used* within the limits placed on it and damages have occurred due to the negligent behaviour of the CSP[684].

6.3.4. Liability caps

Introducing a limit on the value of the transactions does not mean that the CSP could place a limitation cap on its liability[685]. If the certificate is used for transactions below the placed value limit, the CSP shall be fully liable for its negligence; beyond that limit it will not be held liable at all. But such a liability limitation is "relative" – per transaction and per certificate[686]. The Directive does not refer to "absolute" (aggregate) liability, i.e. the liability of the CSP within the limits of transactions indicated in the certificate for all transactions within the operational period of the certificate[687].

In this respect the findings of some authors defining that aggregate liability caps do not seem to be covered by Article 6 is plausible, while it is not possible for the relying party to see the number of previous transactions that have been conducted by the certificate holder or the extent to which the liability for the certificate has already been consumed by these previous transactions.[688]

---

[683] See Proposal for a European Parliament and Council Directive on a common framework for electronic signatures (COM(98)0297 - C4-0376/98 - 98/0191(COD)), Amendment 22

[684] *Ibid.*

[685] For example GlobalSign places liability caps for the different classes of certificates. See the Certification Practice Statement of GlobalSign, Article 7.31 in relation to Article 10.7 and 10.8 (http://www.globalsign.net/repository/CPSv4.pdf)

[686] See Dumortier, J., Kelm, et al., *ibid.*, p.55

[687] See Smedinghoff, T., *ibid.*, p.p. 95 and 105.

[688] Dumortier, J., Kelm, S., Nilsson, H., Skouma, G., Van Eecke, P., *ibid.*, p.55. Also Rinderle, R., *ibid.*, p.53.

Considering the above, it could be concluded that placing of aggregate liability caps is not regulated, nor does the Directive allow it. Nevertheless, the provisions of paragraphs (3) and (4) are "CSP friendly".[689] The minimum liability regime established by Article 6 in general is meant to protect the interest of the parties relying on the certificates, but not the interests of the CSPs[690]. In this respect the possibility for placing limits on the liability exposure under paragraphs (3) and (4) seems to be an exception to this rule.

6.4. Limitation by CPS/CP

Beyond the instrument set by Article 6, paragraphs (3) and (4), the CSPs can successfully manage their liability to a certain extent by introducing limitations into the Certification Practice Statement (CPS) or the Certificate Policy (CP).

Before analyzing the issue, some basics on the concepts of CP and CPS and their relationship should be provided.

6.4.1. Nature of the CPS and the CP

A Certification Practice Statement (CPS) is a statement of the practices which a certification-service-provider employs in issuing and managing certificates[691].

A Certificate policy (CP) is a named set of rules that indicates the applicability of a certificate to a particular community and/or class of application with common security requirements. For example, a particular certificate policy might indicate the applicability of a type of certificate for the authentication of electronic data interchange transactions for the trading of goods within a given price range[692].

---

[689] Rinderle, R., *ibid.*, p.49.

[690] See Chapter IV, section 2, *infra.*

[691] RFC 2527 Internet X.509 Public Key Infrastructure Certificate Policy and Certification Practices Framework. Section 2. Definitions. Almost same definition given in ABA Digital Signatures Guidelines, *ibid.* The X.509 standard defines the CP to be "a named set of rules that indicates the applicability of a certificate to a particular community and/or class of application with common security requirements".

[692] *Ibid.*

A collection of practice and/or policy statements, spanning a range of standard topics, for use in expressing a certificate policy definition or CPS is commonly referred to as a set of provisions.

6.4.1.1. Certificate policy

The industry standards see the CP to be a statement to the relying parties that a particular public key is bound to a particular entity (the certificate holder, or subject). The standards find that the relying party has to choose the extent to which it shall rely on that statement, while different types of certificates can be issued following different practices and procedures, and may be suitable for different applications and purposes[693].

For the liability of the CSPs it is important how the policies are represented in the issued certificate, and particularly, one of the extension fields. There are three extension fields in an X.509 certificate to support the certificate policies: Certificate Policies extension; Policy Mappings extension[694]; and Policy Constraints extension[695].

The CP extension field can be flagged as either critical or non-critical. Depending on how it is flagged the consequences differ. Should the CP is introduced in a non-critical CP field, the usage of the certificate shall not be restricted to the purposes

---

[693] *Ibid.*, Section 3.1. Under the said RFC a certificate policy, which needs to be recognized by both the issuer and user of a certificate (the relying party), is represented in a certificate by a unique, registered Object Identifier. The registration process follows the procedures specified in ISO/IEC and ITU standards. The party that registers the Object Identifier also publishes a textual specification of the certificate policy, for examination by certificate users. Any one certificate will typically declare a single certificate policy or, possibly, be issued consistent with a small number of different policies.

[694] The Policy Mappings extension may only be used in CA-certificates. This field allows a certification authority to indicate that certain policies in its own domain can be considered equivalent to certain other policies in the subject certification authority's domain. See RFC 2527, section 3.3.2.

[695] *Ibid.*, Section 3.3.3. "The Policy Constraints extension supports two optional features. The first is the ability for a certification authority to require that explicit certificate policy indications be present in all subsequent certificates in a certification path. Certificates at the start of a certification path may be considered by a certificate user to be part of a trusted domain, i.e., certification authorities are trusted for all purposes so no particular certificate policy is needed in the Certificate Policies extension. Such certificates need not contain explicit indications of certificate policy. However, when a certification authority in the trusted domain certifies outside the domain, it can activate the requirement for explicit certificate policy in subsequent certificates in the certification path. The other optional feature in the Policy Constraints field is the ability for a certification authority to disable policy mapping by subsequent certification authorities in a certification path. It may be prudent to disable policy mapping when certifying outside the domain. This can assist in controlling risks due to transitive trust, e.g., a domain A trusts domain B, domain B trusts domain C but domain A does not want to be forced to trust domain C."

indicated by the applicable policies[696]. If flagged critical, the CP field shall have an additional role. It indicates that the certificate could only be used in accordance with the provisions of one of the listed certificate policies. When this field was defined by the industry standards, it was intended to protect the certification authority against damage claims by a relying party who has used the certificate for an inappropriate purpose or in an inappropriate manner, as stipulated in the applicable certificate policy definition[697].

The CP extension field may hold the CPS pointer qualified as a URL pointer to the CPS published by the CSP[698]. It may also hold the user notice qualifier to display a text to the certificate holder or the relying party prior to the use of the certificate and thus to invoke a procedure that requires that the certificate user acknowledge that the applicable terms and conditions have been disclosed or accepted[699].

6.4.1.2. Certification practice statement

A certification practice statement is a statement of practices and procedures followed by the CSP. Where the PKI is governed by a CP which sets forth general requirements, a CPS reveals how the CSP meets the requirements appearing in the CP by disclosing practices and procedures. In this respect, the CPS is much more detailed than the CP[700].

On the legal nature of the CPS, an explanation is provided in the ABA Guidelines. They read:

A certification practice statement may take the form of a declaration by the certification authority of the details of its trustworthy system and the practices it employs in its operations and in support of issuance of a certificate, or it may be a statute or regulation applicable to the certification authority and covering similar subject matter. It may also be part of the contract between the certification authority

---

[696] The non-critical CP field is meant to be used by applications pre-configured to identify what policy it requires. When processing a certification path, a certificate policy that is acceptable to the certificate-using application must be present in every certificate in the path, i.e., in CA-certificates as well as end entity certificates.

[697] See RFC 2527, *ibid.*, section 3.3.3.

[698] Defined in PKIX Part I. See Housley, R., Ford, W., Polk, W., Solo, D., "Internet X.509 Public Key Infrastructure, Certificate and CRL Profile", RFC 2459, January 1999.

[699] The text string may be an IA5String or a BMPString - a subset of the ISO 100646-1 multiple octet coded character set.

[700] ABA ISC PAG v0.30 Public Draft for Comment Only, Section B.4.

and the subscriber. A certification practice statement may also be comprised of multiple documents, a combination of public law, private contract, and/or declaration.[701]

Certain forms for legally implementing certification practice statements lend themselves to particular relationships. For example, when the legal relationship between a certification authority and subscriber is consensual, a contract would ordinarily be the means of giving effect to a certification practice statement. The certification authority's duties to a relying person are generally based on the certification authority's representations, which may include a certification practice statement.[702]

As much as possible, a certification practice statement should indicate any of the widely recognized standards to which the certification authority's practices conform. Reference to widely recognized standards may indicate concisely the suitability of the certification authority's practices for another person's purposes, as well as the potential technological compatibility of the certificates issued by the certification authority with repositories and other systems.[703]

With respect to the binding nature and the possibilities for liability management through the CPS/CP, the ABA Guidelines shed light on this, but mainly from a common law perspective. The nature of the CPS/CP shall be examined carefully from a civil law point of view. The legal traditions of jurisdictions following this system of law will not always recognize the possibilities for liability limitations by using the CPS/CP as instruments.

The issue should be examined separately from the subscriber's and relying party's point of view while the legal relationship and thus the legal value of the CPS/CP shall differ[704]. Furthermore, it should be noted that the specific liability regime of the CSPs issuing qualified certificates under the Directive shall be reflected in the possibilities for the CSPs to manage their liability by CP/CSP.

6.4.1. Limitations with respect to the certificate holder

In terms of a contractual relationship, the binding power of the CPS/CP seems to be indisputable. This conclusion shall be valid irrespective of the jurisdiction and legal

---

[701] ABA Digital Signatures Guidelines, *ibid.*, section 1.8.1.

[702] *Ibid.*, section 1.8.2.

[703] *Ibid.*, section 1.8.4.

[704] For the relations between the CSP and the certificate holder, resp. the relying party see sections 2.1 and 2.2, *supra*, in respect to the particular regime of the Directive and Chapter I, sections 2.2.5.1 and 2.2.5.2 for the general regime.

system where the contract is enforced. Thus, limiting the liability of the CSP by the CPS/CP in respect to the certificate holder proves to be possible.

There are different legal techniques for such an effect to be enforced.

Where national legislations provide so, the CPS/CP may take the form of General Terms[705] of contract for certification services[706]. Thus they become part of the contract with respective legal effects to all liability limitations that could be agreed upon among parties pursuant to the national general and specific liability rules[707]. However, the usage and enforcement of General Terms should meet certain statutory requirements established by the national laws, such as the form of acceptance, priority of special terms, particularities in effecting amendments to the contract, particularities in view of the status of the person – merchant or not, restrictions in unification of general terms in view of fair competition, requirements in respect to consumers as contractual parties, special requirements for the General Terms of the CSP where applicable, etc.[708]

Further, liability limitations in the CPS shall be enforceable against the certificate holder should the CSP have communicated them before entering into a contractual relationship. Such a possibility is even imposed as a duty by the very Directive. Annex II (k) rules that before entering into a contractual relationship with a person seeking a certificate to support his electronic signature, the CSP must inform that person by a durable means of communication about the precise terms and conditions regarding the use of the certificate, including any limitations on its use, the existence of a voluntary accreditation scheme and procedures for complaints and dispute settlement. This information is usually part of the CPS and the CP. Suppying the certificate holder with this core information shall undoubtedly make him decide whether or not to enter into a contractual relationship with the CSP and thus to reasonably rely on the certificate pursuant to Article 6. *Per argumentum a fortiori* if the CSP advises the person seeking issuance of a certificate on all policies, procedures and practices

---

[705] In US they are sometimes referred to as ToS – Terms of Service.

[706] Under Article 33 (2) of the Bulgarian Ordinance On The Activities Of Certification-Service-Providers, The Terms And Procedures Of Termination Thereof, And The Requirements For Provision Of Certification Services adopted pursuant to CMD No. 17 dated 31 January 2002 (Promulgated, SG No. 15 dated 8 February 2002) the User's Guide that consists of Certificate Policy and Certification Practice Statement shall have the meaning of general terms and shall be binding upon its issuer.

[707] See *supra* Chapter II, section 5. On the legal value of the CPS as General Terms see Kalaydjiev, A., Belazelkov, B., Dimitrov, G., et al., *ibid.*, p. 182.

[708] *Ibid.*, p.p. 183-185.

employed for a given type of certificate, including certain liability limitations, the latter shall be binding to the certificate holder, the same way they will be binding for the CSP. Should the CSP fail to comply with the representations placed at the CP/CPS, he will be held liable[709]. Under national laws its liability due to *culpa in contrahendo* shall be invoked in the cases when no contract was enforced or validly enforced, the contract was cancelled, or, respectively, contractual liability – should the binding contract be enforced but damages have occurred due to the misrepresentations[710].

Further, it is possible certain liability limitations, as part of the CPS/CP, to become part of the contract upon explicit reference thereto[711]. In this case, depending on the approach of the national civil procedure rules, the interested party may have to prove that the document was made available to the other party in a certain version at the moment of the enforcement of the contract[712].

Finally, the very laws may introduce, by mandatory rules, the binding effect of the CPS/CP and thus all liability limitations as introduced by the CSP shall be enforceable by virtue of law[713]. Some laws even prescribe certain contents of the CPS/CP[714]. The Directive also provides some directions on what the CPS/CP shall consist of by imposing some duties to the CSPs issuing qualified certificates in Annex II.

Considering the said above, the CPS/CP can successfully serve as an instrument for managing the liability of the CSP before the certificate holder. By introducing certain liability limitations, the CSPs can either directly stem rights from the contract, should the CPS/CP be legally enforced by general terms or contractual covenants, or indirectly by making the certificate holder aware of certain limitations before entering into a contractual relationship and thus making him "unreasonably" relying on the

---

[709] In common law doctrine representations and warranties shall be considered promises that a particular state of facts has existed in the past, does exist, or will exist in the future. See ABA ISC PAG v0.30 – Public Draft for Comment, Section D.2.3, p. 117.

[710] On *culpa in contrahendo* concept and the absorption of the pre-contractual liability by the contractual see Chapter II, section 2.4, *supra*.

[711] In common law doctrine the promises to do or refrain from certain actions over a period of time into the future are referred to as *covenants*.

[712] See Article 16 of the Bulgarian LOC.

[713] Such an effect one could identify under Bulgarian law on e-signatures and especially the secondary legislation. The CSP is obliged to develop CP and CPS (Article 30 – 33 of the Ordinance on the activities of CSPs, the terms and procedures of termination thereof, and the requirements for provision Of certification services) to incorporate them into a User's Guide and to enter into contractual relationship under the conditions as set forth therein.

[714] *Ibid.*, Article 32 (1) and (2).

certificate if the certificate is used beyond the policy employed. In any case, the limits of the reasonable reliance shall be the national general liability rules[715] and those specific rules which transpose the ones of Article 6 or go further. The parties may not deviate from statutory imposed duties. The CPS/CP may not prescribe, for example, that the CSP issuing qualified certificates shall not be liable for meeting given requirement of Annex II of the Directive, as transposed, or when issuing qualified certificates shall not be liable for the reasons implied in Article 6. For example, the CPS/CP may not provide that the CSP shall not be liable as regards the accuracy at the time of issuance of all information contained in the qualified certificate[716], or it will be liable up to certain limits for negligent failure to register revocation[717]. The mandatory nature of these rules shall prevail with regard to any clause that might be contradictory whatsoever.

6.4.2. Limitations in respect to the third relying party

While, with respect to the certificate holder, limitations of liability by the CPS/CP prove to be enforceable against the relying party, the case does not seem to be so clear.

Apart from the abovementioned industry standards[718], some studies and examples in the provision of certification services[719] were found to see the reasonableness in knowing certain particularities by the relying party in respect to the certificate policy[720] followed by the CSP. By placing different conditions on when and how

---

[715] See Recital (22) of the Directive. On the possible limits of the freedom to agree on release or limitation of liability see *supra* Chapter II, sections 4.2 and 5.

[716] Article 6 (1) (a).

[717] Article 6 (2).

[718] ETSI TS 101 456 V1.1.1 (2000-12) Policy Requirements for CAs. In section 7.3.4. Dissemination of terms and conditions it is envisaged that "The CA shall make available to relying parties the terms and conditions regarding the use of the certificate including: - the qualified certificate policy being applied...; - information on how to validate the certificate, including requirements to check the revocation status of the certificate, such that the relying party is considered to "reasonably rely" on the certificate; if the CA has been certified to be conformant with the identified qualified certificate policy, and if so through which scheme". Further it notes that "... these terms and conditions may be included in a certification practice statement provided that they are conspicuous to the reader". Under ISO X.509 Standard, *ibid.*, is envisaged that the X.509 Version 3 certificate may contain an indication of certificate policy, which may be used by a certificate user to decide whether or not to trust a certificate for a particular purpose.

[719] For example section 6.20 of the CPS of Information Services PLC (www.stampit.org). It reads that the relying party is obliged to become acquainted with the certificate policy incorporated by hyperlink reference into the certificate issued.

[720] RFC 2527 Internet X.509 PKI Certificate Policy and Certificate Practices Framework defines the Certificate Policy as "a named set of rules that indicates the applicability of a certificate to a particular

trust should be created, the CSPs try to managed their liability towards the relying party.

The ABA guidelines give a direction in this respect – *"whether a certification practice statement is binding on a relying person depends on whether the relying person has knowledge or notice of the certification practice statement. A relying person has knowledge or at least notice of the contents of the certificate used by the relying person to verify a digital signature, including documents incorporated into the certificate by reference. It is therefore advisable to incorporate a certification practice statement into a certificate by reference."*[721]

Following the historical process of development of the concept of e-signatures and the PKI model, it becomes obvious that the European practices are strongly influences by the US solutions and standards. However, the approach of the US, being under a common law regime does not seem to be appropriate from a civil law doctrine point of view and if accepted without reservation, would threaten the security in PKI in these countries.

There is a significant difference in the substantive law between common law jurisdictions like UK, US, et al., and civil law jurisdictions like most of the EU Member States. It refers to the divergences in the possibilities for regimes of limiting the liability by the CSP/CP before the relying party. The civil law regimes grant less recognition (or none whatsoever) to the doctrines of constructive notice and incorporation by reference than do the common law regimes[722]. Thus, just the placement of an OID reference to the CP/CPS followed by the CSP cannot always bind the relying parties and make them "unreasonably" relying on the certificate.

In the dynamic world of electronic communications and open PKI, where parties are often strangers to each other, the relying party may not be expected to be aware, in detail, of the policy followed by the CSP. Reading, understanding and taking into consideration the certificate policy and the CPS seems to fall beyond the due care of the relying party. The CPSs and the CPs are usually long[723] as they contain legal and

---

community and/or class of application with common security requirements. For example, a particular certificate policy might indicate applicability of a type of certificate to the authentication of electronic data interchange transactions for the trading of goods within a given price range."

[721] See Section 1.8.2 of the ABA Digital Signatures Guidelines Legal Infrastructure for Certification Authorities and Secure Electronic Commerce, August 1, 1996 (www.abanet.org)

[722] ABA ISC PAG v0.30 – Public Draft for Comments, section C.1, p.43, *in fine*.

[723] See the CPs of Bankservice (www.b-trust.org), Information Services (www.stampit.org), Globalsign (www.globalsign.be), etc.

technical language is sometimes difficult to understand by people that do not possess such a specialized knowledge[724]. Moreover, the CPSs and the CPs cannot be incorporated into the very certificate, but are made available for dissemination only through web access. For some applications, no HTTP access[725] is required, because information from the directory could be derived through other protocols or means (touch-tone telephone response, LDAP access, OCSP access, etc.[726]). That especially refers to organizations where, for security reasons, no direct internet access is granted to the employees, and the CRLs of the CSPs are frequently downloaded and kept for verification as a local copy[727].

Actually, the facts listed in the qualified certificate and its status, as reflected in the directory, provide enough information for building trust. The relying party should take due care to become aware of these facts. That is why the Directive introduces in its Annex I statutory requirements for the qualified certificate to meet[728]. Further, Annex II rules that the CSPs issuing qualified certificates to the public shall ensure the operation of a prompt and secure directory and that the date and time when a certificate is issued or revoked can be determined precisely[729]. No requirements exist whatsoever for the certificate policy to be made available to the relying party, nor an obligation for the latter to be imposed because it would contradict the spirit of Article 6. The only possibility for the CSP to limit its liability is by placing certain information into the certificate and thus making the relying party "unreasonably" relying on the certificate as envisaged in paragraphs (3) and (4)[730].

---

[724] Problem also identified in ABA ISC PAG v0.30 – Public Draft for Comments, section B.4 also in section D.1.2.2, p. 78.

[725] Hypertext Transfer Protocol (HTTP) is the protocol used to transfer information on the World Wide Web.

[726] See *supra* note 113.

[727] Such a security policy is followed by many organizations, for example the Bulgarian Ministry of Finance.

[728] Annex I of the Directive [Requirements or qualified certificates] reads that qualified certificates must contain: Qualified certificates must contain: (a) an indication that the certificate is issued as a qualified ertificate; (b) the identification of the certification-service-provider and the State in which it is established; (c) the name of the certificate holder or a pseudonym, which shall be identified as such; (d) provision for a specific attribute of the certificate holder to be included if relevant, depending on the purpose for which the certificate is intended; (e) signature-verification data which correspond to signature-creation data under the control of the certificate holder; (f) an indication of the beginning and end of the period of validity of the certificate; (g) the identity code of the certificate; (h) the advanced electronic signature of the certification-service-provider issuing it; (i) limitations on the scope of use of the certificate, if applicable; and (j) limits on the value of transactions for which the certificate can be used, if applicable.

[729] Under Annex II the CSPs must: "… b) ensure the operation of a prompt and secure directory and a secure and immediate revocation service; (c) ensure that the date and time when a certificate is issued or revoked can be determined precisely; … "

[730] See section 4.4.1.4, *infra*.

Despite the fact that the above conclusions are valid for qualified certificates under the meaning of the Directive, the national courts should estimate in every single case, for other types of certificates, whether it would be a fair business or consumer approach to demand the relying parties to be aware of the CP/CPS[731].

7. Conclusions

In Chapter III an examination of the supranational specific liability rules of the main EC instrument regulating the framework of electronic signatures – Directive 1999/93/EC – was made. The correct interpretation of its rules proved to be possible only upon making an overview of the general notion of civil liability and the different aspects of the civil liability theory in Chapter II, and after clarifying in Chapter I the basic aspects of electronic signatures and the key role of the CSPs in the trust-building process, the lines of relations and the liability exposure of the CSPs, and the applicability of the general liability rules to the relationships thus identified.

The chapter focused on: i) producing detailed research of the relationships falling within the scope of regulation of Article 6; ii) identification of the liability exposure of the CSPs to the certificate holders, the relying parties and other parties; iii) studying the concept of reasonable reliance introduced as a precondition for the liability exposure; iv) analyzing the peculiarities of the liability grounds under Article 6; and v) making a precise distinction between limitation and exemption of liability and the means available for successful liability management under the Directive. While researching these issues, a careful, step-by-step approach was taken in interpreting the normative texts, since most of the erroneous conclusions made by different European scholars have been the result of incorrect interpretation of the liability rules.[732] Thus, it became possible to explain whether contractual and non-contractual liability are covered by the Directive, what is the scope of the duty of care, where and to what

---

[731] In many jurisdictions fair business practices are established to govern the business behaviour of companies operating in a given market. In Australia, for example, a Consumer Protection Principles in Electronic Commerce was set to address fair business practices, fair advertising and marketing practices, on-line business identification, and information disclosure requirements. The American Institute of Certified Public Accountants and the Canadian Institute of Chartered Accountants have established a Business Practices/ Transaction Integrity Principle and Criteria in connection with the developed WebTrust Program. In the US a group established by the core Internet players (known as Electronic Commerce and Consumer Protection Group) has established Guidelines for Merchant-to-Consumer Transactions to identify best practices for consumer protection in e-commerce and e-transactions. BBBOnline has established a set of standards known as BBB Code of Online Business Practices to provide guidance for best commercial practices in conducting on-line business. See ABA ISC PAG v0.30 – Public Draft for Comment, section C 5.1.7, p.62.

[732] See supra notes 531, 550, 568, 569, 595, 598, 680.

extent the burden of proof rests, what idea is behind the presumption of fault introduced by the European legislator, whether it is possible to place liability caps and how the CPS/CP can be used by the CSPs to limit or exempt themselves from liability etc. The proper interpretation of the liability rules was based on the knowledge and deductions derived from Chapter II.

The key to the correct analysis of the specific liability rules introduced by the Directive was the ascertaining of the fact that the Directive aims at promoting trust in the electronic world by establishing a wide set of primary rules containing stipulations mainly concerning the use of *qualified signatures*, i.e. requirements in respect of the secure signature creation devices (Annex III) and standards for electronic signatures products (Article 10 and Article 3 (5)); requirements for conformity assessment of the electronic signature products by designated bodies (Article 3 (4)); requirements for the qualified certificates supporting the qualified signature (Annex I); requirements for the certification service-providers issuing qualified certificates to the public (Annex II); and requirements for ensuring appropriate supervisory schemes for the activities of the CSPs issuing qualified certificates to the public (Article 3 (3)).

After analyzing the specific liability rules for the CSPs issuing qualified certificates to the public, in view of the identified wide set of primary measures to promote trust in the use of qualified signatures, the regime of Article 6 gives the impression of being a weak and ineffective instrument for enhancing trust. This deduction is further substantiated in Chapter V, where it becomes evident that after transposition into the national legislation of the country that is the subject of research (Bulgaria), the specific liability does not create a stronger shield and the general national liability rules may successfully protect the interests of the market players.

The conclusions were reached on the basis of the historical-comparative analysis of the final text of the rule of Article 6, and the versions which appeared during the course of the drafting process that demonstrated the metamorphosis of the initial ideas of the Commission.[733] At the beginning of the drafting process, the Commission did not intend to introduce specific secondary liability rules, but rather primary rules that would give rise to effective liability exposure under the national laws. The research in this chapter reveals that in the final text these initial ideas appeared in distorted form. The Directive elaborated on implementation of secondary rules, but

---

[733] Promoted in the Communication of the Commission - Towards a European Framework for Digital Signatures and Encryption. *Supra* note 503.

the essence of the liability rules of Article 6 is in fact establishing statutory obligations for the CSPs. Thus, most of the liability grounds of Article 6 overlap with the statutory requirements and obligations (primary rules) listed in Annex I and II. Other rules (Article 6 (3) and (4)) proved to be incorrectly interpreted in the doctrine,[734] because of their systematic presence in Article 6 - they provide a possibility for the CSPs to issue certificates under certain conditions and thus to exempt themselves from liability rather than achieve limitation of liability.[735]

The analysis of the specific liability rules for the CSPs set out in this chapter makes it possible to understand the problems faced by national legislators, like the Bulgarian one, in transposing the rule. Only after reviewing the practical transposition can a proper assessment of whether or not those rules promote greater trust in the world of electronic signatures or whether they are doomed to be merely rules.

Since Directive 1999/93/EC is not the only legal instrument containing liability rules for CSPs, the next step in the research is to identify other supranational normative instruments, on a European level, that might affect the liability exposure of the CSPs. The knowledge derived from this research in the present and the following chapters serves as a basis for the assessment in Chapter V of the need for the EU to introduce a specific liability regime to achieve better protection for the interests of the users of certification services in the internal market.

---

[734] See *supra* notes 661, 675, 680.

[735] See Chapter III, sections 6.3.1 and 6.3.3, *supra* and Chapter V, sections 2.6 and 2.7, *infra*.

Chapter IV

LIABILITY REGIME UNDER OTHER COMMUNITY ACTS

The analysis of Article 6 of EC Directive 1999/93 shows that the specific liability regime introduced by this Community act imposes obligations on the Member States to enforce rules applicable to the CSPs issuing or guaranteeing qualified certificates to the public. At the same time, recital (20) states that CSPs providing certification services to the public are subject to national rules regarding liability.

National rules, however, should comply with all other Community acts. The research shows that nowadays there are a number of such acts in force that regulate particular aspects of the provision of services or establish protective instruments for certain groups of users (consumers, individuals etc). Thus, they affect the liability exposure of the providers of certification services by becoming part of the general "national rules regarding liability".

In this respect the lawmakers in the different jurisdictions and particularly in Bulgaria being a case-study country faced several problems:

In the first instance, a problem arises in respect of identifying priorities in the application of different specific liability rules introduced by the *acquis communautaire*, while the Community acts, as transposed, sometimes affect the liability exposure of the providers of certification services *beyond* the specific liability regime established by Directive 1999/93/EC.

Secondly, the Community acts in question may conflict further with the specific minimum liability regime governing those CSPs issuing *qualified* certificates to the public, established by Directive 1999/93/EC, and especially with regard to feasible and successful liability management.

The above issues bring about difficulties in the transposition of the rules contained in different and potentially conflicting directives into national laws.

Thus, the present Chapter aims at determining the priority of application of the conflicting rules in respect of the liability of certification-service-providers, where such conflict exists.

Another of this chapter's aims is to analyze particular provisions of the Community acts that establish grounds for invoking the liability of providers of services that might be applicable to the CSPs without conflicting with the rules of Directive 1999/93/EC. Such rules may address a wider field of liability applicable to the CSPs than that regulated by the e-signatures Directive.

Finally, a comparison of the regimes in existence for the protection of the users of certification services under Directive 1999/93/EC and different user groups under the other Community acts would synthesize further knowledge for the purpose of understanding why the European legislator has chosen to establish a specific liability regime for CSPs. This knowledge will provide further evidence to support the author's assetions as to the lack of necessity for establishing a specific liability regime for CSPs.

To summarize, the objectives of this chapter are: i) to complete the liability position of the CSPs by reference to the provisions of these other Community instruments; ii) to identify the conflicting specific liability rules on the *acquis* level; iii) to provide a model for ascertaining priorities in the applicability of different national liability rules as transposed with regard to different users of certification services (consumers, individuals; and iv) to deduce proofs of evidence to support the assetions of the author.

1. Directive 93/13/EEC on Unfair Terms in Consumer Contracts

1.1. Objective

Council Directive 93/13/EEC of 5 April 1993 on unfair terms in consumer contracts has been enacted to eliminate unfair terms from contracts drawn up between a professional and a consumer[736].

---

[736] Communication From The Commission To The Council And The European Parliament On European Contract Law, Brussels, 11.07.2001, COM (2001) 398 final, http://europa.eu.int/comm/consumers/cons int/safe shop/fair bus pract/cont law/cont law 01 en.pdf

It is out of question that any CSP, in a broad sense, falls under the regulatory regime of Directive 93/13[737]. The scope would, however, encompass those cases when the person seeking the issuing of a certificate to support his signature is a natural person – consumer under the meaning of the Directive 93/13.

Under Article 2, for the purposes of Directive 93/13, a 'consumer' shall mean any natural person who, in contracts covered by the said Directive, is acting for purposes outside his trade, business or profession (i.e. the certificate holder), while 'supplier' shall mean any natural or legal person who, in contracts covered by the said Directive, is acting for purposes relating to his trade, business or profession, whether publicly owned or privately owned (i.e. the certification-service-provider).

How do the terms of the Directive affect the liability exposure of the CSPs?

1.2. Unfair terms – indirect limitation of liability

The purpose of Directive 93/13 is to provide a legal shield against non-mandatory, non-negotiated contractual terms incorporated in contracts drawn up between professional and consumer[738].

Being a supplier, the CSP might try to contractually establish rules in the CPS or the contract with the certificate holder, whereby to:

➤ inappropriately exclude or limit the legal rights of the certificate holder, *vis-à-vis* himself, in the event of total or partial non-performance or inadequate performance of any of the contractual obligations (Annex (a)); or

➤ make a binding agreement with the certificate holder whereas provision of certification services is subject to a condition whose realization depends on his own will alone (Annex (b)); or

➤ permit himself to retain sums paid by the certificate holder where the latter decides not to conclude or perform the contract, without providing for the certificate

---

[737] On the scope of the Directive 93/13 see Kelleher, D., Murray, K., *The Law in the European Union*, London: Sweet & Maxwell, 1999, section 10.13.

[738] See Directive 93/13, Article 1.

holder to receive compensation of an equivalent amount where the CSP is the party canceling the contract (Annex (c)); or

➢ authorize himself to dissolve the contract on a discretionary basis where the same facility is not granted to the certificate holder, or permit himself to retain the sums paid for certification services not yet supplied,,, where it is the CSP himself who dissolves the contract (Annex (f)); or

➢ enable the CSP to alter the contract terms and CPS unilaterally without a valid reason which is specified in the contract (Annex (j)); or

➢ enable himself to alter unilaterally without a valid reason any characteristics of the certification service to be provided (Annex (k); or

➢ give himself the right to determine whether the certification services supplied are in conformity with the contract, or giving him the exclusive right to interpret any term of the contract (Annex (m)); or

➢ limit his obligation to respect commitments undertaken by his agents or subcontractors making his commitments subject to compliance with a particular formality (Annex (n); or

➢ oblige the certificate holder to fulfill all his obligations whereas the CSP does not perform his (Annex (o)); or

➢ exclude or hinder the certificate holder's right to take legal action or exercise any other legal remedy, particularly by requiring the certificate holder to take disputes exclusively to arbitration not covered by legal provisions, unduly restricting the evidence available to him or imposing on him a burden of proof which, according to the applicable law, should lie with another party to the contract (Annex (q));

➢ etc.[739]

In all such cases, by reducing its rights to the detriment of the certificate holder, the CSP would reach a more favorable liability exposure. He will indirectly gain limitation of his liability.

---

[739] See the Annex of the Directive.

Under Directive 93/13 any non-mandatory, non-negotiated contractual term shall be considered unfair - it establishes a significant imbalance, to the consumer's detriment between the rights and obligations of the contracting parties (Article 3).

Of course, any such alleged unfair contractual term limiting the CSPs liability should be considered in view of the particularities of the certification service rendered and the whole set of binding contractual instruments – the contract, the CPS, the CP, etc. In any case, should a doubt exist whether the term is unfair or not, the most favorable interpretation to the customer would prevail (Article 5).

As a legal consequence, such an unfair contractual term will not bind the certificate holder and will be considered null (Article 6) - the protection of its interests will be given more priority than the ones of the CSP while limiting its liability[740]. It is understandable to have this protection established. The interests of the society demand the consumers' interests to be protected by a stronger shield than the interests of the CSPs. The consumers do not possess the knowledge, expertise, or the financial possibilities of the merchants or professionally developed organizations being service providers. Therefore, when consumers are involved, statutory protections should be granted[741].

1.3. Conflicting rules - direct limitation of liability

Besides the above, cases might exist whereby certain contractual terms providing direct exemption of liability of the CSP issuing qualified certificates to the public would be considered unfair under the meaning of Directive 93/13, while other Directives may provide specific rules granting the possibility for such an exemption.

For the CSPs that do not issue qualified certificates, or issue such but not to the public, there will not appear to be a problem, because there was no rule found in any directive or other instrument whatsoever granting explicit rights to limitation of liability of the said category of CSPs. For such market players, the rules of Directive 93/13 will apply.

---

[740] See ETSI TS 101 456 V1.1.1 (2000-12), Annex A, Page 37.

[741] On the intervention of statute and regulation see Weigenek, R., *E-Commerce: A Guide to the Law of Electronic Business*, 3rd ed., UK: Butterworths Lexis Nexis, 2002, p.66

An issue could arise, however, with respect to the rules of Article 6 (3) and (4) of Directive 1999/93/EC providing the possibility for the CSP issuing qualified certificates to the public, to limit its liability by either indicating limitations on the use of the certificate in the qualified certificate (provided such limitations are recognizable to third parties)[742] or by indicating in the qualified certificate a limit on the value of the transactions[743]. At the same time, such liability limitations might prove to be unfair under the rules of Directive 93/13.

The European legislator has correctly assumed that the interpretation on the application of the common rules for proper interpretation *lex specialis derogat legi generali* or *lex posteriori derogat legi priori* cannot be successfully applied, because on one side, in view of the public interests, the Directive on the unfair terms in consumer contracts is special as a matter of particularity in respect to the Directive on e-signatures, but on the other hand the latter act is subsequent in time and regulates in a particular manner the activity of providers of special kinds of services.

To resolve this issue, the Commission has provided in Article 6 (5) of Directive 1999/93/EC a specific rule stating that in case of contradiction, the provisions of the Directive 93/13/EEC shall have priority to the ones of the Directive 1999/93/EC – "*The provisions of paragraphs 1 to 4 (i.e. the liability limitation rights) shall be without prejudice to Council Directive 93/13/EEC of 5 April 1993 on unfair terms in consumer contracts.*"

However, it is important to be noted that such a priority would be granted only when consumers under the meaning of Directive 93/13/EEC enter into a contractual relationship with CSPs issuing qualified certificates to the public.

Furthermore, the scope of Article 6 (5) of Directive 1999/93/EC, refers not only to cases when the certificate holder is a consumer, but also to cases when the relying party enters into a contractual relationship with the CSPs issuing qualified certificates to the public, say, for retrieving information on the status of a qualified certificate. This conclusion is valid, provided such a contract is enforceable under local law.[744]

---

[742] See Chapter III, section 6.2, *supra*.

[743] See Chapter III, section 6.3, *supra*.

[744] See Chapter III, section 2.2, *supra*.

2. Directive 97/7/EC on Distance Contracts

2.1. Objective

Directive 97/7/EC of the European Parliament and of the Council of 20 May 1997 on the protection of consumers, in respect to distance contracts, aims at approximating the laws, regulations and administrative provisions of the Member States concerning distance contracts between consumers and suppliers[745].

The Directive establishes a minimum set of rules that should be introduced by the member states in widening the protection as established by the general consumer protection laws.

In respect to analyzing the applicability of the Directive, *vis-à-vis* the CSPs in a broad sense as suppliers of services – the same pattern as the one used for the analysis of Directive 93/13/EC should be followed. The scope of Directive 97/7 undoubtedly encompasses the protection of signatories - natural persons (consumers under Article 2 (2)) against the suppliers (any CSP in a broad sense) in the course of using one or more means of distance communication up to and including the moment at which the contract is concluded (Article 2 (1))[746]. The services provided by the CSPs are not excluded by the explicit provision of Article 3[747].

---

[745] See Kelleher, D., Murray, K., *The Law in the European Union*, London: Sweet & Maxwell, 1999, section 10.15, also Dickie, J., *Internet and Electronic Commerce Law in the European Union,* UK: Hart Publishing, 1999, pp. 91-100.

[746] See Chissik, M., Kelman, A., *Electronic Commerce: Law and Practice*, London: Sweet & Maxwell, 2002, p.31.

[747] Article 3 of Directive 97/7/EC provides that the Directive shall not apply to contracts: relating to financial services, a non-exhaustive list of which is given in Annex II, concluded by means of automatic vending machines or automated commercial premises, concluded with telecommunications operators through the use of public payphones, concluded for the construction and sale of immovable property or relating to other immovable property rights, except for rental, concluded at an auction. Further it states that Articles 4, 5, 6 and 7 (1) shall not apply to contracts for the supply of foodstuffs, beverages or other goods intended for everyday consumption supplied to the home of the consumer, to his residence or to his workplace by regular roundsmen, to contracts for the provision of accommodation, transport, catering or leisure services, where the supplier undertakes, when the contract is concluded, to provide these services on a specific date or within a specific period; exceptionally, in the case of outdoor leisure events, the supplier can reserve the right not to apply Article 7 (2) in specific circumstances.

2.2. Liability grounds

The Directive 97/7 sets a statutory standard for behaviour for the CSPs by enumerating certain duties, the negligent non-performance of which, would lead to the invoking of the CSPs' contractual or pre-contractual liability.

Prior to the conclusion of a distance contract, the person requesting the issuing of a certificate to support his signature must be provided, in a way appropriate to the distance, communication with clear and comprehensible information, complying with the principles of good faith in commercial transactions, particularly in the area of the certification services market[748]. This information should reveal the following:

➢   the identity and, in the case of contracts requiring payment in advance, the address of the CSP;

➢   the main characteristics of the certification services or in the case of any devices or products being provided (i.e. card reader, tokens, smart cards, smart pens, etc.) – their characteristics too;

➢   the price of the products or certification services including all taxes;

➢   delivery costs of devices or other CSP products where appropriate;

➢   the arrangements for payment, delivery or performance;

➢   the existence of the right of withdrawal, except in certain cases referred to in Article 6 (3) of the Directive 97/7[749];

➢   the cost of using the means of distance communication, when it is calculated at other than the basic rate;

---

[748] On the meaning of the prior information requirements and its provision in a comprehensible matter See Chissik, M., Kelman, A., *ibid.*, p.33

[749] Article 6 (3) of the Directive 97/7/EC stipulates that unless the parties have agreed otherwise, the consumer may not exercise the right of withdrawal provided for in paragraph 1 of the same article in respect of contracts: for the provision of services if performance has begun, with the consumer's agreement, before the end of the seven working day period referred to in paragraph 1, for the supply of goods or services the price of which is dependent on fluctuations in the financial market which cannot be controlled by the supplier, for the supply of goods made to the consumer's specifications or clearly personalized or which, by reason of their nature, cannot be returned or are liable to deteriorate or expire rapidly, for the supply of audio or video recordings or computer software which were unsealed by the consumer, for the supply of newspapers, periodicals and magazines, for gaming and lottery services.

➢   the period for which the offer or the price remains valid;

➢   where appropriate, the minimum duration of the contract in the case of contracts for the supply of products or certification services to be performed permanently or recurrently.

In the case of telephone communications, the identity of the caller and the commercial purpose of the call must be made clear at the beginning of the conversation with the potential client[750]. The CSP must address confirmation in writing or in another durable means at the time of performance of the contract[751], as well as any procedures and conditions for exercising the right of withdrawal; the geographical address of the place of business of the CSP to which the certificate holder may address complaints; information relating to after-sales service and guarantees if such exist; the conclusions for canceling the contract when it is of an unspecified duration or such exceeding one year[752].

The Directive 97/7 provides that unless agreed otherwise, the CSP shall be obliged to perform the contract in thirty days. Should he fail to do that, he shall be held liable for refunding the amounts paid (Article 7)[753].

As it becomes clear, Directive 97/7 provides specific mandatory obligations for the CSPs being suppliers under the meaning of the Directive towards the signatories – consumers. Failure to follow the rules of the Directive, as implemented into the local legislations may result in engaging the CSPs liability. Of course this would be the case, provided damages have occurred.

2.2. Limitation of liability

By introducing mandatory contractual rules, the Directive 97/7 deprives the parties in deviating from its provisions by agreement. The certificate holder, for example, could

---

[750] See Article 4 of the Directive.

[751] In some jurisdictions the electronic form is equalized to the written form (especially those that have transposed the UNCITRAL Model Law of Electronic Commerce (i.e. Ireland, Slovenia, Bulgaria) or the Directive 2000/31/EC on E-commerce. Thus confirmation in writing shall be considered met if such is made electronically and the electronic document is stored (see for example Article 3 (2) of the Bulgarian EDESA). In any case confirmation by electronic mail trough the Internet shall be considered a durable mean under the meaning of Article 5 (1).

[752] See Article 5 of the Directive.

[753] Chissik, M., Kelman, A., *ibid.*, p.34-35

not waive the rights conferred on him by transposition of the Directive (Article 12 (q)) into the respective national law. Thus, the Directive 97/7 affects directly, the relationship between the CSPs and the signatories in entering into contracts by distance communication. In such a way, the Directive reduces the available instruments of the CSP to manage its liability through distance contracting by agreeing on certain behaviour.

Any deviation, in contradiction to the rules set forth by the Directive 97/7 where introduced by the Member States, would lead to a serious legal defect in the contract – it would be considered null and would not bind the parties[754].

In the case of a dispute between the certificate holder and the CSP, the burden of proof concerning information, confirmation, time limits and the certificate holder's consent will be born by the CSP, rather than by the certificate holder[755].

2.4. Conflicting rules

As already mentioned, the rules of Directive 97/7 (as transposed) will apply to the CSPs when supplying certification services or products by distance contracts.

However, unlike the case with Directive 93/13/EC, the rules of Directive 97/7, as transposed, would not apply to CSPs issuing qualified certificates to the public by distance contracts. These providers could manage their liability and follow their duties pursuant to the rules of Directive 1999/93/EC. In such respect, the CSPs issuing qualified certificates to the public by distance means would not be bound by the rules of Directive 97/7/EC. The Directive 1999/93/EC would have priority over Directive 97/7/EC.

The reasons for such a conclusion could be found in different directions.

In the first instance, whenever special rules for consumer protection are explicitly envisaged, in respect of the liability of the CSPs issuing qualified certificates to the public, these are meant to have priority over the rules of Directive 1999/93/EC. Article 6 (5) of the latter Directive provides such[756]. *Per argumentum a contrario* should

---

[754] *Per argumentum* of Article 12.

[755] Same opinion supported by Chissik, M., Kelman, A., *ibid.,* p.37

[756] See section 1.3, *supra.*

the provisions of Article 6, paragraphs 1 to 4 granting rights of the CSPs issuing qualified certificates to the public contradict with other directives, than Directive 93/13/EEC, the first would apply.

Secondly, in Annex II of Directive 1999/93/EC is defined the scope of duties to be followed by the CSPs issuing qualified certificates. In view of liability management, the rule of Annex II (k) provides, for example, that the CSPs must, before entering into a contractual relationship with a person seeking certificate to support his electronic signature, inform that person by a durable means of communication of the precise terms and conditions regarding the use of the certificate, including any limitations on its use, the existence of a voluntary accreditation scheme and procedures for complaints and dispute settlement and such information, which may be transmitted electronically, must be in writing and in readily understandable language. This rule differs from the rules of Articles 4 and 5 of Directive 97/7/EC. Should special rules be provided for the particular service rendered – certification service, they should apply in all cases when the CSP issuing qualified certificates to the public enters into a contractual relationship either by distance communications or in a common way.

Thirdly, the conclusions made are supported by the provision of Article 13 (2) of Directive 97/7/EC. It states that where specific Community rules contain provisions governing *only certain aspects of the supply of goods or provision of services* (i.e. certification services for issuing qualified certificates to the public regulated by Directive 1999/93/EC), those provisions, rather than the provisions of Directive 97/7, shall apply to these specific aspects of distance contracts.

3. Directive 95/46/EC on the Protection of Personal Data

3.1. General notes

While regulating the provision of certification services, Directive 1999/93/EC provides in Recital (24) that in order to increase user confidence in electronic communication and electronic commerce, certification-service-providers must observe the data protection legislation and individual privacy.

Furthermore, by recognizing the priority of the protective rules with respect to personal data, the Directive envisages by the special provision of Article 8, that Member States shall ensure that CSPs comply with the requirements laid down in

Directive 95/46/EC of the European Parliament and of the Council of 24 October 1995 on the protection of individuals with regard to the processing of personal data and on the free movement of such data (Article 8 (1))[757]. Particularly Member States shall ensure that a CSP which issues certificates to the public may collect personal data, only directly from the data subject, or after the explicit consent of the data subject, and only insofar as it is necessary for the purposes of issuing and maintaining the certificate. The data may not be collected or processed for any other purposes without the explicit consent of the data subject.

Directive 1999/93/EC reveals some specific obligations, while at the same time, general obligations in respect to the personal data protection it refers to in Directive 95/46/EC.

How does Article 8 of the E-signature Directive and thus the Personal Data Protection Directive affect the liability exposure of the certification-service-providers?

The answer to this question could be found in the potential damages that could occur to the individuals – users of certification services - resulting as an infringement on behalf of the CSP of the rules established for protection of the processing, storing and disclosing of personal data.

3.2. Obligations under Directive 95/46/EC

As already mentioned, Directive 95/46/EC aims at harmonizing the Member States' laws by establishing uniform civil rights of privacy in respect to personal data and its processing[758].

Under the Directive, data processing is permissible if it is necessary for the performance of a contract to which the data subject is party (i.e. certificate holder, or relying party in certain cases[759]) or in order to take steps at the request of the data subject prior to entering into the contract (i.e. the person seeking the issuing of a certificate provides personal data, but further it becomes clear, that the certificate

---

[757] OJ L 281,23.11.1995, page 31

[758] See Dimech, F., *Protecting Yourself ... From Data Protection*, http://www.cdf.com.mt/pages/docs/data%20protefction.pdf

[759] See Chapter I, section 2.2.5, *supra*.

214

holder does not hold the signature-creation data corresponding to the signature-verification data and refuses to issue the certificate) (Article 7).

For the purposes of the PKI, collection and processing of personal data is an inevitable process. Such data is first contained in the personal public key certificates issued by the CSPs[760]. Otherwise, no connection could be made between the identity of the person and his public key and thus the CSP cannot serve as a third relying party – the PKI would not function. On the other hand, before issuing certificates, the CSPs should collect and verify such data by appropriate means, according to the law[761]. In the third place, this data is stored into a directory where all published certificates and the certificate revocation lists are kept. The data is subject to being revealed to any relying party either by using search engines or by retrieving the very certificates[762].

There are many obligations for processing personal data established by the Directive, with which the CSP must comply[763]. The analysis of these obligations is not subject to this study. Among them, however, there should be identified those obligations relevant to the CSPs, that prove to be of utmost importance for the general liability exposure of the different types of CSPs.

For example, the controller must, when the processing is carried out on his behalf, choose a processor providing sufficient guarantees in respect to the technical security measures and organizational measures governing the processing to be carried out, and must ensure compliance with those measures. Therefore, the CSP should always be

---

[760] See Annex I of the Directive 1999/93/EC – Requirements for qualified certificates. Such should contain the name of the certificate holder or a pseudonym, which shall be identified as such (c) and specific attribute of the certificate holder to be included if relevant, depending on the purpose for which the certificate is intended (d). The latter attribute might be personal data pursuant to Article 2 (2) of the Directive 95/46. Despite of the fact, that the Directive on e-signatures establishes requirements for qualified certificates, the name and other applicable attributes will be contained in any personal public key certificates – See Section 2 of RFC 2693, SPKI Certificate Theory, September 1999, The Internet Society.

[761] See Annex II (d) of Directive 1999/93/EC the CSP shall verify, by appropriate means in accordance with national law, the identity and, if applicable, any specific attributes of the person to which a qualified certificate is issued; See also RFC 2527 - Internet X.509 Public Key Infrastructure, Certificate Policy and Certification Practices Framework.

[762] See ITU-T Recommendation X.501 Information technology – Open Systems, Interconnection – The Directory: Models, and IETF RFC 1777 "The Lightweight Directory Access Protocol". See also Annex II (b) – the CSP shall ensure the operation of a prompt and secure directory and a secure and immediate revocation service, and further he shall record all relevant information concerning a qualified certificate for an appropriate period of time, in particular for the purpose of providing evidence of certification for the purposes of legal proceedings - such recording may be done electronically.

[763] For the obligations established by the Directive 95/46/EC see Kelleher, D., Murray, K., *The Law in the European Union*, London: Sweet & Maxwell, 1999, section 14.01.

liable for such misconduct of other CSPs, to which it has outsourced certain activities or certification services. Article 17 provides special provisions ruling that there must be a contract or other legal act between the controller, being the person that determines the purposes and means of the data processing (i.e. the CSP running the CA) and the processor, being the person who processes data on behalf of a controller (i.e. the CSP playing the RA role under agreement with the CSP - CA). The contract should stipulate that the processor CSP should act only upon instructions from the controller CSP, and that the controller's obligations should also be incumbent on the processor.

This does not mean that the processor CSP would be directly liable before the damaged person. His liability would be towards the controller CSP, i.e. he could be engaged on indemnity grounds only by the latter. As an exception, however, in some countries, the liability of the processor CSP could be engaged directly on tort grounds[764].

3.3. Liability for unlawful processing

By introducing respective legislative measures, Member States must secure that any breach of the rights guaranteed to the person whose data is being processed by the national law applicable to such processing, would bring a right of the person to a judicial remedy. This right should arise without prejudice to any administrative remedies for which provision may be made, *inter alia* before the national supervisory authority, prior to referral to the judicial authority.

As can be derived from the rule of Article 23, Member States shall provide that any person (particularly the certificate holder, the relying party, or other whose personal data might be subject to processing) who has suffered damage as a result of an unlawful processing operation or from any act incompatible with the national provisions adopted pursuant to the Directive, is entitled to receive compensation from the controller (CSP) for the damage suffered.

---

[764] See for example Article 49 of the Netherlands Data Protection Act (it refers to all responsible parties). Same approach is followed by the Lithuanian Law on Legal Protection of Personal Data – it refers that "controllers or data processors of personal data" shall be liable towards the damaged person.

Such compensation should encompass all actual direct damages caused by the negligent behaviour[765].

3.4. Exemption and limitation of liability. Burden of proof

The general liability rule of paragraph (1) of Article 23 does not reveal any particularities of interest for this analysis. Very important norm, however, is found in paragraph (2) of the same article. It reads that the controller may be exempted from liability, in whole or in part, if he proves that he is not responsible for the event giving rise to the damage. The approach of the Directive on personal data should be analaysed carefully.

The idea that stays behind Article 23 (2) is to protect the economically weaker party – the natural person whose data is being unlawfully processed (i.e. the certificate holder, relying party or other). Directive 95/46/EC, similarly to Directive 1999/93/EC[766], establishes a burden of proof rule. However, the rebutable presumption is different in the two Directives.

The rule of Article 23 (2) gives the person the advantage of not bearing the burden of proof in a civil proceeding that the behaviour of the controller CSP has caused the damage. Such a presumption would protect its interests, unless the controller CSP proves to the contrary. In other words the Directive on personal data establishes *presumption of causality*.

Thus, the controller CSP may be exempted from liability, in whole or in part, if he proves that he is not responsible for the event giving rise to the damage (Article 23 (2)). By using the term "not responsible" the Directive encompasses all the cases when the behaviour of the person is not in a causality chain to the damages

---

[765] Section III of the Proposed Standard Contractual Clauses for the Transfer of Personal Data from the EU to Third Countries (controller to controller transfers) (of September 2003) refers that "Each Party shall be liable to the other Party for damages it causes by any breach of these clauses. Liability as between the Parties is limited to actual damage suffered. Punitive damages (i.e. damages intended to punish a party for its outrageous conduct) are specifically excluded. Each party shall be liable to Data Subjects for damages it causes by any breach of third party rights under these Clauses. This does not affect the liability of the Data Exporter under its data protection law" (http://www.iccwbo.org/home/e_business/word_documents/ Model%20contract%20Sept%202003%20FINAL.pdf).

[766] Article 6 (1) of Directive 1999/93/EC provides that the CSP issuing or guaranteeing qualified certificates to the public shall be liable for damages caused to any person who reasonably relies on the certificate for diligently performing certain duties, "unless the certification-service-provider proves that he has not acted negligently". See Chapter III, section 6.1.2, *supra*.

occurrence, or despite the behaviour, the event causing the damage would have occurred. Such would be the cases of *force majeur* or accidental events, behaviour of the other party that led to causing the damage[767], etc.

The liability exposure of the CSPs on such grounds would differ from jurisdiction to jurisdiction. This is due to the fact that the presumption has not been transposed in a common way in all member states and the other European countries. In some countries like Finland[768], Lithuania[769], Ireland[770], Bulgaria[771], and others, the presumption is not transposed at all, while the national rules in other countries like the Netherlands[772], Sweden[773], Bosnia and Herzegovina[774], UK[775], Hungary[776], Portugal[777], and others follow the wording of the Directive.

---

[767] See Article 18 (2) of the Bosnian Personal Data Protection Act – "No compensation shall be paid for damage caused by the injured person's intentional or seriously negligent conduct"; Section 18 (2) of the Hungarian Act LXIII of 1992 on Protection of Personal Data and Disclosure of Data of Public Interest – "No compensation shall be paid for that part of damage caused by the injured person's intentional or seriously negligent conduct".

[768] Section 47 of the Data Protection Act of Finland (http://www.tietosuoja.fi/uploads/hopxtvf.HTM) provides, that the controller is liable to compensate for the economic and other loss suffered by the data subject or another person because of processing of personal data in violation of the provisions of this act without establishing reversed burden of proof.

[769] The Lithuanian Law on Legal Protection of Personal Data (http://www.ada.lt/en/docs/lawonlegalprot.doc), articles 28-29 stipulates that any person who has sustained damage as a result of unlawful processing of personal data or other acts or omissions by the data controller or data processor shall be entitled to claim compensation for material and non-material damage caused to him. The data controller, data processor or other person, after compensation for damage caused to the person, shall make a claim, in the manner established by law, for recovery of the loss sustained from the employee processing the data due to whose fault the loss occurred.

[770] See Section 5 (f) of the Irish Data Protection Act (http://www.dataprivacy.ie/6ai-1.htm#7).

[771] See the Bulgarian Personal Data Protection Act (http://xdata.gateway.bg/htmls/en/zakon_protection.htm).

[772] Article 49 of the Netherlands Personal Data Protection Act (http://home.planet.nl/%7Eprivacy1/wbp_en_rev.htm) provide that where a person suffers harm as a consequence of acts concerning him which infringe the provisions laid down by or under this act the responsible parties shall be liable for harm resulting from non-compliance with the statutory provisions. Processors are liable for this harm where this was incurred as a result of their actions. Responsible parties or processors *may be exempted wholly or partially from this liability where they can prove that the harm cannot be attributed to them.*

[773] Section 46 of the Swedish Personal Data Act (http://justitie.regeringen.se/inenglish/pressinfo/pdf/nyengpul.pdf) envisage that the controller of personal data shall compensate the registered person for damages and the violation of personal integrity that the processing of personal data in contravention of this Act has caused. The liability to pay compensation may, to the extent that it is reasonable, *be adjusted if the person providing personal data proves that the error was not caused by him or her.*

[774] The Law on the Protection of Personal Data of Bosnia and Herzegovina (http://www.privacyinternational.org/countries/bosnia/bosnia-dpa.html), Article 18, provides that the data controller shall pay compensation for any damage caused to a data subject as a result of the processing of his or her data. The data controller is liable for any damage to a data subject caused by a data processor. The data controller *may be exempted from this liability, in whole or in part, if he proves that he is not responsible for the event giving rise to the damage.*

Such an exemption cannot be evaded by contractual agreement. The mandatory character of the rule also gives grounds to concluding that no liability limitation could be agreed in this respect, either.

To a contrast – the Directive 1999/93 establishes *presumption of fault* by explicitly allocating the burden of defense in respect to whether the CSP has acted diligently. It does not establish presumption of causality.

As it became evident from the analysis made in Chapter II, the causality is one of the elements of the liability corpus. As a general rule, the causality should be proved by the damaged party in order to have a successful claim against the alleged tortfesor, resp. the debtor in fault. While the general national liability rules usually do not establish reversed burden of proving the causality of the illicit behaviour to the result[778], the rule of Article 23 of Directive 95/46 would serve as an effective protective instrument to the weaker party – the individual. The latter would benefit from the reversed burden since he will not have to prove that the causality. As it has become apparent from Chapter III, section 6.1.2, Directive 1999/93/EC does not establish a presumption of causality. It aims at establishing a "presumption of fault". However, in Chapter V it will be substantiated that this presumption does not in fact "reverse" the burden of proving the negligence while in civil law the fault is presumed both in contract and tort in many jurisdictions. Thus it cannot play essential role to

---

[775] Article 13 of the UK Personal Data Protection Act (http://www.hmso.gov.uk/acts/acts1998/80029--b.htm#13) provides that An individual who suffers damage by reason of any contravention by a data controller of any of the requirements of this Act is entitled to compensation from the data controller for that damage, but in proceedings brought against a person by virtue of this section *it is a defence to prove that he had taken such care as in all the circumstances was reasonably required to comply with the requirement concerned.*

[776] Pursuant to the Hungarian Act LXIII of 1992 on Protection of Personal Data and Disclosure of Data of Public Interest, Section 18, (http://www.osa.ceu.hu/bridge/ access&protection/04.htm) the data controller shall pay compensation for any damage caused to data subject with processing of his or her data or by violation of the technical requirements of data protection. Controller shall be discharged from liability upon proving that the damage was caused inevitable by reasons beyond control of data processing.

[777] Article 34 of the Portuguese Act on Protection of Personal Data (http://www.cnpd.pt/Leis/lei 6798en.htm) provides that any person who has suffered damage as a result of an unlawful processing operation or of any other act incompatible with legal provisions in the area of personal data protection is entitled to receive compensation from the controller for the damage suffered.The controller may be exempted from this liability, in whole or in part, if he proves that he is not responsible for the event giving rise to the damage.

[778] See Chapter II, section 4.2, *supra.*

making the users' protection stronger and to contributing essentially to the trust-building process[779].

4. Directive 2000/35/EC on Late Payments in Commercial Transactions

4.1. Objective

Another legislative document that might affect directly the liability exposure of the CSPs is the Directive 2000/35/EC of the European Parliament and of the Council of 29 June 2000 on combating late payment in commercial transactions.

The aim of the Directive is to establish appropriate legislative measures to fight late payments made as remuneration in commercial transactions. Under the interpreting provision of Article 2a *commercial transaction* shall mean transaction *between undertakings* or *between undertakings and public authorities* which lead to the delivery of goods *or the provision of services* for remuneration. The Directive defines undertaking as "any organization acting in the course of its independent economic or professional activity, even where it is carried out by a single person".

As already analyzed in section 3 of Chapter III, *supra*, under the meaning of the Directive 1999/93/EC a certification-service-provider shall be considered any entity or legal or natural person who issues certificates *or provides other services* related to electronic signatures. In such a sense, the CSP would be "*any organization*" or "*a single person*", acting in the course of its "*economic or professional activity*" – "*undertaking*" under the meaning of the Directive 2000/35/EC.

From the said above, it becomes clear that any contract between CSPs as market players in the PKI market will be considered a commercial transaction (i.e. contract between the CSP running the CA and CSP acting as a RA, CSP outsourcing to another CSP certain services, etc.). In almost all cases under such contract, payments are due for the services rendered.

On the other hand, there is no doubt that any CSP falls under the meaning of "*undertaking*" when entering into commercial transaction with another CSP, regardless of the type of certification or other trust services it provides, and regardless of what role within the PKI it plays – CA, RA, TSA, DSA, etc.

---

[779] See Chapter V, section 2,5, *infra*.

Therefore, the scope of this Directive encompasses all cases where liability for late payments between any CSPs could be invoked.

The Directive will not affect the liability of the CSP within the basic lines of the relationship of the CSP with the certificate holder and the CSP with the relying party. The direction of payments is either always towards the CSP, or there is no obligation for payments at all. The Directive might affect the liability of the certificate holder towards the CSP, when the certificate holder will be considered an undertaking under the meaning of the Directive 2000/35, entering into contractual relationships with another undertaking (the CSP) to issue and maintain a certificate, or to provide other certification services. However, the liability of the certificate holder remains out of the scope of the present research.

4.2. Liability for late payments

The Directive establishes a legal framework to be introduced by the Member States that would affect only one aspect in respect to the liability exposure of the CSPs – the late payments due as remuneration for commercial transactions. For example, the late payment of a CSP running the CA to another CSP performing an RA, or DSA function, would be covered by the Directive.

In burden of such CSP, an interest with a predefined statutory rate will become payable from the day following the date or the end of the period for payment set forth in the contract. The interest rate will be the sum of the interest rate applied by the European Central Bank to its most recent main refinancing operation carried out before the first calendar day of the half-year in question, plus at least seven percentage points, unless otherwise specified in the contract[780].

If the date or period for payment is not fixed in the contract, interest will become payable automatically, without the necessity of a reminder, 30 days following the date of receipt by the CSP - debtor of the invoice or an equivalent request for payment. If the date of the receipt of the invoice or the equivalent request for payment is uncertain, interest will become payable automatically 30 days after the date of receipt of the goods or services; or if the CSP - debtor receives the invoice or the equivalent

---

[780] For a Member State which is not participating in the third stage of economic and monetary union, the reference rate referred to above shall be the equivalent rate set by its national central bank. In both cases, the reference rate in force on the first calendar day of the half-year in question shall apply for the following six months.

request for payment earlier than the goods or the services, 30 days after the receipt of the goods or services.

If there is a statutory or contractually agreed procedure of acceptance by the CSPs or verification by which the conformity of certification services with the contract is to be ascertained, interest will become payable 30 days after the date of the procedure. If the debtor CSP receives the invoice or the equivalent request for payment earlier on or on the date on which such acceptance or verification takes place, the time frame would be 30 days after this latter date.

The creditor CSP will be entitled to interest for late payment to the extent that he has fulfilled his contractual and legal obligations; and he has not received the amount due on time, unless the debtor CSP is not responsible for the delay.

The Directive provides that for certain categories of contracts to be defined by national law, Member States may fix the period after which interest becomes payable to a maximum of 60 days provided that they either restrain the parties to the contract from exceeding this period or fix a mandatory interest rate that substantially exceeds the statutory rate. Research shows that there is no specific national regulation in any Member State in respect to certification services contracts or other contracts that CSPs may enter into, to fix the period above the statutory rate as defined by the Directive 2000/35.

Member States should provide that an agreement on the date for payment or on the consequences of late payment which is not in line with the provisions of the Directive would either not be enforceable or would give rise to a claim for damages if, when all circumstances of the case, including good commercial practice and the nature of the product are considered, it is grossly unfair to the creditor. In determining whether an agreement is grossly unfair to the creditor, it will be taken into account, *inter alia*, whether the debtor has any objective reason to deviate from the provisions of the Directive. If such an agreement is determined to be grossly unfair, the statutory terms will apply, unless the national courts determine different conditions which are fair. The Directive instructs the Member States to ensure, in the interests of creditors and of competitors that adequate and effective means exist to prevent the continued use of terms which are grossly unfair.

Member States are also to provide that, where the debt is not in dispute, an enforceable title can be obtained, irrespective of the amount of the debt, usually within 90 calendar days of the lodging of the creditor's action or application at the court or other competent authority, provided that the debt or aspects of the procedure are not disputed (Article 5).

5. Directive 2000/31/EC on Certain Legal Aspects of Information Society Services, in Particular Electronic Commerce, in the Internal Market

5.1. Overview

The Directive 2000/31/EC of the European Parliament and of the Council of 8 June 2000 on certain legal aspects of information society services, in particular electronic commerce, in the Internal Market ('Directive on electronic commerce')[781] establishes certain rules that, similarly to the approach of Article 6 (1) of Directive 1999/93/EC, define the scope of the liability sources – infringement of certain obligations of the CSPs that might cause damages and thus, might attract their liability.

The objective of this Directive is to create a legal framework to ensure the free movement of information society services between Member States[782], and at the same time, to establish a minimum set of rules to protect the consumers in contractual matters, particularly in respect to the provision of information society services[783]. To achieve this objective, the Directive imposes certain obligations on the providers of information society services[784].

Some of the certification services would fall within the scope of the Directive. That would be the case when, for example, the CSP provides at a distance through the Internet the certification service for issuing or maintaining the certificate to support the certificate holder's public key, or to provide electronic access to the public register to the relying party (in those cases, when this could be considered 'a service'). Under

---

[781] Official Journal L 178 of 17.07.2000

[782] See Recital (8) of the Directive.

[783] In such respect the provisions of the Directive are without prejudice to other analyzed directives establishing rules for protection of consumers that might affect the CSPs liability. Recital (11) explicitly envisages, that the Directive is without prejudice to the level of protection for, in particular, consumer interests, as established by Community acts; amongst others, Directive 93/13/EEC on unfair terms in consumer contracts and Directive 97/7/EC on the protection of consumers in respect of distance contracts; those Directives also apply in their entirety to information society services; that same Community acquis, which is fully applicable to information society services. Thus the Directive complements information requirements established by the abovementioned Directives and in particular Directive 97/7/EC.

[784] Groshieide, F., Boele-Woelki, K., *European Private Law (1999/2000). E-Commerce Issue*, The Netherlands: Molengrafica, 2000, p.11.

the definition of Article 2 "*information society services*" as regulated by the Directive shall mean "*any service normally provided for remuneration, at a distance, by electronic means and at the individual request of a recipient of services*". The notion already exists in Directive 98/34/EC of the European Parliament and of the Council of 22 June 1998 laying down a procedure for the provision of information in the field of technical standards and regulations and of rules on information society services and in Directive 98/84/EC of the European Parliament and of the Council of 20 November 1998 on the legal protection of services based on, or consisting of, conditional access. This definition covers *any service normally provided for remuneration, at a distance, by means of electronic equipment for the processing (including digital compression) and storage of data, and at the individual request of a recipient of a service*. The certification services examined above are not excluded from the indicative list of Annex V to Directive 98/34/EC of services that do not imply data processing and storage. Furthermore, Recital (20) of Directive 2000/31/EC clarifies that the definition of '*recipient of a service*' covers all types of users of information society services, both by persons who provide information on open networks such as the Internet and by persons who seek information on the Internet for private or professional reasons. At the same time, '*consumer*' will be any natural person who is acting for purposes which are outside the scope of his or her trade, business or profession.[785]

Therefore, any certification service provided for remuneration, at a distance, by electronic means, and at the individual request of the recipient of the service, would be considered an information society service and its provision by the CSP would be covered by the Directive[786].

Even though provided without remuneration, the certification service would also be considered an information society service. Recital (18) envisages that information society services are not solely restricted to services giving rise to on-line contracting but also, in so far as they represent an economic activity, extend to services which are not remunerated by those who receive them, such as those offering on-line

---

[785] See Weigenek, R., *E-Commerce: A Guide to the Law of Electronic Business*, 3rd ed., UK: Butterworths Lexis Nexis, 2002, pp. 17-18

[786] See for example the conditions for issuing of Personal Freemail Certificates of Thawte (www.thawte.com) or of B-Trust Certificates Class 1 of Bankservice (www.b-trust.org). Such certificates are issued upon electronic request of the interested person and are provided electronically and at distance only. Furthermore the access to the CRL or the X.509 directory kept by the CSP is sometimes subject to entering into agreement – see the Relying Party Agreement of Globalsign (www.globalsign.be). Sometimes, especially for CSPs providing access to the directory or to some items stored therein (especially when the certification services are provided not to the public) could be made subject to payment of remuneration.

information or commercial communications, or those providing tools allowing for search, access and retrieval of data[787].

The Directive does not apply to certification services provided by CSPs but not by electronic means (Article 2 (ii)).

Considering the above, the certification-service-providers shall be considered an information-society service provider – "*any natural or legal person providing an information society service*" (Article 2) and thus the specific obligations established by the Directive 2000/31/EC towards the recipients of the services shall be binding upon the CSPs.[788]

5.2. Obligations

Each Member State shall ensure that the certification services provided by CSPs established on its territory comply with the national provisions applicable in the Member State in question, which fall within the coordinated field.

In addition to all other statutory information requirements[789] established by Community law, the CSP must render easily, directly and permanently accessible to the recipients of the service and competent authorities, at least the following information:

➢   the CSP's name;

➢   the CSP's address of establishment;

➢   all details of the CSP, including his electronic mail address, which allow him to be contacted rapidly and communicated with in a direct and effective manner;

---

[787] Lodder, A., Kaspersen, H., *eDirectives. Guide to European Union Law on E-commerce*, Kluwer Law International, 2002, p.77. The authors find that contractual relations are covered by the information requirements, but the requirements are also applicable if there is no contract between the provider and the recipient.

[788] For the nature of the Information Service Providers see Groshieide, F., Boele-Woelki, K., *ibid.*, p.13

[789] See Weigenek, R., *E-Commerce: A Guide to the Law of Electronic Business*, 3rd ed., UK: Butterworths Lexis Nexis, 2002, p.19

> where it is registered in a trade or similar public register, the trade register in which the service provider is entered and its registration number, or equivalent means of identification in that register;

> where the activity is subject to an authorization scheme, the particulars of the relevant supervisory authority[790].

In addition, should the certification service refer to prices (i.e. certificate issuance, or certificate suspension or revocation), the CSP should indicate them clearly and unambiguously and, in particular, he should indicate whether they are inclusive of tax and further costs.

Further, the commercial communications which are part of, or constitute, a certification service, should at least comply with the following conditions:

> the commercial communication shall be clearly identifiable as such;

> the natural or legal person on whose behalf the commercial communication is made shall be clearly identifiable;

> promotional offers, such as discounts, premiums and gifts, where permitted in the state where the certification-service-provider is established, shall be clearly identifiable as such, and the conditions which are to be met to qualify for them shall be easily accessible and be presented clearly and unambiguously.

When contracts for provision of certification services are to be concluded electronically[791], the CSP should include the following information:

> the different stages in the course of contract formation;

> whether or not the concluded contract will be filed and whether it will be accessible;

> the expedients for correcting handling errors;

---

[790] This provision would be hardly applicable to CSPs while Article 3 (1) of Directive 1999/93/EC rules that Member States shall not make the provision of certification services subject to prior authorisation. However, this might be cases where some countries may stay out of the EU and make the provision of certification services subject to prior authorization (i.e. Estonia).

[791] On the electronic contracting see Groshieide, F., Boele-Woelki, K., *ibid.*, p.20

> the languages offered for the conclusion of the contract.

There are certain other obligations for the providers of information society services but the CSP would hardly fall in such a role[792]. Therefore these obligations will not be subject of analysis in the present work.

5.3. Legal consequences with respect to liability of CSPs

The way the information requirements are established would raise a question of what would be the legal consequences *vis-à-vis* the civil liability exposure of the CSPs, being providers of information society services?

The question should be examined separately for both the obligation for the general information requirements and those concerning the conclusion of contracts in electronic form.

5.3.1. Legal consequences with respect to non-provision of general information

At first glance, it might appear that the non-fulfillment of any of the obligations established for provision of general information would not lead to invoking of CSP's civil liability. Non-fulfillment of obligation for provision of information on the address or the details of the CSP, for example, would hardly cause direct damages to the recipient of the service and thus would substantiate liability. Even if we assume that the lack of such information would mislead the recipient and he would enter into a contractual relationship, nullity of the contract due to infringement of such obligation seems to be an extremely harsh sanction.

It is true that such provisions are set forth for the protection of the interests of the recipients of information society services and hence peculiarities of the relationships are taken into consideration while drafting the Directive[793]. Thus, those peculiarities crystallize in mandatory rules when it comes to the protection of consumers, i.e. of the economically and knowledgably weaker party to negotiate.

---

[792] Such obligations would address providers of commercial communications, providers of hosting services, intermediaries in electronic communications, etc.

[793] See Recitals (7) and (11) of the Directive.

It should be expressed the view that the European legislator has left the consequences, as regards the non-fulfillment of general information requirements in the civil sphere, to the freedom of the Member States to decide, while the administrative sanctions and other measures are to be introduced in line with the Directive[794].

Therefore, the legal consequences in view of the civil relationships and thus the possibility for liability exposure should be analyzed on a national level and would depend on the national rules in respect to the:

➢ grounds for nullity of the contract;

➢ grounds for voidance of the contract;

➢ grounds for pre-contractual liability;

➢ level of mandatory weight of the general information requirements in view of consumer protection;

➢ general consumer protection rules;

➢ general tort grounds.

The consequences and the liability would in any case differ.

If we look at the Bulgarian law that follows the French model, infringement of certain parts of the general information requirements would lead to nullity of the contract, others - to voidance, third - to pre-contractual liability, fourth – to contractual liability. For example, non-provision of complete information on the correct prices (Article 5(2) of the Directive) might lead to the nullity of the contract, while there would be considered no agreement reached on an essential element of the contract[795]. Any

---

[794] Article 18 (1) provides that Member States shall ensure that *court actions* available under national law concerning information society services activities allow for the rapid adoption of measures, including interim measures, designed to terminate any alleged infringement and to prevent any further impairment of the interests involved. In the same time Article 20 rules that Member States shall determine the *sanctions* applicable to infringements of national provisions adopted pursuant to this Directive and shall take all measures necessary to ensure that they are enforced. The sanctions they provide for shall be effective, proportionate and dissuasive.

[795] See Article 26 (1) of the Bulgarian Law on Obligations and Contracts (LOC). Also Pavlova, M., *General Civil Law*, Vol.II, Sofi-R, 2000, p. 102 and p. 151.

damages that have occurred as a result of entering into such a contract should be repaired – the CSP would be held liable for all direct damages[796].

At the same time, the lack of adequate information or misrepresentations that has caused the recipient to be misled (Article 5 (1) of the Directive) and thus has made him express his will on entering into a contract, would not be considered a ground for nullity but rather to voidance of the contract[797]. Declaring the voidance is a subjective right of the person and whether to exercise it or not would depend on the person[798]. Should he do so, he will be entitled to damages[799].

In both cases specified above, the nature of the liability invoked would be pre-contractual[800]. Parties never enter into a contract (a nugatory contract is not considered a contract at all) or evenmore into a void contract (after declaring the voidance, the contract is considered not to be concluded whatsoever – all consequences are obliterated with reverse effect[801]).

Should the infringement of the general information requirements fall beyond the scope of the nullity or voidance grounds, the contract will be valid. However, in such a case, any damage that might occur due to the non-fulfillment of the obligation should give a right for compensation on contractual grounds. The pre-contractual obligations would migrate into contractual liability[802].

Where there are statutory provisions that might substitute the will of the parties, but the latter is either missing or deviating to the mandatory rules, the statutory provisions would apply[803]. For example, Article 56 (2) of the Bulgarian Law on VAT provides that should no reference in the contract exist on whether the price agreed incurs VAT (i.e. obligation under Article 5 (2) of the Directive), the price should be considered

---

[796] See Article 12 of the Bulgarian LOC. See also Kalaydjiev, A., *ibid.*, p. 354.

[797] See Article 27 (1) of the Bulgarian LOC – "It could be declared void a contract concluded due to mistake, fraud, or under menace". Pavlova M., *ibid.*, 166, et seq. See Article 4:107 of the Principles of the European Contract Law, Article 1116 of the French Code Civil, §123 of BGB.

[798] Article 28 of the Bulgarian LOC.

[799] See Kalaydjiev, A., *ibid.*, p. 339.

[800] See Article 12 of the Bulgarian LOC. When entering into a contract and during the course of negotiations the parties should proceed in *bona fide*. Some authors find that the pre-contractual liability is a type of tort liability in cases when it leads to non-entering into the contract or entering into a void contract.

[801] See Pavlova, M., *ibid.*, p. 126.

[802] See Kalaydjiev, A., *ibid.*, p. 101.

[803] See Article 26 (4) of the Bulgarian LOC. See also Pavlova, M., *ibid.*, p. 131.

VAT inclusive. In such respect the contract would not be considered void due to the lack of an agreement on its essential element – a statutory irrefutable presumption exists to protect the interests of the contractual party.

It becomes obvious that the liability exposure of the CSP due to non-provision of general information should be estimated only on a case by case basis at a national level, taking into consideration the seriousness of the breach and the type of general information which has not been provided.

Provided a given Member State decides to simply transpose the mandatory rules for information provisions into its national legislation, the possibility of the CSPs to manage their liability by placing clauses on releasing of liability due to non-provision of this information would be considered, depending on the mandatory nature of the national rules *vis-à-vis* the civil relationship. In most cases, deviation would not be possible.

5.3.2. Legal consequences with respect to non-provision of information before entering into electronic contracts

In addition to the general information requirements, Article 10 of the Directive establishes specific requirements for provision of information, that should communicated to the recipients of the certification services when entering into electronic contracts prior the orders are being placed.

Contrary to the consequences of non-provision of general information, however, the parties may not deviate from the statutory rule by agreeing otherwise on releasing of responsibility and thus, on managing the liability exposure, unless the parties are not consumers. The provision of Article 10 explicitly restricts such a possibility – Member States shall ensure, *except when otherwise agreed by parties who are not consumers* that certain information is given by the service provider clearly, comprehensibly and unambiguously.

The specific information that should be provided is as follows:

➢ the different technical steps the recipient should follow to conclude the contract;

➢ whether or not the concluded contract will be filed by the service provider and whether it will be accessible;

➢   the technical means for identifying and correcting input errors prior to placing the order;

➢   the languages offered for the conclusion of the contract.

Further, except when otherwise agreed by parties who are not consumers, the service provider indicates any relevant codes of conduct to which he subscribes and information on how those codes can be consulted electronically. The CSP will also have the obligation to make available the contract terms and general conditions provided to the recipient in a way that allows him to store and reproduce them.

Therefore, the CSP may not manage its liability by introducing clauses releasing him of responsibility due to non-distribution of such information. This would only be possible when the contractual party is not a consumer.

The analysis of the provision of Article 10 shows that the mandatory level of the rule is of the highest density. While introduced for protection of consumers, any lack of information provision prior placing the order would lead to nullity of the contract[804]. Invalidity of the contract may undoubtedly constitute grounds for invoking the CSPs liability.

The above conclusions would not be valid in cases when the CSP enters into a relationship with a recipient that is not a consumer. In such a case, he could manage his liability by placing release clauses for information non-provision.

6. Conclusions

The analysis made in this chapter focused on several main objectives.

Firstly, the main Community acts (apart from Directive 1999/93 on e-signatures) which establish specific liability rules applicable to CSPs – as a type of service provider – were identified. In this regard, the following directives were analyzed: Directive 93/13/EEC on unfair terms in consumer contracts; Directive 97/7/EC on distance contracts; Directive 95/46/EC on protection of personal data; Directive 2000/35/EC on late payments in commercial transactions; and Directive

---

[804] Lodder, A., Kaspersen, H., *cit. ibid.*, p.79

2000/31/EC on certain legal aspects of information society services, in particular electronic commerce, in the internal market.

Secondly, the research has identified particular provisions of these Community acts that establish grounds for invoking the liability of providers of services that prove to be applicable to the CSPs without conflicting with the rules of Directive 1999/93/EC. The rules from the following directives were identified as addressing a wider field of liability affecting CSPs than that regulated by the e-signatures Directive: Directive 2000/35/EC, and some provisions from Directives 93/13/EC, 97/7/EC, 2000/31, and 95/46/EC.

Thirdly, a model for assessment of the priorities of application of the conflicting and overlapping rules in respect of the liability of certification service-providers in the different Community instruments was promoted. Such rules were found to exist in relation to certain provisions of Directive 93/13/EC, Directive 97/7/EC, Directive 2000/31 and Directive 95/46/EC. However, it should be noted that, in any case, the priorities in protection of the interests of different subjects should be examined on a case-by-case basis in the light of the principles of European law.

Another group of objectives is achieved in this chapter by deducing substantial proofs of evidence to support the assertions of the author.

The research demonstrates that the European legislator, while intending to introduce a protective legal shield for certain groups of users in the provision of services, uses the introduction of either strict liability or mandatory rules in order to establish given obligations for service providers (Directives 3000/35/EC, Directive 97/7/EC, Directive 93/13/EC, Directive 2000/31/EC). In this way it restricts the possibility of the service providers to derogate by contractual or other means and thus to exempt or limit their liability.

It becomes obvious that the introduction of a legal method such as the establishment of a reversed burden for proving certain facts, in contrast to the general rules, is a rare exception. It is applicable only where the interests of society demand particularly strong protection, making it justifiable to introduce such measures. The analysis shows that such a reversed burden is introduced in Directive 95/46 for the protection of consumers, and refers to the burden of demonstrating the chain of causation (i.e. 'rebuttable presumption of causality'). It is obvious that introducing a reversed burden in this respect has not much to do with enhancing trust in the market. The regime would protect the interest of the consumers whether or not they trust the service providers. In this respect, the regime is not intended to enhance trust. Therefore, the idea held by the supporters of the thesis that the specific liability rules as introduced by Directive 1999/93/EC provide *prima facie* evidence of trust in the trust-building process does not seem to be strongly grounded.

In the forthcoming chapter, when analyzing the peculiarities of the application of the specific liability rule in the national jurisdiction of Bulgaria, as a case study country, the proposition that the presumption of fault was not intended to establish further or more draconian protection is substantiated. This rule is common to most of the EU Member States' jurisdictions and its plain transposition does not affect the liability of the CSPs towards users of certification services. Furthermore, the position that just equalization of the regimes in all Member States is not a good reason for introducing an explicit rule for allocation of the burden of proving the fault is defended.

Chapter V

EFFECTS OF THE TRANSPOSITION OF THE SPECIFIC LIABILITY REGIME

The present work aims at answering the question of whether specific liability rules for the CSPs established on a supranational level do in fact play their role in promoting trust in the electronic world where electronic signatures are involved. This question is analyzed from the point of view of the transposition of the supranational liability rules in one case study jurisdiction - Bulgaria.

Evidence that there are many problematic issues connected with the specific liability regime was produced by clarifying the notion of electronic signature, the role of the CSP and its liability exposure to other market actors in Chapter I, outlining the predominant concepts in the civil liability theory upheld in Bulgaria in Chapter II, analyzing the specific liability regime established by the e-signatures Directive in Chapter III and the specific liability rules applicable to CSPs established by other Community acts in Chapter IV. This evidence, however, were produced solely on the basis of theoretical assumptions and deductions. In the present chapter more solid evidence is presented, based on the analysis of the practical problems and effects of the transposition of the specific liability rules for the CSPs in Bulgarian law. In this respect, the preceding chapters play a preparatory role in order that in-depth analysis may be made in this chapter.

Examination of the problems of the practical transposition could demonstrate to the greatest extent whether in fact the supranational rules, when transposed, establish an effective protective legal shield for the interests of the users of certification services and promote trust in the provision of certification services on a national level.

Since this task is perhaps over-ambitious, this present work focuses on one country instead of attempting to research all the EU jurisdictions. The country chosen is Bulgaria, which has transposed Directive 1999/93/EC. Some references to other jurisdictions are made in order to support the findings and conclusions which are valid for Bulgaria. As envisaged *supra*, Bulgaria seems to be an appropriate subject for examination due to the fact, that as a new Member State of the EU, it has carefully but swiftly transposed the rules of the European legislation in the area of e-signatures, seeking to balance and adjust the new regulatory framework to the nascent e-market. Furthermore, Bulgarian law falls within the scope of the Roman civil law families, following the main principles of the French and the German legal traditions. Thus, proper evaluation of the effects of the transposition of the specific liability regime might produce findings that will also be valid for other European countries. Finally, since Bulgaria has successfully joined the EC, a strong necessity for information on the Bulgarian legal system, especially in the area of e-signatures, will emerge. This work will provide valuable information in the area of liability related to the provision of certification services.

During the course of the negotiations for joining the EU, Bulgaria adopted the vast majority of European normative acts. Therefore, the legislative framework is now to a great extent harmonized with the *acquis communautaire*. This is true especially in the area of information and communication technologies, particularly with regard to the regime in place for electronic documents and electronic signatures.[805]

On 22 March 2001, the National Assembly adopted the Electronic Documents and Electronic Signature Act (referred to as 'EDESA' in this chapter))[806] – the main normative act that regulates the activity of the CSPs. It contains rules transposing the specific liability as introduced by Directive 1999/93/EC[807] (referred to as 'the Directive' in this chapter).

Achieving the aims of this chapter may be possible by analysis of the following issues:

To begin with, in order to properly analyze the liability regime of the CSPs and the effects of the transposition of the supranational liability rules in the national jurisdictions, the priorities for application of the national liability rules relevant to the CSPs established by the different normative acts should be identified. Depending on the legal traditions, the national jurisdictions take different approaches to systematizing the legal rules in codes, general acts, special acts etc. These acts may contain liability rules applicable to the CSPs, but at the same time they might provide protection directed to diverse types of social relations or groups of persons. The level of protection may not be always easily identifiable. For example, there might exist

---

[805] There are number of studies providing assessment on the level of transposition of the *acquis communautaire* into the Bulgarian law in the area of electronic signatures. See Dimitrov, G., Transposition of the EU Electronic Signatures Directive into the Bulgarian Law, Report to the Closed Legal Group Meeting, ECAF/EEMA, 25 September 2001, London (available at http://www.eema.org); also Dumortier, J., et al., *Legal and Market Aspects of Electronic Signatures in Europe, ibid.*

[806] Promulgated in State Gazette No. 34 of April 6, 2001, in force since October 7, 2001. Available in English on http://www.orac.bg/en/resources-links.

[807] For a thorough analysis of the liability of the CSPs under Bulgarian law see Kalaydjiev, A., Belazelkov, B., Dimitrov, G., et al., *ibid.*, p.p. 254 – 259.

both rules for the protection of consumers and rules for the protection of natural persons – users of certification services – all of which might impose specific, sometimes contradictory obligations on the providers of services. A problematic issue on a supranational level was identified in respect of the priority of application of the rules of the different directives. Therefore, in order to properly assess the need for specific liability rules for the CSPs, a view should be taken as to what the priorities should be as to the application on a national level (in Bulgaria) of different overlapping liability rules, *inter alia*, the transposed particular liability rules for the CSPs.

Another issue arises in view of the fact that regardless of whether issuing qualified or other certificates, or issuing certificates to the public or not, the CSPs will be always subject to national rules regarding liability.[808] However, the national laws are based on different principles, concepts and legal traditions, and the specific liability rules of Article 6 of the Directive that should be imposed as a minimum in the national jurisdictions of the EU Member States might contradict or belie the general national civil liability principles. Any given jurisdiction has its own *differentia specifica* and it might not always be possible to transpose the minimum specific liability regime *per se*; or, if transposed, it might conflict with the general liability rules. This chapter will address the issue by investigating the transposition in the jurisdiction that is the subject of this research, and will provide substantial knowledge to support the assetions of the author. The research in Chapter II has already provided an overview on the general civil liability regime in Bulgaria, thus making the task easier.

Secondly, the way in which the principles of the general civil law regarding liability identified in Chapter II will be affected by the specific liability rules imposed by Directive 1999/93/EC should be investigated. The reason for this is that the analysis of Article 6 of the Directive in Chapter III shows that the rules in this respect reveal a number of legal problems concerning the grounds for liability, the burden of proof concept, the reasonable reliance concept, the limitation of liability options etc.

Thirdly, in order to ensure that the conclusions would be just and fair, there should be a clause-by-clause examination designed to assess whether the Bulgarian national rules transpose correctly and in an exhaustive manner the specific liability rules contained in Article 6. Where discrepancies exist, the investigation will provide insight as to the

---

[808] See Recital 19 of Directive 1999/93/EC '"Certification-service-providers providing certification services to the public are subject to national rules regarding liability". On the applicability of the general liability rules to the CSPs issuing qualified certificates not to the public or not qualified certificates see supra Chapter I.

particular problems associated with the Directive's liability rules and its impact on the national general liability regime.

In summary, therefore, the aim of this chapter is to evaluate the necessity for specific liability rules for the CSPs on the national level, by taking the Bulgarian jurisdiction as a case study. The research will show whether beyond the general liability rules, the particular rules of Directive 1999/93/EC as transposed *de facto* contribute to the establishment of better legal protection for the interests of the users of certification services and to enhancement of trust in these services. Hence, the chosen method of research will assist in answering the core question of this work.

To achieve this aim it will first be necessary to take a view as to what the priorities should be in the application of the national liability rules of different normative acts applicable to CSPs. The research will be based on the distinctive features of Bulgarian legislation, but will also draw on the information set out in Chapter IV – though it may be noted that most of the supranational acts containing applicable liability rules have already been transposed into Bulgarian legislation. Furthermore, the transposition of the specific liability rules contained in the Directive will be analyzed to assess whether their transposition on a national level is fair, and thus whether the conclusions as to the lack of necessity for such rules on a supranational level deduced later on may be regarded as reasonable and valid. The transposition analysis will be made by reference to groups of legal problems, following the model used in Chapter III. Finally, various deductions and conclusions will be made.

1. Priority in Application of National Liability Rules

As already mentioned, the liability regime of particular group of market actors in a given jurisdiction is regulated by different normative acts containing general rules applicable to all subjects, and particular rules applicable to specific types of subjects or the relationships they enter into. In this respect, Recital (22) of the Directive states that the 'certification-service-providers providing certification services to the public are subject to national rules regarding liability'. But does Directive 1999/93 mean the general rules applicable to *all subjects* when referring to 'general rules regarding liability'?

Providing the incorrect answer to this question may lead to the making of serious mistakes and wrong assumptions with regard to the transposition and application of the specific liability rules established by the Directive.

'General rules' might mean, in the first instance, those rules that regulate the liability between the subjects when entering in contractual relationships, or when torts are committed. The term might also encompass all national rules that regulate general administrative and criminal liability. General rules might finally cover all national rules regulating the specific liability of given groups of subjects and the relationships they enter into, for example: liability with respect to the protection of consumers, with respect to personal data, with respect to particular means of entering into contractual relations etc.

It is reasonable to assume that the provision of Recital (22) should be broadly interpreted and when referring to 'general rules regarding liability' the European legislator meant all national rules regulating liability – general and particular, applicable to CSPs, excepting the liability rules introduced by Directive 1999/93. 'General rules' will be referred to in this latter meaning for the purposes of the present and the following conclusive chapter.

Thus, to properly analyze the transposition of the specific supranational liability rules and to answer the core question of whether they contribute to better protection of the social relations by enhancing trust in the market, it is first necessary to analyze the Directive liability rules and their level of priority in relation to other international instruments. Secondly, the priority of application of these rules as transposed into national legal systems should be identified. While the first question has already been answered in Chapter IV, the present section aims at giving some basic ideas as to the answer to the second question – i.e. the priority of application of the specific rules as transposed into national legislation from the Directive.

The liability regime governing the activities of CSPs may be derived from the general national rules for liability in contract and tort. The specific liability regime, as introduced, would be applicable with priority over the general regime, pursuant to the common principles *lex specialis derogat legi generali*; i.e. the special law takes precedence over the general law.[809] The levels of 'speciality' of different rules should be assessed depending on the protected interests. The specific liability regime of the CSPs will not always be applicable with priority over the general liability regime. The law may provide protection for particular groups in society, such as consumers, or of different material or non-material wealth (like personal data and the privacy of

---

[809] Pavlova, M., *ibid*, p, 120.

238

natural persons) which will be applied in priority to the specific liability regime established for the CSPs.

Since during the course of harmonization of the Bulgarian legislation with the *acquis communautaire,* a set of directives dealing with the protection of consumers and rules for fair trade etc, as analyzed in Chapter IV, have already been transposed,[810] an overview and analysis of the effects of their transposition into the Bulgarian legislation seems unnecessary. Moreover, being properly transposed, these normative acts will hardly affect the liability exposure of the CSPs beyond the scope of the legal consequences noted in Chapter IV. Therefore, the present Chapter will focus solely on the effects of the transposition of the specific liability rules of Directive 1999/93/EC in Bulgaria.

However, before entering into the core analysis, the level of protection provided by the particular CSPs' liability rules of EDESA on a national level should be at least identified, so that proper assessment may be made of these rules and the impact they might have in promoting trust among market players.

Based on the conclusions of Chapter IV, several assumptions may be made as to the applicability of the particular rules of the CSPs established by EDESA on a national level when conflicting rules drawn from different laws are in existence. As became obvious, the liability rules of EDESA may conflict with other national liability rules that may apply to the CSPs, such as the rules in respect of the regulation of data protection,[811] individual privacy,[812] consumer protection,[813] and other relevant areas.

---

[810] The Law on Consumer Protection and Trade Rules (promulgated in State Gazette, issue 30 of April 2, 1999) which entered into force as of July 3, 1999 is the principal piece of legislation in the field of consumer protection in Bulgaria which transposes into Bulgarian legislation the following European Directives: Directive 98/6/EC on consumer protection in the indication of the prices of products offered to consumers; Directive 84/450 on misleading advertising; Directive 93/13 on unfair terms in consumer contracts; Directive 92/59/EEC on general product safety; Directive 85/374 on liability for defective products; Directive 85/577/EEC to protect the consumer in respect of contracts negotiated away from business premises. The Law on Consumer Protection and Trade Rules introduces partially into Bulgarian legislation some of the essential provisions of the Directive 97/7 on the protection of consumers in respect of distance contracts, and other. See the Regular Report on the Harmonization Process of the Ministry of Economy of the Republic of Bulgaria (http://www.mi.government.bg/integration/eu/docs.html?id=9425). The Law on Protection of Personal Data transposes the rules of Directive 95/46/EC.

[811] Under Article 8 (1) of the Directive "Member States shall ensure that certification-serviceproviders ... comply with the requirements laid down in Directive 95/46/EC of the European Parliament and of the Council of 24 October 1995 on the protection of individuals with regard to the processing of personal data and on the free movement of such data". The Bulgarian law that transposes the Directive of personal data is the Bulgarian Law for Protection of Personal Data.

[812] See Recital (24) of the Directive – "In order to increase user confidence in electronic communication and electronic commerce, certificationservice-providers must observe data protection legislation and individual

It is possible that the liability regime prescribed by EDESA may not contravene, but rather be simultaneously applicable with other specific liability rules. The analysis made in Chapter IV has already shown this applicability on a supranational level and it is obvious that the specific regimes on the national level will be applied in the same way as on a supranational level. Therefore, the research will not dwell further on this issue. Only the basic rules to be followed by the Bulgarian courts and all law enforcement authorities in identifying the priorities in the application of different liability rules will be outlined. These apply if the CSP's liability is triggered by a given type of negligent behaviour, but different grounds apply for the benefit of the aggrieved party in respect of the CSP's liability.

The demand for justice in society calls for the establishment of legal rules relating to the business world that provide legal protection to the economically weaker parties or to persons not possessing the necessary knowledge to protect their own interests. The laws for protection of consumers, personal data, and users of information society services establish, *inter alia*, such specific rules. Despite the fact that, in derogation from the Directive, the Bulgarian EDESA does not make any explicit reference to conflict with other rules that might be applicable in a liability case,[814] the protection provided by those other rules should be considered greater.[815] Such would be the case under Bulgarian law as far as the consumer protection rules are concerned. With respect to the protection of personal data, EDESA leaves no room for uncertainty, since it sets out explicitly the applicable levels of priority. Similarly to the Directive,[816] the law contains a particular chapter in this respect.[817] By way of illustration, the rules

---

privacy". The indivividul privacy in Bulgaria is protected by wide set of normative acts *inter alia* the LPPD, the Telecommunications Act, the Law for the Special Inteligence Devices, the Criminal Code, and others.

[813] Article 6 (5) of the Directive reads that "The provisions of paragraphs 1 to 4 shall be without prejudice to Council Directive 93/13/EEC of 5 April 1993 on unfair terms in consumer contracts.". The Bulgarian Law for Protection of Consumers and Trade Rules transposes the principles of the said Directive.

[814] The Directive explicitly refers in Article 6 (5) that the liability provisions shall be without prejudice to Council Directive 93/13/EEC of 5 April 1993 on unfair terms in consumer contracts.

[815] For example the general liability rules shall govern the liability of the CSP for non-performance of obligations that arise from EDESA but are not covered by the special rule of Article 29 or the obligations arise from other laws or the contract between the CSP and the certificate holder.

[816] Article 8 of the Directive.

[817] Chapter VI of EDESA called Protection of Personal Data envisages that the protection of personal data, collected by the certification-serviceproviders, needed for the activities, carried out by them, and the protection of registers kept shall be regulated by a Law (i.e. the Law for Protection of Personal Data). The protection shall also encompass the personal data known to the Commissions Regulation Commission, collected during the performance of its supervising activities. The certification-service-e providers shall collect personal data about the signatory and the owner of the signature, only to the extent necessary for issuing and using a certificate. Data about a third party may be collected only with the explicit consent of the person it is related to. The collected data may not be used for purposes, different from the ones

of the identified special laws will be applied in priority if damage occurs as a result of the negligent behaviour of the CSP, leading, for example, to illegal disclosure of the user's collected personal data (where the user is a natural person), or to misleading the consumer about price or about certificate usage. Therefore, in first place in the hierarchy of speciality and priority are all national liability rules that regulate the relationships between given particular groups of subjects. These rules grant better legal protection to the economically weaker party or to persons not possessing the necessary knowledge to protect their own interests; thus they should be applied with high priority. Whether special liability rules like the ones for consumer protection and personal data protection exist is subject to careful assessment and judgment by the courts in any single case.

In second place in the hierarchy of speciality and priority usually come other specific liability rules establishing a specific liability regime for given explicitly defined subjects. These rules, however, reveal lower intensity than the particular rules under the above section. When speaking about CSPs, these would include the specific liability rules of EDESA. In other words, except in cases where the application of particular rules is feasible to establish stronger liability protection for given groups of persons or relationships, the liability rules of EDESA would be applicable in priority to all other liability rules. For example, the liability of the CSPs towards the certificate holder as a legal entity would arise on the basis of EDESA being the first level of priority special act, should no infringement of higher priority acts, such as those dealing with consumer protection or data protection,[818] be applicable in contradiction to the liability regime of EDESA.

In third place in the level of priority come all other specific liability rules of other national acts giving a greater degree of protection to the given group of subjects or relationships, but lower than the level of EDESA. For example, should the CSP also simultaneously provide telecommunications services it will be also bound by the requirements and liability regime of the Telecommunications Act. The latter rules will be applied if there are no conflicting liability rules contained in other acts which give a greater degree of protection (EDESA, LPPD, LPCRC, et al).

---

pointed in the EDESA, except with the explicit consent of the person it is related to or if this is permitted by a Law.

[818] See the preceding paragraph.

Fourthly, where no special rules are found to be applicable, the liability regime of the CSPs will be regulated by the general civil law of contract and tort. The general rules will always be applied as subsidiary rules – where the specific liability rules contained in the other acts do not provide comprehensive regulation of the liability. The general rules and theory in this respect are analyzed in Chapter II. This situation would arise, for example, when CSPs provide certification services to closed user groups (e.g. banking institutions) or issue advanced certificates falling outside the scope of regulation of EDESA and no consumers *strictu sensu* are involved, nor is there damage resulting from personal data infringement or from any infringement of rules established by other acts providing a greater degree of protection.

After identifying the main rules that will be followed by the courts in applying the specific liability rules to the CSPs, in the light of their level of priority, it is now possible to analyze the peculiarities of the national specific liability rules established for the CSPs. However, it is possible to draw from the above analysis a very important conclusion to support the assertions of the author: the specific liability rules protecting the users of certification services do not take first priority in terms of application as compared to the other specific national liability rules. The users for which the jurisdiction secures special protection, such as natural persons or consumers, are effectively protected by rigorous liability rules contained in the relevant laws other than EDESA. These rules take precedence over any other specific rules. By revealing a lower level of rigour, it seems questionable whether the specific liability rules established for the CSPs *de facto* promote more trust and confidence among the players on the certification services market.

2. Peculiarities of the EDESA Liability Rules.

Article 29 of EDESA is the main provision containing specific liability regulation of the CSPs, and is therefore considered to transpose the specific provisions of the Directive. The question of whether the transposition of the liability rules on a national level is fair is addressed in this chapter by making a detailed analysis of the rules of Article 29 EDESA and drawing a parallel with the Directive rules in the following sections.. By this means it is possible to substantiate the conclusion that there is no necessity for the Bulgarian legislation to introduce such rules.

Article 29 of EDESA reads:

"Liability of the Certification-service-provider"

Article 29 (1) The certification-service-provider shall be liable before the owner of the qualified electronic signature and all third parties for the damages caused:

1. by non-compliance with the requirements of Article 21 and non-performance of the obligations under Article 22 and 25;

2. by false or missing data in the certificate at the moment of its issuance;

3. in the case where the person, denoted as certificate holder, has not controlled the private key, corresponding to the certified public key at the moment of issuance of the certificate;

4. by non-correspondence of the data for the use of the private key and the data disposed to the person using the public key.

(2) Agreements by which the CSP's liability for negligence is excluded or limited shall not be valid.

(3) The CSP shall not be liable for damages, caused by the use of the certificate beyond the limits of restrictions of its effect, listed therein."

In general, it could be claimed that the Bulgarian EDESA transposes the rules of Article 6 fairly well.[819]

In a similar way to the Directive, Bulgarian law provides for specific regulation of the liability of the CSPs.

In order to properly understand the rule of Article 29 and to assess the accuracy of its transposition, attention should be paid, in the first instance, to the peculiarities of the terminology used in Bulgarian law.

As is evident from the analysis made in Chapter II, Bulgaria follows the 'strict approach' in defining and regulating 'certification-service-providers'.[820] Under Article 19 of EDESA, 'certification-service-providers' are defined as being only those natural or legal persons who: i) issue certificates and maintain registers in relation thereto, and ii) provide access to the published certificates to any third party. Additionally, the CSP

---

[819] See Dimitrov, G., Transposition of the EU Electronic Signatures Directive into the Bulgarian Law, Report to the Closed Legal Group Meeting, ECAF/EEMA, 25 September 2001, London (available at http://www.eema.org).

[820] See Chapter I, section 2.2.1, *supra.*

may provide services for the creation of private and public keys for qualified electronic signatures.[821] Providers of certification or other trust services falling outside the scope of the legally defined notion of 'certification-service-provider'" will not be considered as CSPs in Bulgaria and hence will not be subject to the specific liability regime of Article 29. Their liability will be regulated by the general liability rules applicable to any other provider of information or other services.

Furthermore, Bulgarian law distinguishes two actors staying on the side of the certificate user and outlining the *differentia specifica* of the Bulgarian law with regard to specific liability: the owner of the qualified electronic signature and the signatory.[822] The person on behalf of whom the electronic statement has been performed will be considered the owner of the electronic signature. He could be either a legal or a natural person. The signatory is the person authorized to make electronic statements on behalf of the owner of the electronic signature by virtue of law or by authorization of the owner. Under the law, no one but the signatory has the right of access to the signature-creation data. The signatory can only be a natural person.[823] In cases when the natural person makes electronic statements on his own behalf, the entities of owner and signatory will coincide. The model on which the introduction of the two actors is based derives from the necessity of using electronic signatures on behalf of legal entities. In the paper-based world, legal entities always act through natural persons, who are their representatives. In this respect, natural persons can only express the will of legal entities by affixing their own handwritten signature to the relevant statements. In the electronic world the situation is similar. As a matter of technology, the signature itself is created by using the private key held by the signatory – a natural person – to electronically sign the given message. However, in the high-tech environment it is difficult for previously unknown parties to determine on whose behalf they act. The certificate should serve as a means of clarifying this issue. By putting the name of the owner therein, the addressee of the signed electronic statements becomes aware that the signatory acts not on his or her own behalf, but on behalf of another person. Therefore, once the name of the owner – as a legal entity – is entered into the certificate, the electronically signed statements shall be considered made on behalf of the legal entity, and are binding its legal sphere. Of

---

[821] Article 19 (2) EDESA.

[822] The said notions are translated from Bulgarian. Interpreting provisions are given in Article (4) EDESA.

[823] See Dumortier, J., et al., *The Legal and Market Aspects of Electronic Signatures in Europe, ibid.*, Questionnaire of the Bulgarian National Correspondent.

course, the signatory should be duly authorized to represent the owner and to make relevant electronic statements in this regard.

After having outlined these peculiarities of Bulgarian law, it is now possible to enter into analysis of the specific liability regime that has been introduced.

In order to comply with the minimum regime prescribed by Article 6 of the Directive, the Bulgarian legislator has chosen to transpose the said rule explicitly. However, as it will be seen, the rule does not appear to impact significantly on the general civil liability regime applicable to the CSPs.

To some extent it might be argued that the rule contained in Article 29 establishes a more stringent specific liability regime, to the detriment of the CSP's. As discussed in Chapter III, this approach seems to be allowed by the Directive[824] provided it does not hinder the free provision of certification services in the internal market.[825]

2.1. Scope of liability regulation

In a similar way to Article 6 of the Directive, the rule of Article 29 reveals a dualistic nature.[826] It proves to be simultaneously a legal ground for liability in contract and in tort on the part of the CSPs towards the certificate holders and the third parties relying on the certificates.

EDESA goes further than the Directive, however, by providing in Article 31 particular rules regulating the liability of the certificate holders towards the CSPs.[827] Such an approach is definitely in line with the Directive, while the Community act leaves these relations to be regulated by the national general or specific liability rules. Similarly, Article 30 of EDESA introduces specific rules to regulate the liability exposure of the certificate holder to the relying party. The grounds for such liability include intentional or negligent provision of inaccurate information to the CSP that

---

[824] See section 1.3. of Chapter III, *supra*.

[825] Recital (4) of the Directive.

[826] See section 2 of Chapter III, *supra*. See also Kalaydjiev, A., Belazelkov, B., Dimitrov, G., et al., *ibid.*, p. 248.

[827] Article 31 reads that the owner of the signature, respectively the signatory, shall be liable towards the certification-service-provider, if he or she has accepted the certificate, issued by the certification service-provider on the basis of false data, presented by him or her, respectively on the basis of data concealed by him or her.

results in the issue of a qualified certificate that is intended to mislead the relying party to perform certain acts, failures to request prompt revocation of the certificate while knowing that the private key had been compromised etc.[828] Since these regulations do not affect the specific liability regime of the CSPs introduced by Article 29, they are not discussed further in this work.

As it will become evident, in divergence to the Directive, the liability of the CSP towards *bona fide* third parties[829] and before impersonated persons falls within the scope of specific regulation.[830]

In a similar way to the Directive, regulation of the liability of the relying party towards the CSP,[831] the liability of the impostor towards the CSP,[832] and various other issues remain beyond the scope of the specific regulation. These relationships and the liability arising from them will be governed by the national liability rules on contract or tort.

2.2. Liable persons under EDESA

As is the case with Article 6 of the Directive, Article 29 of EDESA does not provide for specific liability regulation for all CSPs. The scope of Article 29 covers only the certification-service-providers *strictu sensu*, i.e. only those *CSPs that issue qualified or universal certificates*, maintain the relevant directories in relation thereto, provide access to the published certificates to any third party, and additionally provide services for the generation of key pairs for qualified electronic signatures. Bearing this in mind, it may be deduced that the scope of the CSPs under Bulgarian law, subject to the

---

[828] Article 30 of EDESA provides that the owner of the qualified signature shall be liable towards conscientious third parties, when during the creation of the key pair (public and private key) an algorithm not corresponding to the requirements of the Regulation for the algorithms for qualified signatures has been used. Furthermore he shall be liable towards conscientious third parties, if the signatory: does not perform exactly the security requirements, specified by the certification-service-provider, or does not request from the certification-service-provider revocation of the certificate, when he has learned that the private key has been used illegally or a danger of its illegal use exists. The owner, who has accepted the certificate with its issuance, shall be liable towards conscientious third parties if the signatory is not authorized to hold the private key corresponding to the public key pointed in the certificate, and also for false statements made before the certification-service-provider that are related to the content of the certificate. The signatory, who has accepted the certificate with its issuance, shall be liable towards conscientious third parties, if he has not been authorized to request the issuance of the certificate.

[829] See Chapter I, section 2.2.5.3.2, *supra*.

[830] See Chapter I, section 2.2.5.3.1, *supra*.

[831] See Chapter I, sections 2.2.5.3, *supra*.

[832] *Ibid.*

specific liability regime, reflects the scope of CSPs under Article 6 of the Directive. This deduction is valid despite the fact that the CSPs may provide these services by themselves or by outsourcing to other CSPs.

Similarly to the approach of the Directive, the certification provider under Bulgarian law will be subject to specific liability where a certificate is issued as a qualified certificate, but in reality fails to meet the statutory requirements set forth in Article 24.[833] The specific liability will be triggered once the certificate is issued as qualified (or universal) and at least one of the liability causes is present.[834] At first glance one might gain the opposite impression since the European Directive explicitly envisages in Article 6 that the CSP shall be held liable for causing damage to any entity 'by issuing a certificate *as qualified*', where Article 29 of EDESA lacks such wording. This fact should not lead to a misleading interpretation of the actual intention of the Bulgarian legislator. When EDESA regulates the certificates it refers only to qualified and universal certificates, but not to other types. Thus, since the law provides that the '*certification-service-provider shall be liable before the owner of the qualified electronic signature and all third parties for the damages caused … from false or missing data in the certificate at the moment of its issuance*', and the CSP is the person issuing certificates (qualified or universal), then it should be considered that the rule addresses liability specifically to those CSPs issuing qualified or universal certificates as such, i.e. by indicating this on the certificate.[835] A party issuing other types of certificates will not be considered a CSP

---

[833] Article 24 transposes the rules of Annex I. Under Article 24 the qualified certificate as an electronic document, issued and signed by a certification-service-provider must include: 1. the name, address, personal identification number (PIN) or BULSTAT of the certification-service-provider, as well as an indication of its nationality; 2. the name or the trade name, address and court registration data of the owner of the qualified electronic signature; 3. the grounds for authorization, the name and address of the natural person (signatory) that is authorized to make electronic statements on behalf of the owner of the qualified electronic signature; 4. the public key that corresponds to the private key of the owner of the qualified electronic signature; 5. the identifications of algorithms with the help of which the public keys of the owner of the qualified electronic signature and of the certification-service provider are used; 6. the date and the hour of issuance, suspension, renewal, and revocation of the effect; 7. the term of validity; 8. the restrictions of the effect of the signature; 9. the unique identification code of the certificate; 10. the liability and guarantees of the certification-service-provider; and 11. reference to the qualified electronic signature certificate of the certification-service-provider and to its registration at the Communications Regulation Commission. When the authorization of the signatory comes from other authorized persons the certificate should include identification data for these persons as well.

[834] See Kalaydjiev, A., Belazelkov, B., Dimitrov, G., et al., *ibid*, p.194 and p.248.

[835] Indication of the qualified certificate as such was already discussed is made by marking the certificate as such by setting the non-critical field "Qualified Statements". The procedure and the requirements are set forth in ETSI 101 862 - Qualified Certificate Profile. See *supra* note 622. However, in Bulgarian doctrine different theories exist how the indifcation of the universal certificate should be made as far as the ASN.1 and the applicable standards does not provide for such a standardized field. Most of the Bulgarian scholars see the distinguishment between the qualified and the universal certificates in the possibility for the CSPs to enter into the qualified certificate in any non-crtitical and non-mandatory field a link to the register of the Communications Regulation Commission where the CSP that issues universal certificates should is registered. Article 24 (1) (11) of EDESA envisages that the certificate must contain reference the

under Bulgarian law at all and its activity – and therefore its exposure to liability – will not be subject to regulation by EDESA, but to the general law.

In addition, it is noteworthy that the rule in Article 29 does not explicitly address the specific liability regime for the CSPs that have guaranteed qualified certificates. In fact, the rule should be interpreted broadly and in relation to the rule in Article 44 of EDESA that has transposed the provision of Article 7(1)(b) of the Directive. As is evident from the analysis in Chapter III, the scope of Article 6 goes beyond the term 'guaranteeing' *strictu sensu* usually achieved by cross-certification.[836] By transposing the provision, Bulgarian law has provided in Article 44 that a foreign certificate shall be recognized in the territory of Bulgaria, provided a Bulgarian certification-service-provider, that has been accredited or registered, has undertaken the obligation to be liable for actions or failure to take actions by a certification-service-provider, established in another country, in cases falling under Article 29. As clarified in Chapter III, this fact shall be ascertained by the Bulgarian national supervisory body, The Communications Regulation Commission (CRC). Only after this has occurred shall the certificate of the foreign certification-service-provider, in respect of which liability has been accepted and conditions upon which the liability has been undertaken, be entered into a special register kept by the CRC. Therefore the Bulgarian CSP will be held jointly liable with the foreign CSP for the performance of the obligations as set forth in Article 29 pursuant to a unilateral statement to the regulatory body and to the public.[837] The specific liability regime would spread its protective shield so that the liability of Bulgarian CSPs that have guaranteed the qualified certificates issued by other CSP would arise on the same grounds as the liability of CSPs that have issued a certificate as qualified.

Another point of interest is the divergent way the Bulgarian law transposes the rule of Article 6 by not explicitly indicating that the specific rules are intended to regulate the liability of CSPs issuing qualified certificates to the public. Bulgarian legal doctrine unanimously supports the thesis that the law regulates the activity of the CSPs issuing certificates to the public only.[838] To draw a parallel, in the same way as in the Directive, the specific liability of certain CSPs remains beyond the scope of regulation

---

CSP's "registration at the Communications Regulation Commission". See Kalaydjiev, A., Belaselkov, B., Dimitrov, G., et al., *ibid*, p. 202.

[836] See Chapter III, section 3, *supra*.

[837] See Kalaydjiev, A., Belazelkov, B., Dimitrov, G., et al., *Ibid.*, p.p. 334-340.

[838] *Ibid*, p.149.

of the Bulgarian EDESA. This is true of those CSPs that do not issue or guarantee certificates to the public, including banking or financial institutions, companies and private or public bodies that issue certificates to be used within closed systems by customers, employees, clients, and any other person where the purpose of usage may be identified as relating to an internal relationship. Those CSPs that do not issue or guarantee certificates, such as RSPs, DSPs, ASPs etc, also fall beyond the scope of Article 29.[839] Bulgarian law does not introduce a specific liability regime for such providers. Furthermore, the specific liability regime does not cover CSPs that issue or guarantee advanced, basic or other certificates, which are not qualified or universal. The liability of all those CSPs will be regulated by the national rules regarding liability.

The above findings not only demonstrate the accurate transposition of Directive liability rules into Bulgarian law in the light of the scope of the liable parties, but also support the interpretation of Article 6 of the Directive made in Chapter III.

2.3. Liability exposure

As regards the range of persons to whom the CSPs will be liable, Article 29 of EDESA exceeds the scope of the Directive, but does not contradict its principles.

Article 6 of the Directive prescribes that CSPs (that issue or guarantee certificates as qualified to the public) shall be exposed to liability if they cause damage to '*any entity or natural or legal person that reasonably relies on that certificate*'. By way of contrast, Bulgarian law provides simply that the CSPs '*... shall be liable before the owner of the qualified electronic signature and all third parties for the damages caused ...*'

Since the particularities of the reasonable reliance concept prove to be a cornerstone in demonstrating the problems involved in the transposition of the Directive's specific liability rules at national level, the whole section 3 of this chapter is dedicated to analysis of this issue. The present section will examine the range of aggrieved parties who are entitled to the benefit of the specific liability regime affecting CSPs where they negligently cause damage. The analysis will also demonstrate the fair transposition of the Directive's liability rules in this respect.

---

[839] See Chapter II, sections 2.3, 2.4 and 2.6, *supra*.

2.3.1. Liability towards the certificate holder

As noted in Chapter III, some authors are unable to give a clear answer as to whether the certificate holders fall within the scope of the specific liability rules of Article 6 of the Directive,[840] while others find that the scope of the specific liability rules excludes the certificate holders.[841] The vague manner in which the intentions of the European legislator are expressed in Article 6 has led to difficulties in the transposition of this provision into national legal systems.[842] This problem was also encountered during the course of the legislative process of drafting and enacting the Bulgarian EDESA.

Unlike other jurisdictions that have simply copied the wording of Article 6, and thus bypassed the problem,[843] the Bulgarian legislator has chosen to interpret carefully the rule of Article 6. As a result, Article 29 of the Bulgarian EDESA explicitly envisages that the CSPs shall be always liable under the specific liability rule towards the certificate holder. This fact helps substantiate the thesis argued in this work and the conclusions reached in Chapter III *supra.*[844]

The Directive aims at providing minimum liability statutory requirements to be introduced by the Member States in order to have equal minimum protection for all entities and persons that rely on qualified certificates in the EU States.[845] By transposing these rules as mandatory, the national legislations *de facto* reduce by virtue of law the freedom of the parties (particularly the CSPs) to negotiate contractual exemptions or limitations of liability beyond the established options and limits. Any agreement *contra lege* will be void[846] and the mandatory statutory rules will apply.[847] Hence the regime contained in Article 29 EDESA, constituting actual transposition of Article 6 of the Directive, protects the interests of certificate holders who have entered into contractual relationships with the CSP.

---

[840] See *supra* note 569.

[841] See supra note 568.

[842] See Dumortier, J., Kelm, S., Nilsson, H., Van Eecke, P., Skouma, G., *ibid.*, p. 91 – 92.

[843] Such countries are Greece, Ireland, Italy, the Netherlands, et al. See Dumortier, J., Kelm, S., Nilsson, H., Van Eecke, P., Skouma, G., *ibid.*, p. 86-89.

[844] See Chapter III, section 4.1, *supra.*

[845] Communication from the Commission COM (97) 503: Ensuring security and trust in electronic communication: "Towards a European Framework for Digital Signatures and Encryption", available at http://www.swiss.ai.mit.edu/6805/articles/crypto/eu-october-8-97.html, Section 3.2.

[846] Unless the contract could survive without the void clauses. See Article 26 of Bulgarian LOC.

[847] See *supra* note 158. Also Chapter I, section 2.2.5.1, *supra.*

It should be stressed that Bulgarian law refers to '*the owner of the electronic signature*'. As clarified *supra*, the owner shall be considered the person who is envisaged in the certificate to be the party, whose legal sphere is bound by the acts of the signatory, i.e. he or she is the contractual party in the relationship with the CSP. The signatory (the person that actually signs), when not him or herself the owner, holds no direct rights stemming from the contractual relationship between the owner and the CSP – assuming that person always acts on behalf of the owner and never becomes party to this relationship. However, if the signatory suffers damage resulting from the acts of the CSPs, then he or she falls within the scope of '*all third parties for the damage caused*'.[848]

As becomes obvious, the Bulgarian law refers to the 'certificate owner' when it aims to address the 'certificate holder' under the meaning of the Directive. This deduction firstly supports the interpretation of Article 6 in Chapter III with regard to whether the certificate holder falls within the '… *persons reasonably relying on the certificate*';[849] and secondly, demonstrates the correct transposition of Directive rules in the light of the scope of CSPs' exposure to liability towards the certificate holders.

2.3.2. Liability towards third parties relying to the certificate

In the same way as envisaged in the Directive, under Bulgarian EDESA the CSP will undoubtedly be liable towards the relying party. However, Bulgarian law contrary to the Directive, does not explicitly envisage the CSP's exposure in liability towards those persons relying on the certificate. Article 29 stipulates generally that the CSP shall be liable towards '… *any third person*' in respect of the damage caused.[850]

In most cases, the nature of the CSP's liability toward the parties relying on the certificate will be non-contractual (i.e. tortious) since normally these actors do not enter into contractual relationships with the CSPs.[851] The CSP will be liable on tort grounds for any negligent behaviour in breach of the statutory mandatory duties that has caused damage to those relying on the certificate. Thus, the liability claim based on Article 29 of EDESA will be considered as brought on special tort liability grounds.

---

[848] Article 29 EDESA.

[849] See Chapter III, section 4.1, *supra*.

[850] Kalaydjiev, A., Belaselkov, B., Dimitrov, G., et al., *ibid*, p. 248.

[851] See Chapter I, section 2.2.5.2, *supra*.

Under Bulgarian law, while it appears theoretically feasible that a valid contract for accessing the register may be executed between the relying party and the CSP, in practice none of the Bulgarian CSPs was found to follow such an approach.[852] In this theoretical case, if damage were caused due to the CSP's negligent behaviour, the liability based on Article 29 would be of a contractual nature.[853] It is noteworthy that under Bulgarian law the CSP will not be able to deviate contractually or by CPS/CP from its statutory duties (as established in Sections II, III and IV of Bulgarian EDESA). Therefore, it has no means of limiting or excluding its liability. Those rules will be considered mandatory.[854]

As evidenced in chapters I and III, the Bulgarian situation supports the assertions of this work that a contract between the certificate holder and the CSP might be enforceable in most of the jurisdictions. As a result of this, Article 6 of the Directive reveals a dualistic nature and should be broadly interpreted.[855]

In cases when a contract is executed between a CSP and a party relying on the certificate, the relying party may end up in a situation in which it is able to sue the CSP both in contract and in tort in respect of the behaviour that has caused the damage (i.e. 'concurrence of claims'). The general Bulgarian legal theory, as well as court practice, give priority of the contractual claim over the tort claim.[856] The issue of concurrence of the general civil liability theory in Bulgaria and the approaches of the other EU jurisdictions are discussed *supra*.[857]

2.3.3. Liability towards third parties not relying on the certificate that have suffered damage

In respect of the protection of other persons that might suffer damage from the negligent behaviour of the CSPs, Bulgarian law, in its specific liability rules, goes beyond the scope of the Directive. As noted in chapters II[858] and III[859] there may be

---

[852] The author has investigated the only Bulgarian CSPs issuing universal certificates to the public – Information Services PLC and Bankservice PLC.

[853] On the same opinion Biddle, B., *Legislating Market Winners, ibid.*

[854] See Kalaydjiev, A., Belaselkov, B., Dimitrov, G., et al., *ibid*, p. 257

[855] See Chapter III, section 4.2, *supra.*

[856] Pavlova, M. *General Civil Law*, Vol.I, Sofi-R, 1995 ed., p. 193.

[857] See Chapter II, section 2.3, *supra.*

[858] See Chapter I, section 2.2.5.3, *supra.*

[859] See Chapter III, section 4.3, *supra.*

cases where impersonated persons could suffer damage resulting from the fraudulent usage of their identity by impostors that have obtained from the CSPs certificates by using forged or fake identity documents. Furthermore, as is clear from section 2.3.1 of this chapter, the signatories (when acting not on their own behalf but on behalf of the owners) could also suffer damage in cases where due to the negligent behaviour of the CSPs they fail to fulfil their own contractual obligations towards the owner of the certificate.[860]

By envisaging that the CSPs shall be liable for any breach of the statutory obligations towards '... *all third parties for the damage caused* ...' Bulgarian law in fact protects all parties that have suffered damage. That is to say, the Bulgarian EDESA does not distinguish between relying and non-relying persons when it comes to the granting of rights in respect of engaging the CSP's liability. In contrast, the Directive rules establish at the minimum a liability regime for the protection solely of parties that reasonably rely on the certificate. Since neither the impersonated persons who have suffered damage nor the signatories rely on the certificate, they should fall outside the category of parties for whom specific remedies are provided. Despite this derogation, however, the Directive indicates that the prescribed regime should be considered as minimum protection. The Directive aims at providing minimum liability statutory requirements to be introduced by the Member States in order to have equal minimum protection for all entities and persons that rely on qualified certificates in the EU States.[861] Parties are not permitted to negotiate exemption of liability beyond the established limits. If the legislation provides such minimum liability rules, they should be of an 'imperative' nature so the parties cannot derogate from them. If they seek to agree otherwise, disregarding the rules, then the imperative rules apply.[862] Should the national jurisdictions choose to impose stringent protective measures by widening the protective shield of the national law, they are entitled to do this unless it would lead to the imposition of barriers in the way of the free provision of certification services. However, the provision of protection to more groups of persons in cases of negligent behaviour by CSPs than those encompassed by the Directive can hardly be regarded as a barrier in this

---

[860] It is out of question that a valid contract may exist between the signatory and the owner of the certificate to arrange their internal relations so that the signatory be empowered and obliged to act on behalf of the owner. For example – employment contract, management contract, etc.

[861] Communication from the Commission COM (97) 503: Ensuring security and trust in electronic communication: "Towards a European Framework for Digital Signatures and Encryption", available at http://www.swiss.ai.mit.edu/6805/articles/crypto/eu-october-8-97.html, Section 3.2.

[862] The evaluation of the last Report to the EC – The Legal and Market Aspects of E-signatures also supports this conclusion. See *supra* note 158. Also Chapter I, section 2.2.5.1, *supra*.

regard. Therefore, it should be considered that the Bulgarian approach is in line with the rules and principles contained in the Directive.

It could be concluded that in spite of the identified peculiarities, in terms of the range of persons to whom CSPs are liable on specific liability grounds, Bulgarian law transposes the rule in Article 6 fairly well.[863] The analysis of the issues from the point of view of Bulgarian theory also firmly supports the findings made in Chapters I and III on the range of liable parties, the nature of their relationships, the liability exposure of the CSPs; and, finally, it supports the approach to interpretation of the Directive's liability rules made *supra*.[864]

2.4. Liability grounds

Analysis of the liability clauses of the EDESA in this section will provide further evidence of the correctness of the transposition. Should transposition in Bulgaria prove to be fair, then all the identified problems caused by enforcing the specific liability rules of the Directive will provide solid arguments to support the thesis that there is little necessity for the enforcement of such rules on a national level. These arguments will also dispel the idea that specific liability rules are necessary on a supranational level.

In Chapter III, the interpretation of the Directive's liability rules gives some idea that the Directive focused on the implementation of secondary (liability) rules, but the essence of the liability rules of Article 6 was in fact to establish statutory primary obligations for the CSPs. Thus, it was deduced that most of the liability grounds of Article 6 overlap with the statutory requirements and obligations imposed on the CSPs (primary rules) listed in Annex I and II.[865]

How has the Bulgarian legislator approached the issue and does this approach substantiate the theoretical deductions made in Chapter III? A positive answer to this question would demonstrate the serious imperfection of the Directive liability rules.

---

[863] Dumortier, J., Kelm, S., Nilsson, H., Van Eecke, P., Skouma, G., *ibid.*, Country Index Card for Bulgaria, p. 244.

[864] Compare these findings to the ones of sections 2.2.5.1, 2.2.5.2 and 2.2.5.3 of Chapter I in respect to the general liability regime of the CSPs and sections 4.1, 4.2. and 4.3 of Chapter III in respect to the liability regime under the Directive, *supra*.

[865] See Chapter III, section 6, *supra*.

Article 29(1) of Bulgarian EDESA reads that the specific liability rules will be triggered if: 1) the duties under Articles 21, 22 and 25 are infringed; or 2) the data present in the certificate is wrong or incomplete at the moment of issue of the certificate; or 3) the signatory did not hold the private key at the moment of issue of the certificate; or 4) there is a lack of correspondence between the public and the private keys. With regard to the liability grounds of Article 29(1)(1), it is worth noting that the duties to which it refers (Articles 21, 22 and 25 of EDESA) correspond to the requirements listed in Annexes I and II of the Directive. The duties under Article 29(1)(2)-(4) seem to be merely copied from Article 6(1) of the Directive.

This approach leads to the assumption that the Bulgarian legislator had difficulties in understanding the idea of the specific liability rules of Article 6 and in transposing those rules into Bulgarian law. The reasons for this are twofold: firstly because the rules in Article 6 are *de facto* primary rules,[866] and secondly, because they do not bring any 'special' protection whatsoever. Furthermore, the lawmakers found no answer to the question of why a different liability regime was needed for the CSPs towards the relying parties in respect of non-compliance with the duties listed in Article 6(1) and (2), on the one hand; and in respect of non-compliance with the duties listed in Annex II of the Directive, on the other. The same damage could be caused to the relying parties in respect of 'assurance that at the time of the issuance of the certificate, the signatory identified in the qualified certificate held the signature-creation data corresponding to the signature-verification data given or identified in the certificate' (Article 6(1)(i)(b)), and for not using 'trustworthy systems and products which are protected against modification and ensure the technical and cryptographic security of the process supported by them' (Annex II(f)). Why is specific liability exposure needed for the first ground (Article 6(1)), and not for the other (Annex II(f))? No reasonable answer was found to this question.

The author believes that during the drafting process the lawmakers decided to stay in line with the grounds listed in subparagraphs (2), (3) and (4) of the Directive, but only formally, rather to achieve more effective protection for the interest of the users of certification services and the relying parties.[867] This is because Articles 21, 22 and 25,

---

[866] The concept and the distiction between "primary rules" and "secondary rules" is analysed in Chapter II, Section 2.2, *supra*. As "primary rules" should be considered those statutory rules in contract and tort which establish duties and thus give rise to corresponding subjective rights. The rules referring to unfavourable legal concequences should primary rules are infringed shall be considered "secondary". They could not exist without the existence of corresponding primary rules. The latters are referred to as "liability rules". See Van Gerven, et al., *ibid.*

[867] The author has attended some of the sessions of the working group drafting the Bulgarian EDESA.

being primary rules, actually list all mandatory duties and obligations that the CSPs must comply with, and thus encompass all the grounds of Article 29(1)(2)-(4) (being transposed from Article 6(1) (.i)(a)-(c) of the Directive). These findings will be supported by the following analysis.

2.4.1. Liability causes under article 29(1)(1) of EDESA

As already mentioned, the approach of Bulgarian law is to set, by a secondary rule (Article 29(1)(1)) the grounds that trigger the liability of the CSP for non-compliance with given statutory duties (established by the primary rules of Article 21, 22 and 25). These duties are as follows:

Under Article 21, the CSPs must:

1. maintain financial resources that allow operation in conformity with the requirements laid down in the law;[868]

2. obtain insurance during the period of their operation against damage resulting of non-fulfilment of their duties under the law;[869]

3. use trustworthy systems and technologies which ensure the technical and cryptographic security of the processes supported by them;[870]

4. employ personnel who possess expert knowledge, experience, and qualifications necessary for the services provided – in particular, expertise in electronic signature technology and familiarity with proper security procedures;[871]

5. ensure that the date and time when the certificate is issued, revoked, suspended and restored, can be determined precisely;[872]

---

[868] Corresponding to Annex II (h) of the Directive.

[869] *Ibid*;

[870] Corresponding to Annex II (f) of the Directive.

[871] Corresponding to Annex II (e) of the Directive. The Bulgarian law has not transposed explicitly this part of the rule of the Directive whereby the CSPs must also apply administrative and management procedures which are adequate and correspond to recognized standards. However, in respect to the standards, which the CSPs must follow the Bulgarian legislator has issued an Ordinance on the activities of certification-service-providers, the terms and procedures of termination thereof, and the requirements for provision of certification services, adopted pursuant to CMD No. 17 dated 31 January 2002 (Promulgated, SG No. 15 dated 8 February 2002).

[872] Corresponding to Annex II (c) of the Directive.

6. take measures against forgery of certificates, and guarantee confidentiality during the process of generating the data made available to the CSP;[873]

7. use trustworthy systems to store and manage the certificates, so that

➢   only authorized persons can make changes,

➢   the certificates can be verified for authenticity and validity,

➢   restrictions with respect to public access to the certificates may be applied,

➢   any technical problems compromising the security requirements are apparent to the operator, and

➢   upon expiration of the certificates, it is impossible for the private key to be verified;.[874]

8. ensure conditions for prompt suspension and revocation of the certificates;[875]

9. immediately notify the Communications Regulation Commission on commencement of operation.[876]

Under Article 22, the CSPs should:

1.   issue a certificate upon request of a person seeking to support his or her signature, and to inform that person beforehand as to whether it is accredited or registered under Chapter IV of EDESA;

2.   inform the persons seeking issue of a certificate of the terms and conditions of issue and usage of the certificate, including the limitations on its use, as well as the existence of a voluntary accreditation scheme and procedures for complaints and dispute settlement;[877]

---

[873] Corresponding to Annex II (g) of the Directive.

[874] Corresponding to Annex II (l) of the Directive.

[875] Corresponding to Annex II (b) of the Directive.

[876] This rule establishes notification regime for the CSPs. Such an approach is followed also by other jurisdictions. See Dumortier, J., Kelm, S., Nilsson, H., Van Eecke, P., Skouma, G., *ibid.,* p.36 – 37.

[877] Corresponding to Annex II (k) of the Directive. However the second and the third senctence of the said rule were not transposed literally. There exists no relevant wording in Bulgrian EDESA that the information may be transmitted electronically, and it must be in writing and in readily understandable

3.   when issuing a certificate, verify by appropriate means, in accordance with the law, the identity and, if applicable, any specific attributes of the owner of the electronic signatures, and the signatory;[878]

4.   publish the certificate that has been issued, so that third parties are able to access it on the instructions of the owner;[879]

5.   not store or copy data for creation of private keys;[880]

6.   undertake immediate action regarding the suspension, restoration and the revocation of certificates, when the relevant reasons exist;[881]

7.   immediately inform the owner and the signatory of circumstances relevant to the validity or trustworthiness of the certificate;

8.   use a qualified electronic signature for the purposes of the activities of a CSP.

Under Article 25, the CSPs should follow strict procedures when issuing certificates. It guarantees that the CSP has verified: i) the completeness and the accuracy of the information to be entered into the certificate;[882] ii) the identity of the person seeking issue of the certificate; iii) that the signatory holds the private key to be identified in the certificate;[883] iv) the private key can be used through generally accepted standards to create qualified signatures; and v) the private and the public keys can be used in a complementary manner.[884] When the certificate is issued to a signatory other than the owner of the certificate, the above information should be verified for the signatory as well.[885]

---

language, and relevant parts of this information must also be made available upon request to third parties relying on the certificate.

[878] Corresponding to Annex II (d) of the Directive.

[879] Corresponding to Article 6 (2) of the Directive, and Annex II (k), (b) and (i) of the Directive.

[880] Corresponding to Annex II (j) of the Directive.

[881] Corresponding to Annex II (b) of the Directive.

[882] An obligation contained in Article 6 (1) (a) of the Directive.

[883] An obligation contained in Article 6 (1) (b) of the Directive.

[884] An obligation contained in Article 6 (1) (c) of the Directive.

[885] The model of the Bulgarian law to introduce two actors – "owner" and "signatory" was discussed in Section 2, *supra*.

To draw a parallel, Articles 21, 22 and 25 in fact transpose explicitly and completely the duties of the CSPs issuing qualified certificates, established by Annex II and Article 6(1) and (2) of the Directive. It is evident, firstly, that the Bulgarian legislator has chosen to introduce all these duties. Secondly, these duties are introduced systematically aside from the specific liability rules in Article 29. This approach leads to very important deductions in respect of the liability of the CSPs on a supranational level, which will be made only after reviewing the other set of liability causes under Article 29(1)(2)-(4) of EDESA.

2.4.2. Liability causes under article 29(1)(2)-(4) of EDESA

As envisaged above, Article 29(1)(2)-(4) of Bulgarian EDESA provides three causes triggering the specific liability of the CSPs. These causes are:

➢ the data present in the certificate is wrong or incomplete at the moment of its issue;

➢ the signatory did not hold the private key at the moment of issue of the certificate; and

➢ there is lack of correspondence between the public and the private keys.

It was also identified that these rules are a plain transposition of Article 6 (1)(a), (b) and (d) of the Directive.

From the point of view of Bulgarian law, these sets of provisions also establish primary duties for the CSPs. Re-interpreted in this way the rule should read as follows: i) the CSP is obliged to verify and secure the entry of true and complete data in the certificate at the moment of its issue; ii) the CSP is obliged to verify whether the signatory holds the private key at the moment of issue of the certificate; and iii) the CSP is obliged to verify that the private and the public keys can be used in a complementary manner.[886]

---

[886] It is noteworthy that under the Directive, the CSP shall be liable for its assurance that the signature-creation data and the signature-verification data can be used in a complementary manner *only in cases where the certification-service-provider generates them both*. Under Bulgarian law, the CSP shall be liable in all cases when the signature-creation data and the signature-verification data cannot be used in a complimentary manner, even when the signatory has generated them himself. This deviation, however,

Let us now turn to the liability causes under Article 29 (1)(1). This secondary rule reads that the liability of the CSPs shall be invoked if the given primary duties are infringed (i.e. those established by Articles 21, 22 and 25).

The comparative overview of these rules and the causes under Article 29(1)(2)-(4) lead to interesting findings:

1.   The primary rule of Article 29(1)(2) overlaps with the primary rule established by Article 25(2). The latter states that prior to issue of the certificate the CSP must verify the completeness and accuracy of the information to be entered into the certificate.

2.   The primary rule of Article 29(1)(3) overlaps with the primary rule of Article 25(2)(3)(a). The latter reads that prior to issue of the certificate the CSP should verify that the signatory is the one that holds the private key to be identified in the certificate.

3.   The primary rule of Article 29(1)(4) overlaps with the primary rule of Article 25(2)(3)(b) and (c). The latter reads that prior to issue of the certificate, the CSP must verify that the private key can be used through generally accepted standards to create a qualified signature, and the private and the public keys can be used in a complementary manner.

In other words, the liability provisions of Article 29(2)-(4) are ineffectual and worthless because, being primary rules, they reiterate other primary rules that are already in existence. The protection of the market actors was effectively achieved by establishing statutory mandatory duties for the CSPs as primary rules in Articles 21, 22 and 25, and the infringement of these duties would in any case lead to liability on the part of the CSPs.

To substantiate the above contentions, let us assume that Article 29(1)(1), which contains specific liability and transposes Article 6(1) and (2) of the Directive, was not present. Would the CSP be liable on general contractual or tort grounds? –Apparently so. Since mandatory statutory duties are introduced by virtue of law (Articles 21, 22 and 25), the CSP cannot contractually derogate from them and thus the party that has suffered damage under a contract shall be always entitled to claim damages on general

cannot substantially impact the liability exposure of the CSPs on a national level, therefore it should be considered insignificant.

liability grounds under Article 79 *et seq.* of the Bulgarian Law on Obligations and Contracts (LOC)[887] in relation to Article 23 of EDESA.[888] If no contract is executed, the statutory duties outline the CSP's duty of care. Therefore, where the CSP has behaved negligently, in contravention of the legal norms, the aggrieved party has grounds to hold the CSP liable on general tort grounds under Article 45 of LOC.[889] Those liability issues are analyzed from the standpoint of the general liability theory and regime, as discussed in Chapter I, *supra*.[890]

The Bulgarian legislator plainly had difficulties in understanding why the Directive had established liability causes in Article 6(1) and (2), since those provisions evidently introduce duties for the CSPs; i.e. they reveal primary rules. The view taken by the Bulgarian legislator leads to the correct conclusion that those duties should be introduced where the primary rules lay down all the CSP's statutory duties, i.e. where they logically belong – in Articles 21, 22 and 25. The legislator saw no reason for wholesale transposition, but has chosen merely to transpose the provisions of Article 6(1)(a), (b) and (c) of the Directive into Article 29 of EDESA in order for it to be formally in line with the Directive. Such an approach has been followed by other jurisdictions (see *infra* section 2.4).

After demonstrating the lack of necessity for the transposition of Article 6(1) and (2) into Bulgarian law, the question of whether the deductions made in respect of the Bulgarian specific liability rules are relevant for the Community act itself will be investigated. The relevant issues are as follows:

1. Has the Directive established duties for the CSPs issuing qualified certificates as primary rules? Yes. Annex II contains such rules,[891] as well as Article 6(1) and (2).[892]

---

[887] Article 79 *et seq.* of Bulgarian LOC holds the general rules establishing liability for non-performance of contractual obligations. It reads that if the debtor fails to perform his obligation strictly the creditor shall be entitled to seek performance together with damages for the delay or to claim damages for non-performance. See section 2.2 of Chapter I, *supra*.

[888] Article 23 of EDESA reads that the relations between the certification-service-provider and the owner shall be regulated by a written contract.

[889] Article 45 *et seq.* of Bulgarian LOC hold the general liability rules in tort. They apply should no other particular tort rules are applicable to the respective case. Article 45 reads that every person is obliged to repair the damages, which has negligently caused to other person. See section 2.2 of Chapter I, *supra*.

[890] See section 2.2 *et seq.* of Chapter II, *supra*.

[891] See Chapter III, section 3, *surpa*.

[892] See Chapter III, section 5, *surpa*.

2. Has the Directive established some of these primary rules systematically in a secondary liability provision? Yes. Article 6(1) and (2) contain primary duties for the activity of the CSPs.

3. Are Member States obliged to transpose those duties as mandatory? Yes. The wording of the Directive leaves no doubt as to whether such duties should be introduced as mandatory. However, the Directive uses two legislative techniques to achieve this aim. In the first instance, Annex II rules that '*certification-service-providers* **must** ...' meet the listed requirements when issuing qualified certificates. Therefore the Member States should use legislative techniques that preserve the mandatory nature of the rules. In this regard, the Bulgarian legislator has chosen to establish Articles 21, 22 and 25. Secondly, the CSPs would be threatened with exposure to liability if they act in breach of the rules of Article 6(1) and (2). The latter approach seems to be inappropriate, as will become evident from section 3.3 *infra*.

4. Would the CSPs be liable under general national liability rules in cases of misfeasance in respect of established mandatory duties, and the specific liability rule if Article 6 was not present? Yes. Recital (22) explicitly envisages that certification-service-providers providing certification services to the public are subject to national rules regarding liability if mandatory duties are infringed. This statement will be valid both in contract and tort.

Bearing all the above in mind, several cornerstones may be put in place at this stage, in order that a proper base may be laid for the general conclusions made later on:

1) The Directive has established a set of duties by using two legislative techniques: explicitly listing such duties in primary rules, and introducing duties as an integral part of other secondary liability provisions.

2) This approach seems to be inappropriate, since it leads to the existence of mandatory duties which are disunited in the different parts of the Directive (annexes and articles), and this leads to ambiguity.

3) In spite of the approach taken, the mandatory duties should be transposed by the Member States.

4) During the course of transposition, the Bulgarian legislator faced problems in interpreting the intention of the European legislator; in particular in respect of the idea behind Article 6 – i.e. why specific liability provisions are introduced.

5) To resolve vagueness, the Bulgarian legislator chose to follow two approaches – to transpose the Directive by extracting the duties of CSPs from Article 6(1) and (2) and moving them to a logical and correlated place; and to merely and literally transpose the rule in Article 6 in order to be formally in line with the wording of the specific liability provision of the Directive.

6) The second approach proves to be useless since, as has become evident, even without the literal transposition, the general liability rules will secure protection both for the certificate holders and the relying parties on general contractual or tort grounds. The following sections provide more evidence on this issue.

2.4.3. The approach taken in other EU jurisdictions

Since the above deductions are based on analysis of the Bulgarian legislation, it is conceivable that the problems faced by the Bulgarian jurisdiction are isolated, and that therefore no general conclusions may be drawn from the Bulgarian experience in respect of the Directive. Therefore, turning to the comparative overview made in the Report 'Legal and Market Aspects of Electronic Signatures in Europe'[893] on the methods and legal techniques applied in other jurisdictions to tackle the transposition of Article 6 seems an appropriate step in order to shed more light on the problems faced in interpretation of the supranational specific liability rules.

The report demonstrates that most of the countries seem to follow the idea of introducing explicit liability rules simply to be formally in line with the Directive. It is established that there are three identifiable lines in transposing the liability clauses list: countries that have transposed the list of liability grounds of Article 6.1 in an identical or similar way to the Directive (Belgium, Greece, Ireland, Italy, the Netherlands, UK, *et al*); countries which further to the literal transposition have amplified the list by extending the scope of Article 6.2, which deals with omission to register revocation of qualified certificates (Austria, Denmark, Luxembourg, Finland, Sweden, Slovenia, Lithuania, Norway, *et al*); and countries which have extended the scope of the list by adding other liability causes as specific failures or omissions to act (Germany, Czech Republic, Estonia, Hungary, Latvia, Malta, Romania etc).[894]

---

[893] Dumortier, J., Kelm, S., Nilsson, H., Van Eecke, P., Skouma, G., *ibid.*,

[894] *Ibid.*, p.86-89.

The grouping made by the authors of the Report makes it clear that, just like Bulgaria, most of the countries have faced difficulties in understanding and transposing Article 6. While the first two groups of countries have made an almost literal transposition and thus bypass the difficult issue, the third group has identified fundamental problems in the transposition of Article 6.

What lies behind the model of Article 6 of the Directive? The simple answer – 'liability grounds' – does not quite seem satisfactory and correct. As has become obvious, the idea of Article 6 is to establish duties for the CSP. Negligent non-feasance or malfeasance in respect of these duties, giving rise to damage, would constitute grounds for liability, and this would be reflected in the CSP being held liable. Therefore, a fundamental question arises as to whether it is appropriate to list liability clauses, rather than duties.

Although from the point of view of legal technique, the answer to this question seems to be of no great importance, it has specific significance from the point of view of substantive law. The approach of some systems, like Bulgaria, Germany,[895] and, to some extent, Hungary,[896] Romania,[897] and Austria,[898] prove that it should be

---

[895] The German E-signature Law (SIgG) for example does not provide a liability list, but rather provides a general provision and leaves the liability of the CSPs to the general rules. The rules that regulate the issue are § 11 SigG and § 823 BGB. The particular rule of the SigG provides that the CSPs shall be liable for "infringes the requirements under this Law and the statutory ordinance under Section 24, or if his products for qualified electronic signatures or other technical security facilities fail".

[896] Under the Section 15 (1)-(3) of the Hungarian e-signature law it is Law the certification service provider shall be liable to any third person with whom it has no contractual relationship according to the Civil Code of the Republic of Hungary, to the certificate holder according to the rules of liability for breach of contract in respect of the damage caused with the qualified electronic signature or time stamp or the electronic record having the former in the case that the service provider failed to comply with certain provisions of the law. Those rules are to inform the users about the terms and conditions of the certification service and on the publication, revocation, suspension of certificates; keep records related to certificates; maintain a continuous service and use of secure-signature creation devices in the framework of provision of advanced services.

[897] The Romanian law on e-signatures no. 455 of July 18th, 2001 on Electronic Signature, similarly to the Bulgarian EDESA provide that a certification service provider that issues certificates presented as being qualified or guarantees such certificates is liable for damage caused to any person the behaviour of which is based on the legal effects of such certificates concerning: the accuracy at the time of issuance of a certificate of all the information included therein; the assurance that, at the time of issuance of a certificate, the certificate holder identified in the certificate held the signature-creation data corresponding to the signature-verification data referred to in the respective certificate; the assurance that the signature-creation data were consistent with the signature-verification data, if the certification service provider generates them both; the suspension and revocation of the certificate, in cases and conditions provided in Article 24 1st and 2nd paragraphs; fulfillment of every obligation provided by Arts. 13-17 and 19-22 herein (the general rules regulating the activity of the CSP).

[898] Under §23 of the Austrian Electronic Signature Act,the CSPs which issue qualified certificates or which guarantee qualified certificates issued by CSPs established in the EC, the validity of which can be verified shall be liable towrds persons who rely on the certificates. All other negligent actions of the CSPs falling beyond the scope of §23 ESL shall be subject to the general rules on contractual liability and the general tort law rules (see §1295 and the following of the Austrian Civil Code). The same regime shall govern the

taken into consideration that the CSP should comply with all the requirements set forth in national law. There is no reason to release the CSP from liability for causing damages to the party relying on the certificate, if the CSP has infringed any obligation established by law or by contract and such obligation does not fall within the grounds of Article 6(1) and (2). Such grounds will be always present when Annex II of the Directive is fairly transposed. Will the CSPs issuing qualified certificates under any given EU jurisdiction be released from liability for failure to fulfil, say, the requirement of Annex II(l) to use reliable systems for the storage of certificates in a verifiable form, or the requirement of paragraph (j) not to store or copy the signature-creation data of the party to whom the certification-service-provider provided key management services? Obviously not. The CSP will be held liable and will not be able to obtain release from such liability by using contractual instruments or by use of any disclaimers or warranties.[899] In this respect, the list of liability causes set out in Article 6(1) and (2) should be considered exhaustive in view of the specific liability to be established, and indicative in view of the general liability rules that would apply. Otherwise, an incorrect and very dangerous conclusion could be made, to the effect that the CSPs may be held liable only under the hypotheses of Article 6(1) and (2), and not beyond them. The latter problem was widely discussed by legal scholars during the course of drafting the legal provisions of EDESA, and later, in drafting the Commentary to the law.[900]

Considering the above, it is inexplicable why the Directive has chosen to provide specific liability for infringements of the duties listed in Article 6(1) and (2) only and not in cases where any duty listed in the Annexes is infringed. The impossibility of finding a reasonable answer to this question poses serious questions about the adequacy of the Directive's approach.

---

liability of the RSPs, the TSPs, the DSPs and other providers of certification cervices related to electronic signatures.

[899] Similarly, the UNICTRIAL Model Law on Electronic Signatures in Article 9 establishes duties and obligations to be complied with by any certification service provider, and not only those who issue "high value" certificates. However, the authors of the Model Law took care not to require from a certificate holder or a certification service provider a degree of diligence or trustworthiness that bears no reasonable relationship to the purposes for which the electronic signature or certificate is used (See Section 139 of the Guide for Enactment of the UNCITRAL Model Law on Electronic Signatures).

[900] The commentary of EDESA is the first academic legal research in Bulgaria in area of electronic signatures. It is drafted by the drafters of the primary and subsidiary legislation of the e-signatures in Bulgaria – Prof. Anguel Kalaidjiev, Borislav Belaselkov – Supreme justice at the Supreme Court of Cassation, George Dimitrov – Chairperson of the Center for ICT Law, Maria Yordanova – Director of the Law programme at the Center for Study of the Democracy, Dimitar Markov – expert to the Center, and Vessela Stancheva – lawyer. The commentary was published in 2004.

The supporters of the liability concept of Article 6 would probably uphold the thesis that Article 6(1) and (2) provides a 'reversed burden of proof' designed to protect users, and that is why it matters where the liability clauses are listed. Furthermore, they would probably contend that in the hypotheses of Article 6(1) and (2) the parties suffering damage should have placed reasonable reliance on the certificate in order to base their claim on the specific liability grounds.

From the analysis made below, it is evident that the introduction of the concepts of 'reasonable reliance' and 'reversed burden of proof' are also questionable. This fact casts grave doubt on the wisdom of the Directive's approach in introducing specific liability in order to enhance trust in the market.

2.5. Reasonable reliance concept

Bulgarian law does not explicitly copy the wording of the Directive with regard to the concept of 'reasonable reliance'. Article 6(1) and (2) of the Directive provides that the CSPs shall be liable for issuing qualified certificates to the public towards persons who reasonably rely on the certificates. However, Bulgarian law, in common with other EU jurisdictions, would hardly allow liability exposure towards a person who, on the other hand, 'unreasonably' relied on the certificate. The issue of the duty of care towards users (creditors or aggrieved parties), as interpreted in Bulgarian law, will apply to the CSPs' liability exposure, thus mere transposition is unnecessary.

2.5.1. Contributory fault

Under the general Bulgarian liability theory, both in contract and tort, it is unjust to hold the debtor liable in cases when the creditor, likewise the person who has suffered damage, has contributed to the occurrence of the damage.[901] This issue arises where that party's behaviour contradicts the general duty of care. The concept is known as contributory fault. Art 83(1) of the Bulgarian Law on Obligations and Contracts (LOC) provides that should non-performance be due to reasons caused by the creditors' behaviour, the court may reduce the compensation or release the

---

[901] This concept is also set forth as main Principle of European Contract Law. Article 9:504 reads that the non-performing party is not liable for loss suffered by the aggrieved party to the extent that the aggrieved party contributed to the non-performance or its effects. Furthermore, Article 9:505 rules that the non-performing party is not liable for loss suffered by the aggrieved party to the extent that the aggrieved party could have reduced the loss by taking reasonable steps. The aggrieved party is entitled to recover any expenses reasonably incurred in attempting to reduce the loss.

debtor from liability. Article 51(2) provides that if the aggrieved party in respect of the commission of a tort has contributed to the occurrence of the damage the court is entitled to reduce the compensation payable.

The Bulgarian court practice is full of cases in which the damage was caused as a direct result of the creditor's behaviour. In such cases, no liability emerges.[902] At the same time, there are cases in which the creditor may have only contributed to the occurrence of the damage, i.e. they are the consequence of the behaviour of both the debtor and the creditor.

The first rules that refer to the creditor's contribution appear in Roman law.[903] Being relatively general, they were applicable both for contract and tort.[904] The main principle for the compensation of damage was that no compensation should be awarded to the creditor where he or she has contributed to the occurrence of the damage, unless the debtor had acted intentionally. Later, Roman jurisprudence introduced another rule, whereby depending on the contribution made to the causation of the damage, the creditor was alternatively awarded either full compensation or the application was dismissed in its entirety.

Much later, in the countries following Roman civil law traditions, the rule for compensation depending on the 'contributory quota' was accepted. According to this rule, the compensation has to be reduced only to the extent of the actual contribution.[905]

When the damage occurs as a result of the behaviour of other parties besides the debtor, complications cannot arise because all the parties will be jointly liable either in tort or on contractual grounds.

2.5.2. The general concept of reasonable care of the creditor (the aggrieved party)

The contributory fault concept is based on a more general principle of civil liability.

---

[902] Under Decision of the Supreme Court of Republic of Bulgaria №1410–1974–I ГО the tort allowed by the aggrieved person is a ground for reducing of the compensation. *Cit op.* Court Practice of the Supreme Court of Republic of Bulgaria. Civil Division 1993. S., 1996, p.213

[903] See Goleva, P., *Contributive damages in tort*, 1989, Sofia, p. 9–21.

[904] It is quite famous the epigram of Pomponius "Whoever causes damages to himself shall not be considered damaged" – See Goleva, P., *ibid.*, p. 12.

[905] §254 BGB, also Article 83 (1) and Article 51 (2) of the Bulgarian LOC, etc.

Under Article 83(2) of the Bulgarian LOC the debtor shall not be liable for damage which the creditor could have avoided if he or she had acted with due care. This principle is applicable both in contract and tort.[906] Unlike the contributory fault concept, where the behaviour of the creditor/the aggrieved party has contributed to the occurrence of the damage, under the general principle in question the inertness of the creditor, who has failed to act with the necessary due care causes the occurrence of the damage[907] where no causality exists between the behaviour of the debtor/the tortfeasor and the creditor/the aggrieved party. The established court practice also firmly supports the above findings.[908]

2.5.3. The reasonable care of the parties relying on the certificate under the general principles of law

The general principles of Bulgarian law support the idea that it is unjust to hold the debtor, respectively the tortfeasor solely responsible in cases in which the creditor, resp. the aggrieved party does not behave with due care in respect of its own interests and thus contribute to the occurrence of the damage, or does not act diligently in order to avoid the damages. That is to say, the CSP – being the debtor in a contractual relationship with the certificate holder, or being the tortfeasor in respect of a tort committed to the detriment of a relying third party - would be released from liability, or the level of compensation would be reduced, if the certificate holder, respectively the relying party did not act with due care, i.e. reasonably. The fault, or lack of due care, of the creditor/the aggrieved party which leads to the occurrence of the damage is known in all jurisdictions as *culpa creditori*.

Under the general law the relying party must exercise reasonable care in relying on the certificate.[909] The relying party should at least: verify the validity, suspension or revocation of the certificate using current revocation status information;[910] take into

---

[906] The principle is widely applied in insurance relationships. For example the insured person is obliged to exercise due diligence to reduce the damages – Article 389 (2) of the Commercial Act. See Gerdjikov, O., Commercial Transactions. Commentary of Part III of the Commercial Act., Sofia 2000, p. 173–174

[907] See Kalaydjiev, A., *ibid.*, p. 388-390, also Kojuharov, A., *ibid.*, p.285-286.

[908] See decisions of the Supreme Court of Cassation №№ 1641–1983–I ГО, ПП–4–1968, 1696–1974–I ГО, 16–1983–I ГО, 917–1986–II ГО, cit op. Tsachev, L., ibid, p.333-334.

[909] The liability of CAs issuing qualified certificates to the public specified in Article 6 of the Directive 1999/93/EC applies to parties who "reasonably rely" on a certificate. However, the requirement for reasonable reliance applies not only to the relying parties *strictu sensu* but also to the certificate hodlers who may rely on the qualified certificates as well. See Chapter III, section 4.4, *supra*.

[910] Depending on CA's practices and the mechanism used to provide revocation status information, there may be a delay of up to 1 day in disseminating revocation status information.

account any limitations put on the usage of the certificate indicated to the relying party in the certificate; use a secure signature-verification device;[911] take any other precautions prescribed in agreements or elsewhere.[912] These duties should be considered normal, and no contract should be executed in order for the relying party to follow them.[913] Further obligations may be imposed on the relying party to delineate the scope of its due care, should the contract with the CSP be duly executed.

If the relying party does not fulfil its duties in a manner that may be considered reasonable in the particular case at issue, and damage has occurred, the CSP, whether it has acted negligently or not, will be able to successfully defend itself by providing evidence of contributory fault or negligent inertness as a cause.[914]

In the same way, the certificate holder should exercise due care in the following ways: in the provision of accurate information to the CSP, when such information is published in the certificate; in verifying the correctness of the information before and after the certificate has been issued; in verifying the purpose and the limits of transactions placed in the certificate; in notifying the CSP to request suspension and revocation should the private key be compromised; in using standardized algorithms for the creation of the signature; in using secure signature-creation devices[915] etc.[916] Even if those duties are not explicitly listed in the contract for certification services they should be considered within the reasonable due care of the certificate holder. Thus, any unreasonable behaviour on the part of the certificate holder that has led to his or her reliance on the certificate, followed by the occurrence of damage, would give the CSP the possibility of successfully defending itself by providing evidence as to contributive negligence or negligent inertness, whether it has acted negligently or not. [917]

---

[911] See Annex IV of the Directive, also Article 17 (2) of EDESA.

[912] See ETSI 101 456 V1.1.1 (2000-12) Policy Requirements for CAs, section 6.3, p.15.

[913] Further analysis of the reasonable reliance is made in Chapter III, section 4.4, *supra*.

[914] See Chapter II, section 5, *supra*.

[915] See Annex III of the Directive, and Article 17 (1) of EDESA.

[916] See Article 30 of EDESA.

[917] See Chapter II, section 5, *supra*.

2.5.4. The approach taken in other EU jurisdictions

Comparative research shows that in many other countries, the concept of 'reasonable reliance' was not literally transposed as being inherent to the general principles of law.[918] This approach was taken by Sweden, Finland, Hungary, Estonia, Austria, Czech Republic, Germany, Iceland, and Latvia.

Other countries, like Belgium, Denmark, France, Greece, Ireland, Italy, literally transposed the 'reasonable reliance' concept as a precondition for holding a particular CSP liable. However, even in those countries, by deriving justice from the general principles of law, the courts would hardly award compensation where the relying party has acted carelessly, regardless of whether the CSP has acted diligently or not. However, in cases in which both the relying party and the CSP have acted carelessly, the courts would apply the common doctrine of *culpa creditori*[919] and either release the CSP from liability or reduce the level of compensation.[920] Therefore, it becomes evident that the various jurisdictions have literally transposed the rule primarily to ensure that their laws are in line with the exact wording of the Directive, rather than to introduce a specific rule deviating from the general principles of law.

The approach taken by the Bulgarian legislator, of not transposing the Directive literally but to leaving the liability exposure of the CSPs, when *culpa creditori* is involved, to the general principles of law, demonstrates the vagueness of the Directive's requirement for reasonable reliance as a prerequisite for triggering the specific liability of the CSPs, from the perspective of Bulgarian law. However, since the general principle in question is widely accepted in all jurisdictions throughout Europe, it is questionable whether a particular reference to 'reasonable reliance' is needed at all. Thus, the first serious argument of the supporters of the specific liability approach seems ungrounded. The following section contains an analysis of the worth of the second argument – the necessity of the reversed burden of proof.

---

[918] Dumortier, J., et al., *ibid.*, p.85

[919] The German Law refers this to be a re-allocation of the damages in "quota" to the level of co-causation. See §247 of the BGB. In the Bulgarian law the concept of the co-causation is regulated by different rules for the tort and the contractual liability. See Chapter II, section 5, *supra*.

[920] The principle of reducing of the compensation due to contributive fault is known to the Roman law. It is applicable both to tort and contractual liability. It is quite popular the epigram of Pomponius: „The one who suffers damages due to his own fault shall not be considered damaged". (*Op. cit.* Kalaydjiev A., *ibid*).

2.6. Burden of proof concept

Under the Bulgarian law, no 'reversed' burden of proof *strictu sensu* exists. The Bulgarian law does not explicitly copy the wording of the Directive but it is in line with the rule of Article 6. The burden of proving the fault derives from the general civil liability rules. Under those rules, the CSP would always bear the burden of proving that it has acted with due care, both in contract and in tort.[921] For example, Article 45(2) of the Bulgarian Law on Obligations and Contracts provides that, 'in tort the fault is presumed unless the contrary is proved'. In contractual relations, Article 79 provides that the creditor's claim for damages is presupposed only from the non-fulfilment of the obligation and the causality of the occurrence of the damage.[922]

It should be noted that negligence in civil law is not considered to be a psychological attitude, but rather non-compliance of the relevant party's behaviour with the objective criterion for the duty of care required from 'the good merchant'.[923] The illicit behaviour is subject to proof, but no such necessary exist for proving the negligence as a type of fault.

Presuming negligence means that the illegal result was foreseeable and avoidable by exercising the duty of care required from 'the good merchant'[924] In tort, the party that has suffered damage must prove the illicit behaviour, the damage suffered and the chain of causation between the illicit behaviour and the occurrence of the damage. In contract, the burden of proving the performance rests with the debtor.[925] Both in tort and contract, the debtor/the tortfeasor, must prove that he or she has acted with due care.

The rule in Article 6 of the Directive provides that the CSP shall be held liable for non-performance of the listed duties, '*unless he proves that he has not acted negligently*'.[926] It is worth noting that in a number of studies, this rule is considered to establish a reversed burden in respect of proving the occurrence of the damage or the causality

---

[921] See Chapter III, section 6.1.2, *supra*.

[922] The concept is introduced and examined in Chapter II, section 4, *supra*.

[923] See Kalaydjiev, A., *ibid.*, p. 371.

[924] See Konov, Tr., *ibid.*, p. 169

[925] See Kalaydjiev, A., *ibid.*, p. 373.

[926] See Chapter III, section 6.1.2, *supra*.

of the damage rather than a reversed burden in respect of proving the negligence of the CSP.[927] Often the rule allocating the burden of proving non-negligence is referred to as 'presumption of causality'.[928] Such an interpretation seems to widen the scope of Article 6 excessively.

As already discussed, the party suffering damage always bears the burden of proving the actual appearance of the damage and the chain of causation between the behaviour of the CSP and the occurrence of the damage.[929] In tort, the party suffering damage should also prove that the behaviour of the CSP is *contra lege*,[930] but need not prove the negligence of the CSP. The negligent behaviour (the fault) of the provider is a precondition for entitlement to compensation for damage suffered.[931]

It may appear that the rule of Article 6 establishes a rebuttable 'presumption of fault' by explicitly allocating the burden of defence in respect of whether the CSP has acted diligently, but not a 'presumption of causality'.[932] Whether the behaviour of the CSPs is the actual cause of the damage may also be the subject of a presumption under certain legislative acts. For example, Article 23 of Directive 95/46 on the Protection of Personal Data[933] explicitly establishes a presumption of causality, rather than a presumption of fault. The rule provides that the controller may be exempted from liability, either altogether or partially, under the Directive if able to prove that he or she is not responsible for the event giving rise to the

---

[927] Georgia Skouma finds that "any party who relied on the certificate and suffered damages because of this *does not need to demonstrate the cause of the damage if the latter arise from the list of liability clauses set out in Article 6.* The CSP shall be considered *de facto* liable in relation to these liability causes ("presumption of causality"), unless he is able to demonstrate that he has not acted negligently ("refutable presumption")". Skouma, G., et al., *ibid.*

[928] *Ibid.*, p. 90-92

[929] See Chapter II, section 3, *supra.*

[930] Konov, Tr., *ibid.*, p. 169

[931] See Rinderle, R., *ibid.*, section 10.1.1.7. Also Kalaydjiev, A., *ibid.*, section 5.5. See also *supra* Chapter II, section 4.2.

[932] The rules on the burden of proof of causality have an impact as regards issues of negligence (i.e. the breach of a duty of care under the tort of negligence in English law), *faute* (under French law) or *Rechtswidrigkeit and Verschulden* (under German law). See Ius Commune Casebooks for the Common Law in Europe – Tort Law, Note 1, p. 428/13 (http://www.law.kuleuven.ac.be/casebook/tort/heading4.2.3.pdf)

[933] See Chapter IV, section 3.4, *supra.*

damage (i.e. the cause). The burden of proving the negligence (i.e. the fault) under Directive 95/46 is left to the general national liability rules.[934]

This does not seem to be the case under Directive 1999/93/EC. The rule in Article 6(1) and (2) does not establish presumption of causality. The CSP shall be the one to prove that the reason for its conduct is not due to its negligence (fault), i.e. that the CSP has acted with due care. In most EU countries, negligence under the general liability regime will be presumed both in tort and in contract relationships.[935] However, the party suffering damage will not be released from the requirement to prove causality,[936] i.e. that the behaviour of the CSP has caused the damage.[937] In this respect, the rule in Article 6 should be strictly interpreted. Thus it remains unclear why the explicit allocation of the burden to the CSP is considered by some studies to be a 'reversed burden'.

As it has become evident, under Bulgarian law 'reversing' the burden is of no use, since it tallies with the general principles of allocating the burden of proving the negligence both in contract and tort.[938] The comparative research, on the other hand, shows that with some exceptions[939] the general civil liability rules in almost all the jurisdictions of the EU Member States that follow the civil law model take a similar approach in allocating the burden of proving the negligence.[940] Therefore, it appears

---

[934] See Chapter II, section 4.2, *supra*.

[935] See Kalaydjiev, A., *ibid.*, p. 373-374.

[936] In respect to causality in almost all Euroepan legal systems (France, Germany, England, etc.) the plaintiff must bear the burden of proving causation between the conduct of the alleged tortfeasor and the injury which was suffered. See Ius Commune Casebooks for the Common Law in Europe – Tort Law, Chapter 4, section 4.2.3, p. 428/13 (http://www.law.kuleuven.ac.be/casebook/tort/heading4.2.3.pdf)

[937] In the famous case *Wilsher* v. *Essex Area Health Authority*, House of Lords [1988] 1 AC 1074, it is clearly delineated what is the burden of proof of causality: "*The plaintiff must prove on a balance of probabilities that the conduct of the alleged tortfeasor was a cause-in-fact ("but for" test) of the injury which he or she suffered.*"

[938] See *supra* note 428. The presumption of negligence in tort law is provided by Article 45 (2) of the Bulgarian LOC and the similar rule in contract exist in Article 79 of LOC.

[939] Under the UK general rules the plaintiff has to prove that the defendant has acted negligently. See Hindelang S, *No Remedy for Disappointed Trust – The Liability Regime for Certification Authorities Towards Third Parties Outwith the EC Directive in England and Germany Compared*, Refereed article, The Journal of Information, Law and Technology (JILT), 2002 (1), http://elj.warwick.ac.uk/jilt/02-1/hindelang.html. "This might be a cumbersome or even an impossible task due to the complexity of technical processes and the ignorance of the organisational structure of a CA. Finally, the EC Directive on a Community framework for electronic signatures (Article 6 (1), (2)) requires for qualified certificates that the CA has to prove that it did not act negligently. Therefore, the present English rules need to be brought in line with the EC provisions (see also DTI, 2001a), as already outlined above."

[940] In countries like Finland, Sweden, Denmark (the Nordic Approach) the fault not need to be proved – Ius Commune Casebook – Tort Law, p. 68/4. See also Kalaydjiev, A., *ibid.*, section 5.5. Also Harrison, R., *Public Key Infrastructure: Risks of Being Trusted*, 2000 11 C & L 28.

that the Directive in fact reiterates the common general civil liability approach of most of the EU Member States rather than introducing deviation and 'reversing' the burden. Therefore, it is questionable whether such explicit allocation referral is needed at all. Even if we assume that in some countries, such as the UK,[941] the concept is different and thus Article 6 would affect the general principles, it is unreasonable to claim that explicit introduction of the allocation of the burden of proof would promote 'trust and confidence in electronic signatures' which otherwise would not exist. The Bulgarian approach demonstrates that even without transposition of the specific liability rule, the burden of proving due care falls to the CSP in any case and trust and confidence in electronic signatures will not be in any way undermined. It would appear that the arguments of the supporters of the specific liability regime weaken in this respect as well.

2.7. The limitation of liability concept

The preceding sections of this chapter contain weighty arguments on the serious imperfections in the rules of Article 6(1) and (2) from the perspective of the transposition of the Directive into Bulgarian law. These arguments cast grave doubt on the necessity of the specific liability rules.

The following section is dedicated to analysis of the problems involved in the transposition into national law of paragraphs (3) and (4) of Article 6, and aims at identifying whether serious imperfections exist that might threaten the adequacy of Article 6 in its entirety.

The interpretation of the Directive liability rules in Chapter III gives some indication that the rules of the Directive (in Article 6(3) and (4)) are improperly interpreted. The reason for this is due to their place of presence in Article 6 - they provide a possibility

---

[941] In the UK DTI Consultation document on the Implementation on EU Electronic Signatures Directive of 19 March 2001 the Department of Trade and Industry envisage: "We believe that this will require that the claimant will need to establish that the service provider issued or guaranteed a qualified certificate to the public, that the claimant reasonably relied on it and that such reliance was for any of the specified purposes and that damage was caused by such reliance. The final words of Article 6 (1) make it clear that the onus is on the service provider to prove that he had not acted negligently. We have looked at the obligations imposed by Article 6.1 against the existing requirements of the English, Northern Irish and Scots law of tort and delict and contract. *We have concluded that existing law does not provide a comprehensive solution to the requirements of the Directive and therefore provision will need to be made which would ensure that in the circumstances set out in Article 6.1 a certification service provider is liable unless he proves that he has not acted negligently and that this liability is not dependent on the existence of a duty of care.".* The full text of the consultation paper is available at http://www.dti.gov.uk/industry_files/pdf/esigs_consult.pdf

for the CSPs to issue certificates under certain conditions and thus to exempt themselves from liability rather then achieve limitation of liability.

How has Bulgarian law approached the liability management concept?

Bulgarian law has introduced specific rules in respect of the possible management of liability by CSPs.

Under Article 29(3) of EDESA, the CSP shall not be held liable for damage caused by use of the certificate in a manner contrary to the denoted purpose or by exceeding the limitations as to value of transactions stipulated in the certificate.[942] The rule is mandatory. Where the certificate contains limitations, a presumption of knowledge of these limitations by relying third parties exists. If the relying party has trusted the e-signature anyway and has undertaken given actions, it would not be entitled to compensation for the damage that has occurred.[943]

In respect of the types of fault within the limits of the liability exposure under the general Bulgarian civil law, as is the case in the laws of many other EU jurisdictions, exemption of liability can be agreed upon between the parties by contract.[944] Such an exemption cannot, however, be agreed upon for wilful misconduct or gross negligence (Article 94 of the Law on Obligations and Contracts).[945] There are further limitations for the CSPs. Under Article 29(3), apart from wilful misconduct, parties cannot agree upon exemption of liability for the CSP for any type of negligence. This limitation concerns only the hypotheses listed in Article 29. In contractual terms, the CSP can limit its liability for the non-performance of other obligations outside the scope of Article 29.[946]

Most of the countries that have transposed the Directive into their national law also recognize the possibilities for liability limitations by placing limits on the value of transactions or the usage of the certificate (Belgium, Denmark, Luxembourg, Austria,

---

[942] Kalaydjiev, A., Belazelkov, B., Dimitrov, G., et al., *ibid.*, p. 252.

[943] *Ibid.*

[944] Dumortier, J., et al., *The Legal and Market Aspects of Electronic Signatures in Europe,* Questionnaire of the Bulgarian Correspondent, section 19.

[945] Kojuharov, A., *ibid.*, p. 257.

[946] Kalaydjiev, A., Belazelkov, B., Dimitrov, G., et al., *ibid.*

Germany, Spain etc). The words of the Directive are transposed almost literally into the national laws of these countries.[947]

There are a few exceptions where limitations have not been explicitly provided (this is the case in the United Kingdom, Switzerland and Estonia[948]).

Some national laws were identified in which further possibilities for limitations have been introduced.[949] Some jurisdictions go even further, by making the placing of any limitation possible, at the request of the certificate holder, and even such limitations as are placed in the certificate policy of the CSP.[950]

The evaluation of the transposition of the liability limits rules of Article 6 (3) and (4) of the Directive shows that there is both lack of clarity and improper interpretation in the way in which the intentions of the European legislator have been interpreted. As discussed in sections 6.2.1 and 5.3.3 of Chapter IV, *supra*, the idea of the rule was to make the CSP able to manage the conditions under which certificates are issued by placing limits on the use and validity of the certificate.[951] Therefore, the usage of the certificate beyond these purposes and the established limitations does not make the CSP liable whether or not it has acted with due care. The above conclusions are strongly supported by the historical comparative analysis of the normative texts of the Directive made in section 1.2 of Chapter III, *supra*.

---

[947] Dumortier, J., et al., *The Legal and Market Aspects of Electronic Signatures in Europe, ibid.*, Appendix 4.

[948] Estonian law provides that CSPs cannot be held liable for damages resulting from the certificate's use or misuse since certificate holders are presumed to bear such a risk. *Op. cit.* Dumortier, J., et al., *The Legal and Market Aspects of Electronic Signatures in Europe, ibid.*, p.91

[949] Hungarian Law, for example, provides a possibility for geographical limitations or other limits on the legal value of the certificate to be placed . According to Section 15 (2) of the Hungarian Law the CSP shall not be liable for claims associated with electronic records issued and signed in respect of transactions exceeding the restrictions identified in Article 9 (2) and for the resultant damage. According to latter article the CSP may determine in the qualified certificate the restrictions applicable to the certificate in terms of scope, geographical or other limits and the maximum liability assumed for one occasion.

[950] Article 11 of the Polish Act on Electronic Signatures, for example, provides that the certificate holdersshall not hold the CSP responsible for the losses arising from the use of the certificate outside the scope provided for in the certification policy which was determined in the certificate. Particularly he will not be held responsible for the losses arising from the exceeding of the greatest boundary value of the relevant transaction, provided that value was indicated in the certificate. Further it is envisaged that the certificate holders shall not hold the certification-service-provider responsible for the losses arising from the falsity of the data revealed in the certificate at the request of the person to have put his electronic signature. The certificate holders shall finally hold the certification-service-provider who signed the certificate responsible for all the losses arising from the use of this certificate unless the loss arises from the use of this certificate outside the scope provided for in the certification policy which was determined in the certificate.

[951] See Proposal for a European Parliament and Council Directive on a common framework for electronic signatures (COM(98)0297 - C4-0376/98 - 98/0191(COD)), Amendment 22.

Logically, the rules contained in Article 3 and 4 should be moved away from Article 6 because they lead to confusion as to what is meant by the provision. The norm that underpins Article 6 is that the CSPs are entitled to issue certificates that may be used in certain conditions, which are explicitly noted in the certificate itself. The certificates do not appear to be valid if used beyond their indicated purpose.[952] Thus, the effect on the liability exposure comes only afterwards – what would happen if the certificate is used in a manner contrary to its purpose and the CSP has acted negligently?

A clear answer to this question could be derived from the general national principles of civil liability even without introducing special rules. The CSP may not be held liable if the certificate holder decides to use the certificate without regard to its purpose. The CSP may be held liable only in respect of what it certifies, and not beyond that point. As already explained, the assessment as to when, how, and under what conditions the CSP would issue a qualified certificate is made prior to the enforcement of the certification practice statement and the certificate policy[953]. Pursuant to the CPS and the CP, the CSP develops and follows a special security policy.[954] The certificates are issued for use in relation to low-value transactions, usually when the security controls are lower (for example, without face control – i.e. visual identification – issuing the certificate via the Internet etc),[955] while those of higher value are issued subject to stricter security control (verification of personal documents, face control, other biometric identification etc).[956] The review of the certificate policy and security policies of different CSPs shows that the requirements for issue of certificates of a higher value are not simply more stringent than those that apply to certificates issued in relation to lower value transactions. In fact, they are of completely different character. Thus the CSP may not be held liable if the certificate is used in respect of a transaction of a higher value than the one placed into the

---

[952] See Kalaydjiev, A., Belazelkov, B., Dimitrov, G., et al., *ibid.*, p. 199.

[953] See for example the CPS and the CP of the CSP Bankservise (www.b-trust.org). The security procedures that are followed by the CSP and its Registration authorities to issue certificates of Class 1 (of lower value of transactions usage) differes substantially of the procedure for issuing certificates of Class 2 (of higher value of transactions usage). Thus the prices for obtaining certificates of Classes 1 and 2 differs.

[954] See for example the Security Policy of Bankservice - http://www.b-trust.org/documents/Bankservice,%20Security%20Policy.pdf.

[955] See for example the Certificate Policy for issuance of Personal Certificate Class 1 and Professional Certificate Class 1 of Bankservice (www.b-trust.org), also the conditions fur issuance of personal certificates of GlobalSign - PersonaSign 2™ (http://www.globalsign.net/digital_certificate/personalsign/index.cfm)

[956] See the Certificate Policy for issuance of Personal Certificate Class 2 and Professional Certificate Class 2 of Bankservice (www.b-trust.org), also the conditions fur issuance of personal certificates of GlobalSign - PersonalSign 3™ and PersonalSign 3 Qualified™ (http://www.globalsign.net/digital_certificate/personalsign/index.cfm)

certificate, because if the certificate had been issued for a higher amount, different security policies would have been followed.[957] Hence, if the certificates have an indicated purpose, they can be used only for this purpose. If limits are placed on usage, transactions or other issues, then once the relying party receives a document signed with an e-signature supported by such a certificate, it should be considered notified as to the conditions for usage of the certificate. Thus, it should not be considered to be 'reasonably relying' on the certificate anymore, and the CSP may not be held liable under the provision of Article 6(1).[958]

Considering the results of the transposition, it is clear that the rules of Article 6, paragraphs 3 and 4 also reveal serious imperfections that lead to confusion and vagueness. As became evident from the analysis, the essence of the rules is not to provide possibilities for the limitation of liability but rather to regulate the legal option for the CSPs to limit the certification power of the issued certificates by placing limitations on the usage of the certificate and on the value of transactions recognizable to relying third parties. Management of liability by using this instrument comes only afterwards, as a consequence of the limited certification power of the certificates. Therefore, the rules in paragraphs (3) and (4) do not have any logical place in a specific liability rule, since they are of primary nature in the way in which they provide rights, and do not affect in any way the liability regime of the CSPs.

By identifying in this section the irrelevance of the rules in paragraphs (3) and (4) to the liability regime governing the CSPs, and by establishing the imperfections and the ineffectiveness of the rules in paragraphs (1) and (2), it becomes evident that the specific liability regime of article 6 in fact does not effectively promote trust and confidence in the usage of electronic signatures, and is thus unnecessary.

---

[957] On the same opinion Briddle, Br., The Role of Certification Authorities in Consumer Transactions: A Report of the ILPF [Internet Law and Policy Forum] Working Group on Certification Authority Practices, published by the ILPF and online at http://www.ilpf.org (co-authored with Eric Goldman and Terry Maher) (1996). http://www.ilpf.org/groups/ca/draft.htm: "CAs may want to establish classes of certificates that, based on the different levels of effort exerted by the CA and differential pricing, have different dollar caps on liability. The rationale is entirely understandable -- a cheap certificate which contains unverified information provided by a consumer is not comparable with an expensive, extensively-verified certificate. With respect to consumers, while it makes sense for CAs to limit their liability for authorized certificates, it is unreasonable for a CA to unduly limit its liability for issuing unauthorized certificates".

[958] See Chapter IV, section 4.4 and Chapter V, section 3, *supra*.

3. Conclusions

In this chapter, an evaluation of the transposition of the Directive's liability rules into the Bulgarian national legislation has been made. In so doing, the practical problems involved in the transposition of the liability rules and the effect of this process on the national general liability regime of the case study country have been identified. As a result, it has been possible to assess the correctness of the approach of the Directive in establishing specific liability rules, and the adequacy of the rules themselves, from the point of view of the Bulgarian national legislation.

The analysis provided knowledge on the issue of the priority in application of the national liability rules in respect of different normative acts applicable to the CSPs. This knowledge is essential for identifying the circumstances in which the specific liability of EDESA applies and when the liability rules of the other normative acts apply. The research was based on the peculiarities of the Bulgarian legislation, but also on the knowledge acquired in Chapter IV, while most of the supranational acts containing applicable liability rules have already been transposed into the Bulgarian legislation. It is clear from the analysis that when it is justifiable to introduce specific liability, such rules establish derogation from the general rules only where the interests of the society demand particular and stronger protection.

The analysis also supports the general conclusions of the preceding chapter, and shows that the regime transposed by the e-signature Directive does not lead to reversing the burden of proof or to imposing further duties for reasonable care, or to deviations from the general rules in respect of the scope of compensation for damage, the range of parties who may held the CSPs liable, and so on. The specific rules transposed from the other Community acts, or elaborated by the Bulgarian legislator, already provide effective protection for the interests of those users of certification services (consumers, natural persons etc) whose rights needed strengthening to the detriment of the interests of the certification-service-providers. Thus, the specific liability rules transposed from Directive 1999/93 in fact do not promote more trust in the market. Therefore, the idea held by the supporters of the thesis that the specific liability rules as introduced and transposed by Directive 1999/93/EC serve as *prima facie* evidence for enhancing the trust in the market seems to remain ungrounded.

The transposition of the specific liability rules of the Directive is analyzed systematically in this chapter. The overview on the topic provides evidence that transposition of the liability rules on a national level is satisfactory and complete.

Thus, the conclusions as to the lack of necessity for such rules to be elaborated on a supranational level should be assumed to be reasonable and valid.

In the first instance, the analysis made it clear that, with some slight deviations,[959] the Bulgarian law transposes Article 6 in its entirety as far as the scope of regulation of liability, the range of liable parties, liability exposure, and liability grounds are concerned. The fair transposition of all requirements with respect to mandatory duties for the CSPs listed in Annex II and Article 6(1) and (2) of the Directive was also ascertained. The chapter also demonstrated the way in which the liability rules of Article 29 of EDESA would be triggered if a negligent infringement of any of the mandatory duties of the CSPs listed in Articles 21, 22 and 25 of EDESA occurred. Since the transposition is fair, the analysis of the problems and the deductions on the necessity of specific liability rules on a national and, thus, on a supranational level, by taking Bulgaria as an example and case study country, should be regarded as relevant and acceptable.

Secondly, it became evident that the Bulgarian legislator has chosen to transpose all the requirements for the activity of the CSP established by the Directive in Annex II and Article 6(1) and (2) as primary statutory duties in Articles 21, 22 and 25 EDESA. Under Bulgarian law, liability always arises if these duties are breached, and not only in the cases covered by Article 6(1) and (2) of the Directive (transposed in Article 29(3)-(5) of EDESA). It was ascertained that this approach of the Bulgarian legislator reveals to the greatest extent the difficulties involved in understanding the idea and thus in transposing the specific liability rules of Article 6(1) and (2) of the Directive into Bulgarian legislation. This is largely due to the primary nature of these rules. On the other hand, vagueness exists in the Directive due to lack of directness in addressing the same liability exposure for the CSPs should the duties set out in Annex II be infringed, while the users need the same level of protection as that prescribed in respect of breaching the duties under Article 6(1) and (2) of the Directive. It was demonstrated that besides the decision to transpose all statutory duties for the activity

---

[959] The Bulgarian law was found not to transpose explicitly the requirements of Annex II (a) and (i). Under those rules the CSP issuing qualified certificates must demonstrate the reliability necessary for providing certification services, and must record (even electronically) all relevant information concerning a qualified certificate for an appropriate period of time, in particular for the purpose of providing evidence of certification for the purposes of legal proceedings. However those requirements are explicitly listed in the Ordinance on the activities of certification-service-providers, the terms and procedures of termination thereof, and the requirements for provision of certification services, adopted pursuant to CMD No. 17 dated 31 January 2002 (Promulgated, SG No. 15 dated 8 February 2002). Therefore it should be considered that the rules of Directive 1999/93/EC in view of these requirements are met. See also the preceding note.

of the CSP (listed in Annex II and Article 6(1) and (2)) as primary statutory duties in Articles 21, 22 and 25 of EDESA, the Bulgarian lawmakers decided to reiterate the grounds listed in Article 6(1) and (2) purely in order to ensure that the legislation was formally in line with the Directive, rather than to achieve better and more effective protection for the interest of the users of certification services and the relying parties.

Thirdly, it was shown that the approach of the Directive in Article 6(1) and (2) of referring to 'reasonable reliance' to exclude the application of the specific liability of the CSPs is of no practical use and does not require transposition. The general principles of Bulgarian law provide a balanced defence in respect of the interests of the CSPs where the parties relying on the certificates act carelessly and damage results from this, regardless of whether the CSPs have acted with due care or not. The way in which the general principles of 'contributive fault' and 'due care of the creditor' apply was demonstrated. *Culpa creditori* will be examined by the courts in all cases in which the liability of CSPs is at issue. The comparative analysis demonstrated the same applicability of these principles in the other EU countries. None of the national general regimes, whether they have transposed the 'reasonable reliance' requirement exactly permit CSPs to be exposed in liability towards a party who has 'unreasonably' relied on the certificate and brought a claim against the CSP.

Fourthly, in respect of the so-called 'rebuttable presumption' of Article 6(1) and (2) that introduces a 'reversed burden of proof' for the CSP seeking to prove its diligence, it was demonstrated that under Bulgarian law 'reversing' the burden is of no use, since it tallies with the general principles of allocating the burden of proving the negligence both in contract and tort.[960] These principles are grounded on those contained in the drafts for the Principles of the European Contract Law and the Principles of the European Tort Law.[961] The upshot of this is that the Directive in fact reiterates these common general principles without introducing legal novelty by actually 'reversing' the burden. Even if there are exceptions (as is the case in the UK), and Article 6(1) and (2) would affect the national general principles as a result, the argumentation in this chapter demonstrates that this reason is insufficient to

---

[960] Proving of the negligence as a type of fault by the claimant (the certificate holder) in contractual relationships does not exist as a concept in any jurisdiction. Negligent non-fulfillment of contractual obligations constitutes non-provision of due care and is an objective criterion. Proving negligence in tort also unconsistent because the common approach in almost all EU jurisdictions analyzed, is not to require proving the type of fault (in civil law context), but rather the wrongful behaviour (*contra lege* or in some countries *contra bonos mores*) and the causality.

[961] v. Bar, Ch., *Principles of European Law: Non-Contractual Liability Arising out of Damage Caused to Another (PEL Liab.Dam.)*, Study Group on a European Civil Code, Osnabrück 2005 (www.cgecc.net)

substantiate the claim that by introducing explicit allocation and 'reversing' the burden from the point of view of these jurisdictions, greater 'trust and confidence in the electronic signatures' would be promoted in the internal market, which otherwise would not exist. On the contrary, in these countries even the ambiguity of the 'reversed burden of proof' has led to a 'complete lack of confidence on how this would be handled in a legal dispute, given that it was outside the general experience of the courts'.[962]

It was demonstrates that even without transposition of the specific liability rule, the burden of proving diligence is preserved to be borne by the CSPs without affecting trust and confidence in electronic signatures in any way. Furthermore, the analysis also deposed the widely accepted theory that Article 6(1) and (2) introduces a 'rebuttable presumption of causality', but it was substantiated that it refers to presumption of fault.

Fifthly, it became obvious that the rules of Article 6(3) and (4) also reveal serious imperfections that lead to confusion and vagueness[963]. The analysis of the essence of the rules, supported by analysis of the historical overview of the drafting process of Article 6 in Chapter III, section 1.2, proved that the idea of these paragraphs is not to provide possibilities for limitation of liability. Instead, they regulate the legal option of the CSPs to limit the certification power of the issued certificates by placing limitations on the certificate usage and on the value of transactions which may be seen by third parties. Management of liability by using this instrument comes only afterwards, as a consequence of the limited certification power of the certificates. In fact, it was substantiated that these rules lead to exemption of liability rather than 'limitation of liability' - a term used in the provisions themselves, and by many academics. If the limitation of the legal value of the certificates may be seen by third parties, then those parties should be considered to be 'unreasonably' relying on the certificate if the certificate is used in a way which exceeds those limitations – and thus the CSP would be exempted from liability. Since the rules of paragraphs (3) and (4) do not affect in any way the specific liability regime governing the CSPs, they do not have any logical place in a specific liability rule.

---

[962] The Impact in UK of the EU E-signature Directive DTI TFBJ/003/0061X Report issue 1.0.0 (Final), p.24.

[963] The authors of the UK DTI TFBJ/003/0061X Report issue 1.0.0 (Final), when assessing the rules of Article 6 evisage that "the provisions were confusing and unclear ...".

As a general conclusion to this chapter the deduction may be made that the transposition of the rule of Article 6 establishing a specific liability regime for the CSPs into the Bulgarian legislation, in spite of being fairly transposed, introduces no novelties or deviations into the general national liability regime – and, by extension, into the liability exposure of the CSPs – but rather brings vagueness and confusion. The analysis of the transposition clearly evidenced: i) the irrelevance of the rules in paragraphs (3) and (4) of Article (6) of the Directive to the liability regime governing the CSPs; and ii) the imperfections and ineffectiveness of the rules in paragraphs (1) and (2) of the same article. Therefore, it may be deduced that the specific liability regime of Article 6 of the Directive does not in fact effectively promote more trust and confidence in the usage of electronic signatures on a national level, and thus its necessity is questionable.

Chapter VI

CRITICAL EVALUATION AND GENERAL CONCLUSIONS

The present work aims at identifying the legal and market necessity for the establishment of a specific liability regime for the certification-service-providers by making an analysis of the current specific liability rules established on a supranational level and their transposition and effects on the national jurisdictions. For the purposes of this analysis Bulgaria has been selected as a case study jurisdiction. This final chapter will summarize the deductions made during the course of the whole work and will synthesize the conclusions in support of the assertions of the author.

From a structural point of view, the conclusive chapter comprises three sections.

The *first section* summarizes the main findings of the research and provides an overview of the goals achieved in the preceding chapters. Based on all findings, an evaluation is made as to the necessity of having a specific liability regime for the certification-service-providers in order to enhance trust in electronic signatures as established by Directive 1999/93/EC. The section also synthesizes the main conclusions of the work.

Considering the substantiated final conclusion on the imperfections and lack of real market need for specific liability rules for the CSPs, the *second section* contains more general theoretical conclusions about the approach to be followed when specific liability regimes in respect of given groups of relationships are to be established on a supranational level.

Despite the critical evaluation of the specific liability regime established for the CSPs by Directive 1999/93/EC, the latter proves to be a binding Community instrument, and all EU Member States and Accession countries are obliged to transpose it and to keep their legislation in line with the Directive. Since amending the specific liability regime might affect the basic pillars of the Directive regulation of e-signatures, a thorough revision seems unrealistic for the time being. Therefore, the author has chosen to provide in the *third section* guidelines for national legislatures on how to transpose the Directive's liability rules in order to achieve compliance with the Directive by suggesting a viewpoint for proper re-interpretation and clarification of the liability concept. Several simple and practical recommendations in this respect are offered.

1. Conclusions with Respect to the Specific Liability Regime for the CSPs

1.1. General overview of the problems analyzed

To substantiate his assertions, the author has focused on systematically analyzing different main groups of problems and issues that might promote knowledge and evidence as to the necessity for specific liability rules for the CSPs.

The research made in Chapter I shed light on the context of the work. This introductory chapter provided knowledge on how the electronic signatures work, the essence of the concept of trust in electronic communications, and the role of the CSPs in the trust-building process. The overview of the concept of trust demonstrated that trust is one of the basic pillars for the functioning of the public key infrastructure and the usage of electronic signatures in open networks. The research of the trust concept produced three main deductions:

i) A key role in the trust-building process is played by the certification-service-providers being trusted third parties.

ii) Trust in the PKI is promoted by certain factors, *inter alia*: the presence of an effective supervisory scheme, legal rules establishing statutory duties for the activities of the CSPs, mandatory rules, national accreditation schemes etc.

iii) One, but not the most important factor, for instilling trust is also the presence of a clear and effective national liability regime to guarantee the protection of aggrieved parties' interest if trust is undermined due to the negligent behaviour of the CSPs.

The analysis of the role of the CSPs led to establishing further necessary viewpoints for investigating the liability of the CSPs, and to several deductions:

i) A clear perspective was given on the trusted third party, whose liability is the subject of the research – the certification-service-provider. The different notions involved were clarified in order to make it possible to properly interpret, in the following chapters, the statutory liability rules established on national and supranational levels.

ii)   The role of the CSPs was examined from the perspective of the relationships with the other PKI actors – the relationships between the CSPs and the other parties using or relying on certification services were identified. These consist of relationships between the CSP and the certificate holder, and between the CSP and the relying party. The scope of the research was narrowed down by excluding the relations between the certificate holder and the CSPs and between the relying party and the CSPs providing outsourced services or activities, since no direct liability could arise in this situation.

iii)   The nature of the relations and liability exposure between the CSP and the other main actors was analyzed. These include contractual liability towards the certificate holder; contractual or non-contractual liability towards the relying party; and contractual liability towards other CSPs to whom certain functions are outsourced. This analysis provided a perspective for the proper interpretation of the liability provisions of Directive 1999/93/EC in Chapter III and the national rules transposing the Directive rules.

Understanding the specific liability regime of the CSPs was also grounded on the making of a theoretical overview of the general notion and main principles of civil liability. At this introductory stage, the legal 'instruments' through which the research had to be elaborated were pre-defined. Thus, the analysis in Chapter II focused on the different aspects of the civil liability theory – notion, types of liability (contractual and tortious), concurrence of claims, pre-contractual liability, types of damage and causation, meanings of unlawfulness and fault, particularly presumptions of causality and fault, as well as liability without fault and liability for the conduct of others. The basic aspects of the different means by which liability is extended or limited were also overviewed. Illustrative examples related to the CSPs were introduced at this stage to outline the types of problematic issues discussed further and to demonstrate the applicability of the general liability regime to the activity of the certification-service-providers in the absence of a specific liability regime.

Making such an analysis at the beginning of the survey was of utmost importance since no Community instrument was found to be in force which might harmonize the general principles of civil liability or provide interpreting provisions or valid directions in respect of the notion of liability. It was impossible to proceed further and deduce valid conclusions as to the necessity of the specific liability regime of the certification-service-providers as directed by the Community acts, particularly Directive 1999/93/EC, and to properly analyze the Directive's rules without precisely defining beforehand a clear viewpoint from which to understand and interpret the *acquis'* liability rules. Furthermore, apart from the specific liability rules introduced, the liability of the CSPs shall be regulated by the national rules regarding liability.[964] It was impossible to commence the analysis of the supranational specific liability regime of the CSPs to be transposed without having a good basis for identifying where deviations from the general national liability regime might arise. The analysis shed light on the theoretical perspectives on the general liability regime from the point of view of the Bulgarian legal doctrine – an acceptable approach, since the Bulgarian legislation falls within the Continental law family and follows the traditions of the French legal system. Therefore, the conclusions and deductions made could be successfully used as a general reference on an EU level for building knowledge for the understanding of the liability rules of the *acquis*.

In Chapter III, an examination was made of the supranational specific liability rules established by the main EC instrument regulating the framework of electronic signatures – Directive 1999/93/EC. The Chapter elaborated on the following issues:

i)   making a thorough research of the relationships falling within the scope of regulation of Article 6;

ii)   identifying the CSPs as liable parties and their liability exposure to the certificate holders, the relying parties and other parties;

iii)   studying the concept of reasonable reliance introduced as a precondition for the liability exposure;

iv)   analyzing the peculiarities of the liability grounds under Article 6;

v)   making a precise distinction between limitation and exemption of liability and the legal means provided for successful liability management under the Directive.

The approach employed for researching the above issues was based on a step-by-step careful and just interpretation of the normative texts, since most of the erroneous conclusions made by different European scholars are the result of inaccurate interpretation of the liability rules.[965] Thus it became possible to explain whether contractual and non-contractual liability are covered by the Directive, what is the scope of the due care, where and to what extent the burden of proof lies, what idea is

---

[964] Recital (22) of the Directive 1999/93/EC.

[965] See supra notes. 531, 550, 568, 569, 595, 598, 680.

behind the presumption of fault introduced by the European legislator, whether it possible to put in place liability caps, how the CPS/CP can be used by the CSPs to limit liability or exempt themselves of liability etc.

The proper interpretation of the liability rules was based on the knowledge and deductions contained in Chapter I and Chapter II. The key to the correct analysis of the specific liability rules introduced by the Directive was the ascertaining of the fact that the Directive aims at promoting trust in the electronic world by establishing a wide set of primary rules containing requirements mainly in respect of the usage of qualified signatures, e.g. requirements as to secure signature creation devices and standards for electronic signatures products, requirements for conformity assessment of the electronic signature products by designated bodies, requirements for the qualified certificates supporting the qualified signature, requirements for the certification-service-providers issuing qualified certificates to the public, and requirements for ensuring appropriate supervisory schemes for the activities of the CSPs issuing qualified certificates to the public.

After analyzing the specific liability rules for the CSPs issuing qualified certificates to the public in the light of the identified wide set of primary measures to promote trust in the usage of qualified signatures, the regime of Article 6 gave the impression of being a relatively weak and to some extent ineffective instrument for promoting trust. Searching for further evidence to substantiate this deduction was left to Chapter V, which analyzes the transposition of the Directive liability rules into Bulgarian law and the effects of this process.

The deductions derived from the historical-comparative analysis of the final text of the rule of Article 6 and its versions created during the course of the drafting process, demonstrated the metamorphosis of the initial idea of the Commission not to introduce specific secondary liability rules, but rather primary rules that would give rise to effective liability exposure under the national laws – and how this initial idea became distorted in practice. The way in which the Directive elaborated on the implementation of secondary rules while the essence of the liability rules in Article 6 is to establish statutory obligations for the CSPs was demonstrated. Thus, it became evident that most of the liability grounds of Article 6(1) and (2) overlap with the statutory primary rules set forth as requirements and obligations in Annex I and II. The other provisions of Article 6 – those of paragraphs (3) and (4) – were shown to be inaccurately interpreted in the theory, due to their illogical presence in Article 6; it was demonstrated that they provide in fact a possibility for the CSPs to issue certificates under certain conditions and thus to exempt themselves from liability rather than to achieve limitation of liability.

A detailed analysis of the specific liability rules for the CSPs is made in this chapter, which facilitates understanding, later in the work, of the problems faced by the national legislators, including the Bulgarian legislator, in transposing the rule.

Since Directive 1999/93/EC was found not to be the only act containing liability rules directly applicable to the CSPs, the next step in the research was the identification of the other main Community instruments that might affect the liability exposure of the CSPs. This permitted the creation of a solid platform on which to base the assessment contained in Chapter V as to the necessity for a specific liability regime to be introduced by the *acquis communautaire* in order to achieve better protection of the interests of the users of certification services in the internal market.

Therefore, the analysis contained in Chapter IV was carried out in order to attain two groups of objectives. The first group of objectives were: to complete the liability position of the CSPs with the provisions of the other Community instruments apart of Directive 1999/93; to identify the conflicting specific liability rules on the *acquis* level; and to provide a model for ascertaining priorities in the applicability of different national liability rules as transposed with regard to different users of certification services. The second group of objectives aimed at producing evidence to support the thesis that there is no necessity for specific liability rules for the CSPs on a supranational level for enhancing trust in electronic signatures.

With respect to the first group of objectives, the main Community acts (apart from Directive 1999/93) which have established specific liability rules applicable to service providers, and thus to the CSPs as a type of service provider, were identified. In this regard, the following were analyzed: Directive 93/13/EEC on unfair terms in consumer contracts, Directive 97/7/EC on distance contracts, Directive 95/46/EC on the protection of personal data, Directive 2000/35/EC on late payments in commercial transactions, and Directive 2000/31/EC on certain legal aspects of information society services, in respect of particular electronic commerce, in the internal market.

During the course of the research, the author identified the particular provisions of these Community acts that establish grounds for invoking the liability of providers of services that prove to be applicable to the CSPs without conflicting with the rules of Directive 1999/93/EC. The rules contained in Directive 2000/35/EC, and some rules from Directives 93/13/EC, 97/7/EC, 2000/31/EEC and 95/46/EC were identified as rules addressing a wider scope of liability than that regulated by the e-signatures Directive.

The analysis finally promoted a model for assessment of the priorities of application of the conflicting and overlapping rules in respect of the liability of certification-service-providers in the different Community instruments. Such were found to exist with respect to certain provisions of Directive 93/13/EC, Directive 97/7/EC, Directive 2000/31 and Directive 95/46/EC.

With respect to the second group of objectives – to elaborate on collecting evidence to support the assertions made in this work – the analysis also achieved its aim. It demonstrated that the European legislator, while intending to introduce a protective legal shield over certain groups of users, uses as a legal technique the introduction either of strict liability or of mandatory rules imposing given obligations for the providers of services.[966] It became evident that these techniques in fact restrict the possibilities of the service providers to derogate, by contractual or other means, from the mandatory rules, and thus to exempt themselves from or limit their liability.

It became obvious that introducing a legal technique such as the establishment of reversed burden for proving certain facts, as a contrast to the general rules, is a rare exception. Only where the interests of society demand high-level and stringent protection will it be justifiable to introduce rules that deviate from general legal norms. The analysis shows that the reversed burden was established by Directive 93/13 for the protection of consumers, and refers to the burden of proving of the causality chain.[967] Evidently, introduction of the reversed burden in this respect has not much to do with enhancing the trust in the market. The regime of this directive would protect the interest of the consumers whether or not they trust the service providers. In this respect, it was ascertained that such a regime was never intended to promote trust. Therefore, it was deduced that the idea held by the supporters of the thesis that the specific liability rules as introduced by Directive 1999/93/EC serve as *prima facie* evidence of the trust-building process does not appear well grounded.

It was further ascertained that no Community instrument whatsoever, even those establishing legal regimes revealing the most stringent protection for given groups of subjects, establish a presumption of fault, and it became evident that this presumption

---

[966] Directives 3000/35/EC, Directive 97/7/EC, Directive 93/13/EC, Directive 2000/31/EC.

[967] I.e. "rebutable presumption of causality".

does not in fact lead to enhancement of the level of trust – these conclusions are strongly substantiated in Chapter V.

Finally, the analysis in Chapter V focused on the identification of the practical problems involved in the transposition of the specific liability regime of Article 6 of the Directive 1999/93/EC in Bulgaria, as a case study country, and the impact of these problems on the national general liability regime. By using inductive methods, the analysis made possible the making of a balanced assessment of the necessity of having a specific liability regime on a supranational level, i.e. it sought to establish a viewpoint for fair evaluation of the correctness of Directive's approach to the establishment of specific liability rules and derived knowledge for assessing their adequacy when transposed.

The analysis promoted understanding on the priorities in application of the national liability rules of different normative acts applicable to the CSPs as a precondition for identification of the priority levels of the specific liability rules of EDESA. The research was based on the peculiarities of the Bulgarian legislation, but also on the knowledge derived from Chapter IV, while almost all supranational acts holding applicable liability rules are already transposed into the Bulgarian legislation. It became clear from the analysis that it is justifiable to introduce specific liability rules in derogation from the general rules, only where the interests of society demand more stringent and more specific protection. It also became clear that the specific rules transposed from the other Community acts as analyzed in Chapter IV, or elaborated by the Bulgarian legislator, already provide effective protection for those interests of the users of certification services (consumers, natural persons etc) that require stronger protection to the detriment of the interests of the certification-service-providers. Thus serious doubt emerges as to whether the specific liability rules as transposed from Directive 1999/93 in fact promote more protection and trust in the market.

The transposition of the specific liability rules of the Directive was analyzed systematically.

It was substantiated that the Bulgarian law transposes fairly well the specific liability rules of Article 6 in terms of the scope of liability regulation, range of liable parties, liability exposure, and liability grounds. Therefore, any deductions on the necessity for specific liability rules on a national level would be relevant also on a supranational level. It also became evident that the Bulgarian legislator has chosen to transpose all the mandatory requirements for the activities of CSPs established by the Directive in

Annex II and Article 6(1) and (2) as primary statutory mandatory duties in the corresponding provisions of EDESA. It was demonstrated that under the Bulgarian law liability would arise if these duties are infringed, and not only in the cases covered by the transposed rules of Article 6(1) and (2) of the Directive. The analysis made it plain that this approach of the Bulgarian legislator reveals to the greatest extent the difficulties inherent in understanding the idea and thus in transposing the specific liability rules of Article 6(1) and (2) of the Directive into the Bulgarian legislation. This is because of the primary nature of these rules and because of lack of direct supranational level rules establishing the same liability exposure for the CSPs should the duties set out in Annex II be breached. The users need the same level of protection in case of breach of the obligations under Annex II as is provided in respect of breaching the duties under Article 6(1) and (2) of the Directive. It was deduced that the Bulgarian lawmakers have decided to reiterate the grounds listed in Article 6(1) and (2) purely in order to bring Bulgarian law into line with the provisions of the Directive, rather than to achieve more effective protection of the interests of the users of certification services and the relying parties.

Chapter V also provided evidence that the 'reasonable reliance' concept established by the Directive as a precondition for engaging the CSPs' liability needs no transposition since the general principles of the law in Bulgaria – 'contributive fault' and 'due care of the creditor' – provide a balanced defence of the CSP's interests should the party relying on the certificate act carelessly and unreasonably, and damage ensues. The usefulness of the so-called 'rebuttable presumption', employed as a legal technique in Article 6(1) and (2) to allocate to the CSPs the burden of proving their due care, was strongly criticized. The analysis demonstrated that under the Bulgarian law no reversal of burden is achieved by means of transposition, since the general principles of allocating the burden of proving the negligence both in contract and tort traditionally regulate this principle. The same approach was shown to be followed by other EU Member States and is laid down in the draft Principles of the European Contract Law and the Principles of the European Tort Law. It was demonstrated that even without transposition of the specific liability rule, the burden of proving due care falls to the CSPs without affecting in any way the trust and confidence in electronic signatures. Thus, another basic pillar of the liability rule of Article 6 was severely shaken.

The analysis of the transposition of the Directive led to important deductions in respect of the essence of Article 6(3) and (4). It was demonstrated that these rules reveal terminological imperfections and have no logical place in the liability rule, since they do not in fact provide for possibilities for limitation of liability for the CSPs, but rather introduce a legal option for the CSPs to limit the certification power of the issued certificates by placing limitations on the usage of certificates and on the value of transactions recognizable to third parties. It became evident that in this way the CSPs have the legal means to exempt themselves from liability rather than to achieve limitations on their liability. It became evident that since the possibility for the CSPs to place limits on the usage and value of transactions is already introduced in Annex I, and the latter is fairly transposed, then the transposition of the rules in paragraphs (3) and (4) of Article 6 also seems questionable.

1.2. Evaluation of the necessity of specific liability rules

Based on the findings made in the course of the above research, the following evaluation of the impact on trust in electronic signatures made by introducing a specific liability regime for the certification-service-providers by Directive 1999/93/EC could be made:

A) By reviewing the development of the legislative process in the initial stages of drafting the liability rule of Directive 1999/93/EC the roots of the liability rule were examined. The historical-comparative method of analysis has shown that the European Commission never intended to introduce any specific liability rules, but had intended rather to identify the problems that should had been taken into consideration during the drafting process.[968] The research evidenced that the core idea during the first stages of the legislative process in respect of the so-called 'liability rule' was the establishment of statutory obligations for the CSPs,[969] rather than liability rules *strictu sensu*, to regulate the unfavourable consequences that might ensure if the imposed duties are breached.[970] These initial ideas of the Commission appear to have been misunderstood, and later resulted in the enforcement of a distorted general

---

[968] Communication from the Commission COM (97) 503: Ensuring security and trust in electronic communication: "Towards a European Framework for Digital Signatures and Encryption", available at http://www.swiss.ai.mit.edu/6805/articles/crypto/eu-october-8-97.html.

[969] Those listed in Annex II, and in respect to requisites of the qualified certificate – Annex I.

[970] See Amendment 20 of the Proposal to the European Parliament and Council Directive on a common framework for electronic signatures (COM(98)0297 - C4-0376/98 - 98/0191(COD)) - http://europa.eu.int/information_society/topics/ebusiness/ecommerce/8epolicy_elaw/law_ecommerce/lega l/1signatures/index_en.htm

liability concept.[971] The Commission enforced 'secondary' ('sanction'), rather than 'primary' ('obligation') rules.[972]

In this respect, the approach of the drafters of another international instrument establishing a uniform regime for e-signatures – the UNCITRAL Model Law on Electronic Signatures – seems to be much more appropriate.[973] The Model Law does not deal with the issues of liability that may affect the various parties involved in the operation of electronic signature systems. Those issues are left to the applicable national laws. However, the Model Law sets out the criteria against which one can assess the conduct of the certification-service-providers.[974] The Model Law establishes general duties for the activities of the CSPs – to utilize reliable systems, procedures and human resources, to act in accordance with the representations that it makes with respect to its policies and practices. In addition, the certification-service-provider is expected to exercise reasonable care to ensure the accuracy and completeness of all material representations it makes in connection with a certificate.[975] In the certificate, the supplier should provide essential information allowing the relying party to identify the supplier. It should also represent that the person who is identified in the certificate had control of the signature device at the time of signing, and the signature device was operational on or before the date when the certificate was issued. In its dealings with the relying party, the certification-service-provider should provide additional information as to the method used to identify the signatory, any limitation on the purpose or value for which the signature device or the certificate may be used etc.[976] Obviously, in contrast to the Directive, the Model Law rightly encourages the implementing jurisdictions to establish statutory duties rather than liability rules.

B) Further deviations were detected in reviewing the course of the historical implementation of the idea of granting to the CSPs the possibility of managing their

---

[971] See Chapter III, section 1.1, *supra*.

[972] On the conept of "primary" and "secondary" rules see Chapter II, section 2.2, *supra*. Also Van Gerven, W., et al., *ibid.*, p.32.

[973] The text of the UNCITRAL Model Law on Electronic Signatures was adopted on 5 July 2001 on the thirty-fourth session of the United Nations Commission on International Trade Law held at Vienna, from 25 June to 13 July 2001.

[974] Guide to Enactment of the UNCITRAL Model Law on Electronic Signatures, A/CN.9/WG.IV/WP.88, Section 78, p.28 (http://www.uncitral.org/english/travaux/ecommerce/ml-ecomm/travaux-ml-ecomm-index-e.htm)

[975] See Article 9 of the UNICITRAL Model Law.

[976] Guide to Enactment of the UNCITRAL Model Law on Electronic Signatures, *ibid.*, Section 80.

business risk exposure by issuing certificates under certain conditions (key usage and value of transactions). This issue was strongly substantiated by analyzing the difficulties in the transposition of Article 6(3) and (4) into the Bulgarian legislation in Chapter V. The intention of the European legislator was definitely not to provide possibilities for limitation of liability, but to regulate the legal option for the CSPs to limit the certification power of the issued certificates by placing limitation on the certificate usage and on the value of transactions recognizable to third parties. Usage of certificates beyond the indicated purpose or conditions should lead to revocation of the validity of the qualified e-signature because of lack of any certification power of the supporting qualified certificate. The legal effect would be the exemption of CSPs from liability, rather than limitation of their liability.[977] In this respect, the successful management of the liability by employing the envisaged instrument comes only afterwards, as a consequence of the limited certification power of the certificates. The final text of Article 6 of the Directive inaccurately pursues this idea by placing substantive primary rules into a liability clause, which resulted in most academics as well as national legislators misunderstanding the provision. Inaccurate placing the rules of Article 6, paragraphs (3) and (4) in Article 6 seems to be improper.

C) The evaluation of the transposition of the specific liability rules of the Directive into Bulgarian law made in Chapter V, the comparative overview on the transposition in other jurisdictions, and the review of the draft Principles of the European Contract Law and the Principles of the European Tort Law demonstrated that the difficulties and problems faced by the national legislatures result from the imperfections of the rule of Article 6 also in other respects.

In order to be formally in line with the Directive, Member States simply copy almost literally the requirement for 'reasonable reliance', despite the fact that such a transposition seems to be unnecessary. The research shows that under the general rule of law in Bulgaria, and probably under the laws in the other EU jurisdictions, where parties relying on the certificate do so in an unreasonable way this will not be permitted to cause detriment to the CSP. As noted *supra*, when the party relying on the certificate has acted unreasonably,[978] the CSP may build a successful defence on certain general legal grounds, such as 'contributive fault' and 'due care of the creditor', even when it had acted carelessly. *Culpa creditori* will always be examined by the national courts if the CSP's liability is at issue. All national general regimes, whether or

---

[977] See   Chapter III, sections 6.3.1 and 6.3.3 and Chapter V, sections 6 and 7, *supra*.

[978] See Chapter II, section 4 and 5, Chapter I, sections 2.2.5.3, and Chapter IV, section 7, *supra*.

not they have fairly transposed the 'reasonable reliance' requirement would hardly allow liability exposure towards a person who has 'unreasonably' relied on the certificate and has brought a claim against the CSP in pursuance to this.

D) Furthermore, it became clear that under Bulgarian law no 'reversed' burden of proof is established in respect of causality, but rather a normal burden of proof of fault when the Directive rule is transposed on a national level (in other jurisdictions this seems not to be the case).[979] This concept does not reveal a deviation from the common general allocation of burden, when it comes to fault, where liability is invoked either in contract or in tort.[980] If a reversed burden of proof in respect of causality were to have been established, then the rule would have made sense, as it would then have resembled the approach of the consumer protection laws, which provide for such a deviation to protect the weaker party in the transaction. It was substantiated however, that the rule does not introduce a presumption of causality but rather a presumption of fault. Thus, in its present wording, the rule in Article 6 would hardly fulfil its role of establishing protection for the users of certification services by imposing an explicitly reversed burden of proof of fault. But even if there are exceptions and Article 6(1) and (2) would affect the national general principles by actually reversing the burden of proof in respect of fault, it was argued that this reason seems not weighty enough to claim that by following this approach more trust and confidence would be promoted in the electronic signatures in the internal market, which would otherwise not exist. On the contrary, in these countries, the vagueness of the 'reversed burden of proof' led to a complete lack of certainty as to how this would be handled in a legal dispute, given that it was outside the general experience of the courts.[981]

Moreover, if we assume the necessity of 'reversing the burden' from the perspective of the market – particularly as regards those countries whose legal systems deviate from the common principles as to bearing the burden of proof of fault – it is clear that the rule would be reiterated in the upcoming unification of the Principles of the European Contract Law and Principles of the European Tort Law. This means that those countries would in any case have to harmonize their legislation with common standards. Thus, addressing the burden of proof of fault in Article 6 would again be to no purpose.

---

[979] See Chapter II, section 4.2, Chapter III, section 6.1.2, Chapter V, section 5, *supra*.

[980] See Chapter V, section 7, *supra*.

[981] See *supra* note 962.

In addition, strong arguments as to the misleading effect of the 'reversed burden' concept were made in the work. Even if we assume that a protective shield is established, directed to those Member States, which do not allocate the burden of proof of fault to the alleged tortfeasor/debtor, the rule would reveal another imperfection. There is no reason to impose liability on the CSPs liable under the 'reversed burden of proof' for non-performance or breach of the duties listed in Article 6(1) and (2), while at the same time allowing them to evade liability for non-compliance with any of the other duties in Annex II. Breach of the latter duties may result in the same or even more serious damage than breach of the former. Examples to this effect include the requirement to use reliable systems (Annex II (f)), or not to store or copy signature-creation data when providing key generation services (Annex II (j)).[982]

Considering the matters noted above, it becomes evident that even without transposition of the specific liability rule, the burden of proving due care will be borne by the CSPs without affecting in any way the trust and confidence in electronic signatures. The regulation of the burden of proof should be left to the general national liability rules, and therefore, the rule of Article 6 should be revised.

E) Another issue of crucial importance to the assessment of the appropriateness of the specific liability rules in promoting trust is their review from the market point of view. The relationships between the subjects on the market usually call for a degree of legal regulation. In this sense, in private relationships, the law comes normally after the necessity for regulation has arisen. The Directive follows a different approach. By trying to forecast behaviour in an undeveloped market, it seeks to establish legal regulation before the actual social relationships have emerged.[983] The European legislator provides legal regulation of the liability of the market players without being certain whether this will actually 'build trust in electronic signatures',[984] or how this will 'ensure the proper functioning of the internal market'[985] by affecting the willingness of the CSPs to accept this liability and offer qualified certificates at all.[986]

---

[982] See Chapter V, section 4.3, *supra*.

[983] Known in the theory as "pre-regulation".

[984] See Recital (5) of the Directive.

[985] See Article 1 (1) of the Directive.

[986] While in some countries the transposition of the Directive's liability rules does not seem to affect the market behaviour of the CSPs, in other countries it proves to have predeterminated the model of their business. In the United Kingdom, for example, the liability provisions deterred the CSPs from claiming qualified certificate status for their certificates, even though they may meet the requirements of Annexes I

This does not always seem to be an appropriate approach, especially when new technologies are involved. Pursuant to the requirements of the Directive, two years after its implementation the Commission should have carried out a review of this Directive with the aim, *inter alia*, of ensuring that neither the advance of technology nor changes in the legal environment have created barriers to achieving the aims stated in this Directive. In this regard, the review should have examined the implications of associated technical areas and submitted a report to the European Parliament and the Council on this subject.[987] Such a survey was prepared by a team of experts and submitted to the Commission in the autumn of 2003.[988]

The survey shows that there is no practical use for qualified e-signatures in Europe and there is currently no natural market demand for qualified certificates and related services.[989] The largest application area in Europe for electronic signatures is generally linked to e-banking applications in a closed user PKI environment, and thus remains outside the scope of the Directive. Very few applications within the scope of the Directive are in use today and these are almost completely limited to e-government.[990] The reasons for this market situation remain outside the scope of the present work.[991] In such an undeveloped market, any regulation that provides obstacles in the way of, or vagueness as to, the provision of certification services, including the prescription of specific liability rules, might lead to suffocation of the market.[992]

Furthermore, the rule of Article 6 is meant to regulate liability in the provision of qualified certificates only. The approach to qualified signatures is essentially not as

---

and II: this was to the detriment of users who were likely to have enhanced confidence in "qualified" certificates and inhibited the growth of the industry. See DTI TFBJ/003/0061X Report issue 1.0.0 (Final).

[987] Recital (27) of the Directive.

[988] See Dumortier, J., et al., *The Legal and Market Aspects of Electronic Signatures in Europe, ibid.*

[989] *Ibid.*, p.8

[990] See Dumortier, J., *The European Regulatory Framework for Electronic Signatures: A Critical Evaluation* at Nielsen, R., Jacobsen, S., Trzaskowski, J. (editors), *EU Electronic Commerce Law*, Djøf Publishing (2004), p.79.

[991] For more information about the current situation of the market on qualified certificates and services thereof see the Report, and also the views of Dumortier, J., *The European Regulatory Framework for Electronic Signatures: A Critical Evaluation, Ibid.*, pp. 75-93.

[992] In this respect the Report Prepared on Behalf of the Department of Trade and Industry into the Impact in the United Kingdom of the EU Electronic Signatures Framework Directive DTI TFBJ/C/003/0061X reveals that "legislative attempts to regulate a new industry in the absence of any market experience were premature.". In the Report it is also envisaged, that "the overall view was that services and certificates equivalent in terms of assurance would be offered, but that service providers in the U.K. would not claim "qualified" because the liability aspects were unclear."

technologically neutral as indicated in the Directive.[993] The process is based on asymmetric cryptography by usage of signature-creation-data (the private key) and signature-verification data (the public key). The technological development trend during the last few years and the forecast as regards future developments will probably bring into being new technical instruments and solutions for electronic signatures, such as biometric alternatives to PKI-based signatures, more secure PC environments, mobile signatures, signature servers etc.[994] The aim of the Directives is to establish regimes that, when transposed into the national legislations, provide long-term regulation of a particular social relationship. From this angle, it seems improper to establish liability regulations for provision of certain services that might disappear in the near future.

On the other hand, by forecasting the course of the development of the electronic world, the whole concept of qualified e-signatures might become stillborn. The Directive has established a concept whereby only an advanced electronic signature that is supported by a qualified certificate shall be recognized as the legal equivalent of a handwritten signature.[995] Thus, the legal value of the qualified electronic signature is dependent on the legal status of the handwritten signature in given national jurisdictions.[996] The research shows that in some countries such a reference is inconsistent with the general law.[997] Also in the longer term, such a concept might prove to be inadequate. More and more applications use electronic communications, in respect of which no possibility exists whatsoever to make use of paper-based documents. If, in the next ten to twenty years, paper-based forms lose their applicability and present value, the handwritten signature will also lose its value as an authentication tool. Therefore, relating the qualified electronic signature to the

---

[993] *Ibid.*, p.32. The authors find that the language and most of the content of the Directive is heavily PKI biased.

[994] Dumortier, J., *The European Regulatory Framework for Electronic Signatures: A Critical Evaluation, Ibid.*, p.79.

[995] Article 5 (1) of the Directive.

[996] Recital (20) of the Directive.

[997] In the UK, for example, the legal system does not regulate the handwritten signature as an authentication tool. Thus the UK legislator found no reasons to regulate the status of the qualified electronic signature. To solve this problem the Department of Trade and Industry in its Consultation on the Directive (*ibid*) proposes in section 38 "to provide under regulations made under section 2(2) of the European Communities Act that where a person in relation to data in electronic form uses an advanced electronic signature which is based on a qualified certificate and is created by a secure signature creation device, any legal requirement for a signature in respect of such data is satisfied. This would not alter the substantive English, Northern Irish or Scots law on when writing is required for a transaction. Its practical impact should be limited given that requirements as to form usually specify both writing and signature. Implementation in Scotland and Northern Ireland would be a devolved matter to be dealt with by Scottish and Northern Irish Ministers, the Scottish Parliament and the Northern Irish Assembly."

handwritten signature will no longer be meaningful, as there will be no reference point for this.[998] From this point of view, the establishment of liability as applied to the use of certification services related to qualified electronic signatures will also prove to be futile.

F) One of the main principles enshrined in the Directive is the striking of a balance between consumer and business needs by introducing a specific regulatory framework for this purpose.[999] But does that principle really require the establishment of the specific liability rules?

When it comes to consumers, the *acquis communautaire* has already established a wide set of general rules that impact on and regulate the liability exposure of all providers of services, including the CSPs. The liability rules arising out of these directives are thoroughly analyzed in Chapter IV above. From the analysis made, it is evident that the specific regimes in these Directives give grounds for invoking the liability of providers of services, and thus, the liability of the CSPs, with or without entering into conflict with the rules contained in Directive 1999/93/EC. Furthermore, such rules address a wider range of CSPs and cases than those regulated by the e-signatures Directive. The protective rules are widely transposed in Bulgarian law and in the laws of all EU Member States.[1000] From sections 2, 3, 4 and 6 of Chapter IV it becomes apparent that the liability principles are sufficient for achieving firm consumer and user protection in the electronic environment. Thus, introducing specific liability rules in the e-signature Directive seems be questionable, or the present model might require serious revision.

From the analysis of the transposition it becomes evident that the general liability regime under the Bulgarian law and the specific liability regimes for consumer

---

[998] The tendency identified by Dumortier, J., *The European Regulatory Framework for Electronic Signatures: A Critical Evaluation, ibid.*, pp. 86-87, *supra* note 994.

[999] Recital (14) of the Directive. See also Opinion of the Committee of the Regions on the 'Proposal for a European Parliament and Council Directive on a common framework for electronic signatures' (1999/C 93/06) - http://europa.eu.int/information_society/topics/ebusiness/ecommerce/8epolicy_elaw/law_ecommerce/legal/1signatures/index_en.htm

[1000] See Report from the Commission on the implementation of Council Directive 93/13/EEC of 5 April 1993 on unfair terms in consumer contracts [COM (2000) 248 final] (http://europa.eu.int/scadplus/leg/en/lvb/l32017.htm); Report to the Council and the European parliament on Consumer complaints in respect of distance selling and comparative advertising (Article 17 of Directive 97/7/EC on distance contracts and Article 2 of Directive 97/55/EC on comparative advertising) [COM (2000) 127 final] http://europa.eu.int/scadplus/leg/en/lvb/l32014.htm; Report from the Commission - First report on the implementation of the Data Protection Directive (95/46/EC) COM (2003) 265(01) http://europa.eu.int/eur-lex/en/com/rpt/2003/com2003_0265en01.pdf

protection, personal data protection etc. provide a wide set of rules that give fair and just protection for the interests of the users of certification services, even without the specific liability regime of Article 6. Therefore, defining the scope of the CSPs' duties and introducing relevant mandatory rules adjusted to the particularities of the provision of certification services is sufficient for achieving an adequate liability exposure, without the need for specific liability rules in addition.

From all that has been said above, it may be concluded that the specific liability regime for the CSPs issuing qualified certificates, going beyond the general national liability rules, does not seem to promote more trust in using electronic signatures.[1001] Instead of 'bringing trust and confidence in the usage of e-signatures'[1002] and establishing 'a legal framework for electronic signatures and certain certification services in order to ensure the proper functioning of the internal market',[1003] the liability provisions introduce vagueness of a kind that might create market barriers. In a nascent market which lacks relevant experience this scarcely seems a felicitous approach. It is clear from assessment of the Bulgarian situation that even if the specific rules analyzed are not transposed into national legislation, the general national liability rules provide good protection for the interests of the users of certification services. Thus, the specific liability rules established by Directive 1999/93/EC do not fulfil the allotted role, and therefore the concept should be revised.[1004]

[1001]   The general attitude towards Article 6 varies. In the DTI TFBJ/003/0061X Report issue 1.0.0 (Final), there was a proposal to DTI to lobby before the EC that "liability clause should be simply removed."

[1002]   An aim placed by the Commission in its first deliverables - See Chapter III, section 1.1, *supra*.

[1003]   Article 1 (1) of the Directive.

[1004]   The earlier drafts of the liability grounds of the UNCITRAL Model Law (Article 9) contained an additional paragraph, which addressed the consequences of liability as set forth in the article. In section 141 of the Draft Guide for Enactment of the Model Law it is envisaged that during the course of the preparation of the Model Law, it was observed that suppliers of certification services perform intermediary functions that are fundamental to electronic commerce and that *the question of the liability of such professionals would not be sufficiently addressed by adopting a single provision along the lines of paragraph (2)*. The said paragraph may not be sufficient for addressing the professional and commercial activities covered by Article 9. One possible way of compensating such insufficiency would have been *to list in the text of the Model Law the factors to be taken into account in assessing any loss resulting from failure by the certification service provider to satisfy the requirements of paragraph (1)*. It was finally decided that a *non-exhaustive list of indicative factors should be contained*.

2. Theoretical Deductions with Regard to the Introduction of Specific Liability Rules on a Supranational Level

The final conclusion on the lack of a positive impact of the specific liability rules established in Directive 1999/93 in promoting trust in the usage of electronic signatures, viewed from the perspective of a national jurisdiction, however, gives rise to further general theoretical deductions as to whether the establishment of specific liability regimes should be approached on a supranational level.

The civil liability regime impacts not only the usage of the electronic signatures, but also on the functioning of the whole internal market. By entering into different legal relationships people have faith in the rule of law in terms of the belief that 'someone will be liable' for the misconduct which has caused damage to their tangible or intangible property. In other words, if the regulations are not followed, the statutory law enforcement instruments and mechanisms will be executed to ensure justice and balance in society.

Therefore, the presence of a clear regime for invoking liability promotes trust for the market players. When relationships between people come into being, alter and come to an end in an electronic environment by means of electronic signatures, uncertainty as to whether and how the general liability regime could be effectively enforced might undermine trust and hamper the usage of electronic means of communications.

When the European legislator finds that certain groups of relationships require special regulation and the interests of given groups of the legal subjects need to be protected to a greater degree, to the detriment of other groups of subjects, it usually chooses to put specific liability rules into effect. *Prima facie* evidence thereof is provided by the liability regimes that have been established in relation to personal data protection, consumer protection, contracts for distance selling etc, and this approach was also chosen for protection of the interests of the users of certification services.

However, the establishment of a specific liability regime does not always seem to be an appropriate approach. On the contrary, as this work strongly argues, instead of playing its role in promoting trust and confidence in the market sometimes it leads to legal vagueness and causes difficulties for national jurisdictions.

The general reasons for such an effect were found during the course of developing the analysis of the specific liability of the CSPs in different directions:

In the first instance, it became evident that the notion of 'civil liability' has different aspects and meanings in the different jurisdictions. Not only has the doctrine found different explanations for the legal substance of the liability throughout Europe, but also the national legislations. It was ascertained that the *acquis communautaire* uses certain terminology in the different Community acts but does not provide clear directions on a supranational level as to what should be considered liability, negligence, reasonableness, fault etc. Thus, it became evident that in Directive 1999/93 the European legislator misleadingly referred to the liability of the CSPs instead of referring to statutory duties, or uses legal techniques that do not introduce novelties or deviations into the national liability regimes. These facts sometimes lead to formally accurate and proper transposition of the *acquis* liability rules, without, however, providing essential synchronization with the local national laws. The review of the Bulgarian doctrine and law made in this work undoubtedly proves this statement.

Secondly, the *acquis communautaire* does not provide for harmonization of the general rules for liability.

Nowadays, we are witnessing the co-existence of several private law regimes in the EU Member States which differ considerably. The most important of these is the conceptual difference between common law and the continental civil law systems. In second place, however, substantial differences are encountered between the countries following one and the same system as a fundament. Depending on the legal traditions, the national jurisdictions follow diverse approaches to systematize the legal rules in codes, general acts, special acts etc. The theory also finds different explanations on the essence of the legal rules and principles, particularly as regards civil liability. The legal system of France and the countries following its traditions, for example, sometimes take significantly different approaches to those taken by the systems falling within the German law family, where tort law is concerned. In the third place, the difficulties in transposition of the Community acts establishing civil liability regimes by the different legal systems identified are worsened by the fragmentary approach currently taken by the European legislator. One of the key problems related to the supranational instruments involving civil liability rules concerns the regulation of the definite scope of relationships and activities (for example, consumer contracts, distance selling, personal data protection etc), whereas the national legal systems focus

303

on general legal concepts.[1005] When speaking of specific liability for the CSPs, the analysis undoubtedly supports these deductions – Directive 1999/93/EC establishes specific liability rules, but leaves the general regulation of the liability to the national jurisdictions. In spite of the fact that all legal systems throughout Europe are based on common values, however, the concepts and rules introduced by the directives may not always be known or easily translatable, and may not also be relevant to a given jurisdiction. The transposition of the specific liability rules into the Bulgarian legislation demonstrates the difficulties faced by the case study jurisdiction, but the problems identified are also faced by almost all EU Member States. The main problem is that the present Community private law has left the core material private law, particularly in the area of liability, untouched and non-harmonized.

It becomes evident that these two factors – the difference between the private legal regimes of the various Member States and the insufficient and inadequate Community legislation – form the basis of the adverse effect on the internal market and competition in the EU.[1006] This leads to the conclusion that introducing specific liability rules cannot play a role in promoting trust in the market as long as the main issue – the harmonization of EU civil law rules, and particularly the general rules regarding liability – remain unresolved.

The Commission on European Contract Law and the Study Group on a European Civil Code in a Joint Response to Communication on European Contract Law identify differences between the laws of the Member States that can have negative repercussions for the participants in the internal market in four ways. Those ways refer to the liability of the CSPs and any specific liability regime as follows:

➤ Firstly, the differences may effectively prevent certain modes of organizing activity of the CSPs in the European market. For example, mandatory rules in the national legal systems may be irreconcilable and so preclude the marketing of identical certification services or on identical terms and conditions.

➤ Secondly, the need to find out about foreign law may involve significant additional costs for businesses or, if they are passed on, for consumers. In some cases these costs may dissuade a business from undertaking cross-border commercial

---

[1005] Lando, O., Von Bar, Ch., et al., *Communication on European Contract Law. Joint Response of the Commission on European Contract Law and the Study Group on a European Civil Code*, Commission on European Contract Law Study Group on a European Civil Code, Osnabrück 2001, v. (www.sgecc.net)

[1006] *Ibid.*

activity, particularly involving the use of certification services, and this would affect competition.

➢ Thirdly, whether from oversight or because obtaining legal advice would not be cost-effective or simply due to the complexity of the matter, users of certification services and the relying parties may enter into legal relationships on the basis of a deficient understanding of the legal rules applicable to their relationship with the CSP. Businesses and people do not always reckon on many peculiarities that may exist in foreign contract or tort law. In relation to the rules of private international law, which are based on the diversity of private law in the EU, there is plenty of scope for businesses to be taken by surprise, simply because the rules are complex and may not always be rigorously applied in practice.

➢ Finally, the fear of legal surprises in providing trans-border certification services may be a reason for not risking foreign trade. In this way, the diversity of contract law may deter businesses, especially small or medium-sized enterprises (SMEs), from entering the European market.

Furthermore, in the Joint Response the Commission and the Study Group stress the adverse consequences on competition of the existence of varying levels of protection for consumers between nations. Where the terms of a bargain hinge on a choice of law, there is a real risk that an unsuspecting party will make a prejudicial decision simply out of ignorance of the different legal rules being offered and their comparative merits.

Although the above-listed adverse effects on the internal market and competition are predominantly related to the differences in contractual law between Member States in general, other areas of the law of obligations and core aspects of tort law play an equally critical role in the conclusion and performance of contracts or when transactions backfire.[1007]

The following conclusion can be easily reached on the basis of the stated information: the proper functioning of the internal certification services market and competition within the European Union and, related to this function, the extension of economic and social prosperity, is hardly possible without comprehensive harmonization of

---

[1007]   *Ibid*, p.18.

private law and a commitment to structure, general approach and terminology in the Community's legislation.[1008]

It is obvious that the absence of common principles on a supranational level to equalize the EU Member States' liability rules regimes causes difficulties for the national jurisdictions in dealing with liability rules established on a supranational level, particularly as regards the liability of the CSPs. It is necessary for a framework designed to harmonize the common principles of civil liability in contract and tort to be developed at Community level.

Thirdly, the analysis shows that introduction of a specific liability regime on a supranational level (particularly for the CSPs) is justifiable where the general national liability regimes are not suited to guarantee the interests of given groups of subjects and thus to promote trust in the market. However, when dealing with a nascent market like the electronic signatures market, it must be acknowledged that the introduction of a specific liability regime may not anticipate the real needs of the market. A risk exists that rather than promoting trust and confidence in the market, such a regime will in fact adversely affect the willingness of the market agents to provide services, thus causing fragmentation of the market. In general terms, the consumer protection and data protection laws have a number of years of history and as a result social relations have crystallized the needs of the markets. However, this is not the situation with the electronic signatures regulations. This particular market is undeveloped and already highly fragmented, and the Community instrument itself – Directive 1999/93 – contains serious imperfections. These have been identified in a report entitled 'Legal and Market Aspects of Electronic Signatures'. Therefore, it is highly advisable to approach the enactment of specific liability regulations in respect of any undeveloped market – particularly the e-signatures market – conservatively and only as an exception.

3. Recommendations for Transposition of the Directive 1999/93 Liability Rules

Since the specific liability regime established by Directive 1999/93/EC has been introduced by a binding Community instrument, all EU Member States and Accession countries are obliged to transpose it and to keep their legislations in line with its provisions as regards their liability regimes.

[1008]   *Ibid*, p.20.

The above critical evaluation reveals the idea that the specific liability regime should be substantially revised. However, this particular regime is based on other criticized concepts (such as the concept of the qualified signature[1009]) and no significant change could be made to the qualified signature concept without thorough revision of the whole Directive. Since such revision seems unrealistic for the time being,[1010] the national jurisdictions require guidance on how to transpose the Directive liability rules in such a way as to make their national legislations compliant with the Directive. What is needed in this regard, essentially, is the provision of a standpoint for re-interpretation and clarification of the liability concept.

The following simple and practical recommendations may be made in this respect:

3.1. Main recommendation

As a first point, the literal transposition of Article 6 should be avoided. The above analysis provided a number of arguments in this respect. The Directive does not provide a model rule but rather gives directions on what the Member States should seek to ensure in their national legal regulations. The rules of the Directive are not consistent with the legal traditions, codification techniques, principles of the general law, or types of legal system of the Member States' jurisdictions. Simple transposition, when it produces disharmony with national legal traditions, may result in vagueness for all market agents – the providers of certification services, the users, and the law enforcement authorities.

Instead of implicitly labelling the national provisions as 'liability', it is advisable for the national legislatures to focus on systematizing all statutory duties of the CSPs by excerpting the essence of the rules of Article 6(1) and (2) and the Annexes to the Directive. Defining the scope of the CSPs' duties and introducing relevant, mandatory

---

[1009]   For critical evaluation of the qualified signature concept see Dumortier, J., *The European Regulatory Framework for Electronic Signatures: A Critical Evaluation, Ibid.*, p.71

[1010]   The Report "Legal and Market Aspects of Electronic Signatures" advises that "a number of issues have nevertheless been identified as problematic. These problems can mainly be attributed to a misinterpretation of the Directive's wording, which in turn leads to divergences in national laws and/or divergences in the practical application of the rules", p.4. The authors of the Report also advise that their "first recommendation is not to amend the Directive. Such amendments would have to be considered as an ultimate solution, only to be used when all other measures are deemed to be insufficient. Amending the Directive is a long and cumbersome operation that should be avoided if at all possible. As with all EU Directives, the Electronic Signature Directive is by no means a perfect legal text. It is a compromise which has been reached after long and difficult negotiations between 15 Member States all of whom have very divergent views on these issues. Our main conclusion is that the text of the Directive is adequate enough to serve its purpose in the near future but that it needs re-interpretation and clarification."

primary rules, adjusted to the particularities of the provision of certification services, would be sufficient for achieving adequate exposure of the CSPs liability by means of the general national secondary liability rules.[1011] Therefore, it is advisable to introduce explicit provisions in which the intention of the legislator as to the mandatory nature of these duties becomes clearly apparent unless, even without explicit referral by using the national legal techniques, such nature would undoubtedly become evident in any case.

3.2. Recommendation for transposition of Article 6(1)

The author's advice is that Article 6(1) of the Directive should be transposed extremely carefully. Literal transposition should be avoided. This regulation obliges the Member States to ensure that where a certification-service-provider issues a certificate, indicated as a qualified certificate to the public, or where it guarantees such a certificate to the public, then it must fulfil given statutory duties, and if fails to do so it will exposed to liability.

As discussed, the primary role of the provision of Article 6(1) of the Directive is to introduce statutory duties for the CSP issuing qualified certificates to the public. These include the following duties: to issue certificates with accurate and complete information (i.(a)); to verify the ownership of the signature-creation data (i.(b)); and to verify the cryptographic correspondence of the signature-creation and signature-verification data where it provides the generation service (i.(c)). These duties, together with the rules of Annex I and Annex II, being clearly transposed as mandatory (see section 3.1), makes direct transposition of the provision of paragraph 1 useless. Under the general rule of law, negligent failure to fulfil statutory requirements will result in exposure to liability. The author recommends the employment of a systematical approach in grouping the statutory duties on a national level by transposing the duties of the CSPs listed in Article 6(1) and 2, and those listed in Annexes I and II. However, attention should be paid to the fact that most of the duties established by Article 6 and the Annexes overlap. Thus a simple combination of the duties in Article 6(1) with those in the Annexes also does not seem to be an appropriate approach.

The duties of the CSPs to secure 'accuracy at the time of issuance of all information contained in the qualified certificate' and 'the fact that the certificate contains all the

---

[1011]   See Chapter II, section 2.2 and Chapter V, section 7, *supra*.

details prescribed for a qualified certificate' prescribed in Article 6 (1) are covered in Annex I. If the national legislatures accurately transpose the Annex, then the national laws, in the same way as the Directive, would contain explicit stipulations about what the qualified certificate 'must contain', i.e. what the CSP must put into the qualified certificate if it decides to issue such a certificate. In this respect, should a qualified certificate be issued with inaccurate or incomplete information, the certificate will lose its value as a qualified certificate.[1012] In such circumstances, the CSP would be acting wrongfully by misleading the certificate holder and the relying parties as to the legal value of the certificate. The general national liability rules, without exception, will sanction such behaviour on the basis of contractual liability towards the certificate holder (non-fulfilment of the obligation to issue qualified certificates holding all the details prescribed in the national rule that transposes Annex I),[1013] or on the basis of tort or contractual liability towards the relying party (by making a certification statement in the certificate, the CSP would be misleading the relying party as to the legal value of the certificate to be qualified, as it omits or misrepresents certain data).[1014]

It is advisable to transpose the duty of the CSP set out in Article 6(1)(i)(b) as a separate duty, and insert it, logically, in the same place as the rule transposing Article II. Article 6(1)(i)(b) stipulates a duty to assure 'that at the time of the issuance of the certificate, the signatory identified in the qualified certificate held the signature-creation data corresponding to the signature-verification data given or identified in the certificate'.

It is recommended that the same approach be followed with respect to the transposition of Article 6(1)(i)(c) which imposes a duty on the CSP to assure 'that the signature-creation data and the signature-verification-data can be used in a complementary manner in cases where the certification-service-provider generates them both'.

The allocation of the so-called 'reversed burden of proof' of negligence ('...unless the certification-service-provider proves that it has not acted negligently') should also be approached carefully. In most of the countries, simple transposition seems

---

[1012]   See Chapter III, section 6.3.3, *supra,* also Kalaydjiev, A., Belazelkov, B., Dimitrov, G., et al., *ibid.,* p. 194.

[1013]   See Chapter I, section 2.2.5.1, *supra.*

[1014]   See Chapter I, section 2.2.5.2, *supra.*

unnecessary, while, as already mentioned, the presumption of negligence persists either explicitly or implicitly in almost all EU jurisdictions as a general rule in relation both to contract and to tort.[1015] Simple transposition would not introduce any innovations or deviations into the liability regime governing the CSPs and thus would not promote more trust and confidence in the provision of certification services. Those countries that do not establish the presumption of fault as a general rule, despite this being more an exception than a rule,[1016] should definitely make explicit transposition.

3.3. Recommendation for transposition of Article 6(2)

Article 6(2) of the Directive provides a minimum liability requirement for certification-service-providers. It stipulates that Member States shall ensure that a certification-service-provider which has issued a certificate indicated as a qualified one to the public, is liable for damages caused to any entity or legal or natural person that reasonably relies on the certificate, for failure to register revocation of the certificate. The certification-service-provider can avoid liability only by proving that it has not acted negligently. It seems that by introducing the concept of duty to comply with the mandatory requirements transposing Annex II of the Directive the rule will be covered by the national rule transposing Annex II (b). This provides that the CSP must ensure the operation of a prompt and secure directory and a secure and immediate revocation service.

Transposition of the model providing that CSPs shall be liable 'to any entity or legal or natural person who reasonably relies on the certificate' appears redundant, unless the concepts of contributory fault and due care of the creditor/aggrieved party[1017] are unknown in given national legal systems, which is hardly likely to be the case. If the relying party behaves carelessly with regard to reliance on the certificate, the CSP will be in a position to build a successful defence on the basis of contributory fault or the careless behaviour of the creditor/aggrieved party. The author is unaware of the existence of any jurisdiction that would permit the party relying on the certificate to behave unreasonably to the detriment of the CSP.

[1015]   See Chapter II, section 4.2, Chapter III, section 6.1.2, and Chapter V, sections 5 and 7, *supra*.
[1016]   *Ibid.*
[1017]   See Chapter V, sections 2.5.1, 2.5.2 and 2.5.3, *supra*.

With respect to the transposition of the presumption of negligence, what is said in the preceding section should be taken into consideration.

3.4. Recommendation for transposition of Article 6(3) and (4)

As became clear, the rules in paragraphs (3) and (4) do not have a logical place in Article 6. It was deduced that the actual norm that stands behind Article 6 is that the CSPs are entitled to issue certificates that could be used upon certain conditions, as explicitly noted in the certificate.[1018] Certificates do not seem to be valid if used contrary to the indicated purpose.[1019] Thus, the effect on the liability exposure comes only afterwards – the CSP cannot be held liable if the certificate is used contrary to its purpose regardless of whether the CSP has acted negligently or not.

The idea of a CSP being able to manage its business risk by placing limits on the use and the value of the transactions will be encompassed by the national rule transposing Annex I. Therefore, a simple transposition seems to be useless. The qualified certificate must contain, Annex I stipulates, '... *(i) limitations on the scope of the use of the certificate, if applicable; and (j) limits on the value of transactions for which the certificate can be used, if applicable*'. Should the CSP choose to exercise this right granted by law by placing certain limitations on the use or the value of transactions, it will be entitled to do this by virtue of the rule itself, transposing Annex I. Thus, the certificate may be used only within its 'scope of use' or 'the limits on the value of transactions'. Beyond these limits, the certificate would not certify any fact contained therein, and thus, the CSP would not be held liable.

3.5. Recommendation for transposition of Article 6(5)

The rule of Article 6(5) of the Directive should be preserved unless under the national legislation it is in any event applicable without explicit transposition. While the protection of consumers in contract must be achieved by stronger means than are provided by the mandatory draft rule of Article 6(1) as proposed, they should be applicable in priority to the requirements of the Directive in case conflict arises.

[1018] See Chapter V, section 7 and Chapter IV, sections 6.2.1 and 5.3.3, *supra*.

[1019] See Kalaydjiev, A., Belazelkov, B., Dimitrov, G., et al., *ibid.*, p. 199.

BIBLIOGRAPHY

Books and Academic Journals

Aliyah, P., *The Basis of Contract*, 46 Harvard LR 553, 1986

Akdeniz Y., et al., *Cryptography and Liberty: Can the Trusted Third Parties be Trusted? A Critique of the Recent UK Proposals*, 1997, The Journal of Information, Law and Technology (JILT)

Andreev, M., *Roman civil law*, Sofia, 1975

Anson, B., *Contract Law*, 1984.

Antonov, D., *Unjust injury*, 1965, Sofia

Apostolov, A., *Law on Obligations. First part. General theory of obligation*, Sofia, 1990

v. Bar, Ch., *Principles of European Law: Non-Contractual Liability Arising out of Damage Caused to Another (PEL Liab.Dam.)*, Study Group on a European Civil Code, Osnabrück 2005 (www.cgecc.net)

Beale, H., Hartkamp, A., Kötz, H., Tallon, D., *Cases, Materials and Text on Contract Law*, Hart Publishing, Oxford and Portland, Oregon, 2002

Biddle, B., *Digital Signature Legislation: Flawed Efforts Will Hurt Consumers and Impede the Development of a Public Key Infrastructure*, The PSR [Computer Professionals For Social Responsibility] Newsletter (Fall, 1995).

Bohm N., *Response to the DTI Consultation Paper*, Comment, 1997 (3) JILT

Borrows, A., *Remedies for Torts and Breach of Contract*, 2nd ed., Butterworth, London.

Black's Law Dictionary, 7th ed., West Group, St.Paul, 1999.

Cane, P., *The Anatomy of Tort Law*, Hart Publishing, Oxford, 1997

Cane P., Stapelton, J., *The Law of Obligations: Essays in Celebration of John Fleming*, Oxford University Press, 1999

Clerk & Lindsell *on Torts*, 15th ed., London: Sweet and Maxwell, 1982

Chissik, M., Kelman, A., *Electronic Commerce: Law and Practice*, London: Sweet & Maxwell, 2002

Cornu, G., *Vocabulaire Juridique Henri Capitant*, 8th ed., Paris, PUF, 2000

Demogue, R., *Modern French Legal Phylosophy*, Boston, The Boston Book Company, 1916.

Dickie, J., *Internet and Electronic Commerce Law in the European Union*, UK: Hart Publishing, 1999

Dikov, L., *Civil Law Course. Law on Obligation. General Part*, Vol. III, 1934

Dimitrov, G., *Electronic Signatures: Basic Electronic Signature*, Market & Law Journal, vol.2, 2003.

Dimitrov, G., *Electronic Signatures: Advanced Electronic Signature*, Market & Law Journal, vol.3, 2003.

Dumortier., J., *The European Regulatory Framework for Electronic Signatures*, an article in Nielsen, R., Sandfeld S., Jacobson, Trzaskowski, J., editors, *EU Electronic Commerce Law*, Djøf Publishing, Copenhagen, 2004, p. 69-95

Dumortier, J., *Judicial Electronic Data Interchange in Belgium*, p 125-136, in Judicial Electronic Data Interchange in Europe: Applications, Policies and Trends, IRSIG-CNR, Italy, Bologna, 2004,483 p. Grotius Civil Programme, EC support.

Dumortier, J., Dekeyser, H., Loncke, M., *Legal Aspects of Trusted Time Services in Europe*, Leuven, ICRI, 51 p., Research Paper commissioned by Amano

Dumortier, J., *Directive 1999/93/EC on a Community framework for electronic signatures*, Lodder, A.R., Kaspersen, H.W.K.,: *eDirectives: Guide to European Union Law on E-Commerce*. Commentary on the Directives on Distance Selling, Electronic Signatures, Electronic Commerce, Copyright in the Information Society, and Data protection. In de reeks Law and Electronic Commerce, Vol 14, Kluwer Law International

Dumortier, J., *Evaluation of the Standardization Procedures in the Context of the European Electronic Signatures Standardization Initiative (EESSI)*, Report for the European Commission, May 2002.

Dumortier, J., Van Den Eynde, S., *Electronic signatures and trusted archival services*, in Proceedings of the DLMForum 2002, Barcelona 6-8 May 2002, Luxembourg, Office for Official Publications of the European Communities, 2002

Dumortier, J., Libon, O., Mitrakas, A., Rinderle, R., Schreiber, A., Van Eecke, P., *European Electronic Signature Standardization Initiative - Signature Policies*, European Commission.

Dumortier, J., Libon, O., Mitrakas, A., Rinderle, R., Schreiber, A., Van Eecke, P., *European Electronic Signature Standardization Initiative - Certificate Path Validation , European Commission.*

Edwards, Ch., Savage, N., Walden, I., *Information Technology & the Law*, UK: Macmillan Publishers Ltd., 1990

Edwards, L., Waelde, Ch., *Law and the Internet: A framework for Electronic Commerce*, 2nd ed., UK: Hart Publishing, 2001

Ellison, C., Schneier, B., *Ten Risks of PKI: What You're not Being Told about Public Key Infrastructure*, Computer Security Journal, Vol. XVI, N. 1, 2000.

Eorshi, G., *Comparative Civil (Private) Law*, Budapest, 1979

Fuller and Purdue, *"The reliance interest in contract damages"*, 46 Yale LJ 52, 1936

Ganzaroli, A., Mitrakas, A., *Trusted Third Parties in open electronic commerce: The phase of negotiations in the International Trade Transactions model*, EURIDIS, 2002

Goleva, P., *Contributive damages in tort*, 1989, Sofia

Goleva, P., *Remedies of victims in car accidents*, 1991, Sofia

Gotsev, V., *Contractual and tort liability*, 1979, Sofia

Groshieide, F., Boele-Woelki, K., *European Private Law* (1999/2000). E-Commerce Issue, The Netherlands: Molengrafica, 2000

Howing, P., *Positive and Negative Interest in Law*, Deventer: Kluwer, 192

Housley, R., Ford, W., Polk, W., Solo, D., *"Internet X.509 Public Key Infrastructure, Certificate and CRL Profile"*, RFC 2459

Hunter, B., et al., *The Role Of Certification Authorities In Consumer Transactions*, A Report Of The ILPF Working Group On Certification Authority Practices, Draft, April 14, 1997.

Kalaydjiev, A., Belaselkov, B., Dimitrov, G., Yordanova, M., Stancheva, V., Markov, D., *Electronic Document. Electronic Signature. Legal Regime*, Sofia, Ciela Publishing Ltd., CSD, 2004.

Kalaydjiev, A., *Contract for the Benefit of a Third Person*, Market and Law Magazine, 2003, Vol.3

Kalaydjiev, A., *Law on Obligations. General Part*, Sibi Publishing, Sofia, 2001

Kalaydjiev, A., *Electronic Statement and Electronic Document*, Market & Law Journal, 2002, vol.1

Kalaydjiev, A., *Contract for Certification Services*, Market & Law Journal, 2003, vol.6

Kelleher, D., Murray, K., *The Law in the European Union*, London: Sweet & Maxwell, 1999

Kojuharov, A., *Law of Obligations. General Study of the Obligation,* Vol. I, New Edition by Gerdjikov, O., Sofi-R, 1992,

Kojuharov, A., *Culpa in contrahendo, Legal research dedicated to prof. Venelin Ganev on the occasion of 30-years academic activity*, Sofia, 1939

Konov, T., *Grounds for Civil Liability,* University Publishing House 'St.Kliment Ohridski', 1995

Konov, T., *The Notion Unlawfulness in the Area of Delicts under the Bulgarian Civil Law*. Almanach of Sofia University, Vol. 79, 1986, Book 1

Kuner C., Barcelo R., Baker S., Greenwald, E., *An Analysis of International Electronic and Digital Signature Implementation Initiatives*, A Study Prepared for the Internet Law and Policy Forum (ILPF), September, 2000

Lando, O., Von Bar, Ch., et al., *Communication on European Contract Law. Joint Response of the Commission on European Contract Law and the Study Group on a European Civil Code*, Commission on European Contract Law Study Group on a European Civil Code, Osnabrück 2001, v. (www.sgecc.net)

Lee, R.W., *The Elements of Roman Law*, 4th ed., 1956.

Lodder, A., Kaspersen, H., *eDirectives. Guide to European Union Law on E-commerce*, The Netherlands, Kluwer Law International, 2002.

Loubser, M., *Concurrence of Contract and Tort*, Law in Motion, Kluwer Law International, Dordrecht, 1996

Masse, D., Fernandes, A., *Economic Modelling and Risk Management in Public Key Infrastructures*, Version 3.0, Apr. 15, 1997, p. 178 (http://www.chait-amyot.ca/docs/pki.html)

Martine, E., *L'option entre la responsabilité contractuelle et la responsabilité délictuell*, Paris, 1967

Mazeaud, H., Mazeaud., L., *Traité théorique et pratique de la responsabilité civile délictuelle et contractuelle.*, V. 1. Paris, 1947

McLaughlin M., *Scrambling for Safety - Privacy, security and commercial implications of the DTI's proposed encryption policy*, Conference Report , 1997, JILT.

McRoberts' Comments on the UK Consultation Paper of 5th of March.

Mehren, A., *International Encyclopedia of Comparative Law*. Volume VII. Contracts in General. The Formation of Contracts. Chapter 9. J. C. B. Mohr (Paul Siebeck) Tübingen. Martinus Nijhoff Publishers. Dordich-Boston-Lancaster, 1991.

Menzel, T., Schweighofer, E., *Liability of Certification Authorities, User Identification & Privacy Protection*, Joint IFIP WG 8.5 and WG 9.6 Working Conference 1999, Kista Schweden, DSV

Mitrakas, A., *Legal Aspects of Time Stamping*, Globalsign NV/SA, January 2002

Pavlova, M. *General Civil Law*, Vol.I, Sofi-R, 1995

Pavlova, M. *General Civil Law*, Vol.II, Sofi-R, 1996

Poulett, Y., Julia-Barcelo, R., *Healt Telematics Networks: Reflections on Legislative and Contractual Models Providing Security Solutions*, The EDI Law Review, 1997

Pound, R., *Jurisprudence*. V. IV. West Publishing Co. St. Paul, Minn. 1959

European Group on Tort Law, *Principles of European Tort Law*, Text and Commentary, Springer-Verlag/Wien, 2005.

Public Consultation Paper, *Licensing of Trusted Third Parties for the Provision of Encryption Services*, June 1997, JILT

Reed, C., Angel, J., *Computer Law*, 4th ed., UK: Blackstone Press Limited, 2000.

Rouschev, I., *Liability for eviction*, Regouli, Sofia, 1995.

Ryan, P., *Revisiting the United States' Application of Punitive Damages: Separating Myth from Reality*, ILSA Journal of International and Comparative Law, Volume 10:1 (2003)

Showcase Europe, *Guide to Internet Security Markets in Europe*, 2001

Smedinghoff, T., *Certification Authority Liability Analysis in the USA*, A survey assigned by the American Bankers Association, 1999

Street, F., Grant, M., *Internet Law*, Lexis Publishing, 2001

Treitel, G., *Remedies for Breach of Contract (Courses of Action Open to a Party Aggrieved)*. *Contracts in General*. Chapter 16. International Encyclopaedia of Comparative Law. Volume VII. J. C. B. Mohr (Paul Siebeck). Tübingen-Mouton- the Hague-Paris, 1976

Tsachev, L., *Law of Obligations and Contracts. Text, court cases, literature and notes*, 1990, Sofia

Tunc, A., *Introduction*, International Enciclopedia of Comparative Law, Vol. XI/I, Torts, Mohr, Tübingen, 1974

Van Eecke, P., Dumortier, J., *A common legal framework for Electronic Signatures within the European Union*, Electronic Commerce & Law Report, the Bureau of National Affairs (BNA), Washington

Van Gerven, W., Lever, J., Larouche, P., *Cases, Materials and Text on National, Supranational and International Tort Law*, Hart Publishing, Oxford and Portland, Oregon, 2000

Visoiu, D., *Digital Signature Legislation in Central Europe*, International Business Lawyer, March 2002

Weigenek, R., *E-Commerce: A Guide to the Law of Electronic Business*, 3rd ed., UK: Butterworths Lexis Nexis, 2002

Weir, T., *Complex Liability*, International Encyclopedia ot Comparative Law, Torts, XI/12, Mohr, Tübingen, 1974

Yossifov, B., Balabanov, B., *Tort*, 1989, Sofia.

Zweigert, K., Kötz, H., *An Introduction to Comparative Law*, Clarendon Press, Oxford, 1987

Zimmermann, R., *Comparative Foundations of a European Law of Set-Off and Prescription*, Cambridge University Press, 2002

Electronic Editions and other Academic Sources on Internet

Biddle, B., _In Defense of E-SIGN,_ published online on Red Rock Eater, 2000 (http://commons.somewhere.com/rre/2000/RRE.In.Defense.of.E-Sign.html)

Biddle, B., _Legislating Market Winners: Digital Signature Laws and the Electronic Commerce Marketplace,_ 34 San Diego Law Review 1225 (1997) (modified version in 2:3 World Wide Web Journal 231 (1997)). (http://bradbiddle.com/LMW.htm)

Biddle, B., _Misplaced Priorities: The Utah Digital Signature Act and Liability Allocation in a Public Key Infrastructure,_ 33 San Diego Law Review 1143 (1996). (http://bradbiddle.com/MP.htm)

Biddle, B., _Short History of Digital and Electonic Signature Legislation,_ in Simson Garfinkel, Web Security, Privacy And Commerce (2nd Edition, O'Reilly, 2001). (http://bradbiddle.com/history.html)

Biddle, B., _Public Key Infrastructures and Digital Signature Legislation: 10 Public Policy Questions,_ 2:2 Cyberspace Lawyer 10 (April, 1997); reprinted in Simson Garfinkel and Eugene Spafford, Web Security And Commerce (O'Reilly, 1997). (http://www.state.ma.us/itd/legal/biddle1.htm)

Biddle, B., _The Problem with Certification Practice Statements_ (unpublished, 2000). (http://bradbiddle.com/CPS.html)

Buono, F., Friedman, J., _Maximizing the Enforceability of Click-Wrap Agreements,_ 4.3 J. TECH. L. & POL'Y 3, 2000, (http://journal.law.ufl.edu/~techlaw/4-3/friedman.html)

David G., Masse and Andrew D. Fernandes, _Economic Modelling and Risk Management in Public Key Infrastructures_ (Version 3.0, Apr. 15, 1997) (http://www.chait-amyot.ca/docs/pki.html).

Dimech, F., _Protecting Yourself ... From Data Protection,_ http://www.cdf.com.mt/pages/docs/data%20protefction.pdf

Dimitrov, G., _Legal Protection of Domains,_ WIPO, 2001 (www.wipo.org).

Dumortier, J., Kelm, S., Nilsson, H., Skouma, G., Van Eecke, P. (2003) *The Legal and Market Aspects of Electronic Signatures in Europe*, Study for the European Commission within the eEurope 2005 framework (http://europa.eu.int/information_society/eeurope/2005/all_about/secur ity/electronic_sig_report.pdf).

Francis, B., Friedman, J., *Maximizing the Enforceability of Click-Wrap Agreements*, 4.3 J. TECH. L. & POL'Y 3, 2000, (http://journal.law.ufl.edu/~techlaw/4-3/friedman.html)

Froomkin, M., *The Essential Role of Trusted Third Parties in Electronic Commerce*, Published at 75 Oregon L. Rev. 49, 1996, (http://www.law.miami.edu/~froomkin/articles/)

Gerck, Ed., *Toward Real-World Models of Trust:Reliance on Received Information*, 1998 by E. Gerck and MCG, (http://mcwg.org/mcg-mirror/trustdef.htm)

Goldman, E., Maher, T., Biddle, B., *The Role of Certification Authorities in Consumer Transactions*: A Report of the ILPF [Internet Law and Policy Forum] Working Group on Certification Authority Practices, published by the ILPF and online at http://www.ilpf.org (1996). (http://www.ilpf.org/groups/ca/draft.htm)

Harrison, R., *Public Key Infrastructure: the risks of being trusted*, "Computers and Law", the magazine of the Society for Computer and Law, August/September 2000, Volume 11 issue 3 (http://www.laytons.com/ publications/rmh_article.htm)

Hindelang S., *No Remedy for Disappointed Trust – The Liability Regime for Certification Authorities Towards Third Parties Outwith the EC Directive in England and Germany Compared*, Refereed article, The Journal of Information, Law and Technology (JILT), 2002 (1) (http://elj.warwick.ac.uk/jilt/02-1/hindelang.html).

Introduction to Cryptography in PGP documentation, Network Associates Inc., 1990-1999, Chapter 1, (http://www.pgpi.org/doc/pgpintro/#p1)

Ius Commune Casebooks for the Common Law in Europe – Tort Law, (http://www.rechten.unimaas.nl/casebook/)

McCullagh, A., *The establishment of 'TRUST' in the electronic comerce environment*, The 1998 Information Industry Outlook Conference, 7 November 1998 – Canberra, (http://www.acs.org.au/president/1998/past/io98/etrust.htm)

Norden, A., *Liability of CSP under the Directive*, Speech before the Legal Workshop of ECAF/EEMA, Brussels, 29-30 November 2001 (https://www.eema.org/legal/norden.pdf)

On-line Tort Law Dictionary (http://lexnet.bravepages.com/tortdict.htm#-C-

Polk, W., Hasting, N., *Bridge Certification Authorities: Connecting B2B Pubic Key Infrastructures*, National Institute of Standards and Technology (http://csrc.nist.gov/pki/documents/B2B-article.pdf).

Reagle, Joseph M. Jr., *Trust in Electronic Markets. The Convrgence of Cryptographers and Economists*, First Monday Internet Journal, 1996, (http://www.firstmonday.dk/issues/issue2/markets/)

Rinderle, R., Legal Aspects of Certification Authorities, A Study – Part of the TIE Project, 2000, (www.tie.org.uk/tie_project.htm)

Samson, M., *Internet Law – Click-Wrap Agreement*, 2002, (http://www.phillipsnizer.com/int-click.htm)

Short Survey of the Principles of European Contract Law: Introduction to the Principles of European Contract Law Prepared by The Commission on European Contract Law (http://www.cbs.dk/departments/law/staff/ol/commission_on_ecl/survey_pecl.htm).

Sneddon, M., Partner, Clayton UTZ, NEAC - Legal Liability and E-transactions, A scoping study for the National Electronic Authentication Council, August 2000 (http://www.noie.gov.au)

Strategy for Consumer Protection Policy of Bulgaria (http://www.mi.government.bg/integration/eu/docs.html?id=81715)

The 'Lectric Law Library's Lexicon (http://www.lectlaw.com/def/g020.htm)

Turnbull, J., *Cross-Certification and PKI Policy Network*, Entrust, 2000, p. 3 (http://www.entrust.com/resources/download.cfm/21143/cross_certification.pdf);

Windows Knowledge Database, Glossary of Terms, (www.microsoft.com)

Winn, J., *The Emerging Law of Electronic Commerce* (http://www.smu.edu/~jwinn/mbachapter.htm)

European Commission and Council Decisions, Communications, Proposals and Reports

Amended Proposal for a European Parliament And Council Directive on a common framework for electronic signatures, COM (1999) 195 final, 98/0191(COD)   –
(http://europa.eu.int/information_society/topics/ebusiness/ecommerce/8epolicy_elaw/law_ecommerce/legal/1signatures/index_en.htm)

Commission Green Paper, _Legal Protection of Encrypted Services in the Internal Market,_ 6/3/96, COM (96) 76, ILPF

Communication from the Commission COM (97) 503: Ensuring security and trust in electronic communication: "Towards a European Framework for Digital   Signatures   and   Encryption"   –
(http://www.swiss.ai.mit.edu/6805/articles/crypto/eu-october-8-97.html)

Communication on European Contract Law: Joint Response of the Commission on European Contract Law and the Study Group on a European Civil Code,   2001,   (http://www.sgecc.net/media/download/stellungnahme_kommission_5_final1.pdf)

ECAF Model, Part I – Introduction /Strategy, Section B – _Introducing the Elements of Cryptography_, Version 1 – 12/00

EU Commission, _Communication on the Law of Non-contractual Obligations_, DG JAI D (99) 495, 1999, Internet Law and Policy Forum (ILPF)

European Commission, ICRI – K.U.Leuven, _Digital Signatures: A Survey of Law and Practice in the European Union_, Woodhaed Publishing, 1998

European Electronic Signature Standardization Initiative, _Final Report of the EESSI Expert Team_, 20th July 1999, (http://www.eema.org/ecaf/ Frep.pdf)

Opinion of the Committee of the Regions on the 'Proposal for a European Parliament and Council Directive on a common framework for electronic signatures'   (1999/C   93/06)   –
(http://europa.eu.int/information_society/topics/ebusiness/ecommerce/8epolicy_elaw/law_ecommerce/legal/1signatures/index_en.htm)

Opinion of the Economic and Social Committee on the 'Proposal for a European Parliament and Council Directive on a common framework for electronic signatures' (1999/C 40/10) (http://europa.eu.int/information_society/topics/ebusiness/ecommerce/8epolicy_elaw/law_ecommerce/legal/1signatures/index_en.htm)

Proposal for a European Parliament and Council Directive on a common framework for electronic signatures (COM(98)0297 - C4-0376/98 - 98/0191(COD)) – (http://europa.eu.int/information_society/topics/ebusiness/ecommerce/8epolicy_elaw/law_ecommerce/legal/1signatures/index_en.htm)

Proposed Standard Contractual Clauses for the Transfer of Personal Data from the EU to Third Countries (controller to controller transfers) of September 2003 (http://www.iccwbo.org/home/e_business/word_documents/Model%20contract%20Sept%202003%20FINAL.pdf)

Report from the Commission - First report on the implementation of the Data Protection Directive (95/46/EC) COM (2003) 265(01) http://europa.eu.int/eur-lex/en/com/rpt/2003/com2003_0265en01.pdf

Report from the Commission on the implementation of Council Directive 93/13/EEC of 5 April 1993 on unfair terms in consumer contracts [COM (2000) 248 final] (http://europa.eu.int/scadplus/leg/en/lvb/l32017.htm).

Report on the communication from the Commission to the Council, the European Parliament, the Economic and Social Committee and the Committee of the Regions on ensuring security and trust in electronic telecommunication - towards a European framework for digital signatures and encryption (COM(97)0503 - C4-0648/97) Committee on Legal Affairs and Citizens' Rights – (http://europa.eu.int/information_society/topics/ebusiness/ecommerce/8epolicy_elaw/law_ecommerce/legal/1signatures/index_en.htm)

Report to the Council and the European parliament on Consumer complaints in respect of distance selling and comparative advertising (Article 17 of Directive 97/7/EC on distance contracts and Article 2 of Directive 97/55/EC on comparative advertising) [COM (2000) 127 final] http://europa.eu.int/scadplus/leg/en/lvb/l32014.htm.

Normative Acts, International Treaties, Court Cases

Austrian Federal Law on the Electronic Signatures - Promulgated: Bundesgesetzblatt from 19 August 1999, Teil I. (http://www.sng.it/acrobat/it%20security/Signaturgesetz%20Austria%20 19_8_1999.pdf)

Belgium, Loi fixant certaines régles relatives au cadre juridique pour les signatures électroniques et les services de certification, (http://www.sng.it/acrobat/it%20security/Loi%20signatures%20électroni ques.zip)

Bulgarian Law on Electronic Documents and Electronic Signatures - Promulgated in State Gazette №34 from 06 April 2001, in force as of 07 October 2001. (http://www.orac.bg/en/resources-links)

Bulgarian Ordinance On The Activities Of Certification-Service-Providers, The Terms And Procedures Of Termination Thereof, And The Requirements For Provision Of Certification Services adopted pursuant to CMD No. 17 dated 31 January 2002 (Promulgated, SG No. 15 dated 8 February 2002)

Court practice of the Supreme Court of Cassation. Civil law section 1997, 1999, Sofia

Council Directive 93/13/EEC of 5 April 1993 on unfair terms in consumer contracts, OJ L 176/37 of 15/7/2003

Directive 1999/93/EC of the European Parliament and the Council of 13 December 1999 on a Community framework for electronic signatures, JOCE L13/12, 19 January 2000.

Directive 95/46/EC of the European Parliament and of the Council of 24 October 1995 on the protection of individuals with regard to the processing of personal data and on the free movement of such data, OJ L 281,23.11.1995, page 31

Directive 97/7/EC of the European Parliament and of the Council of 20 May 1997 on the protection of consumers in respect of distance contracts, OJ L 281,23.11.1995, page 31

Directive 2000/31/EC of the European Parliament and of the Council of 8 June 2000 on certain legal aspects of information society services, in particular electronic commerce, in the internal market OJ L 178, 17.07.2000

Directive 2000/35/EC of the European Parliament and of the Council of 29 June 2000 on combating late payment in commercial transactions.

Electronic Commerce Act 2000 of Ireland, No.27 of 2000 (http://www.sng.it/acrobat/it%20security/Electronic%20Commerce%20Bill.pdf)

Electronic Commerce and Electronic Signatures Act of Slovenia (http://www.sng.it/acrobat/it%20security/Electronic%20commerce%20and%20electronic%20signature%20act.PDF)

Electronic Commerce Law of 14 August 2000 of Luxembourg (http://www.sng.it/acrobat/it%20security/Law%20of%2014%20August%202000%20relating%20to%20electronic%20commerce%20Luxembourg.pdf)

Electronic Commerce Promotion Council of Japan (ECOM), *Proposal for Liability of Certification Authorities*, Authentication and Notary WG Report, 2000 (http://www.ecom.or.jp/ecom_e/report/full/_proposalfor.pdf)

France, Loi n. 2000_230 Droit de la preuve e signature électronique (http://www.sng.it/acrobat/it%20security/Loi%20n.%202000_230%20Droit%20de%20la%20preuve%20e%20signature%20électronique%20(français).PDF)

Government of Canada PKI Cross-Certification Policy (www.cio-dpi.gc.ca/pki-icp/crosscert/crosscert_e.asp).

Law Governing Framework Conditions for Electronic Signatures of Germany - Promulgated in Bundesgesetzblatt – BGBl. Teil I S. 876 from 21 May 2001 (http://www.sng.it/acrobat/it%20security/German%20Digital%20Signature%20law%202001%2005%2021.pdf)

Law on Electronic Signatures of Portugal (http://www.sng.it/acrobat/it%20security/Portuguese%20Legislation%20on%20electronic%20signature.pdf)

Qualified Electronic Signatures Act (SFS 2000:832), Sweden (www.pts.se)

Royal Decree-law №14 of the Digital Signatures of Spain (http://www.sng.it/acrobat/it%20security/Reglamento%20de%20acredita ciòn%20(espanol).PDF)

The Bill on Electronic Signatures - Bill No. L 229 Of Denmark, introduced on 22 March 2000 by the Minister of Research and Information Technology (http://www.fsk.dk/cgi-bin/doc-show.cgi?doc_id=41719&leftmenu=LOVSTOF)

The Principles of the Euroepan Contract Law at http://www.cbs.dk/departments/law/staff/ol/commission_on_ecl/PE CL%20engelsk/engelsk_partI_og_II.htm.

UK Electronic Communications Act, Received Royal Assent on 25 May 2000. (http://www.hmso.gov.uk/acts/acts2000/20000007.htm/)

Standardization Deliverables, Guidelines, Reports and CPS

ABA *Digital Signatures Guidelines*, Legal Infrastructure for Certification Authorities and Secure Electronic Commerce, American Bar Association, (http://www.abanet.org/ftp/pub/scitech/ds-ms.doc)

ABA ISC PKI Assessment Guidelines – PAG v0.30, American Bar Association, Information Security Committee, Electronic Commerce Division, Section of Science & Technology Law, 2001, (http://www.abanet.org/scitech/ec/isc/pag/pag.html)

AICPA/CICA, *WebTrust Program for Certification Authorities*, Ver. 1.0, August 2000

AICPA/CICA, BBB Code of Online Business Practices, 2000

BS ISO/IEC 17799 (BS 7799-1): Information technology – Code of practice for information security management

CEN/ISSS CWA 14172, Parts 1-5, WS/E-Sign: EESSI Conformity Assessment Guidances

CEN/ISSS CWA 14172-3: "Trustworthy systems managing certificates for electronic signatures"

CEN/ISSS CWA 14167, WS/E-Sign: CWA 14167-1: "Security Requirements for Trustworthy Systems Managing Certificates for Electronic Signatures"

Certificate Authority Rating and Trust Guidelines (CARAT), NACHA Internet Council (27 Oct. 1998), (http://internetcouncil.nacha.org/projects/default.html)

Certification Practice Statement of GlobalSign, (http://www.globalsign.net/repository/CPSv4.pdf)

Certification Practice Statement of Bankservice PLC (www.b-trust.org)

Certification Practice Statement of Information Services PLC (www.stamp-it.org)

Certification Practice Statement of Verisign (www.verisign.com)

Certification Practice Statement of Thawte (www.thawte.com)

Common Criteria / ISO 15408 at (http://www.iso.ch) or (http://www.commoncriteria.org/cc/cc.html)

ECAF Model, Part I – Introduction /Strategy, *Section C – PKI Security – A Market Overview,* Version 1 – 12/00

ECAF Model Part 1 – Introduction/Strategy, Section B Introducing the Elements of Crytpography

ECAF Model, Part II – *Planning / Choose,* Version 1 – 12/00

ECAF/EEMA Security Best Practice Paper, PKI costs, V.03 final, 2003

ETSI TS 101 456 V1.1.1 (2000-12) *Policy requirements for certification authorities issuing qualified certificates* (http://portal.etsi.org/sec/ ts%5F101456v010101p.pdf)

ETSI TS 101 862 V1.1.1 (2000-12) *Qualified certificate profile* (http://portal.etsi.org/sec/ts_101862v010201p.pdf)

ETSI TS 102 023 V1.1.1 (2002-04) Policy requirements for time-stamping authorities

ETSI TR 102 041 V1.1.1 (2002-02) *Signature Policies Report*

ETSI, DTR/SEC 004 010|STF 178 V0.0.14 (D3) (2001-08) - *Provision of harmonised Trust Service Provider status information* (http://www.apectel24.org/down/ESTG/2%20ETSI%20Project%20on %20Status%20of%20TSPs.doc)

Guide to Enactment of the UNCITRAL Model Law on Electronic Signatures (2001), A/CN.9/WG.iV/WP.8 (http://www.uncitral.org/english/workinggroups /wg_ec/wp-88e.pdf)

ILPF, The Role Of Certification Authorities In Consumer Transactions. A Report Of The ILPF Working Group On Certification Authority Practices, Draft, April 14, 1997 (http://www.ilpf.org/groups/ca/draft.htm)

ISO/IEC TR 13335: Information technology - Guidelines for the management of IT Security (GMITS)

ISO/IEC 9594–8: 1993 (E) Recommendation X.509 Information technology - Open Systems Interconnection - The Directory: Authentication Framework, Introduction

ITU-T Recommendation X.501 Information technology – Open Systems, Interconnection – The Directory: Models

ITU-T Recomendation X.519 | ISO/IEC 9594-5

Network Certification Authority WG, *Cross Certification Guidelines*, Japan, (http://www.ecom.jp/ecom_e/report/summary/wg08-2.pdf);

Regular Report on the Harmonization Process of the Ministry of Economy of the Republic of Bulgaria (http://www.mi.government.bg/integration/eu/ docs.html?id=9425)

Relying Party Agreement of GlobalSign (http://www.globalsign.net/ repository/rel_party.pdf)

RFC 1777: The Lightweight Directory Access Protocol

RFC 2527: Internet X.509 Public Key Infrastructure, Certificate Policy and Certification Practices Framework, The Internet Society (1999)

RFC 2693: SPKI Certificate Theory, September 1999, The Internet Society

Security Policy of Bankservice (http://www.b-trust.org/documents/Bankservice,%20Security%20Policy.pdf)

T7&TeleTrusT: Common Industrial Signature Interoperability and MailTrusT Specification (ISIS-MTT Specification): Part 2: PKI Management

Time-stamping Policy of Unizeto Certum (www.certum.pl)

TScheme, *Approval Profile for Registration Services,* Ref. tSd0042, Issue 2.00, 2001-11-13 (www.tscheme.org)

TScheme, *Glossary of Terms,* Ref. tS0226, Issue 1.00, 2001-08-17 (www.tscheme.org)

TTP.NL Framework for Certification of Certification Authorities against ETSI TS 101 456: 2000, ECP.NL

UK DTI Consultation on EC Directive 1999/93/EC of the European Parliament and Council on a community framework for electronic signatures, Department of Trade and Industry, March 2001, (http://www.dti.gov.uk/industry_files/pdf/esigs_consult.pdf)

UK DTI TFBJ/003/0061X Report issue 1.0.0 (Final)

LIST OF FIGURES

www.ingramcontent.com/pod-product-compliance
Lightning Source LLC
La Vergne TN
LVHW022301060326
832902LV00020B/3211

* 9 7 8 3 6 3 9 0 0 8 2 4 1 *